The Charlton
Standard Catalogue of

ROYAL
DOULTON
ANIMALS

First Edition

By
Jean Dale

Introduction
by
Louise Irvine

W. K. Cross
Publisher

The Charlton Press

Toronto, Ontario ✦ Birmingham, Michigan

Canadian Cataloguing In Publication Data
Main entry under title:
The Charlton standard catalogue of Royal Doulton animals
1994-
Biennial.
ISSN 1195-5384
ISBN 0-88968-122-8 (1st ed.)
1. Royal Doulton figurines--Catalogues
2. Porcelain animals--Catalogues
NK4660.C515   738.8'2'0294   C94-900404-9

**Printed in Canada
in the Province of Quebec**

**Editorial Office
2010 Yonge Street
Toronto, Canada. M4S 1Z9
Telephone (416) 488-4653 Fax: (416) 488-4656**

EDITORIAL

Editor	Jean Dale
Assistant Editor	Davina Rowan
Design	Janet Cross
Layout	Frank van Lieshout
Advertising Manager	Donald Lorimer

ACKNOWLEDGEMENTS

The Charlton Press wishes to thank those who have helped and assisted with the first edition of the Charlton Standard Catalogue of Royal Doulton Animals.

SPECIAL THANKS

The publisher would like to thank Louise Irvine for her research work in the Royal Doulton Archives and for writing the introduction to this First Edition. Louise is an independent writer and lecturer on Royal Doulton's history and products and is not connected with the pricing in this catalogue.

Our thanks also go to Royal Doulton (U.K.) Limited and Royal Doulton (Canada) Ltd., who helped with additional technical information and photography, expecially Valerie Baynton, Kate Ellis, Ian Howe, Pat O'Brien, Graham Tongue and Robert Tabbenor.

CONTRIBUTORS

The Publisher would like to thank the following individuals or companies who graciously supplied photographs or allowed us access to their collections for photographic purposes. We offer sincere thanks to:

DEALERS

Arnie and Judi Berger, Yesterday's South, Miami, Florida; Alan Blakeman, Collecting Doulton, Elsecar, England; Mr. Bowan, Yesteryear Antiques, Norfolk, England; Al and Nicki Budin, Curio Cabinet, Worthington, Ohio; Laura Campbell, Site of the Green, Dundas, Ontario; Anthony Cross, Anthony Cross, The Englishman, Blackburn, England; Richard Dennis, Somerset, England, Charles and Joanne Dombeck, Plantation, Florida; Edith Jackson, E & J Antiques, Freeport, Illinois; Arnold and Margaret Krever, Marnalea Antiques, Campbellville, Ontario; Walter Laidler, White Rock, B.C.; Jocelyn Lukins, London, England; Mark Oliver, Phillips, London, England; Ed Pascoe, Pascoe and Co., Miami, Florida; Tom Power, The Collector, London, England; Mr. and Mrs. Jack Shanfield, Shanfield-Meyers, Windsor, Ontario; Nick Tzimas, U.K. International Ceramics, Suffolk, England; Stan Worrey, Colonial House Antiques and Gifts, Berea, Ohio; Betty J. Weir, Doulton Divvy, Joliet, Illinois; Princess and Barry Weiss, Yesterdays, New City, New York

COLLECTORS

Jo Ellen Arnold; Ann Cook; Fred S. Dearden Jr., Boynton Beach, Florida; B. Esporite; John Fornaszewski; Helen Fortune, Ashtabula, Ohio; Robert Fortune Jr., Ashtabula, Ohio; Carol Levy, White Rock, B.C.; Steve Ross, New York; Joseph Schenberg, St. Louis, Missouri; Peter and Marilyn Sweet, Bolton, England.

A SPECIAL NOTE TO COLLECTORS

We welcome and appreciate any comments or suggestions in regard to the Charlton Standard Catalogue of Royal Doulton Animals. If you would like to participate in pricing or supply previously unavailable data or information, please contact Jean Dale at (416) 488-4653.

HOW TO USE THIS CATALOGUE

THE LISTINGS

Like the other Standard Catalogues in Charlton's Royal Doulton family of price guides, this book has been designed to serve two specific purposes. First, to furnish the Doulton enthusiast with accurate listings containing vital information and photographs to aid in the building of a rewarding collection. Secondly, this publication provides Royal Doulton collectors and dealers with current market prices for the complete line of Doulton animal figures.

Royal Doulton produced in excess of 1,400 animal figures over some 90 years so a note on the organization of this catalogue is in order.

The Royal Doulton animal figures are listed in this catalogue in the following Series order: HN Series, K Series, D Series, Royal Adderley Bird Studies, Bronze Menagerie Series, DA Series and Flambé Series.

Within the individual listings, animal figures are listed in order of their HN, K, D, or DA numbers. After this number comes the figure's Name. Next comes the Style Designation (Sitting - Style One, etc.). When animal figures have the same name but different physical modelling characteristics they are listed as Style One, Style Two and so on. The Model Number of the figure appears next. This number was assigned by Royal Doulton and usually appears impressed in the base of the figurine. However there are figures which do not show the model number. Only varieties of a particular animal figure can have the same model number.

Next comes Designer, Height, Size (if more than one of the same mould type), Colour, and the date of Issue and Withdrawal. The Series to which the figure belongs is listed next. Varieties of the figure then follow. Only colour differences, minor decorative alterations and slight changes in size due to firing constitute genuine varieties. Different physical modelling characteristics constitute different styles.

Lastly, the suggested retail price is given in American, Canadian and British funds.

A NOTE ON PRICING

In addition to providing accurate information, this catalogue gives readers the most up-to-date retail prices for Royal Doulton animal figures in American, Canadian and British currencies.

To accomplish this, The Charlton Press continues to access an international pricing panel of Royal Doulton experts that submits prices based on both dealer and collector retail price activity as well as current auction results in the U.S., Canadian and U.K. markets. These market prices are carefully analysed and adjusted to reflect accurate valuations for the listed Doulton figures in each of these three markets.

Please be aware that all prices given in a particular currency are for figures within that particular country. The prices published herein have not been calculated using exchange rates exclusively. They have been determined solely by supply and demand within the country in question.

A necessary word of caution. No pricing catalogue can be, or should be, a fixed price list. This catalogue, therefore, should be considered as a pricing guide only - showing the most current retail prices based on market demand within a particular region for the various figures.

Current figures, however, are priced differently in this catalogue. Such pieces are priced according to the manufacturer's suggested retail price in each of the three market regions. Be aware that dealer discounting is always possible.

Prices published herein are for figures in mint condition. Collectors are cautioned that a repaired or restored piece may be worth as little as 50 per cent of the value of the same figure in mint condition. The collector interested strictly in investment potential will avoid damaged or restored figurines.

As mentioned above, this is a catalogue giving prices for figures in the currency of three particular markets (Canadian dollars for the Canadian markets; U.S. dollars for the American market and Sterling for the U.K. market.) The bulk of the prices given herein are not determined by straight currency exchange calculations but by actual market activity in the market concerned. This point bears repeating.

One exception, however, occurs in the case of current figurines and very recent limited editions issued in only one of the three markets. Since such items were priced by Royal Doulton only in the country in which they were to be sold, prices for the other countries have been shown as N/A (not applicable).

Additionally, collectors must remember that all relevant information must be known to make a proper valuation. When comparing auction prices to catalogue prices, collectors and dealers must remember two important points.

Firstly, to compare 'apples and apples'. Be sure that realized auction prices for figures include a buyer's premium if one is due. Prices realized for figures in auction catalogues may not include this additional amount. Buyer's premium can range from 10% to 15% and on an expensive piece this amount can be significant. Secondly, if a figure is restored or repaired, this fact may not be noted or explained anywhere in the listings and as a result, its price will not be reflective of that same piece in mint condition. Please be aware of repairs and restorations and the effect they may have on published figure values.

A NOTE ON THE PHOTOGRAPHS

In some cases, photographs of models have been used to represent unobtainable varieties of that particular piece. The reader is cautioned that all photographs so utilized are to be used for model characteristics only. More specific details concerning a figure (i.e. colourway) should be determined from the information listed below the photograph. Readers are cautioned that colours, patterns and glazes may differ within individual figurines. Due to the number and variety of figures represented in this catalogue, readers must assume that photographs are not to scale.

A NOTE ON THE INDICES

At the back of this book the reader will find both an alphabetical index and a model number index. These will allow readers to locate and identify virtually every figure. In the alphabetical index, naturally, figures are listed alphabetically by name. Exceptions, however, exist for figures with more detailed names (barn owl, snowy owl, tawny owl for example). These figures are listed under the generic name of the animal (owl, in this instance). When a figure has a name that does not connote the type of animal represented (Spirit of the Wind, for example), that figure is listed alphabetically under 'S' for "Spirit".

The model number index allows readers to correlate model numbers with both the names and the various other numbers of the figures.

INSURING YOUR FIGURES

As with any other of your valuables, making certain your figures are protected is a very important concern. It is paramount that you display or store any porcelain items in a secure place - preferably one safely away from traffic in the home.

Your figures are most often covered under your basic homeowner's policy and there are generally three kinds of such policies - standard, broad and comprehensive. Each has its own specific deductible and terms.

Under a general policy, your figurines are considered 'contents' and are covered for all of the perils covered under the contractual terms of your policy (fire, theft, water damage and so on).

However, since figurines are extremely delicate, breakage is treated differently by most insurance companies. There is usually an extra premium attached to insure figures against accidental breakage or the carelessness of the owner. This is sometimes referred to as a 'fine arts' rider.

You are advised to contact your insurance professional to get all the answers.

In order to help you protect yourself, it is critical that you take inventory of your figures and have colour photographs taken of all your pieces. This is the surest method of clearly itemizing, for the police and your insurance company, the pieces lost or destroyed. It is also the easiest way to establish their replacement value in the event of such a tragedy.

FIGURE NUMBERING SEQUENCING

In this catalogue an asterisk (*) in the lower left corner of a listing indicates that one or more of the following numbers was either unassigned by Royal Doulton or used for a piece other than an animal figure.

TABLE OF CONTENTS

Fig. R36. Squirrel
13″ high
25/-

Regd. No. 735237
Fig. R17. Rabbit
18″ high
17/6

Fig. R21. Cat
16″ high
16/-

APPROPRIATELY
PLACED IN THE
GARDEN, THESE
BEAUTIFULLY
MODELLED
FIGURES
GIVE A
CHEERFUL NOTE
OF ANIMATION
AND INTEREST

Fig. R24. Duck
15″ high
17/6

Regd. No. 736048
Fig. R16. Fox. 16″ high
25/-

Fig. R25. Hare. 24″ long × 11″ high
17/6

INTRODUCTION
by Louise Irvine

THE HISTORY OF ROYAL DOULTON ANIMALS

The Lambeth Studio

The Doulton factory was founded in London in 1815 and in the early years they made drainpipes for the growing sanitary industry and domestic stonewares, such as bottles and jars. Occasionally useful items took the form of animals, for example a crocus pot in the shape of a hedgehog, but it was not until the Lambeth Art Studio was flourishing in the late 19th century that animals began to inspire a wide range of models. Often they continued to fulfil a practical purpose: owls serve as tobacco jars or perch on the edge of ashtrays; bears dip their paws into honey pots; rabbits crouch into little paperweights and mice hold menus aloft. Most bizarre of all, a life-size kangaroo obligingly holds umbrellas.

This last piece was modelled by George Tinworth, the first full-time artist at the Lambeth Studio. He made his reputation as a sculptor of monumental religious works but, in between his major commissions, he sought inspiration in the animal kingdom. Water birds and marine creatures were incorporated into his fountain designs and, on a smaller scale, he produced paperweights depicting incidents from Aesop's fables. His most famous animal studies, however, feature the cheeky mice which occasionally invaded his studio. In his imagination they assumed human personalities and he modelled them enjoying many popular pursuits of the Victorian period. Frogs often join in the fun and together they participate in sports, play musical instruments and, on one scandalous occasion, get drunk! Tinworth's little mouse and frog groups were moulded in salt glaze stoneware during the 1880's and, as the editions were very small, they are extremely desirable today.

Carraraware Polar Bear c.1890

"The Cockneys at Brighton"
by George Tinworth 1886

Fellow artist Mark Marshall preferred weird and wonderful monsters which seem to spring from the pages of a Gothic horror story. Slimey reptilian creatures claw their way around his vases or slither over rocky crags to form free-standing sculptures. A fish transmutes into seaweed to form a jug whilst a rabbit shaped vase is half lettuce. Marshall's preoccupation with monstrous hybrids and mutations was shared by many Victorians and literature of the time abounds with strange creatures, notably Tenniel's Alice in Wonderland, which inspired Marshall to produce paperweights of the Cheshire Cat and the Mock Turtle as well as a strange vase in the form of the pig-like Rath. One of his most hideous monsters was intended as a garden seat, obviously for those undeterred by lurid warts and fangs!

Garden ornaments were often modelled in the form of animals and the Lambeth factory catalogues show a wide range of species in terracotta and, to a lesser extent, salt glaze stoneware. Marshall was responsible for some of the designs, notably the *lizard (R31)* and the *pelican (R19)*, but most were by the younger artist Harry Simeon and include studies of a *squirrel (R36)*, a *fox (R16)*, a *rabbit (R22)* and other garden visitors. Simeon became the most prolific modeller of animal subjects at the Lambeth Studio, producing several colourful stoneware ornaments which could also be used as bookends. He also contributed to a range of ashtrays, soap dishes and trinket holders adorned with birds and animal models. These colourful stoneware bibelots, as they are known, were introduced in the mid 1920's and are now widely sought after.

Royal Doulton also advertised their own products with animal models, choosing a polar bear, a cat and a stylised

Group of Lambeth stoneware animal models and bibelots c.1913-1925

horse to promote their white Carraraware architectural glaze. The polar bear was the work of Leslie Harradine, who is better known to collectors as a figure modeller. In the early 1900's he was apprenticed at the Lambeth studio and produced several animal models for their slip cast stoneware process. His studies of parakeets on a rock (H58) and polar bears on an ice floe (H35) are illustrated in a Doulton catalogue of 1914 and presumably they were reproduced in some numbers but they are not easy to find today. Some of his designs were reissued in the animals collection produced at the Burslem factory, notably the *Polar Bear on a Cube* and the *Cuddling Monkeys* and it is possible that he also designed pieces specifically for this range. However, attributions can only be made on stylistic grounds as records about the Burslem animal designers are virtually non-existent.

The Burslem Studio

Doulton's factory at Burslem, Stoke-on-Trent was established in 1877 and a few years later the first animal subjects began to appear. John Slater, the first Art Director, introduced a range of vases with models of birds perched on the sides but these strange designs were short-lived. In 1889 he recruited Charles Noke from the Worcester factory as his chief modeller and Noke's earliest vases are dominated by fabulous oriental-style dragons which writhe around the surface in high relief and leer down from the top. Dragons continued to be an important feature of Noke's work when he was experimenting with the Chinese rouge flambé glazes in the early 1900's as they were appropriate subjects for the fiery red effects achieved with his Sung and later his Chang glazes.

It was for the new flambé range that Noke first considered producing free-standing animal models and a catalogue page of 1908 shows four tiny flambé creatures squeezed in between exotic vases. These early designs have four digit model numbers - the frog (1162), three finches (1163), mouse on a cube (1164) and lop-eared rabbit (1165), but a new modelling system for figure and animal sculptures was introduced around 1910. By 1912 more than 60 different animals had been modelled for the flambé process and a

dozen of them were included in an article which appeared in the Connoisseur magazine in 1912. Noke also experimented with vivid monochrome glazes on these early models including blue, yellow, orange, red, brown and black.

Unfortunately the modellers responsible for this menagerie are not recorded although it is believed that Harry Tittensor and Leslie Harradine assisted Noke on the early development of the animal collection. It is known that Charles Noke was responsible for the elephant (65) as it was one of his favorite animals. He started modelling them as a boy and continued throughout his life, producing huge fighting elephants in flambé and naturalistic colours, a small stylised example for the Chinese Jade range and some cute character elephants in humanistic poses. Charles Noke frequently endowed animals with human personalities, sometimes even dressing them in clothes, as with the very first model in this book, *Pedlar Wolf HN7*, which was probably inspired by a character in Fontaine's fables. A succession of amusing characters followed, including *A Fox in Hunting Dress HN 100*, *A Rabbit in Morning Dress HN 101* and a *Granny Owl* wrapped in a shawl HN 173. The animal which provided him with the most scope for caricature was the bulldog, symbolising the spirit of Britain at war, which appears in battle dress or patriotically draped in a Union Jack and bearing a marked resemblance to Winston Churchill. Examples of these very collectable bulldogs can be found in both the HN and the D series.

There are only a few animal models listed in the D series of earthenware models which was usually used to record Series ware patterns or Character Jugs. The vast majority of animals, whether they be in an earthenware or china body, were included in the HN series along with all the Royal Doulton figures. The HN pattern numbers record the different colours used to decorate each figure or animal and models can be produced in many different colourways. The first animals in the HN collection tend to be subtly decorated with muted naturalistic tones. Subjects range from domestic pets, notably dogs and cats, to wild animals including foxes, rabbits and the more exotic monkeys and bears. Birds seem to have been very popular, whether it be chubby chicks, dabbling ducks or sleek penguins.

In the 1920's miniature animals predominated; some have the tactile qualities of Japanese netsuke, for example HN 820, 834 and 837, whilst others are of a humorous nature, notably HN 913-918. *Bonzo*, the popular cartoon dog of the period, was modelled in several guises together with his feline friend *Ooloo HN 827*, who was later renumbered K12 as part of a new series of miniature animals. The K series, which was introduced in 1931, included a number of tiny dogs, birds and hares, some of which stayed in production until 1977. Tiny dog's heads were modelled for use as brooches and larger busts were mounted on alabaster or wooden stands to serve as pen holders. Practicality was obviously an important consideration at the time as several other dog models adorn ashtrays and tobacco jars and birds were incorporated into flower holders.

Models of dogs became increasingly popular in the late 1920's and many different breeds were introduced in a variety of poses. In 1930 Frederick Daws, the celebrated

PORTRAIT MODELS OF CHAMPIONSHIP DOGS

ENGLISH SETTER
Ch. "Flaesydd Mustard"
Large   Medium   Small

COCKER AND PHEASANT
Large   Medium   Small

Also in Liver and
White colouring

COCKER SPANIEL
Ch. "Lucky Star of Ware"

	Height	Length
Large	6½"	9"
Medium	5"	7"
Small	3½"	4½"

The other models are
proportionate to the
above.

SEALYHAM
Ch. "Scotia Stylist"
Large   Medium   Small
Also made lying in the three sizes.

AIREDALE
Ch.
"Cotsford Topsail"
Large
Medium
Small

SCOTTISH TERRIER
Ch. "Albourne Arthur"
Large   Medium   Small
Also made sitting in three sizes.

ROUGH HAIRED TERRIER
Ch. "Crackley Startler"
Large   Medium   Small

PEKINGESE
Ch. "Biddee of Ifield"

BULL DOG
Large   Medium   Small

CAIRN
Ch. "Charming Eyes"
Large   Medium   Small

FOXHOUND
"Tring Rattler"
Large   Medium   Small

Extra large
Large
Medium not made
Small
Also sitting

Miniature Model Dogs, measuring approximately 2½"

K1   K10   K5   K9   K11   K3   K8   K2   K4   K7   K6

Advertising leaflet for the Championship Dogs, date c.1935

xi

animal sculptor, was invited to model a collection of Championship Dogs, mainly in show stances. He visited the kennels of award-winning dogs to work from life and his sculptures were approved by the owners before being reproduced in the HN collection. Most breeds were offered in three sizes and different colours and many stayed in continuous production for over 50 years. Daws also produced a very successful model of a famous racehorse of the day called *Merely a Minor* HN 2530 but most of the horse studies in the Royal Doulton collection were the work of another freelance artist, William Chance.

Chance was a regular exhibitor at the Royal Academy and his work was equally well known and respected in North America. Most of his horses were offered in different colourways and sizes and they continued in the collection until the 1960's. *Monaveen*, his most prestigious commission was not available in the general range as it was made specially for presentation to Princess Elizabeth during her visit to the Royal Doulton factory in 1949. It is a particularly complex action model of the famous steeplechaser, which the princess owned jointly with her mother, and Chance spent a lot of time working with the horse's trainer to ensure it was an accurate portrait.

The freelance artists usually liaised with resident designer Cecil Jack Noke, who ultimately succeeded his father as Art Director. He commissioned Raoh Schorr, a well known animal sculptor with work in the national art galleries, to produce a collection for reproduction in ceramic. The Schorr subjects were launched in 1937 and most were available in white and black matt glazes, simulated green bronze and natural colours. Although they were favourably reviewed in artistic circles, they did not appeal to the general public. Consequently all the lively lambs, goats, calves, horses and donkeys were made for about five years only so they are not easy to find. Even more elusive are his unusual wild animals, such as the *Cerval* HN 2500, *Lynx* HN 2501 and *Asiatic Elephant* HN 2506 which do not appear to have been produced for any length of time.

From 1939, Jack Noke was fortunate to have the services of a new resident modeller, Peggy Davies, who had joined the company to assist Noke senior in his modelling studio. Although she is best known today for all her crinoline ladies, she concentrated initially on animal studies and produced a delightful collection of kittens in playful poses which were introduced in 1941. Peggy went on to model several collections of little animals, including the six piglets, HN 2648-53 and the K series of penguins. She probably modelled many other series, including the character puppies HN 2585-90, but unfortunately there are no surviving records of designers to clarify her role. Shortly before she died in 1988, she talked about some of the prestige birds she had modelled including the *Indian Runner Drake* HN 2636 and a falcon for display in the company showrooms. She also remembered working on the range of championship dogs and she assisted the new Art Director Jo Ledger on his Chatcull range of animals.

Jo Ledger joined Royal Doulton in 1955 and began experimenting with many new design directions for the company. For the animals collection, he envisaged a stylish new range, which he named after his house of the time, Chatcull Hall. Modellers Peggy Davies and David Lovegrove worked from his detailed drawings and produced some very elegant studies, mainly of exotic wildlife, which were launched in 1960. Perhaps the choice of species was too obscure as the collection was not a commercial success and soon withdrawn, with the exception of the *Siamese cats*, HN 2655, 2660 and 2662 which stayed in production until 1985.

It was many years before any new animal collections were commissioned but, in 1972, freelance artist Robert Jefferson was invited to model some large, prestige porcelain sculptures of animals and birds in their natural habitats. Jefferson had enjoyed a distinguished career at the Poole Potteries, where he produced many successful animal models but the impressive scale of the new Royal Doulton sculptures was an exciting new challenge for him. He spent many hours in field study, observing, taking photographs

Advertising leaflet for Raoh Schorr animals, 1937

and making drawings before embarking on the original models, which were executed in wax to preserve the fine detail of the animal's coats and the bird's plumage. Jefferson later produced some studies of otters for the Images of Nature collection, which was launched in 1982. These highly stylised sculptures represented a radical new design direction for Royal Doulton. The streamlined silhouettes of the animals, fashioned in white bone china, have proved particularly effective in contemporary settings and new subjects by a variety of modellers have been introduced to the collection on a regular basis. In 1987 the Images of Fire collection combined these trend-setting sculptures with a traditional Doulton finish, the dramatic flambé glaze. To date four large size models have been available in either white or flambé and new smaller subjects have been modelled especially for the flambé treatment, for example the *Elephant and Young* HN 3548 by Art Director Eric Griffiths and Robert Tabbenor's *Dragon* HN 3552 which was an exclusive offer to members of the Royal Doulton International Collectors Club.

In 1985, the success of the Images animals encouraged Royal Doulton to withdraw all the naturalistically coloured animals remaining in the HN collection. As many of the models had been in continuous production for over 50 years, it was felt that all the potential customers had been satisfied and it was time for something different. The DA series of animals, featuring the work of Design Manager Graham Tongue and his team at the John Beswick Studio of Royal Doulton, was launched in 1989. These artists take a highly detailed, realistic approach to animal modelling. The textures of fur and feathers are painstakingly reproduced as well as the gnarled wood and mossy stones of their environment.

All the young artist in Graham's team are encouraged to be versatile and they spend a lot of time visiting aviaries, stables, kennels, farms and zoos to study their subjects, returning with copious photographs and notes from their encounters to ensure accuracy. In 1990, Warren Platt modelled some fine birds to raise funds for the World Wide Fund for Nature whilst Martyn Alcock has recently produced a delightful collection of puppies and kittens in appealing poses, such as *Give Me A Home* DA 196. A more unconventional pet Martha, the *Vietnamese Pot Bellied Pig* DA 189 has been immortalised by Amanda Hughes-Lubeck and she has recently followed this with the equally unorthodox *Nigerian Pot Bellied Pygmy Goat* DA 223.

Most of Graham Tongue's own models of birds, dogs, cattle and horses are featured in the prestigious Connoisseur collection and he has a considerable reputation for his portraits of famous racehorses, such as *Desert Orchid* DA 134 and *Arkle* DA 227. Graham has worked in the John Beswick modelling studio since 1966, a few years before it was taken over by the Royal Doulton group. During his long career he has modelled a wide variety of animals for the Beswick backstamp and many of these were transferred to the new DA range in 1989, together with models by earlier Beswick artists, such as Arthur Gredington and Albert Hallam. This is not the first time that backstamps have been changed on products made by other companies within the Royal Doulton group. In 1979, a series of birds produced at the Royal Adderley studio were given Royal Doulton

backstamps but they only remained in production in this form until 1982.

Currently two design studios within the group contribute to the Royal Doulton animals collection, under the guidance of Art Director Amanda Dixon. Graham Tongue and his team at the Beswick Studio continue to produce realistic interpretations of the animal kingdom whilst at the Burslem Design Studio, the emphasis is on the stylised Images of Nature and the traditional flambé subjects. Alan Maslankowski has had the experience of working with both studios and is one of the company's most versatile animal modellers, creating subjects as diverse as *Pegasus* the flying horse, HN 3547 and a pair of chickens hatching from an egg in the *Images* style, HN 3551. All this varied talent and subject matter has revitalised the animals collection in recent years and has created lots of collecting opportunities.

BUILDING A COLLECTION

Since 1908, more than 1,000 animals have been introduced to the HN, DA and K series and these are now avidly collected in many parts of the world, Most collectors specialise in one category or another as it would be virtually impossible to acquire them all. Fox collectors can have a field day chasing more than a dozen models in various sizes, whilst elephant collectors can look out for at least ten types in lots of different sizes, colours and glazes, including flambé and Chinese Jade. No doubt there are other collectors pursuing rabbits, monkeys or pigs but some of the most popular collecting categories are discussed in detail below.

Collecting Dogs

Dogs are by far the most collectable animals in the Royal Doulton range. Appealing puppies cocking their ears, playing with bones or rolling on their backs were amongst the first models and it would appear that Art Director Charles Noke was more concerned with the character of the dog than its pedigree. This has led to some confusion in identifying the various breeds represented in the early years, for example HN 127 has often been listed as a Pekinese but Noke's notebook describes it as a Blenheim Spaniel, in other words a liver and white coloured Cavalier King Charles. The conformation of this breed has altered over the years and in the early 1900's it had a flatter muzzle like the pekinese hence the confusion. Another puzzle is HN 231 which some dog experts say looks most like an English St Bernard and others a foxhound. To confuse matters even more the pattern books describe it variously as a setter and a bloodhound. Whatever the breeds, these early models are hard to find and would be welcomed in most dog collections.

The most desirable Royal Doulton breed is undoubtedly the bulldog, which has been portrayed in many different guises. During the First World War, the breed symbolised the dogged determination of the British people and is now regarded as the country's national animal. Bulldogs, patriotically draped with the Union Jack, were introduced at the end of the 1914-18 war and they were reintroduced during World War Two in three sizes, D5913A, B & C. Cartoons of the period picked up the breed's resemblance to Winston Churchill and Charles Noke responded with new versions of the Union Jack bulldog smoking a cigar and wearing a derby hat or Trinity cap in the manner of the great war leader. The popularity of the great British bulldog has ensured its widespread use in advertising and there are several rare Royal Doulton models promoting various brands of drinks. Bar accessories, such as ashpots and match holders, were modelled in the form of bulldog's heads and sometimes complete miniature dogs are posed on top of bowls or pintrays. Keen canine collectors often seek out all the different types of dog derivatives which were produced in the 1920's and 30's. Various breeds were adapted to decorate tobacco jars, ashtrays, bookends, calendars, pen holders, wall plaques, brooches and they are all hard to find today.

Terriers seem to have been the most popular type of dogs with Doulton artists in the mid 1920's and from HN 900 onwards they produced a succession of Fox Terriers, Scottish Terriers, Sealyhams and Airedales in standing or seated poses. Most were offered in a choice of colourings and, although they might not have the same amount of detail as the later Championship series, they are still very collectable and it is quite a challenge to complete the series

as most had disappeared from the range by 1946. The rarest terrier of all is the white *West Highland Terrier* HN 1048 which seems to have been produced for one year only in 1931. It is very similar to the *Cairn* Terrier HN 1104 in the Championship series but the head is at a different angle and the ears are smaller.

New standards were set for Royal Doulton dog sculptures when the celebrated animal artist Frederick Daws became involved in the collection. He strove for complete accuracy in his representations of named champions and he liaised with the breeders on precise details of conformation. Most of his portraits are in show poses but he occasionally modelled the same dog sitting or lying, although these were not promoted with the champion names. The first show dog to join the range was *Lucky Star of Ware* HN 1000, a blue roan Cocker Spaniel, which was twice overall champion at Crufts in 1930 and 1931. Later models feature the name *Lucky Pride of Ware* - perhaps the owner had reservations about the change of colouring to plain black. Another name change

Advertising leaflet for the Championship Dogs c.1935

occurred with the Rough Haired Terrier *Crackley Starter* HN 1007 who is also known as *Crackley Hunter*.

When Frederick Daws retired, other artists contributed to the series. Peggy Davies modelled the Doberman Pinscher *Rancho Dobe's Storm* HN 2645 and the *French Poodle* HN 2631, which was originally going to be offered in a plain white decoration in three different sizes HN 2625-7, but in the end only one model was introduced. Perhaps Peggy was responsible for the Chow champion *T'Sioh of Kin-Shan* HN 2628-30 but judging from the scarcity of this model it is doubtful if it actually went into production. The last championship dog in this series was the black labrador *Bumblekite of Mansergh* HN 2667 modelled by John Bromley in 1967.

After a gap of some years, dogs are once again an important part of the Royal Doulton range. Many breeds originally modelled for the Beswick backstamp were transferred to the DA series in 1989 and the design team at the Beswick studios are regularly introducing new subjects, including a charming series of dogs and their puppies. Design Manager Graham Tongue has also recently revived the idea of modelling famous dogs with his portrait of *Mick the Miller* DA 214, the famous 1930's racing greyhound, which has become the first ever limited edition dog in the collection

Collecting Cats

Feline fanciers are well served in the Royal Doulton collection with around 40 cat models to find in various colours and glaze effects. The earliest is model number 9 which was issued in flambé in 1908 and is still in production today. It was also offered for a while in naturalistic colours as HN 109. Collectors can choose from miscellaneous moggies or pedigree Persians (HN 999) and Siamese (HN 2655). There are playful cats about to pounce on unsuspecting mice (HN 203) as well as studies of these popular pets in equally familiar pose, catnapping on the best seat of the house (HN 210). The antics of a kitten inspired one of the most popular series ever (HN 2579 - 84) and the artist, Peggy Davies, recalled that her model threatened to cause havoc in the studio, weaving in and out of Charles Noke's precious flambé vases. Fortunately he was an animal lover and welcomed the kitten's invasion.

Two of the cats in the HN collection were inspired by famous cartoon characters; *Kateroo*, the creation of David Souter, who appeared in the Sydney Bulletin and little *Ooloo* from George Studdy's comic strips of the 1920's, who is perhaps better known to collectors as *Lucky* from the miniature K series. Other miniature cats, less than 1 inch tall, were included in the HN collection but these are very hard to find today. At the other end of the scale, Alan Maslankowski modelled a large stylised cat, 11 1/2 inches tall, for the flambé range in 1977 and he has recently produced two new models for the DA series, the haughty *Cat (Walking)* DA 148 and the stealthy *Cat (Stalking)* DA 149. The most recent introduction, *Cat with Bandaged Paw* DA 195 by Martyn Alcock, takes a new sentimental approach and tugs at the heartstrings of all cat lovers. The detailed, realistic approach in the DA series contrasts greatly with the modern streamlined sculptures *Shadowplay* HN 3526 and *Playtime* HN 3544 in the Images range and ensures that Royal

Doulton's interpretations of cats are as varied as the animals themselves.

Collecting Horses

Royal Doulton was the name of the first horse portrayed in the HN collection. Owned by the Roulston Brothers of New Zealand, this successful racehorse was modelled in action by a French freelance artist G. D'Illiers and launched as *The Winner* HN 1407 in 1930. Sadly, it is now virtually impossible to find. More accessible is the portrait of another famous racehorse *Merely a Minor* HN 2530, which was modelled by Frederick Daws, who is better known for his championship dogs.

Most of the early horse models were the work of the distinguished sculptor William Chance, who was responsible for the exceptional model of the royal steeplechaser *Monaveen*. He also paid tribute to the gentle giants of the horse world in *Pride of the Shires* HN 2563 and *Chestnut Mare* HN 2565, portraying them with and without their foals. Some of his first studies also included riders who were later removed to produce independent horses, for example the mount in *Farmer's Boy* HN 2520 became *Dapple Grey* HN 2578.

Occasionally stylised horse models have been included in the HN collection, for example Raoh Schorr's *Prancing Horse* HN 1167 and *The Gift of Life* HN 3524 from the Images series. There have also been legendary horses such as *Pegasus* HN 3547 and *The Unicorn* HN 3549 modelled by Alan Maslankowski.

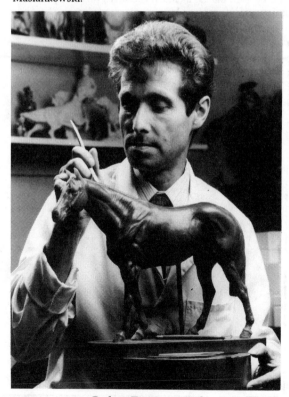

Graham Tongue at work

The range of Royal Doulton horses was expanded when models were transferred from the Beswick range in 1989. Horses had long been the speciality of the John Beswick factory and modellers such as Arthur Gredington and Albert Hallam were renowned in the industry for their portraits of famous racehorses. *Arkle* DA15 and *Nijinski* DA16 are just two examples of their work now in the DA series. When Albert Hallam retired, Graham Tongue became head modeller at the Beswick Studio and continued the tradition with portraits of *Red Rum* DA18 and *Troy* DA37 amongst others. In more recent years he has modelled Britain's favourite racehorse *Desert Orchid* DA134.

AS well as all his famous models, Graham has endeavoured to capture the essential qualities of horses in general with his evocative *Spirit* range, contrasting subjects such as the powerful *Spirit of the Earth* DA61 with the playful *Young Spirit* DA70. His young assistants are now contributing to all these established collections, for example Warren Platt has recently portrayed *Mr. Frisk* DA190 and Amanda Hughes-Lubeck has modelled several *Spirit* horses as well as *My First Horse* DA193B, an ideal purchase to start a collection.

Collecting Birds and Butterflies

Birds have always formed an important part of the Royal Doulton collection, beginning with Charles Noke's models of fledglings for the flambé glaze in 1908. A flock of feathered friends followed in the first few years of the HN collection and by 1920 the list included cockerels, pigeons, pelicans, guinea fowl, eagles, kingfishers, budgies, ducks and penguins, not forgetting all the miscellaneous chicks. Some are realistically rendered like the *Cockatoo* HN 185, which

was modelled by Leslie Harradine, whilst in Noke's hands others assume human characteristics, like *Granny Owl* HN 187 and the *Toucan in Tails* HN 208. The comic approach continued during the 1920's with a series of tiny character toucans and penguins but generally a naturalistic style of modelling prevailed over the years.

During the war years two series of birds (HN 2540-2556 and HN 2611-2619) were made specially for export to the USA but these were short lived and are hard to find today. The same applies to the miniature models of birds which, for some reason, were added to both the HN and the K series in the early 1940's. Some of the K birds are so rare that they have eluded discovery in time for this publication.

In 1952 several large bird models were added to the Prestige range and in the 1970's Robert Jefferson produced some magnificent limited edition sculptures of birds specifically for the US market. A few years later, in 1979, the Lem Ward series of decoy ducks was also produced with American collectors in mind. Ward's carvings of wildfowl counterfeits are very sought after in the USA and Design Manager Harry Sales was asked to interpret the wooden originals in a matt glazed ceramic body.

For a brief period, between 1979 and 1982, the birds produced at the Royal Adderley factory, now one of the companies in the Royal Doulton group, were given Royal Doulton backstamps. There are 50 models in this range and they are quite different in style, body and texture from the earlier Royal Doulton birds.

Birds have regularly provided inspiration for the stylised *Images of Nature* collection and some have been produced in both white bone china and fiery flambé. In contrast, Graham

Group of bird models c.1950

Tongue and his team at the John Beswick studio, aim to recreate the feel of the bird's feathers and they are regular visitors to aviaries and falconry displays as well as avid bird watchers. Since 1989 they have introduced a variety of familiar garden birds to the DA range as well as endangered species such as kestrels and owls.

Bird collectors can also find lots of different derivatives from the 1930's. Ashtrays and bowls often have birds perched on top and flower holders were frequently adorned with birds. Some of these were designed to be placed in the floating flower bowls which were fashionable at the time. Models of butterflies on rocks were made for the same purpose and there are also clip-on varieties for attaching to the side of the bowls. During the Second World War a collection of six different species of butterflies alighting in foliage was introduced but, like the birds of the period, they came and went and are consequently very hard to find today.

Collecting Prestige, Limited Editions and Special Commissions

Art Director Charles Noke specialised in large, ambitious sculptures of wild animals. Massive fighting elephants are depicted with their trunks aggressively outstretched, as in HN 1120, whilst others are shown in repose, HN 1121. Big cats, including lions, tigers and leopards, stalk their prey or crouch ready to pounce from rocks. Most of these impressive studies were first introduced to the HN collection during the 1920's and 1930's but, in 1952, a few of them were given new HN numbers and a new prestige status. *Tiger on Rock* HN 2639, *Leopard on Rock* HN 2638, *Lion on Rock* HN 2641 and *Fighter Elephant* HN 2640 could also be purchased on a special order basis until 1989 and were the most expensive models in the range.

Raoh Schorr's large fox model HN 2634 was also re-classified as a prestige piece in 1952, together with the large *Peruvian Penguin* HN 2633 and the *Drake* HN 2635. Peggy Davies modelled *Indian Runner Drake* HN 2636 especially for the new prestige range and a large study of a polar bear and cub was offered in naturalistic colouring as HN 2637 instead of its earlier flambé finish. With the exception of the fox, these prestige pieces had all been discontinued by the early 1970's.

In 1974 freelance artist Robert Jefferson was commissioned to model Royal Doulton's first limited edition animal sculptures. His studies of animals and birds in their habitats were observed in minute detail and finely executed in matt porcelain to enhance the different textures of fur and feathers. The artistic and technical virtuosity of Jefferson's work is much appreciated by collectors today but examples are hard to find as most were only made in editions of 75-250, exclusively for the US market.

In recent years Design Manager Graham Tongue has been responsible for most of the prestige and limited edition models in the Royal Doulton range. Many of his studies of prize bulls and famous race horses were originally produced for the Beswick Connoisseur range but since 1989 they have had Royal Doulton backstamps and DA numbers. Connoisseur sculptures are generally mounted on polished wooden bases with metal name plaques to reinforce their prestige status.

In 1989 several prestige sculptures of wild animals and birds were launched to raise funds for the World Wide Fund for Nature and a percentage of sales from *The Majestic Stag* DA32 and *The Watering Hole* DA39, amongst others, went to help save endangered species and stop environmental destruction. Lawleys by Post, the mail order division of Royal Doulton, continued this gesture with the limited edition *Kestrel* DA144, which was commissioned exclusively for their customers in 1991. Since that date they have added several limited editions and prestige pieces to their catalogue.

On occasion, Royal Doulton have been approached by independent companies to produce an animal model for promotional or commemorative purposes. In recent years a turkey has been made for the well known poultry company Bernard Matthews and a limited edition paperweight, in the form of a partridge, was produced for the Financial Times. Because of the limited distribution of these pieces to staff and customers of the organisations concerned, they are often difficult to find in the marketplace. This is also the case with the older advertising pieces such as the liqueur containers made for Ervan Bols in the 1930's and National Distillers in the 1950's.

Collecting Miniatures

Tiny collectables have always had a special appeal and animals are no exception. They have the advantage of not taking up too much space and a wide range of animal species can be accommodated in a single cabinet. Lots of little models, including frogs, mice and fledglings, were produced in the early 1900's for the flambé glaze and some were later coloured naturalistically for the HN collection. These models are generally less than 2 1/2 inches tall but even small pieces, around 1 inch in height, were introduced during the 1920's. Collectors can have fun looking for all the tiny character birds, which are comic interpretations of owls, puffins, penguins and toucans. There are 11 different models to find in the first series, some in alternative colour schemes (HN 256-66 and 290-93) but unfortunately only a few were located in time for this publication. Also very rare are the 6

Group of Miniature dogs from
the HN and K series, c.1925-1935

character toucans in the second series (HN 913-918), the character pigs (HN 892-7) and the young elephants (HN 949-952).

Some of the designs resemble Japanese netsuke, in particular the tiny curled up kittens (HN 820-825) and puppies (HN 834-839) which nestle comfortably in the palm of your hand. Some slightly larger seated and standing puppies followed and the star of this group is undoubtedly *Bonzo*. The creation of George Studdy, this popular cartoon dog, appeared in comic strips, films, advertisements and postcards during the 1920's. Bonzo collectables became all the rage and in 1923 Doulton offered four different models of the famous character in several different colourways plus a very rare Chinese Jade version (HN 804, 808-15, 826). His feline friend *Ooloo* was sold in five different colours (HN 818, 819, 827-29) and later joined the K series as *Lucky*, K12, continuing in production until 1977.

The new K numbering system for miniatures was launched in 1931 and applied to twelve little dogs, less than 3 inches tall, and *Lucky* the cat. Six more dogs joined the series in 1940 along with three hares, six penguins and eleven other types of birds. These birds are the hardest of all to find as they were withdrawn within a few years of issue. Three of the K dogs are more elusive than the others as they were withdrawn in 1959 compared to 1977 for the rest. K dogs were frequently mounted on calendars, ashtrays and pen trays and they were sometimes offered in conjunction with figures, for example the *Old Balloon Seller* with the K1 bulldog on a wooden stand was sold as HN 1791

More miniature birds were introduced in 1941 but for some reason they were given HN numbers rather than K ones. To add to the confusion the Drake Mallard is numbered HN 2572 whilst his mate the duck is K26. Subsequent miniatures were also numbered in the HN series. In the late 1940's and 50's, Peggy Davies modelled some collections of baby animals, including kittens, piglets and lambs. The kittens, in particular, proved very popular and stayed in the range until 1985 together with a collection of little puppies. Sadly there have been no new miniature animals in recent years but, given Royal Doulton's successful revival of tiny character jugs and figures, there would surely be an enthusiastic reception for tiny animals too.

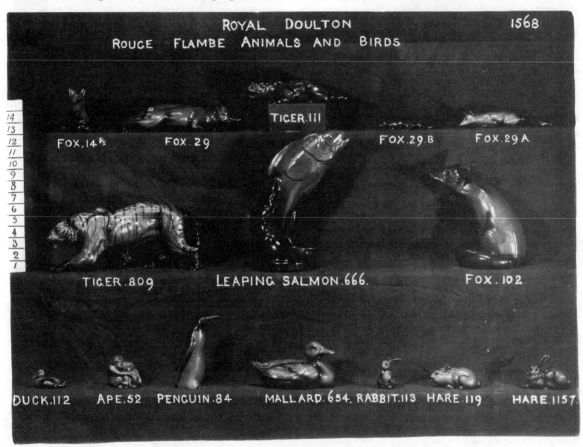

Publicity photograph for the Flambé animals range c.1950

Collecting Animals in Flambé and other Experimental Glazes

The fiery red flambé glaze was inspired by Oriental ceramics and was perfected by Royal Doulton, after many years of experimentation, in 1904. The precise recipe has always been a closely guarded secret but essentially the glaze consists of copper and iron oxides which fire to a glorious red colour when the kiln is deprived of oxygen.

Within a few years of the launch, Charles Noke was applying this lustrous glaze to little animal models and it continues to be used for new designs to this day. Some of the earliest models, including the cat, the foxes, the ducks and the penguin, have been in continuous production for more than 80 years.

The flambé models that were illustrated in the early catalogues and publicity photographs turn up most frequently in the market place and must have been produced in some quantities, for example the cuddling apes (52) the guinea fowl (69) and the leaping salmon (666). Many other animals were decorated with the flambé glaze purely as an experiment and there may be only one or two in existence. Charles Noke was constantly trying out new ideas and some designs turned out to be more suitable for the effect than others.

As well as the monochrome flambé glaze, Noke also developed lots of mottled and veined variations, including Sung and Chang. In most cases, these effects were too capricious to be used on a regular basis but spectacular Sung and Chang animals do come on to the market from time to time. Many of these special pieces bear the monograms of Charles Noke and his assistants Harry Nixon and Fred Moore. Chinese Jade was another of Noke's special effects, perfected in 1920, and he modelled a range of stylised animals especially for this tactile, soft green glaze, including some fish (625 and 632), an elephant (633) and a pair of cockatoos (630). Production of this unpredictable glaze was very short lived so examples are hard to find. Also for a brief period between the wars, animals were decorated with Noke's Titanian glaze, which ranges from a pale, smoky blue to a deep midnight hue but again only a few examples of each would ever have been produced. Occasionally models appear with a dark blue veining on a white ground, which is the second stage in the flambé decoration so, although interesting, these are actually unfinished pieces.

In the course of his glaze experimentation, Noke produced various bright yellow, orange, and red glazes and a greenish brown which was intended to simulate bronze. These effects turn up on animal models from time to time but they will be isolated examples. During the late 1950's and 60's, the new Art Director, Jo Ledger, also produced some interesting flambé glaze effects, including a mottled blue and green colour which he called Mandarin. Some of the animals in his Chatcull range can be found with this finish but they did not go into commercial production.

After a gap of many years, three large models went into the general flambé range in 1973. The owl (2249), the rhinoceros (615), and the dragon (2085) are still in production today, together with the cat (2269) which joined them a few years later. The Royal Doulton International Collectors Club helped promote interest in flambé again when they launched their exclusive Dog of Fo in 1982 and they have recently commissioned an exotic flambé Dragon. Since 1987 new subjects have periodically joined the dramatic Images of Fire collection ensuring a promising future for the flambé range.

MAKING ROYAL DOULTON ANIMALS

Many different creative processes are involved in the production of Royal Doulton animals but essentially they all start the same way with an image in the designer's mind. If the model is to represent a specific breed then the artist will visit the stable, kennel or farm to study the animal in detail. Many photographs will be taken for reference and sometimes sketches will be made of important details. Having decided on the most appropriate pose, the modeller will set to work in clay, recreating the personality of his subject, as well as the precise details of its bone structure, muscles and finally the texture of its skin, fur or feathers. Even if the sculpture is destined for the stylised Images of Nature collection, the artist must study the animal in action to capture the essence of its character and abstract the leading lines of the design.

**Assembling the sculpture of
Rosate Terns by Robert Jefferson**

When the original clay sculpture has been completed and approved, the block maker will divide the model into appropriate sections in order to make the master mould. A few prototype pieces will be cast from this mould to produce colour trials and once these have been approved by the marketing, design and production teams, together with the animal's owner, working moulds will be made of plaster of Paris.

Over the years both earthenware and bone china have been used to make animals at Royal Doulton's factories in Stoke-on-Trent. Bone china is a traditionally British body, with a high proportion of bone ash, which creates the much admired translucency when the body is fired to a high temperature. Earthenware is fired at a lower temperature than china and remains porous. Earthenware is usually painted under the glaze and bone china on top, creating different decorative effects. In the early 1900's, the same models were often offered in both bodies. Since the early 1970's earthenware models have been made at the John

Beswick factory, which has a long tradition in animal production, and bone china models are made at the Royal Doulton factory in Burslem.

Different ingredients and firing techniques are used to produce the two ceramic bodies but the casting process is the same. Liquid clay, known as slip, is poured into the plaster of Paris moulds and, once the body has set to the required thickness, the excess slip is poured out. The pieces are carefully removed from the mould as the clay is still very fragile at this stage and the various parts are jointed together using slip as an adhesive. The seams are then gently sponged away by a process known as fettling and the piece is ready for its first firing, during which the water is driven off and it shrinks to its 'biscuit' state.

The Lem Ward Decoy Ducks
on the kiln truck

Earthenware animal models are decorated at this stage by a combination of spraying and hand painting. For instance, a horse model will have its coat sprayed to the required colour and then all the details, such as head, mane, tail, hooves, etc. will be painted by hand. The Connoisseur collection obviously has a high proportion of hand painting to recreate the animal's distinctive markings, for example the leopard's spots in *The Watering Hole* DA39 and the variegated plumage on the *Barn Owl* DA1. Once the painted decoration has dried, some animals are finished with a matt glaze to best capture their natural appearance. Others are coated with a high gloss glaze, creating a typical ceramic look when fired. In some cases the same models are offered with a choice of glaze effects.

Bone china animals are dipped or sprayed with liquid glaze and then fired again before decoration. In the past these would then have been hand painted by specialists in on-glaze colours. However, most of the bone china figures produced today are for the Images of Nature collection and they are left undecorated in their pure white bone china or finished with flambé glazes.

A complex process is used to create the flambé effect and the precise recipe is still a closely guarded secret. The unglazed pieces are taken to the flambé studios in their biscuit state and the features are painted in touches of blue, which will eventually shine through the flambé glaze. The

Painting the Lem Ward Decoy Ducks

flame effect on larger pieces is achieved by arranging thin strands of hemp over the piece to act as a template and then spraying on various colours. The hemp is removed leaving a unique veined effect and the piece then undergoes the various flambé glaze and firing procedures. In the final stage the kiln is deprived of oxygen which results in the fiery red finish.

The Gift of Life in the early stages
of the Flambé process

CARE AND REPAIR

Careful handling and cleaning of Royal Doulton animal models will ensure that a collection can be enjoyed for many years to come. Tails, ears and other protruding features are particularly prone to damage when transporting, displaying and cleaning the collection. The Championship Dogs, in particular, have very vulnerable tails as they were modelled to portray the show stance as accurately as possible. When purchasing dogs like the Dalmatian HN 1111, always check for restoration to the tail and seek the dealer's opinion. A reputable dealer will stand by any guarantees he gives regarding restorations.

Take care not to damage the animal models during cleaning by following these basic procedures. When dusting in situ, a soft cosmetic brush or photographic lens brush is useful for getting into tight corners. Make sure the animals do not knock against each other causing chips or imperceptable cracks in the glaze which could open up at a later date. When necessary, models should be sponged with luke-warm water, using a mild liquid detergent, and then sponged again with clean water to rinse. It is important that water does not get inside the animal so block up the holes in the bottom before washing. Allow the piece to dry naturally and then, if the piece is glazed, buff gently with a soft cloth.

If the worst happens and a piece gets broken, seek the help and advice of a professional restorer. A skilled practitioner can repair chipped, cracked and shattered models so that the original damage is invisible to all but the most experienced eye.

With the right approach, Royal Doulton animals are much easier to take care of than real pets as they do not need to be walked, fed or house-trained so make the most of them.

CURRENT AND DISCONTINUED ANIMALS

Animals which are produced at the Royal Doulton factories today are referred to as 'current' and most of the range can be purchased in specialist china shops or from mail order companies. Royal Doulton publishes catalogues of their general range and these are obtainable from their Headquarters in England or their distribution companies around the world. Occasionally models have been commissioned exclusively for independent organisations and distribution of these varies. Lawleys by Post, the direct mail division of Royal Doulton, publishes an annual catalogue for their customers which often features animal offers. The Royal Doulton International Collectors Club usually publishes details of these private commissions in their quarterly magazine *Gallery* and they may have, on occasion, offered animal models exclusively to their members. They also provide information on new introductions to the general range and the pieces being withdrawn to make way for the new models.

Once a piece has been withdrawn from production, it is referred to as 'discontinued' or 'retired' and it enters the secondary market. Many dealers around the world carry discontinued Royal Doulton animals as part of their general stock but some specialise in the field more than others. They regularly exhibit at antique fairs, some of which are exclusively for Royal Doulton products, and many run mail order services. Specialist animal dealers will often help

collectors find specific models but it is still fun to scour general antique fairs and flea markets in case there are animals to be found. Auction rooms and estate sales sometimes feature Royal Doulton animals and successful purchases can be made if there is the time to view the lots, armed with techniques for spotting restorations and a good knowledge of prices.

A GUIDE TO DATING AND BACKSTAMPS

The Royal Doulton archive has very little information about the introduction and withdrawal dates of the animals in the HN collection so dating has been based on the study of model numbers, HN numbers and dated examples. Many animals have an impressed model number on the base which tallies with a photographic record book of shapes held at the Sir Henry Doulton Gallery in Stoke-on-Trent. Often the number is indistinct but by close examination of the shape book, it has been possible to match most model numbers with HN numbers. Occasionally photographs are missing from the shape books hence the gaps which still exist - hopefully they can be filled by keen collectors.

The model numbers are entered chronologically and animals are interspersed with figures. Existing information on figure introduction dates has therefore helped in establishing dates when the animals were first modelled. In 1936, many master moulds were destroyed and these are recorded in the shape book thus giving a number of withdrawal dates, Catalogues and price lists have provided further information but there are still several grey areas which have been filled with educated guesses. It is known, for instance, that most early models had been withdrawn by 1946, Collectors are invited to send details of dated pieces in their possession for further editions of this book.

The HN pattern numbers refer to the decorative treatment and many models were offered in a variety of colourways, some over a long period of time. Sequences of HN numbers were reserved for the animals: HN 100 - 300 were all allocated by 1922; HN 800 - 1200 allocated by 1937; HN 2500 - 2670 allocated by 1976 and HN 3500 - 3552 to the present.

The DA numbering system has been in use since 1989 although DA numbers are not found on the base of the piece unless it is a limited edition or prestige piece. There are no seperate model numbers for new introductions. Animals transferred from the Beswick range have model numbers relating to the shape book held at the John Beswick Studio. Some of these models can be found with both Royal Doulton and John Beswick backstamps, which has led to some confusion in the market place. Similarly birds transferred from the Royal Adderley range can be found with both company trademarks.

Sometimes early Royal Doulton animals have a date code on the base which enables the piece to be dated to a specific year. Until around 1927, an impressed date was sometimes used to denote the day, month and year of production. Between 1928 and 1957 a date code was printed adjacent to the lion and crown symbol. To calculate the date, add the number beside the backstamp to 1927 eg the 14 numeral found on the Union Jack bulldogs denotes 1941.

Decorator's initials are often found adjacent to the backstamps. E.W stands for Eric Webster, who was the leading animal painter for many years. He painted the first Championship Dogs and he also worked on special commissions, such as the royal steeplechaser Monaveen. F. C is Fred Clark, who painted a variety of animals from prestige penguins to the K series. He remembers that the painters were paid 2 1/2 pence each for each K dog that they painted in the early years. T. stands for Stan Jones, K. for Ken Taylor and X for Roy Booth - all prolific animal painters. There are many other painter's marks to be found but those mentioned are the most notable.

Many different types of Royal Doulton backstamps have been used on animals over the years and these can also help with the dating process. Some of the most commonly found examples are illustrated below.

Blue Bird

At the same time, details of the body were incorporated underneath eg "Bone China" "Flambé". If there is no reference then the model is made of earthenware.

The earliest mark found on animals is the basic lion and crown trademark which was in use from the launch of the collection until the early 1930's.

"Lucky"

Often the complete lion and crown trademark would not fit on to the base of the animals and so only the bottom part of the mark, incorporating the interlacing D device, was used. In many cases this small circular mark was printed on one of the animal's feet, and the HN number written on another. In the early years of the Championship series, the dog's name was also printed on one of the feet if there was sufficient space.

Between 1923 and 1927 the lion is sometimes found without the crown.

DOULTON
MADE IN
ENGLAND

Some early miniature pieces just say 'DOULTON' or 'DOULTON ENGLAND' or 'DOULTON MADE IN ENGLAND'.

The words 'Made in England' were first added to the Royal Doulton trademark in the 1920's and this new style of backstamp has been used on animals since the early 1930's.

A half moon shaped backstamp with the words 'ROYAL DOULTON MADE IN ENGLAND' was sometimes used on the dogs of character.

WHERE TO BUY

Discontinued Royal Doulton animals can be found in antique shops, markets and fairs as well as auction houses. Specialist dealers in Royal Doulton figures attend many of the venues and events below.

UNITED KINGDOM
Auction Houses

Phillips
101 New Bond Street
London W1

Christie's South Kensington
85 Old Brompton Road
London SW5

Bonhams
Montpelier Street
London SW7

Sotheby's
Summer's Place
Billingshurst, West Sussex

Louis Taylor
Percy Street
Hanley, Stoke-on-Trent

Peter Wilson
Victoria Gallery
Market Street
Nantwich, Cheshire

Antique Fairs

Doulton and Beswick Collectors Fair
National Motorcycle Museum
Meriden, Birmingham

Stafford International Doulton Fair
Stafford Country Showground
Stafford

UK Doulton Collectors Fair
Park Lane Hotel
Piccadilly
London W1

Antique Markets

Alfie's Antique Market
13-25 Church Street
London NW8
Tuesday-Saturday

Camden Passage Market
(of Upper Street)
London N1
Wednesday and Saturday

New Caledonian Market
Bermondsey Square
London SE1
Friday morning

Portobello Road Market
London W11
Saturday only

USA
Auction Houses

Phillips New York
406 East 79th Street
New York, NY 10021

Antique Fairs

Doulton Show
Sheraton Poste House
Cherry Hill, New Jersey

Doulton Show
Holiday Inn
Independence, Ohio

Florida Doulton Convention
Sheraton Design Centre
Fort Lauderdale, Florida

CANADA
Auction Houses

D & J Ritchie Inc.
288 King Street East
Toronto, Ontario, M5A 1K4

Antique Shows

The Canadian Royal Doulton & Beswick Collectors Fair
Sheraton Toronto East Hotel
2035 Kennedy Road
Scarborough, Ontario

Antique Markets

Harbourfront Antique Market
390 Queen's Quay West
Toronto, Ontario
(Tuesday - Sunday)

PLACES TO VISIT

John Beswick Factory Tour
Gold Street
Longton, Stoke-on-Trent
ST3 2JP
For opening times and tour information telephone
(0782) 292292

Royal Doulton Factory Tour
and the Sir Henry Doulton Gallery
Nile Street
Burslem, Stoke-on-Trent
For opening times and tour information telephone
(0782) 744766

CLUBS AND SOCIETIES

The Royal Doulton International Collectors Club was founded in 1980 to provide an information service on all aspects of the company's products, past and present. The Club's magazine 'Gallery' is published four times a year and local branches also publish newsletters. There are also several regional groups in the USA, which meet for lectures and other events and some publish newsletters. Contact the USA branch for further information.

Headquarters and UK Branch

Royal Doulton
Minton House
London Road
Stoke-on-Trent, ST4 7QD

Australian Branch

Royal Doulton Australia Pty Ltd.
17-23 Merriwa Street, Gordon,
Australia NSW 2072

Canadian Branch

Royal Doulton Canada Inc.
850 Progress Avenue,
Scarborough, Ontario, M1H 3C4

New Zealand Branch

Royal Doulton
P.O. Box 2059
Auckland, New Zealand

USA Branch

Royal Doulton USA Inc.
P.O. Box 1815
Somerset, New Jersey 08873

FURTHER READING

Animals

Collecting Doulton Animals by Jocelyn Lukins
Doulton Flambé Animals by Jocelyn Lukins

Figures and Character Jugs

Royal Doulton Figures by Desmond Eyles, Louise Irvine and Valerie Baynton
The Charlton Standard Catalogue of Royal Doulton Jugs by Jean Dale
The Character Jug Collectors Handbook by Kevin Pearson
Collecting Character and Toby Jugs by Jocelyn Lukins
The Doulton Figure Collectors handbook by Kevin Pearson

General

Discovering Royal Doulton by Michael Doulton
The Doulton Story by Paul Atterbury and Louise Irvine
Royal Doulton Series Wares by Louise Irvine (Vols 1-4)
Royal Doulton Bunnykins Figures by Louise Irvine
Bunnykins Collectors Book by Louise Irvine
Beatrix Potter Figures edited by Louise Irvine
Limited Edition Loving Cups and Jugs by Louise Irvine and Richard Dennis
Doulton for the Collector by Jocelyn Lukins
Doulton Kingsware Flasks by Jocelyn Lukins
Collecting Doulton Animals by Jocelyn Lukins
Doulton Burslem Advertising Wares by Jocelyn Lukins
Doulton Lambeth Advertising Wares by Jocelyn Lukins
The Doulton Lambeth Wares by Desmond Eyles
The Doulton Burslem Wares by Desmond Eyles
Hannah Barlow by Peter Rose
George Tinworth by Peter Rose
Sir Henry Doulton Biography by Edmund Gosse
Phillips Collectors Guide by Catherine Braithwaite
Collecting Doulton Magazine Edited by Alan Blakeman, BBR Publishing
Royal Doulton by Jennifer Queree

HN SERIES

H.N. 197. H.N. 163. H.N. 133. H.N. 205. H.N. 158.

H.N. 116. 12. H.N. 147. H.N. 125. H.N. 176. H.N. 151.

H.N. 117. 231. H.N. 168. 61. H.N. 802.

H.N. 181. H.N. 27. H.N. 128. H.N. 134. H.N. 132.

H.N. 276. H.N. 161. H.N. 118. H.N. 280. H.N. 137. H.N. 145.

ROYAL DOULTON BIRDS AND ANIMALS.

HN 7
Pedlar Wolf

Model No.: 76
Designer: Charles Noke
Height: 5 1/2", 14.0 cm
Colour: Black wolf wearing blue cloak
Issued: 1913-1938
Varieties: Flambé

Price: U.S. $ Can. $ U.K. £
Extremely Rare

*

HN 100
Fox In Hunting Dress

Model No.: 151
Designer: Charles Noke
Height: 6", 15.2 cm
Colour: Brown fox wearing hunting pink riding coat, white shirt and cravat, gold stud
Issued: 1913-1942

Price:

	U.S.$	Can. $	U.K. £
	1,400.00	1,600.00	650.00

HN 101
Rabbit In Morning Dress

Model No.: 152
Designer: Charles Noke
Height: 6 1/2", 16.5 cm
Colour: Red coat, white trousers, black and white checkered cravat
Issued: 1913-by 1938
Varieties: Also called "Hare In White Coat", HN 102

Price: U.S. $ Can. $ U.K. £
Extremely Rare

HN 102
Hare In White Coat

Model No.: 152
Designer: Charles Noke
Height: 6 1/2", 16.5 cm
Colour: White coat
Issued: 1913-by 1938
Varieties: Also called "Rabbit In Morning Dress", HN 101

Price: U.S. $ Can. $ U.K. £
Extremely Rare

HN 103
Penguins

Model No.:	103
Designer:	Unknown
Height:	6", 15.2 cm
Colour:	Grey, white and black
Issued:	1913-by 1946
Varieties:	HN 133, Flambé

Price:	*U.S. $*	*Can. $*	*U.K. £*
	600.00	750.00	295.00

HN 104
Penguin
Style One

Model No.:	85
Designer:	Unknown
Height:	4 1/2", 11.4 cm
Colour:	Black and white (earthenware)
Issued:	1913-by 1946
Varieties:	HN 134, Flambé

Price:	*U.S. $*	*Can. $*	*U.K. £*
	350.00	450.00	250.00

HN 105
Collie
Seated - brown

Model No.:	47
Designer:	Unknown
Height:	7 1/2", 19.1 cm
Colour:	Brown with black markings, white chest and feet
Issued:	1912-by 1946
Varieties:	HN106, 112, Flambé

Price:	*U.S. $*	*Can. $*	*U.K. £*
	750.00	1,000.00	400.00

HN 106
Collie
Seated - blue

Model No.:	47
Designer:	Unknown
Height:	7 1/2", 19.1 cm
Colour:	Blue-grey coat, white chest, brown head (earthenware)
Issued:	1912-by 1946
Varieties:	HN 105, 112, Flambé

Price:	*U.S. $*	*Can. $*	*U.K. £*
	750.00	1,000.00	450.00

HN 107
Hare
Crouching - Style One

Model No.:	119
Designer:	Unknown
Height:	2", 5.1 cm
Colour:	Brown (earthenware)
Issued:	1913-by 1946
Varieties:	HN 126, 142, 273, 803, Flambé, Sung

Price:	*U.S. $*	*Can. $*	*U.K. £*
	350.00	450.00	195.00

HN 108
Lop-eared Rabbit

Model No.:	113
Designer:	Charles Noke
Height:	4", 10.1 cm
Colour:	White
Issued:	1913-by 1946
Varieties:	HN 151, 276, Flambé; Matt red glaze, HN 1091B on Fluted Ashtray, HN 1091A on Plain Ashtray

Price:	*U.S. $*	*Can. $*	*U.K. £*
	750.00	950.00	450.00

HN 109
Cat
Seated - Style One

Model No.:	9
Designer:	Charles Noke
Height:	4 1/2", 11.4 cm
Colour:	White with black highlights (earthenware)
Issued:	1912-by 1946
Varieties:	HN 120, 967, Flambé, Sung

Price:	*U.S. $*	*Can. $*	*U.K. £*
	600.00	800.00	350.00

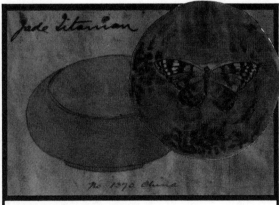

HN 110
Titanian Bowl Decorated with a Butterfly

Model No.:	Unknown
Designer:	Unknown
Height:	3", 7.6 cm
Colour:	Lid of bowl decorated in turquoise with brown and orange butterfly (china)
Issued:	1912

Price:	*U.S. $*	*Can. $*	*U.K. £*
		Extremely Rare	

HN 111
Cockerel
Crowing
Model No.:   25
Designer: Unknown
Height: 3 1/4", 8.3 cm
Colour: White with black wing tips, tail and
              feathers, red comb
Issued: 1912-1936
Varieties: Flambé

Price:	U.S. $	Can. $	U.K. £
	400.00	550.00	250.00

HN 112
Collie
Seated
Model No.:   47
Designer: Unknown
Height: 7 1/2", 19.1 cm
Colour: Blue-grey and white coat,
              brown head (china)
Issued: 1912-by 1946
Varieties: HN 105, 106, Flambé

Price:	U.S. $	Can. $	U.K. £
	750.00	1,000.00	450.00

HN 113
Emperor Penguin
Model No.:   84
Designer: Unknown
Height: 6", 15.2 cm
Colour: Black, white and grey
Issued: 1913-by 1946
Varieties: HN 296, Flambé

Price:	U.S. $	Can. $	U.K. £
	550.00	750.00	350.00

HN 114
Mallard Drake
Standing - Malachite
Model No.:   137
Designer: Unknown
Height: 5 1/2", 14.0 cm
Size: Medium
Colour: Malachite head, green feathers, white breast
Issued: 1913-by 1946
Varieties: HN 115, 116, 956, 1191, 2555, 2647,
              Flambé

Price:	U.S. $	Can. $	U.K. £
	400.00	550.00	250.00

HN 115
Mallard Drake
Standing - Blue head

Model No.:	137
Designer:	Unknown
Height:	5 1/2", 14.0 cm
Size:	Medium
Colour:	Blue head, green feathers and white breast
Issued:	1913-by 1946
Varieties:	HN 114, 116, 956, 1191, 2555, 2647, Flambé

Price:	*U.S. $*	*Can. $*	*U.K. £*
	400.00	550.00	250.00

HN 116
Mallard Duck
Standing - Green head

Model No.:	137
Designer:	Unknown
Height:	5 1/2", 14.0 cm
Size:	Medium
Colour:	Green head and back, white breast
Issued:	1913-by 1946
Varieties:	HN 114, 115, 956, 1191, 2555, 2647, Flambé

Price:	*U.S. $*	*Can. $*	*U.K. £*
	400.00	550.00	250.00

HN 117
Foxes
Curled - Style One

Model No.:	6
Designer:	Unknown
Height:	3 1/2", 8.9 cm
Colour:	Grey, light brown highlights
Issued:	1912-by 1946
Varieties:	HN 179, Flambé, Sung, Treacle glaze

Price:	*U.S. $*	*Can. $*	*U.K. £*
	600.00	800.00	375.00

HN 118
Monkey
Seated, arms folded

Model No.:	53
Designer:	Unknown
Height:	3", 7.6 cm
Colour:	Grey (china)
Issued:	1912-by 1946
Varieties:	HN 253, Flambé, Titanian

Price:	*U.S. $*	*Can. $*	*U.K. £*
	350.00	425.00	230.00

HN 119
Polar Bear on Cube

Model No.:	67
Designer:	Leslie Harradine
Height:	4", 10.1 cm
Colour:	Grey bear with yellow highlights on a green cube
Issued:	1912-1936
Varieties:	Flambé

Price:	U.S. $	Can. $	U.K. £
	500.00	625.00	250.00

HN 120
Cat
Seated - Style One

Model No.:	9
Designer:	Charles Noke
Height:	4 1/2", 11.4 cm
Colour:	White with black highlights (china)
Issued:	1912-by 1946
Varieties:	HN 109, 967, Flambé, Sung

Price:	U.S. $	Can. $	U.K. £
	600.00	800.00	350.00

HN 121
Polar Bear
Seated

Model No.:	39
Designer:	Unknown
Height:	3 3/4", 9.5 cm
Colour:	White (china)
Issued:	1912-1936
Varieties:	Flambé
Derivitive:	Polar bear on dish, Model No. 40

Price:	U.S. $	Can. $	U.K. £
	500.00	625.00	250.00

HN 122
Fantail Pigeons

Model No.:	46
Designer:	Unknown
Height:	4", 10.1 cm
Colour:	Grey-blue with black tail feathers
Issued:	1912-1936
Varieties:	Flambé

Price:	U.S. $	Can. $	U.K. £
	450.00	600.00	325.00

HN 123
Pelican
Beak Up

Model No.:	109
Designer:	Unknown
Height:	4", 10.1 cm
Colour:	White with black highlights, orange beak
Issued:	1913-1936
Varieties:	Flambé

Price:	*U.S. $*	*Can. $*	*U.K. £*
	675.00	850.00	425.00

HN 124
Cockerel
Crouching

Model No.:	30
Designer:	Unknown
Height:	3 1/4", 8.3 cm
Colour:	Cream with black tail feathers, red comb
Issued:	1912-1936
Varieties:	HN 178, 180, 267, Flambé
Derivitive:	Flambé with hollow centre and Sterling silver rim

Price:	*U.S. $*	*Can. $*	*U.K. £*
	300.00	450.00	175.00

HN 125
Guinea Fowl

Model No.:	69
Designer:	Unknown
Height:	3 1/4" x 5 1/4", 8.3 x13.3 cm
Colour:	Grey-pink checkered body, red brown head
Issued:	1912-by 1946
Varieties:	Flambé

Price:	*U.S. $*	*Can. $*	*U.K. £*
	400.00	500.00	225.00

HN 126
Hare
Crouching - Style One

Model No.:	119
Designer:	Unknown
Height:	2", 5.1 cm
Colour:	Brown (china)
Issued:	1913-by 1946
Varieties:	HN 107, 142, 273, 803, Flambé, Sung

Price:	*U.S. $*	*Can. $*	*U.K. £*
	350.00	450.00	195.00

HN 127
Cavalier King Charles Spaniel
Style One

Model No.:	82
Designer:	Charles Noke
Height:	3 1/2", 8.9 cm
Colour:	Light brown coat, dark brown and black head, white nose (Blenheim)
Issued:	1912-1936
Varieties:	Chinese Jade, Flambé

Price:	*U.S. $*	*Can. $*	*U.K. £*
	1,150.00	1,550.00	600.00

HN 128
Puppy
Seated

Model No.:	116
Designer:	Unknown
Height:	4", 10.1 cm
Colour:	Light brown, white chest, dark brown ears (china)
Issued:	1913-by 1946
Varieties:	Flambé, Sung
Derivitive:	Flambé puppy on onyx pin tray

Price:	*U.S. $*	*Can. $*	*U.K. £*
	900.00	1,200.00	550.00

HN 129
Bulldog
Seated - Style Four

Model No.:	135
Designer:	Unknown
Height:	6", 15.2 cm
Colour:	White with black patches
Issued:	1913-by 1946
Varieties:	HN 948, Flambé

Price:	*U.S. $*	*Can. $*	*U.K. £*
	2,500.00	*3,300.00*	*1,500.00*

HN 130
Fox
Seated - Style Three

Model No.:	102
Designer:	Charles Noke
Height:	8 1/2", 21.6 cm
Size:	Large
Colour:	Light brown with dark brown highlights
Issued:	1913-by 1946
Varieties:	Flambé

Price:	*U.S. $*	*Can. $*	*U.K. £*
	1,000.00	1,200.00	600.00

HN 131
Kingfisher on Rock
Style One

Model No.:	44
Designer:	Unknown
Height:	4", 10.1 cm
Colour:	Malachite blue head, blue and green feathers, red-orange breast, brown rock
Issued:	1913-1936
Varieties:	HN 152, Flambé

Price:	*U.S. $*	*Can. $*	*U.K. £*
	250.00	350.00	160.00

HN 132
Drake on Rock

Model No.:	138
Designer:	Unknown
Height:	3 1/2", 8.9 cm
Colour:	Turquoise head, white breast, blue-green and brown wings, pearl rock
Issued:	1913-1936
Varieties:	Flambé; Colourways: Brown rock
Derivitive:	Chinese Jade pin tray

Price:	*U.S. $*	*Can. $*	*U.K. £*
	275.00	375.00	170.00

HN 133
Penguins

Model No.:	103
Designer:	Unknown
Height:	6", 15.2 cm
Colour:	Black, white and brown
Issued:	1913-by 1946
Varieties:	HN 103, Flambé

Price:	*U.S. $*	*Can. $*	*U.K. £*
	600.00	750.00	295.00

HN 134
Penguin
Style One

Model No.:	85
Designer:	Unknown
Height:	4 1/2", 11.4 cm
Colour:	Black and white (china)
Issued:	1913-by 1946
Varieties:	HN 104, Flambé

Price:	*U.S. $*	*Can. $*	*U.K. £*
	350.00	450.00	250.00

HN 135
Raven

Model No.:	43
Designer:	Unknown
Height:	3", 7.6 cm
Colour:	Blue, green and purple
Issued:	1913-1936
Varieties:	Flambé

Price:	*U.S. $*	*Can. $*	*U.K. £*
	Extremely Rare		

HN 136
Swallow on Rock

Model No.:	196
Designer:	Unknown
Height:	4 1/2", 11.4 cm
Colour:	Blue feathers, brown head, red, grey and white breast, beige rock
Issued:	1917-1936
Varieties:	HN 149; Also called "Blue Bird on Rock" HN 269

Price:	*U.S. $*	*Can. $*	*U.K. £*
	300.00	400.00	175.00

HN 137A
Fledgling
Style Four - yellow

Model No.:	99
Designer:	Unknown
Height:	2", 5.1 cm
Colour:	Yellow with black wing tips
Issued:	1917-1936
Varieties:	HN 137B, Flambé

Price:	*U.S. $*	*Can. $*	*U.K. £*
	175.00	225.00	95.00

HN137B
Fledgling
Style Four - blue

Model No.:	99
Designer:	Unknown
Height:	2", 5.1 cm
Colour:	Blue with black wing tips
Issued:	1917-1936
Varieties:	HN 137A, Flambé

Price:	*U.S. $*	*Can. $*	*U.K. £*
	175.00	225.00	95.00

HN137C
Fledgling
Style Two - yellow

Model No.:	1238
Designer:	Unknown
Height:	1 1/4", 3.2 cm
Colour:	Yellow with black wing tips
Issued:	1917-1936
Varieties:	HN 137D, Flambé

Price:	*U..S. $*	*Can. $*	*U.K. £*
	175.00	225.00	95.00

HN137D
Fledgling
Style Two - blue

Model No.:	1238
Designer:	Unknown
Height:	1 1/4", 3.2 cm
Colour:	Blue, black dot on head with black wing tips
Issued:	1917-1936
Varieties:	HN 137C, Flambé

Price:	*U.S. $*	*Can. $*	*U.K. £*
	175.00	225.00	95.00

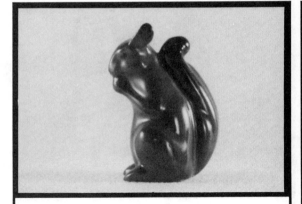

HN 138
Squirrel

Model No.:	115
Designer:	Unknown
Height:	2 1/4", 5.7 cm
Colour:	Brown
Issued:	1917-by 1946
Varieties:	Flambé; HN 1093B on Fluted Ashtray, HN 1093A on Plain Ashtray

Price:	*U.S. $*	*Can. $*	*U.K. £*
	425.00	575.00	225.00

HN 139
Eagle on Rock

Model No.:	145
Designer:	Unknown
Height:	9", 22.9 cm
Colour:	Brown head with orange, yellow and blue highlights, beige rock
Issued:	1917-1936
Varieties:	Titanian

Price:	*U.S. $*	*Can. $*	*U.K. £*
	Extremely Rare		

HN 140
Ape

Model No.:	147		
Designer:	Unknown		
Height:	6", 15.2 cm		
Colour:	Brown with orange highlights		
Issued:	1917-1936		

Price:	*U.S. $*	*Can. $*	*U.K. £*
	1,400.00	1,500.00	750.00

HN 141
Rhinoceros
Standing

Model No.:	107
Designer:	Unknown
Height:	3" x 6 1/2", 7.6 x 16.5 cm
Colour:	Grey with black ear tips, white horn
Issued:	1917-by 1946
Varieties:	Light brown glaze, orange-brown glaze

Price:	*U.S. $*	*Can. $*	*U.K. £*
	800.00	1,000.00	475.00

HN 142
Hare
Crouching - Style One

Model No.:	119
Designer:	Unknown
Height:	2", 5.1 cm
Colour:	Brown (china)
Issued:	1917-by 1946
Varieties:	HN 107, 126, 273, 803, Flambé, Sung

Price:	*U.S. $*	*Can. $*	*U.K. £*
	250.00	350.00	145.00

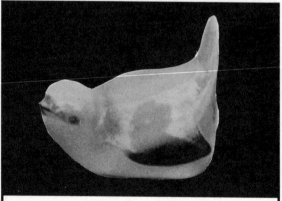

HN 143A
Fledgling
Style Three - yellow

Model No.:	98
Designer:	Unknown
Height:	2", 5.1 cm
Colour:	Yellow
Issued:	1917-by 1946
Varieties:	HN 143B, Flambé

Price:	*U.S. $*	*Can. $*	*U.K. £*
	175.00	225.00	95.00

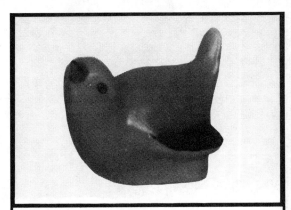

HN143B
Fledgling
Style Three - blue

Model No.:	98
Designer:	Unknown
Height:	2", 5.1 cm
Colour:	Blue and yellow
Issued:	1917-by 1946
Varieties:	HN 143A, Flambé

Price:	*U.S. $*	*Can. $*	*U.K. £*
	175.00	225.00	95.00

HN 144
Robin
Style One

Model No.:	104
Designer:	Unknown
Height:	2", 5.1 cm
Colour:	Dark brown feathers, red breast
Issued:	1917-by 1946
Varieties:	Flambé, HN 1089B on Fluted ashtray; HN 1089A on Plain ashtray, also called "Wren", HN 277

Price:	*U.S. $*	*Can. $*	*U.K. £*
	400.00	550.00	195.00

HN 145A
Fledgling
Style One - yellow

Model No.:	1236
Designer:	Unknown
Height:	1 1/2", 3.8 cm
Colour:	Yellow with black wing tips
Issued:	1917-1936
Varieties:	HN145B, Flambé

Price:	*U..S. $*	*Can. $*	*U.K. £*
	175.00	225.00	95.00

HN145B
Fledgling
Style One - blue

Model No.:	1236
Designer:	Unknown
Height:	1 1/4", 3.2 cm
Colour:	Blue with green dot on head; yellow breast, black wing tips
Issued:	1917-1936
Varieties:	HN 145A, Flambé

Price:	*U..S. $*	*Can. $*	*U.K. £*
	175.00	225.00	95.00

HN 145C
Fledgling on Rock
Style One - yellow

Model No.:	139
Designer:	Unknown
Height:	3 3/4", 9.5 cm
Colour:	Yellow feathers, black wing tips, yellow rock
Issued:	1917-1936
Varieties:	HN 145D, 145E, 145F, Flambé
Derivitives:	Flambé on onyx base

Price:	*U.S. $*	*Can. $*	*U.K. £*
	250.00	350.00	145.00

HN 145D
Fledgling on Rock
Style One - green

Model No.:	139
Designer:	Unknown
Height:	3 3/4", 9.5 cm
Colour:	Green-turquoise feathers, yellow breast, beige rock
Issued:	1917-1936
Varieties:	HN 145C, 145D, 145F, Flambé
Derivitives:	Flambé on onyx base

Price:	*U.S. $*	*Can. $*	*U.K. £*
	250.00	350.00	145.00

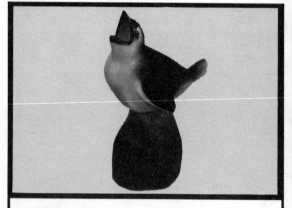

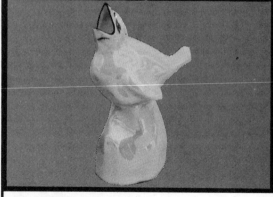

HN 145E
Fledgling on Rock
Style One - blue

Model No.:	139
Designer:	Unknown
Height:	3 3/4", 9.5 cm
Colour:	Dark blue feathers, yellow breast, dark blue rock
Issued:	1917-1936
Varieties:	HN 145C, 145D, 145F, Flambé
Derivitives:	Flambé on onyx base

Price:	*U.S. $*	*Can. $*	*U.K. £*
	250.00	350.00	145.00

HN 145F
Fledgling on Rock
Style One - pearl

Model No.:	139
Designer:	Unknown
Height:	3 3/4", 9.5 cm
Colour:	White bird, cream rock, overall pearl glaze
Issued:	1917-1936
Varieties:	HN 145C, 145D, 145E, Flambé
Derivitives:	Flambé on onyx base

Price:	*U.S. $*	*Can. $*	*U.K. £*
	250.00	350.00	145.00

HN 145G
Fledgling
Style Five - yellow

Model No.:	1237
Designer:	Unknown
Height:	2", 5.1 cm
Colour:	Yellow feathers with black markings
Issued:	1917-by 1946
Varieties:	HN 145F

Price:	*U.S. $*	*Can. $*	*U.K. £*
	175.00	225.00	95.00

Colourways: Yellow with brown markings

HN 145H
Fledgling
Style Five - blue

Model No.:	1237
Designer:	Unknown
Height:	2", 5.1 cm
Colour:	Blue and yellow feathers with black wing tips
Issued:	1917-by 1946
Varieties:	HN 145E

Price:	*U.S. $*	*Can. $*	*U.K. £*
	175.00	225.00	95.00

HN 146
Bulldog with Helmet and Haversack (Old Bill)

Model No.:	Unknown
Designer:	Unknown
Height:	6 1/2", 16.5 cm
Size:	Large
Colour:	Brown body, bronze helmet
Issued:	1918-c.1925

Price:	*U.S. $*	*Can. $*	*U.K. £*
	900.00	1,000.00	475.00

HN 147A
Fox
Stalking - large

Model No.:	29A
Designer:	Unknown
Height:	2 1/2" x 12 1/2", 6.4 x 31.7 cm
Size:	Large
Colour:	Light brown face, dark brown coat
Issued:	1918-by 1946
Varieties:	Flambé

Price:	*U.S. $*	*Can. $*	*U.K. £*
	800.00	950.00	450.00

HN 147A-1
Fox
Stalking - Small

Model No.:	29B
Designer:	Unknown
Height:	1" x 5 1/4", 2.5 x 13.3 cm
Size:	Small
Colour:	Brown and light brown with black highlights
Issued:	1918-by 1946
Varieties:	Chinese Jade, Flambé, Sung

Price:	U.S. $	Can. $	U.K. £
	475.00	550.00	300.00

HN 147B
Fox
Seated - Style Two - small

Model No.:	14
Designer:	Unknown
Height:	4 1/2", 11.4 cm
Size:	Small
Colour:	Brown and cream with black ear tips
Issued:	1918-by 1946
Varieties:	Flambé, Sung

Price:	U.S. $	Can. $	U.K. £
	450.00	550.00	225.00

HN 147C
Fox
Seated - Style One - medium

Model No.:	12
Designer:	Unknown
Height:	4 3/4", 12.1 cm
Size:	Medium
Colour:	Brown and white with black ear tips
Issued:	1918-by 1946
Varieties:	Flambé, Sung; Also decorated with transfer prints of grapes and vines.

Price:	U.S. $	Can. $	U.K. £
	500.00	650.00	275.00

HN 147C-1
Fox
Seated - Style One - small

Model No.:	12A
Designer:	Unknown
Height:	3", 7.6 cm
Colour:	Brown and light brown with black highlights
Issued:	1918-by 1946
Varieties:	Flambé
Derivitive:	Fox seated on Sterling silver tray

Price:	U.S. $	Can. $	U.K. £
	450.00	550.00	225.00

HN 147D
Fox
Curled - Style One

Model No.: 15
Designer: Unknown
Height: 4 3/4", 12.1 cm
Colour: Brown and light brown with black ear tips
Issued: 1918-by 1946
Varieties: Flambé, Treacle glaze

Price:	*U.S. $*	*Can. $*	*U.K. £*
	450.00	550.00	245.00

HN 147E
Fox
Stalking - medium

Model No.: 29
Designer: Unknown
Height: 1 1/2" x 8 1/4", 5.1 x 21.0 cm
Size: Medium
Colour: Brown and light brown
Issued: 1918-by 1946
Varieties: Flambé

Price:	*U.S. $*	*Can. $*	*U.K. £*
	650.00	750.00	325.00

HN 148A
Duck
Preening - Style Two

Model No.: 4
Designer: Unknown
Height: 1 1/2" x 3 1/2", 3.8 x 8.9 cm
Colour: Blue and green head, brown and white body (china)
Issued: 1913-1936
Varieites: HN 271, 299

Price:	*U.S. $*	*Can. $*	*U.K. £*
	300.00	400.00	195.00

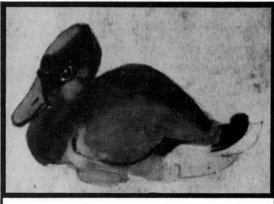

HN 148B
Duck
Resting

Model No.: 112
Designer: Unknown
Height: 2", 5.1 cm
Size: Small
Colour: Blue and green head, brown, green and white body
Issued: 1918-by 1946
Varieites: Flambé

Price:	*U.S. $*	*Can. $*	*U.K. £*
	300.00	400.00	195.00

HN 149
Swallow on Rock

Model No.:	196
Designer:	Unknown
Height:	4 3/4", 12.1 cm
Colour:	Dark blue-black feathers, red markings on head, white breast, beige rock
Issued:	1918-by 1946
Varieties:	HN 136; Also called "Blue Bird on Rock" HN 269

Price:	*U.S. $*	*Can. $*	*U.K. £*
	300.00	400.00	175.00

HN 150
Duck
Head stretched forward

Model No.:	207
Designer:	Unknown
Height:	4", 10.1 cm
Size:	Large
Colour:	Light and dark brown with cream and blue highlights
Issued:	1918-by 1946
Varieties:	HN 229, 2556, Flambé

Price:	*U.S. $*	*Can. $*	*U.K. £*
	375.00	450.00	225.00

HN 151
Lop-eared Rabbit

Model No.:	113
Designer:	Unknown
Height:	4", 10.1 cm
Colour:	White with black patches
Issued:	1918-by 1946
Varieties:	HN 108, 276, Flambé; Matt red glaze HN 1091B on Fluted Ashtray, HN 1091A on Plain Ashtray

Price:	*U.S. $*	*Can. $*	*U.K. £*
	450.00	525.00	275.00

HN 152
Kingfisher on Rock
Style One

Model No.:	44
Designer:	Unknown
Height:	4", 10.1 cm
Colour:	Turquoise-blue and yellow-orange plummage; beige rock
Issued:	1918-1936
Varieties:	HN 131, Flambé

Price:	*U.S. $*	*Can. $*	*U.K. £*
	250.00	350.00	160.00

HN 153
Bulldog With Tam O'Shanter and Haversack

Model No.: Unknown
Designer: Unknown
Height: 7", 17.8 cm
Colour: Brown body, bronze Tam O'Shanter
Issued: 1918-c.1925

Price:	*U.S. $*	*Can. $*	*U.K. £*
	1,000.00	1,200.00	550.00

HN 154A
'Kateroo' Character Cat - black

Model No.: 214
Designer: Charles Noke
Height: 12 3/4", 32.0 cm
Colour: Black and white (china)
Issued: 1918-c.1925
Varieties: HN 154B

Price:	*U.S. $*	*Can. $*	*U.K. £*
		Extremely Rare	

HN 154B
'Kateroo' Character Cat - green

Model No.: 214
Designer: Charles Noke
Height: 12 3/4", 32.0 cm
Colour: Green
Issued: 1918-c.1925
Varieties: HN 154A

Price:	*U.S. $*	*Can. $*	*U.K. £*
		Extremely Rare	

HN 155
Owl
Style One

Model No.: 153
Designer: Charles Noke
Height: 5", 12.7 cm
Colour: Light and dark brown
Issued: 1918-by 1946

Price:	*U.S. $*	*Can. $*	*U.K. £*
		Very Rare	

HN 156
Monkey
Hand to ear

Model No.:	16
Designer:	Unknown
Height:	3 1/2", 8.9 cm
Colour:	Brown with dark brown face
Issued:	1918-by 1946
Varieties:	Flambé

Price:	*U.S. $*	*Can. $*	*U.K. £*
	600.00	725.00	350.00

HN 157
Cockerel
Seated - Style One

Model No.:	50
Designer:	Unknown
Height:	Unknown
Colour:	Blue and purple
Issued:	1918-1936

Price:	*U.S. $*	*Can. $*	*U.K. £*
		Extremely Rare	

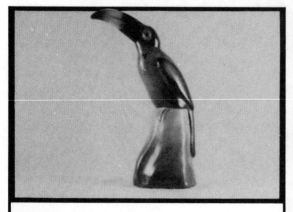

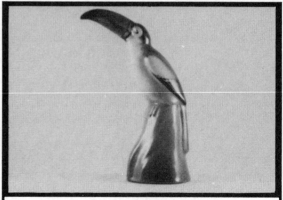

HN 158
Toucan on Perch - green

Model No.:	212
Designer:	Unknown
Height:	7 1/2", 19.1 cm
Colour:	Green, blue and black plummage, orange and black beak; black perch
Issued:	1918-1936
Varieties:	HN 159, 196, 294

Price:	*U.S. $*	*Can. $*	*U.K. £*
	400.00	550.00	265.00

HN 159
Toucan on Perch - black

Model No.:	212
Designer:	Unknown
Height:	7 1/2", 19.1 cm
Colour:	Black, green, yellow and orange
Issued:	1918-1936
Varieties:	HN 158, 196, 294

Price:	*U.S. $*	*Can. $*	*U.K. £*
	400.00	550.00	265.00

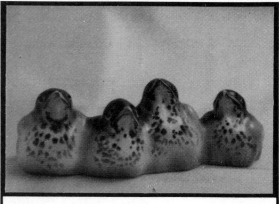

HN 160
Owl With Owlet Under Wing

Model No.:	71
Designer:	Charles Noke
Height:	4 3/4", 12.1 cm
Colour:	Browns
Issued:	1918-1936
Varieties:	Flambé
Derivitive:	Flambé on onyx base

Price:	*U.S. $*	*Can. $*	*U.K. £*
	Extremely Rare		

HN 161
Thrush Chicks (four)

Model No.:	208
Designer:	Unknown
Height:	2" x 5 1/2", 5.1 x 14.0 cm
Colour:	Yellow and black spotted breasts, brown feathering
Issued:	1918-by 1946
Varieties:	Flambé; Also known as "Four Fledglings" HN 171

Price:	*U.S. $*	*Can. $*	*U.K. £*
	350.00	400.00	200.00

HN 162
Butterfly on Stump

Model No.:	141
Designer:	Unknown
Height:	3", 7.6 cm
Colour:	Light blue wings, dark blue markings, gold body; beige rock
Issued:	1918-1936

Price:	*U.S. $*	*Can. $*	*U.K. £*
	225.00	300.00	150.00

HN 163A
Budgerigar on Tree Stump - green

Model No.:	221
Designer:	Unknown
Height:	7", 17.8 cm
Colour:	Green feathers, yellow head; black tree stump
Issued:	1918-1936
Varieties:	HN 163B, 199, Flambé, Sung
Derivitive:	Onyx pin tray

Price:	*U.S. $*	*Can. $*	*U.K. £*
	400.00	550.00	250.00

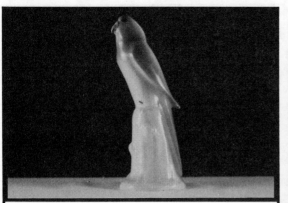

HN 163B
Budgerigar on a Tree Stump - pearl
Model No.:   221
Designer: Unknown
Height: 7", 17.8 cm
Colour: White pearl glaze on bird, green pearl
             glaze on tree stump
Issued: 1918-1936
Varieties: HN 163A, 199, Flambé, Sung
Derivitive: Onyx pin tray

Price:	*U.S. $*	*Can. $*	*U.K. £*
	400.00	550.00	250.00

HN 164
Rooster
Style One
Model No.:   225
Designer: Unknown
Height: 9", 22.9 cm
Colour: Orange back, brown breast, red head
Issued: 1918-by 1946
Varieties: HN 184

Price:	*U.S. $*	*Can. $*	*U.K. £*
	500.00	650.00	325.00

HN 165
Kingfisher on Tree Stump (flower holder)
Style One
Model No.:   227
Designer: Unknown
Height: 3", 7.6 cm
Colour: Blue, turquoise and orange bird,
             brown tree stump
Issued: 1918-1936
Varieties: HN 858, Flambé

Price:	*U.S. $*	*Can. $*	*U.K. £*
	425.00	500.00	250.00

HN 166
Foxhound
Seated - Style One
Model No.:   209
Designer: Unknown
Height: 4", 10.1 cm
Colour: White with brown markings
Issued: 1918-by 1946
Varieties: Flambé

Price:	*U.S. $*	*Can. $*	*U.K. £*
	750.00	900.00	450.00

HN 167
Tern (female)

Model No.:	231
Designer:	Unknown
Height:	2 1/2" x 8 1/2", 6.4 x 21.6 cm
Colour:	Grey and white feathers, red beak
Issued:	1918-by 1946
Varieties:	HN 1194, Flambé; Also called "Tern (male)", HN 168, 1193

Price:	U.S. $	Can. $	U.K. £
	300.00	350.00	175.00

HN 168
Tern (male)

Model No.:	231
Designer:	Unknown
Height:	2 1/2" x 8 1/2", 6.4 x 21.6 cm
Colour:	Blue-grey and white feathers, black head
Issued:	1918-by 1946
Varieties:	HN 1193, Flambé; Also called "Tern (female)", HN 167, 1194

Price:	U.S. $	Can. $	U.K. £
	300.00	350.00	175.00

HN 169
Barn Owl
Style One

Model No.:	148
Designer:	Harry Tittensor
Height:	3", 7.6 cm
Colour:	Cream breast, dark brown feathering with gold highlights (china)
Issued:	1918-by 1946
Varieties:	Flambé

Price:	U.S. $	Can. $	U.K. £
	550.00	700.00	350.00

HN 170
Comic Brown Bear

Model No.:	58
Designer:	Charles Noke
Height:	5", 12.7 cm
Colour:	Brown
Issued:	1918-1936
Varieties:	HN 270, Flambé

Price:	U.S. $	Can. $	U.K. £
	575.00	700.00	375.00

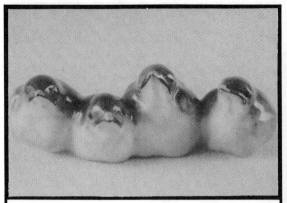

HN 171
Four Fledglings
Model No.:   208
Designer: Unknown
Height: 2", 5.1 cm
Colour: Light brown-cream breasts with dark
             brown feathering
Issued: 1918-by 1946
Varieties: Also called "Thrush Chicks (four)"
             HN 161, Flambé

Price: *U.S. $*   *Can. $*   *U.K. £*
                    350.00   400.00   200.00

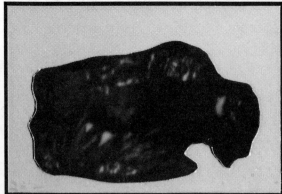

HN 172
Bison
Style One
Model No.:   136
Designer: Unknown
Height: 5", 12.7 cm
Colour: Light and dark brown
Issued: 1918-1936

Price: *U.S. $*   *Can. $*   *U.K. £*
                                  Rare

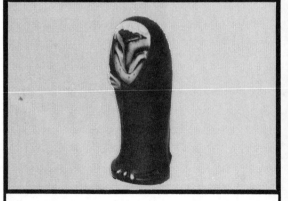

HN 173
Granny Owl
Model No.:   228
Designer: Charles Noke
Height: 7 1/2", 19.1 cm
Colour: Red cloak and ermine collar
Issued: 1918-1936
Varieties: HN 187; also called "Wise Old Owl"

Price: *U.S. $*   *Can. $*   *U.K. £*
                    2,000.00   2,500.00   1,350.00

*

HN 175
Great-Crested Grebe
Model No.:   233
Designer: Unknown
Height: 12", 30.5 cm
Colour: Green back and beak, pale breast
Issued: 1918-by 1946

Price: *U.S. $*   *Can. $*   *U.K. £*
                    Extremely Rare

HN 176
Bloodhound

Model No.: 48
Designer: Unknown
Height: 5 3/4", 14.6 cm
Colour: Brown
Issued: 1919-by 1946
Varieties: Flambé

Price:

	U.S. $	Can. $	U.K. £
	1,750.00	2,250.00	950.00

*

HN 178
Cockerel
Crouching - green

Model No.: 30
Designer: Unknown
Height: 3 1/4", 8.3 cm
Colour: Green
Issued: 1919-1936
Varieties: HN 124, 180, 267, Flambé

Price:

	U.S. $	Can. $	U.K. £
	300.00	450.00	175.00

HN 179
Foxes
Curled - Style One

Model No.: 6
Designer: Unknown
Height: 4", 10.1 cm
Colour: Brown with orange patches
Issued: 1919-by 1946
Varieties: HN 117, Flambé, Sung, Treacle glaze

Price:

	U.S. $	Can. $	U.K. £
	600.00	800.00	375.00

HN 180
Cockerel
Crouching - red

Model No.: 30
Designer: Unknown
Height: 3 1/4", 8.3 cm
Colour: Red and orange
Issued: 1919-1936
Varieties: HN 124, 178, 267, Flambé

Price:

	U.S. $	Can. $	U.K. £
	300.00	450.00	175.00

HN 181
Elephant
Trunk down, curled

Model No.:	65
Designer:	Charles Noke
Height:	4", 10.1 cm
Size:	Small
Colour:	Pale grey with black highlights, white tusks (china)
Issued:	1920-by 1946
Varieties:	HN 186, Flambé, Sung

Price:	U.S. $	Can. $	U.K. £
	400.00	550.00	250.00

HN 182
Character Monkey - green

Model No.:	213
Designer:	Charles Noke
Height:	7", 17.8 cm
Colour:	Green jacket and hat
Issued:	1920-1936
Varieties:	HN 183, Flambé

Price:	U.S. $	Can. $	U.K. £
		Very Rare	

HN 183
Character Monkey - blue

Model No.:	213
Designer:	Charles Noke
Height:	7", 17.8 cm
Colour:	Blue jacket and hat
Issued:	1920-1936
Varieties:	HN 182, Flambé

Price:	U.S. $	Can. $	U.K. £
		Very Rare	

HN 184
Rooster
Style One

Model No.:	225
Designer:	Unknown
Height:	9", 22.9 cm
Colour:	White and grey body, black tail feathers, red comb
Issued:	1920-by 1946
Varieties:	HN 164

Price:	U.S. $	Can. $	U.K. £
	500.00	650.00	325.00

HN 185
Cockatoo on a Rock

Model No.:	68
Designer:	Leslie Harradine
Height:	6", 15.2 cm
Colour:	Yellow and white feathers, green and black rock base
Issued:	1920-1936
Varieties:	HN 191, 192, 200, 877, Flambé
Derivitive:	Onyx pin tray

Price:	U.S. $	Can. $	U.K. £
	400.00	550.00	275.00

HN 186
Elephant
Trunk down, curled

Model No.:	65
Designer:	Charles Noke
Height:	4", 10.1 cm
Size:	Small
Colour:	Brown
Issued:	1920-by 1946
Varieties:	HN 181, Flambé, Sung

Price:	U.S. $	Can. $	U.K. £
	400.00	550.00	250.00

HN 187
Granny Owl

Model No.:	228
Designer:	Charles Noke
Height:	7 1/2", 19.1 cm
Colour:	Blue-grey check shawl with white mob cap
Issued:	1920-by 1946
Varieties:	HN 173; also called "Wise Old Owl"

Price:	U.S. $	Can. $	U.K. £
	2,000.00	2,500.00	1,350.00

HN 188
Duckling
New born - yellow/brown

Model No.:	3
Designer:	Unknown
Height:	3", 7.6 cm
Colour:	Yellow and brown
Issued:	1920-1936
Varieties:	HN189, 190, Flambé

Price:	U.S. $	Can. $	U.K. £
		Rare	

HN 189
Duckling
New born - yellow/black
Model No.:   3
Designer: Unknown
Height: 3", 7.6 cm
Colour: Black and yellow
Issued: 1920-1936
Varieties: HN 188, 190, Flambé

Price: *U.S. $*   *Can. $*   *U.K. £*
                                Rare

HN 190
Duckling
New born - green
Model No.:   3
Designer: Unknown
Height: 3", 7.6 cm
Colour: Green and blue
Issued: 1920-1936
Varieties: HN 188, 189, Flambé

Price: *U.S. $*   *Can. $*   *U.K. £*
                                Rare

HN 191
Cockatoo on a Rock - blue
Model No.:   68
Designer: Leslie Harradine
Height: 6", 15.2 cm
Colour: Blue and purple
Issued: 1920-1936
Varieties: HN 185, 192, 200, 877, Flambé
Derivitive: Onyx pin tray

Price: *U.S. $*   *Can. $*   *U.K. £*
                      400.00   550.00   275.00

HN 192
Cockatoo on a Rock - red
Model No.:   68
Designer: Leslie Harradine
Height: 6", 15.2 cm
Colour: Red and orange
Issued: 1920-1936
Varieties: HN 185, 191, 200, 877, Flambé
Derivitive: Onyx pin tray

Price: *U.S. $*   *Can. $*   *U.K. £*
                      400.00   550.00   275.00

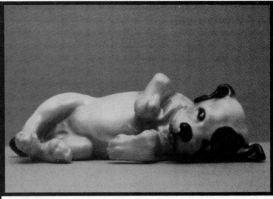

HN 193
Tortoise

Model No.:	101
Designer:	Unknown
Height:	2" x 4 3/4", 5.1 x 12.1 cm
Colour:	Red head, grey shell
Issued:	1920-by 1946
Varieties:	Flambé, Sung

Price:	*U.S. $*	*Can. $*	*U.K. £*
	500.00	500.00	250.00

HN 194
Terrier Puppy
Lying

Model No.:	121
Designer:	Unknown
Height:	3" x 7 3/4", 7.6 x 19.7 cm
Colour:	White with black patches over ears and eye
Issued:	1920-by 1946
Varieties:	Flambé

Price:	*U.S. $*	*Can. $*	*U.K. £*
	1,500.00	1,500.00	650.00

HN 195
Gannet

Model No.:	243
Designer:	Unknown
Height:	6 1/2", 16.5 cm
Colour:	Blue-grey feathers, white bill and chest
Issued:	1920-by 1946
Varieties:	HN 1197, Flambé

Price:	*U.S. $*	*Can. $*	*U.K. £*
	700.00	800.00	395.00

HN 196
Toucan on Perch

Model No.:	212
Designer:	Unknown
Height:	7 1/2", 19.1 cm
Colour:	Blue and purple toucan on brown perch
Issued:	1920-1936
Varieties:	HN 158, 159, 294

Price:	*U.S. $*	*Can. $*	*U.K. £*
	400.00	550.00	265.00

HN 197
Weaver Bird on Rock

Model No.:   251
Designer: Unknown
Height: 5" 12.7 cm
Colour: Black with orange breast
Issued: 1920-by 1946
Varieties: HN 220

Price:	*U.S. $*	*Can. $*	*U.K. £*
		Rare	

HN 198
King Penguin and Chick

Model No.:   239
Designer: Unknown·
Height: 5 1/2", 14.0 cm
Colour: Black and white
Issued: 1920-by 1946
Varieties: HN 297, 998, Flambé

Price:	*U.S. $*	*Can. $*	*U.K. £*
	850.00	1,150.00	475.00

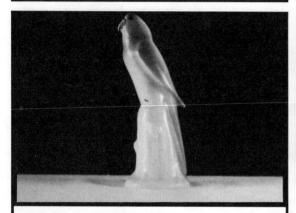

HN 199
Budgerigar on Tree Stump

Model No.:   221
Designer: Unknown
Height: 6 3/4", 17.2 cm
Colour: Light blue and yellow
Issued: 1920-1936
Varieties: HN 163A, 163B, Flambé
Derivitive: Onyx pin tray

Price:	*U.S. $*	*Can. $*	*U.K. £*
	400.00	550.00	250.00

HN 200
Cockatoo on a Rock

Model No.:   68
Designer: Unknown
Height: 6", 15.2 cm
Colour: Blue and green
Issued: 1920-1936
Varieties: HN 185, 191, 192, 877, Flambé
Derivitive: Onyx pin tray

Price:	*U.S. $*	*Can. $*	*U.K. £*
	400.00	550.00	275.00

HN 201
Cat with Mouse on Tail
Tabby

Model No.:	216
Designer:	Unknown
Height:	4 1/4", 10.8 cm
Colour:	Tabby
Issued:	1920-by 1946
Varieties:	HN 202, Flambé, Sung

Price:	*U.S. $*	*Can. $*	*U.K. £*
	1,750.00	2,000.00	950.00

HN 202
Cat with Mouse on Tail
Black

Model No.:	216
Designer:	Unknown
Height:	4 1/4", 10.8 cm
Colour:	Black cat with white face; grey mouse
Issued:	1920-by 1946
Varieties:	HN 201, Flambé, Sung

Price:	*U.S. $*	*Can. $*	*U.K. £*
	1,500.00	1,750.00	2,950.00

HN 203
Cat on a Pillar

Model No.:	240
Designer:	Unknown
Height:	7", 17.8 cm
Colour:	Tabby cat on brown pillar
Issued:	1920-by 1946
Varieties:	HN 244, 245

Price:	*U.S. $*	*Can. $*	*U.K. £*
	2,000.00	2,500.00	1,200.00

HN 204
Persian Kitten
Style One

Model No.:	242
Designer:	Unknown
Height:	5", 12.7 cm
Colour:	Tabby
Issued:	1920-by 1946
Varieties:	HN 221, Sung

Price:	*U.S. $*	*Can. $*	*U.K. £*
		Extremely rare	

HN 205
Ducklings
Standing - black

Model No.:	247
Designer:	Unknown
Height:	2 3/4", 7.0 cm
Colour:	Black and light yellow
Issued:	1920-by 1946
Varieties:	HN 206, 275, Flambé

Price:	*U.S. $*	*Can. $*	*U.K. £*
	500.00	650.00	300.00

HN 206
Ducklings
Standing - brown

Model No.:	247
Designer:	Unknown
Height:	2 3/4", 7.0 cm
Colour:	Brown, light brown and white
Issued:	1920-by 1946
Varieties:	HN 205, 275, Flambé

Price:	*U.S. $*	*Can. $*	*U.K. £*
	500.00	650.00	300.00

HN 207
Country Mouse

Model No.:	250
Designer:	Charles Noke
Height:	Unknown
Colour:	Cream coat, brown head and tail
Issued:	1920-1936

Price:	*U.S. $*	*Can. $*	*U.K. £*
		Very Rare	

HN 208
Toucan in Tail Coat and Bow Tie

Model No.:	234
Designer:	Charles Noke
Height:	4 1/2", 11.4 cm
Colour:	Black and white
Issued:	1920-by 1946
Derivitive:	Place name holder (illustrated)

Price:	*U.S. $*	*Can. $*	*U.K. £*
		Rare	

HN 209
Rabbits

Model No.:	249
Designer:	Unknown
Height:	3 1/2", 8.9 cm
Colour:	Brown, one with dark head
Issued:	1920-by 1946
Varieties:	HN 217, 218, 219, 969, Flambé

Price:	*U.S. $*	*Can. $*	*U.K. £*
	850.00	1,000.00	500.00

HN 210
Cat Asleep, Head on Paw

Model No.:	23
Designer:	Unknown
Height:	1 1/2", 3.8 cm
Colour:	Black and white
Issued:	1920-1936
Varieties:	HN 227

Price:	*U.S. $*	*Can. $*	*U.K. £*
	Rare		

HN 211
Black-Headed Gull (male)

Model No.:	235
Designer:	Unknown
Height:	4", 10.1 cm
Colour:	Black-head, grey feathers, white breast
Issued:	1920-by 1946
Varieties:	HN 1195; also called "Seagull" HN 212, 1196

Price:	*U.S. $*	*Can. $*	*U.K. £*
	300.00	350.00	175.00

HN 212
Seagull (female)

Model No.:	235
Designer:	Unknown
Height:	4", 10.1 cm
Colour:	White head and breast, grey feathers, red beak
Issued:	1920-by 1946
Varieties:	HN 1196; Also called "Black-headed Gull" HN 211, 1195

Price:	*U.S. $*	*Can. $*	*U.K. £*
	300.00	350.00	175.00

HN 213
Pigs
Snoozing - Ears Up

Model No.:	61
Designer:	Unknown
Height:	4" x 7", 10.1 x 17.8 cm
Colour:	Green and mauve
Issued:	1920-1936
Varieties:	HN 238, 802, Flambé

Price:	*U.S. $*	*Can. $*	*U.K. £*
		Rare	

HN 214
Bird with Five Chicks
Black

Model No.:	246
Designer:	Unknown
Height:	3 1/4", 8.3 cm
Colour:	Black, pink and brown
Issued:	1920-1936
Varieties:	HN 215, 216, 272

Price:	*U.S. $*	*Can. $*	*U.K. £*
	400.00	550.00	225.00

HN 215
Bird with Five Chicks
Grey

Model No.:	246
Designer:	Unknown
Height:	3 1/4", 8.3 cm
Colour:	Grey, blue and lemon
Issued:	1920-1936
Varieties:	HN 214, 216, 272

Price:	*U.S. $*	*Can. $*	*U.K. £*
	400.00	550.00	225.00

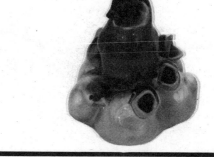

HN 216
Bird with Five Chicks
Green

Model No.:	246
Designer:	Unknown
Height:	3 1/4", 8.3 cm
Colour:	Green, blue and lemon
Issued:	1920-1936
Varieties:	HN 214, 215, 272

Price:	*U.S. $*	*Can. $*	*U.K. £*
	400.00	550.00	225.00

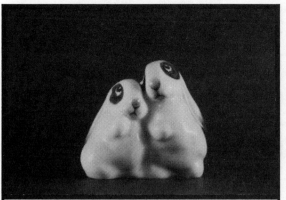

HN 217
Rabbits
Brown patches

Model No.:	249
Designer:	Unknown
Height:	3 1/2", 8.9 cm
Colour:	Brown patches on faces
Issued:	1920-by 1946
Varieties:	HN 209, 218, 219, 969, Flambé

Price:	*U.S. $*	*Can. $*	*U.K. £*
	850.00	1,000.00	500.00

HN 218
Rabbits
Black patches

Model No.:	249
Designer:	Unknown
Height:	3 1/2", 8.9 cm
Colour:	Brown and black patches on faces
Issued:	1920-by 1946
Varieties:	HN 209, 217, 219, 969, Flambé

Price:	*U.S. $*	*Can. $*	*U.K. £*
	850.00	1,000.00	500.00

HN 219
Rabbits
Yellow patches

Model No.:	249
Designer:	Unknown
Height:	3 1/2", 8.9 cm
Colour:	Brown, black and yellow patches on faces
Issued:	1920-by 1946
Varieties:	HN 209, 217, 218, 969, Flambé

Price:	*U.S. $*	*Can. $*	*U.K. £*
	850.00	1,000.00	500.00

HN 220
Weaver Bird on Rock

Model No.:	251
Designer:	Unknown
Height:	5", 12.7 cm
Colour:	Red and brown
Issued:	1920-by 1946
Varieties:	HN 197

Price:	*U.S. $*	*Can. $*	*U.K. £*
	Rare		

HN 221
Persian Kitten
Style One

Model No.:	242
Designer:	Unknown
Height:	5", 12.7 cm
Colour:	Black and white
Issued:	1920-by 1946
Varieties:	HN 204, Sung

Price:	*U.S. $*	*Can. $*	*U.K. £*
	Extremely Rare		

HN 222
Owl in a Crescent Moon-Shaped Dish

Model No.:	37
Designer:	Unknown
Height:	4", 10.1 cm
Colour:	Yellow and green lustre
Issued:	1920-1936
Varieties:	Flambé

Price:	*U.S. $*	*Can. $*	*U.K. £*
		Rare	

HN 223
Lion
Seated

Model No.:	59
Designer:	Unknown
Height:	6 1/2", 16.5 cm
Colour:	Brown
Issued:	1920-by 1946
Varieties:	Flambé, Treacle glaze

Price:	*U.S. $*	*Can. $*	*U.K. £*
	Very Rare		

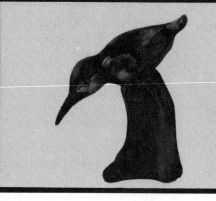

HN 224
Kingfisher on Rock
Style Two

Model No.:	258
Designer:	Unknown
Height:	3 1/2", 8.9 cm
Colour:	Blue
Issued:	1920-by 1946

Price:	*U.S. $*	*Can. $*	*U.K. £*
	Very Rare		

HN 225
Tiger
Crouching

Model No.:	111		
Designer:	Charles Noke		
Height:	2" x 9 1/2", 5.1 x 24.0 cm		
Colour:	Brown with dark brown stripes		
Issued:	1920-1936		
Varieties:	Flambé		

Price:	*U.S. $*	*Can. $*	*U.K. £*
	500.00	675.00	250.00

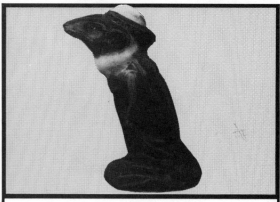

HN 226
Town Mouse
Blue

Model No.:	256		
Designer:	Charles Noke		
Height:	2 1/2", 6.4 cm		
Colour:	Blue coat; blue hat with yellow and green feather, green and yellow scarf		
Issued:	1920-by 1946		
Varieties:	HN 228		

Price:	*U.S. $*	*Can. $*	*U.K. £*
	1,000.00	1,100.00	550.00

HN 227
Cat Asleeping, Head on Paw

Model No.:	23
Designer:	Unknown
Height:	1 1/2", 3.8 cm
Colour:	Tabby
Issued:	1920-1936
Varieties:	HN 210

Price:	*U.S. $*	*Can. $*	*U.K. £*
		Rare	

HN 228
Town Mouse
Yellow

Model No.:	256
Designer:	Charles Noke
Height:	2 1/2", 6.4 cm
Colour:	Yellow coat
Issued:	1920-by 1946
Varieties:	HN 226

Price:	*U.S. $*	*Can. $*	*U.K. £*
	1,400.00	1,500.00	900.00

HN 229
Duck
Head stretched forward

Model No.:	207
Designer:	Unknown
Height:	4", 10.1 cm
Colour:	Dark and light brown, green head with green wing tips, dark brown beak
Issued:	1920-by 1946
Varieties:	HN 150, 2556, Flambé

Price:	U.S. $	Can. $	U.K. £
	375.00	450.00	225.00

HN 231
English St. Bernard

Model No.:	262
Designer:	Unknown
Height:	7", 17.8 cm
Colour:	White with brown markings on face, ears and back
Issued:	1920-by 1946
Varieties:	Flambé

Price:	U.S. $	Can. $	U.K. £
	1,500.00	1,700.00	950.00

HN 232
Puppy with Bone

Model No.:	118
Designer:	Unknown
Height:	4", 10.1 cm
Colour:	Light brown with dark brown markings
Issued:	1920-by 1946
Varieties:	Flambé

Price:	U.S. $	Can. $	U.K. £
		Very Rare	

NOTE ON PRICING

This is a first edition and for the first time a complete list of Doulton animals is being priced. These prices have been arrived at by concensus among knowledgeable dealers. They are not to be considered the final word. An animal figure that is common, appears more often that not in every dealer's inventory and is easy to price. However, when a figure is seldom (if ever) seen its scarcity becomes a problem in establishing its value.

We have used two methods to record prices:
1. Rarity classifications
2. Italicized prices

The rarity classification provides a price range. This simply means that the item should sell in the range given. Italicized prices zero in a little closer than the price range. Italicized prices are the level of the last known sale and serve as a basis for the possible current price. However, it still is an indication only and the next transaction may be higher or lower depending on market demand. When dealing with rare animal figures you always need two willing parties, a willing buyer and a willing seller.

Popularity of a series will exert market pressure that will cause price increases for rare figures. An extremely rare character bird cannot and should not be compared with an extremely rare dog in price level due to the popularity of the dog series. Italicized prices and rarity classifications are interchangeable to a certain degree.

Rarity Classification	Rare	Very Rare	Extremely Rare
U.S. $	1,000./1,500.	1,500./2,000.	2,000./3,000.
Can. $	1,500./2,000.	2,000./3,000.	3,000./4,500.
U.K. £	750./1,000.	1,000./1,500.	1,500./2,250.

N/A (not available) in the pricing table indicates that the item was not available in that particular market.

HN 233
Cat
Lying
Model No.:   70
Designer: Unknown
Height: 3 1/2", 8.9 cm
Colour: Yellow and orange patches, black tail
Issued: 1920-1936
Varieties: Flambé

Price:	*U.S. $*	*Can. $*	*U.K. £*
	650.00	750.00	400.00

HN 234
Cats
Model No.:   259
Designer: Unknown
Height: 5", 12.7 cm
Colour: Black, brown and white
Issued: 1920-1936

Price:	*U.S. $*	*Can. $*	*U.K. £*
	1,200.00	*1,500.00*	*550.00*

HN 235
Duck
Preening - Style One
Model No.:   2
Designer: Unknown
Height: 2 1/2", 6.4 cm
Colour: Orange and black
Issued: 1920-1936
Varieties: HN 298, Flambé

Price:	*U.S. $*	*Can. $*	*U.K. £*
		Rare	

HN 236
Chicks (two)

Model No.:	1163A
Designer:	Charles Noke
Height:	2 1/2", 6.4 cm
Colour:	Unknown
Issued:	1920-by 1946
Varieties:	Flambé, Sung

Price:	*U.S. $*	*Can. $*	*U.K. £*
	300.00	400.00	125.00

HN 237
Mrs Gamp Mouse

Model No.:	257
Designer:	Charles Noke
Height:	Unknown
Colour:	Unknown
Issued:	1920-by 1946

Price:	*U.S. $*	*Can. $*	*U.K. £*
		Extremely Rare	

HN 238
Pigs
Snoozing - Ears Up

Model No.:	61
Designer:	Unknown
Height:	4" x 7", 10.1 x 17.8 cm
Colour:	Unknown
Issued:	1920-1936
Varieties:	HN 213, 802, Flambé

Price:	*U.S. $*	*Can. $*	*U.K. £*
		Rare	

HN 239
Ducklings
Resting

Model No.:	97
Designer:	Unknown
Height:	1 3/4" x 5 1/2", 4.5 x 14.0 cm
Colour:	Light brown
Issued:	1920-by 1946
Varieties:	Flambé

Price:	*U.S. $*	*Can. $*	*U.K. £*
	350.00	475.00	150.00

HN 240
Thrush on Rock

Model No.:	253
Designer:	Unknown
Height:	Unknown
Colour:	Unknown
Issued:	1920-1936

Price:	*U.S. $*	*Can. $*	*U.K. £*
		Rare	

HN 241
Eagle Crouching on Rock
Brown

Model No.:	265
Designer:	Unknown
Height:	5", 12.7 cm
Colour:	Brown and gold
Issued:	1920-by 1946
Varieties:	HN 242

Price:	*U.S. $*	*Can. $*	*U.K. £*
		Very Rare	

HN 242
Eagle Crouching on Rock
Light brown

Model No.:	265
Designer:	Unknown
Height:	5", 12.7 cm
Colour:	Light brown and gold, white head and neck
Issued:	1920-by 1946
Varieties:	HN 241

Price:	*U.S. $*	*Can. $*	*U.K. £*
		Very Rare	

HN 243
Pig Bowl
Style One

Model No.:	Unknown
Designer:	Unknown
Height:	3 1/2", 8.9 cm
Colour:	Brown and cream, Sterling silver rim
Issued:	1920-1936
Varieties:	Flambé

Price:	*U.S. $*	*Can. $*	*U.K. £*
	750.00	850.00	395.00

HN 244
Cat on a Pillar

Model No.:	240
Designer:	Unknown
Height:	7", 17.8 cm
Colour:	Black and white cat on brown base
Issued:	1920-by 1946
Varieties:	HN 203, 245

Price:	*U.S. $*	*Can. $*	*U.K. £*
	2,000.00	2,500.00	1,200.00

HN 245
Cat on a Pillar

Model No.:	240
Designer:	Unknown
Height:	7", 17.8 cm
Colour:	Black cat on brown base
Issued:	1920-by 1946
Varieties:	HN 203, 244

Price:	*U.S. $*	*Can. $*	*U.K. £*
	2,000.00	2,500.00	1,200.00

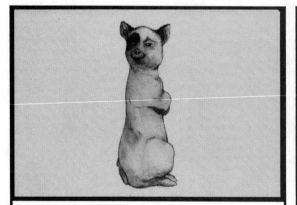

HN 246
Comic Pig

Model No.:	57
Designer:	Charles Noke
Height:	Unknown
Colour:	Unknown
Issued:	1920-1936

Price:	*U.S. $*	*Can. $*	*U.K. £*
		Very Rare	

HN 247
Peahen

Model No.:	270
Designer:	Unknown
Height:	4 1/2", 11.4 cm
Colour:	Grey and pink checkered body with black wing tips, red comb
Issued:	1921-by 1946
Varieties:	Flambé

Price:	*U.S. $*	*Can. $*	*U.K. £*
	500.00	600.00	275.00

HN 248
Duck
Standing - white / blue

Model No.: 307
Designer: Unknown
Height: 13", 33.0 cm
Size: Large
Colour: White and blue
Issued: 1921-by 1946
Varieties: HN 249, 252, 1198, 2635

Price:	*U.S. $*	*Can. $*	*U.K. £*
		Very Rare	

HN 249
Drake
Standing - blue / white

Model No.: 307
Designer: Unknown
Height: 13", 33.0 cm
Size: Large
Colour: Blue and white
Issued: 1921-by 1946
Varieties: HN 248, 252, 1198, 2635

Price:	*U.S. $*	*Can. $*	*U.K. £*
		Very Rare	

HN 250
Heron (flower holder)

Model No.: 314
Designer: Unknown
Height: Unknown
Colour: Unknown
Issued: 1921-1936
Varieties: HN 251

Price:	*U.S. $*	*Can. $*	*U.K. £*
		Rare	

HN 251
Heron (flower holder)

Model No.: 314
Designer: Unknown
Height: Unknown
Colour: Unknown
Issued: 1921-1936
Varieties: HN 250

Price:	*U.S. $*	*Can. $*	*U.K. £*
		Rare	

HN 252
Duck
Standing - white
Model No.:	307
Designer:	Unknown
Height:	13", 33.0 cm
Size:	Large
Colour:	White
Issued:	1921-by 1946
Varieties:	HN 248, 249, 1198, 2635

Price:	*U.S. $*	*Can. $*	*U.K. £*
		Very Rare	

HN 253
Monkey
Seated, arms folded
Model No.:	53
Designer:	Unknown
Height:	3", 7.6 cm
Colour:	Brown and orange
Issued:	1921-by 1946
Varieties:	HN 118, Flambé, Titanian

Price:	*U.S. $*	*Can. $*	*U.K. £*
	375.00	475.00	250.00

HN 254
Monkies, Mother and Baby
Model No.:	52
Designer:	Unknown
Height:	3", 7.6 cm
Colour:	Brown and orange
Issued:	1921-by 1946
Varieties:	Flambé, Sung, Yellow and gold matt glaze

Price:	*U.S. $*	*Can. $*	*U.K. £*
	400.00	550.00	245.00

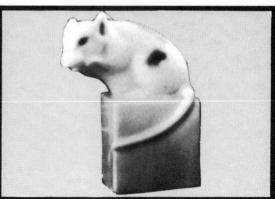

HN 255
Mouse on a Cube
Model No.:	1164
Designer:	Charles Noke
Height:	2 1/2", 6.4 cm
Colour:	Unknown
Issued:	1921-by 1946
Variations:	Flambé

Price:	*U.S. $*	*Can. $*	*U.K. £*
	900.00	1,000.00	450.00

For illustration of HN 256
see page number 48

For illustration of HN 257
see page number 48

HN 256
Character Bird
Style One - green / blue

Model No.:	333		
Designer:	Unknown		
Height:	1", 2.5 cm		
Colour:	Green and blue		
Issued:	1922-by 1946		
Varieties:	HN 283		

Price:	*U.S. $*	*Can. $*	*U.K. £*
	400.00	500.00	250.00

HN 257
Character Bird
Style Two - yellow / red

Model No.:	334		
Designer:	Unknown		
Height:	1 1/2", 3.8 cm		
Colour:	Yellow with red head		
Issued:	1922-by 1946		
Varieties:	HN 284		

Price:	*U.S. $*	*Can. $*	*U.K. £*
	400.00	500.00	250.00

For illustration of HN 258
see page number 48

For illustration of HN 259
see page number 48

HN 258
Character Bird
Style Three - yellow / black

Model No.:	335		
Designer:	Unknown		
Height:	1", 2.5 cm		
Colour:	Yellow with black head		
Issued:	1922-by 1946		
Varieties:	HN 285		

Price:	*U.S. $*	*Can. $*	*U.K. £*
	400.00	500.00	250.00

HN 259
Character Bird
Style Four - grey / red

Model No.:	336		
Designer:	Unknown		
Height:	1", 2.5 cm		
Colour:	Grey with red head and beak and green eyes		
Issued:	1922-by 1946		
Varieties:	HN 286		

Price:	*U.S. $*	*Can. $*	*U.K. £*
	400.00	500.00	250.00

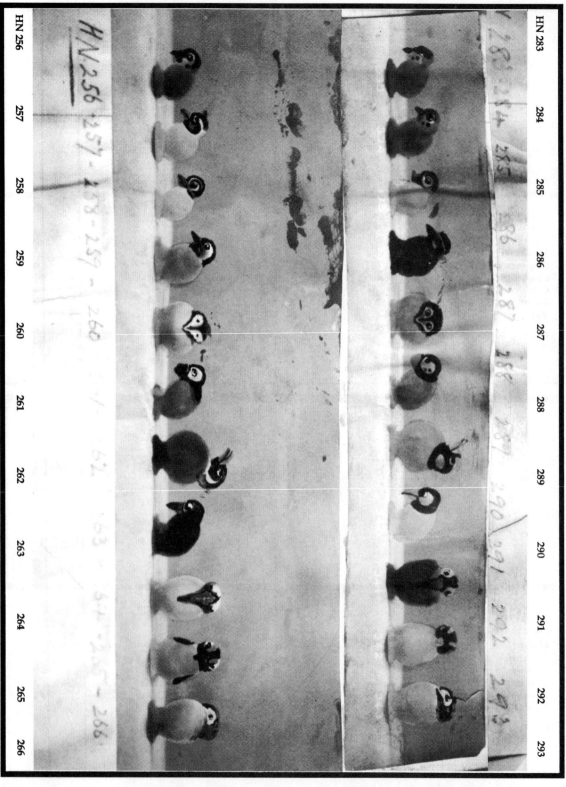

HN 260
Character Bird
Style Five - orange

Model No.:	337
Designer:	Unknown
Height:	1", 2.5 cm
Colour:	Orange
Issued:	1922-by 1946
Varieties:	HN 287
Derivitive:	Ashtray

Price:	*U.S. $*	*Can. $*	*U.K. £*
	400.00	500.00	250.00

HN 261
Character Bird
Style Six - green / red

Model No.:	338
Designer:	Unknown
Height:	1", 2.5 cm
Colour:	Green with red beak
Issued:	1922-by 1946
Varieties:	HN 288

Price:	*U.S. $*	*Can. $*	*U.K. £*
	400.00	500.00	250.00

For illustration of HN 262
see page number 48

For illustration of HN 263
see page number 48

HN 262
Character Bird
Style Seven - orange

Model No.:	339
Designer:	Unknown
Height:	1", 2.5 cm
Colour:	Orange
Issued:	1922-by 1946
Varieties:	HN 289

Price:	*U.S. $*	*Can. $*	*U.K. £*
	400.00	500.00	250.00

HN 263
Character Bird
Style Eight - turquoise

Model No.:	340
Designer:	Unknown
Height:	1", 2.5 cm
Colour:	Turquoise
Issued:	1922-by 1946
Varieties:	HN 290

Price:	*U.S. $*	*Can. $*	*U.K. £*
	400.00	500.00	250.00

HN 264
Character Bird
Style Nine - orange / black

Model No.:	341
Designer:	Unknown
Height:	1 3/4", 4.4 cm
Colour:	Pale orange with black highlights
Issued:	1922-by 1946
Varieties:	HN 291
Derivitive:	Onyx pin tray

Price: | | U.S. $ | Can. $ | U.K. £ |
|---|---|---|---|
| | 400.00 | 500.00 | 250.00 |

HN 265
Character Bird
Style Ten - grey / black

Model No.:	342
Designer:	Unknown
Height:	1 1/2", 3.8 cm
Colour:	Grey, black and orange
Issued:	1922-by 1946
Varieties:	HN 292

Price: | | U.S. $ | Can. $ | U.K. £ |
|---|---|---|---|
| | 400.00 | 500.00 | 250.00 |

For illustration of HN 266
see page number 48

HN 266
Character Bird
Style Eleven - orange / black

Model No.:	343
Designer:	Unknown
Height:	1", 2.5 cm
Colour:	Pale orange with black beak
Issued:	1922-by 1946
Varieties:	HN 293

Price: | | U.S. $ | Can. $ | U.K. £ |
|---|---|---|---|
| | 400.00 | 500.00 | 250.00 |

HN 267
Cockerel
Crouching

Model No.:	30
Designer:	Unknown
Height:	3 1/4", 8.3 cm
Colour:	Brown, blue and black
Issued:	1922-1936
Varieties:	HN 124, 178, 180, Flambé

Price: | | U.S. $ | Can. $ | U.K. £ |
|---|---|---|---|
| | 300.00 | 450.00 | 175.00 |

HN 268
Kingfisher
Style One

Model No.:	91
Designer:	Unknown
Height:	2 1/2", 6.4 cm
Colour:	Blue and yelllow
Issued:	1922-by 1946
Varieties:	Flambé

Price:	*U.S. $*	*Can. $*	*U.K. £*
		Rare	

HN 269
Blue Bird on Rock

Model No.:	196
Designer:	Unknown
Height:	4 1/2", 11.4 cm
Colour:	Blue and yellow
Issued:	1922-by 1946
Varieties:	Also called "Swallow on Rock"
	HN 136, 149

Price:	*U.S. $*	*Can. $*	*U.K. £*
	400.00	500.00	250.00

HN 270
Comic Brown Bear

Model No.:	58
Designer:	Charles Noke
Height:	5", 12.7 cm
Colour:	Brown
Issued:	1922-1936
Varieties:	HN 170, Flambé

Price:	*U.S. $*	*Can. $*	*U.K. £*
	575.00	700.00	375.00

HN 271
Duck
Preening - Style Two

Model No.:	4
Designer:	Unknown
Height:	1 1/2", 3.8 cm
Colour:	Green
Issued:	1922-1936
Varieties:	HN 148A, 299

Price:	*U.S. $*	*Can. $*	*U.K. £*
	300.00	400.00	195.00

HN 272
Bird with Five Chicks

Model No.:	246
Designer:	Unknown
Height:	3 1/4", 8.3 cm
Colour:	Bird: Jade green and brown with red head
	Chicks: pale blue with brown heads
Issued:	1922-1936
Varieties:	HN 214, 215, 216

Price:	U.S. $	Can. $	U.K. £
	400.00	550.00	225.00

HN 273
Hare
Crouching - Style One

Model No.:	119
Designer:	Unknown
Height:	2", 5.1 cm
Colour:	Yellow with black ear tips
Issued:	1922-by 1946
Varieties:	HN 107, 126, 142, 803, Flambé, Sung

Price:	U.S. $	Can. $	U.K. £
	350.00	450.00	195.00

HN 274
Chick

Model No.:	1163B
Designer:	Charles Noke
Height:	2 1/4", 5.7 cm
Colour:	Green
Issued:	1922-by 1946
Varieties:	HN 282, Flambé

Price:	U.S. $	Can. $	U.K. £
	275.00	375.00	165.00

HN 275
Ducklings
Standing

Model No.:	247
Designer:	Unknown
Height:	2 3/4", 7.0 cm
Colour:	Orange
Issued:	1922-by 1946
Varieties:	HN 205, 206

Price:	U.S. $	Can. $	U.K. £
	500.00	650.00	300.00

HN 276
Lop-eared Rabbit

Model No.:	113
Designer:	Unknown
Height:	4", 10.1 cm
Colour:	Bright yellow with black markings
Issued:	1922-by 1946
Varieties:	HN 108, 151, Flambé, Matt red glaze, HN 1091A on Plain Ashtray, HN 1091B on Fluted Ashtray

Price:	*U.S. $*	*Can. $*	*U.K. £*
	450.00	525.00	275.00

HN 277
Wren
Style One

Model No.:	104
Designer:	Unknown
Height:	2", 5.1 cm
Colour:	Unknown
Issued:	1922-by 1946
Varieties:	Also called "Robin", HN 144

Price:	*U.S. $*	*Can. $*	*U.K. £*
	400.00	550.00	195.00

Photograph
Not Available
At Press Time

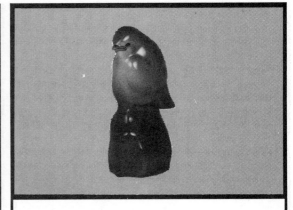

HN 278
Finches (two young)

Model No.:	263
Designer:	Unknown
Height:	2 3/4", 7.0 cm
Colour:	Green and yellow
Issued:	1922-by 1946
Varieties:	Flambé

Price:	*U.S. $*	*Can. $*	*U.K. £*
	500.00	650.00	300.00

HN 279
Fledgling on Rock
Style Two - green

Model No.:	140
Designer:	Charles Noke
Height:	4 1/2", 11.4 cm
Colour:	Green
Issued:	1922-1936
Varieties:	HN 281

Price:	*U.S. $*	*Can. $*	*U.K. £*
	350.00	425.00	200.00

HN 280
Finches (three)

Model No.:	264
Designer:	Charles Noke
Height:	2" x 3 3/4", 5.1 x 9.5 cm
Colour:	Yellow with brown highlighting on centre chick
Issued:	1922-by 1946
Varieties:	Flambé

Price:	U.S. $	Can. $	U.K. £
	300.00	400.00	195.00

HN 281
Fledgling on Rock
Style Two - yellow

Model No.:	140
Designer:	Charles Noke
Height:	4 1/2", 11.4 cm
Colour:	Yellow
Issued:	1922-1936
Varieties:	HN 279

Price:	U.S. $	Can. $	U.K. £
	350.00	425.00	200.00

For illustration of HN 283
see page number 48

HN 282
Chick

Model No.:	1163B
Designer:	Charles Noke
Height:	2 1/4", 5.7 cm
Colour:	Blue
Issued:	1922-by 1946
Varieties:	HN 274, Flambé

Price:	U.S. $	Can. $	U.K. £
	275.00	375.00	165.00

HN 283
Character Bird
Style One - green

Model No.:	333
Designer:	Unknown
Height:	1", 2.5 cm
Colour:	Green with green beak
Issued:	1922-by 1946
Varieties:	HN 256

Price:	U.S. $	Can. $	U.K. £
	450.00	500.00	250.00

For illustration of HN 284
see page number 48

For illustration of HN 285
see page number 48

HN 284
Character Bird
Style Two - mauve / green

Model No.:	334
Designer:	Unknown
Height:	1 1/2", 3.8 cm
Colour:	Mauve and green head with orange beak
Issued:	1922-by 1946
Varieties:	HN 257

Price:

U.S. $	Can. $	U.K. £
450.00	500.00	250.00

HN 285
Character Bird
Style Three - yellow / green

Model No.:	335
Designer:	Unknown
Height:	1", 2.5 cm
Colour:	Yellow with green head
Issued:	1922-by 1946
Varieties:	HN 258

Price:

U.S. $	Can. $	U.K. £
450.00	500.00	250.00

For illustration of HN 286
see page number 48

HN 286
Character Bird
Style Four - blue / red

Model No.:	336
Designer:	Unknown
Height:	1", 2.5 cm
Colour:	Blue with red head and beak
Issued:	1922-by 1946
Varieties:	HN 259

Price:

U.S. $	Can. $	U.K. £
450.00	500.00	250.00

HN 287
Character Bird
Style Five - green / black

Model No.:	337
Designer:	Unknown
Height:	1", 2.5 cm
Colour:	Green with black head
Issued:	1922-by 1946
Varieties:	HN 260
Derivitive:	Ashtray

Price:

U.S. $	Can. $	U.K. £
450.00	500.00	250.00

HN 288
Character Bird
Style Six - purple / green

Model No.:	338
Designer:	Unknown
Height:	1", 2.5 cm
Colour:	Purple with green beak
Issued:	1922-by 1946
Varieties:	HN 261

Price:	*U.S. $*	*Can. $*	*U.K. £*
	450.00	*500.00*	*250.00*

For illustration of HN 289
see page number 48

HN 289
Character Bird
Style Seven - orange / green

Model No.:	339
Designer:	Unknown
Height:	1", 2.5 cm
Colour:	Orange with green beak
Issued:	1922-by 1946
Varieties:	HN 262

Price:	*U.S. $*	*Can. $*	*U.K. £*
	450.00	*500.00*	*250.00*

For illustration of HN 290
see page number 48

HN 290
Character Bird
Style Eight - yellow / green

Model No.:	340
Designer:	Unknown
Height:	1", 2.5 cm
Colour:	Yellow with green head and orange beak
Issued:	1922-by 1946
Varieties:	HN 263

Price:	*U.S. $*	*Can. $*	*U.K. £*
	450.00	*500.00*	*250.00*

HN 291
Character Bird
Style Nine - blue / green

Model No.:	341
Designer:	Unknown
Height:	1 3/4", 4.5 cm
Colour:	Blue with green head and yellow eyes
Issued:	1922-by 1946
Varieties:	HN 264
Derivitive:	Onyx pin tray

Price:	*U.S. $*	*Can. $*	*U.K. £*
	450.00	*500.00*	*250.00*

HN 292
Character Bird
Style Ten - yellow / blue

Model No.:	342
Designer:	Unknown
Height:	1 1/2", 3.8 cm
Colour:	Yellow with blue and yellow striped head
Issued:	1922-by 1946
Varieties:	HN 265

Price:	U.S. $	Can. $	U.K. £
	450.00	500.00	250.00

For illustration of HN 293
see page number 48

HN 293
Character Bird
Style Eleven - yellow / orange

Model No.:	343
Designer:	Unknown
Height:	1", 2.5 cm
Colour:	Yellow with orange spot on head
Issued:	1922-by 1946
Varieties:	HN 266

Price:	U.S. $	Can. $	U.K. £
	450.00	500.00	250.00

HN 294
Toucan on Perch

Model No.:	212
Designer:	Unknown
Height:	7 1/2", 19.1 cm
Colour:	Black and white, red beak
Issued:	1922-by 1946
Varieties	HN 158, 159, 196

Price:	U.S. $	Can. $	U.K. £
	400.00	550.00	265.00

HN 295A
Pelican
Beak Down - red beak

Model No.:	125
Designer:	Unknown
Height:	6 1/4", 15.9 cm
Colour:	Black and green, red beak
Issued:	1922-by 1946
Varieties:	HN 295B, Flambé

Price:	U.S. $	Can. $	U.K. £
	400.00	550.00	265.00

HN 295B
Pelican
Beak Down - brown beak

Model No.: 125
Designer: Unknown
Height: 6 1/4", 15.9 cm
Colour: Black and green, brown beak
Issued: 1922-by 1946
Varieties: HN 295A, Flambé

Price:	*U.S. $*	*Can. $*	*U.K. £*
	400.00	550.00	265.00

HN 296
Emperor Penguin

Model No.: 84
Designer: Unknown
Height: 6", 15.2 cm
Colour: Black and grey
Issued: 1922-by 1946
Varieties: HN 113, Flambé

Price:	*U.S. $*	*Can. $*	*U.K. £*
	550.00	750.00	350.00

HN 297
King Penguin and Chick

Model No.: 239
Designer: Unknown
Height: 5 1/2", 14.0 cm
Colour: Black and white
Issued: 1922-by 1946
Varieties: HN 198, 998, Flambé

Price:	*U.S. $*	*Can. $*	*U.K. £*
	850.00	1,150.00	475.00

HN 298
Duck
Preening - Style One

Model No.: 2
Designer: Unknown
Height: 2 1/2", 6.4 cm
Colour: Unknown
Issued: 1922-1936
Varieties: HN 235, Flambé

Price:	*U.S. $*	*Can. $*	*U.K. £*
		Rare	

HN 299
Drake
Preening - Style Two

Model No.:	4
Designer:	Unknown
Height:	1 1/2", 3.8 cm
Colour:	Green, brown and white
Issued:	1922-by 1946
Varieties:	HN 148A, 271

Price:	U.S. $	Can. $	U.K. £
	300.00	400.00	195.00

*

HN 800
Pig
Snoozing - Large

Model No.:	110
Designer:	Unknown
Height:	Unknown
Size:	Large
Colour:	Unknown
Issued:	1922-by 1946
Varieties:	Flambé, Sung

Price:	U.S. $	Can. $	U.K. £
	600.00	800.00	350.00

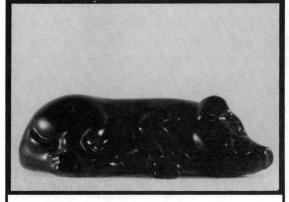

HN 801A
Pig
Snoozing - Medium

Model No.:	110A
Designer:	Unknown
Height:	2" x 4 1/2", 5.1 x 11.4 cm
Size:	Medium
Colour:	Unknown
Issued:	1922-by 1946
Varieties:	Flambé, Sung

Price:	U.S. $	Can. $	U.K. £
	450.00	500.00	295.00

HN 802
Pigs
Snoozing - Ears Up

Model No.:	61
Designer:	Unknown
Height:	4" x 7", 10.1 x 17.8 scm
Colour:	Black and white
Issued:	1923-1936
Varieties:	HN 213, 238, Flambé

Price:	U.S. $	Can. $	U.K. £
	550.00	650.00	325.00

HN 803
Hare
Crouching - Style One

Model No.: 119
Designer: Unknown
Height: 2", 5.1 cm
Colour: Black and white
Issued: 1923-by 1946
Varieties: HN 107, 126, 142, 273, Flambé, Sung

Price: *U.S. $*   *Can. $*   *U.K. £*
                  350.00   450.00   195.00

HN 804
'Bonzo' Character Dog
Style One - orange / cream

Model No.: 392
Designer: Charles Noke
Height: 1", 2.5 cm
Colour: Pale orange and cream
Issued: 1922-1936

Price: *U.S. $*   *Can. $*   *U.K. £*
                       Very Rare

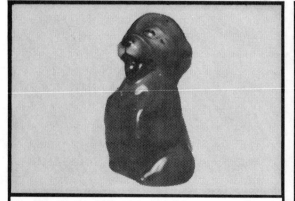

HN 805A
'Bonzo' Character Dog
Style Two - large mouth - green / purple

Model No.: 389
Designer: Charles Noke
Height: 2 1/2", 6.4 cm
Colour: Green and purple
Issued: 1923-1936
Varieties: HN 809, 811

Price: *U.S. $*   *Can. $*   *U.K. £*
                     Very Rare

HN 805B
'Bonzo' Character Dog
Style Three - small mouth - blue

Model No.: 387
Designer: Charles Noke
Height: 2", 5.1 cm
Colour: Blue with brown face and highlights
Issued: 1923-1936
Varieties: HN 808, 810, 812

Price: *U.S. $*   *Can. $*   *U.K. £*
         1,000.00   1,350.00   550.00

HN 806
Duck
Standing - white

Model No.:   395
Designer: Unknown
Height: 2 1/2", 6.4 cm
Size: Small
Colour: White with light brown and black
               highlights
Issued: 1923-1968
Varieties: HN 807, 2591, Flambé

Price:	U.S. $	Can. $	U.K. £
	150.00	200.00	100.00

HN 807
Drake
Sstanding - green

Model No.:   395
Designer: Unknown
Height: 2 1/2", 6.4 cm
Size: Small
Colour: Green, brown and white
Issued: 1923-1977
Varieties: HN 806, 2591, Flambé

Price:	U.S. $	Can. $	U.K. £
	150.00	200.00	100.00

HN 808
'Bonzo' Character Dog
Style Three - small mouth - yellow / brown

Model No.:   387
Designer: Charles Noke
Height: 2", 5.1 cm
Colour: Yellow with brown spots
Issued: 1923-1936
Varieties: HN 805B, 810, 812

Price:	U.S. $	Can. $	U.K. £
	1000.00	1,350.00	500.00

HN 809
'Bonzo' Character Dog
Style Two - large mouth - yellow

Model No.:   389
Designer: Charles Noke
Height: 2 1/2", 6.4 cm
Colour: Yellow
Issued: 1933-1936
Varieties: HN 805A, 811

Price:	U.S. $	Can. $	U.K. £
		Very Rare	

HN 810
'Bonzo' Character Dog
Style Three - small mouth - green
Model No.:   387
Designer: Charles Noke
Height: 2", 5.1 cm
Colour: Green
Issued: 1923-1936
Varieties: HN 805B, 808, 812

Price: *U.S. $*   *Can. $*   *U.K. £*
                  1000.00   1,350.00   500.00

HN 811
'Bonzo' Character Dog
Style Two - large mouth - blue
Model No.:   389
Designer: Charles Noke
Height: 2 1/2", 6.4 cm
Colour: Blue
Issued: 1923-1936
Varieties: HN 805A, 809

Price: *U.S. $*   *Can. $*   *U.K. £*
                                Very Rare

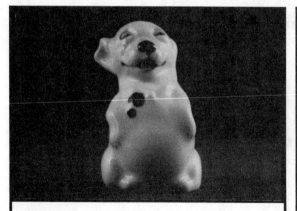

HN 812
'Bonzo' Character Dog
Style Three - small mouth - orange
Model No.:   387
Designer: Charles Noke
Height: 2", 5.1 cm
Colour: Orange
Issued: 1923-1936
Varieties: HN 805B, 808, 810

Price: *U.S. $*   *Can. $*   *U.K. £*
                  1,000.00   1,350.00   500.00

HN 813
Miniature Bird
Model No.:   396
Designer: Unknown
Height: Unknown
Colour: White
Issued: 1923-by 1946
Varieties: HN 867, 868, 869, 870, 871, 872, 873, 874

Price: *U.S. $*   *Can. $*   *U.K. £*
                                Very Rare

HN 814
'Bonzo' Character Dog
Style Four - black buttons

Model No.:	393
Designer:	Charles Noke
Height:	2", 5.1 cm
Colour:	Cream-yellow with black buttons and jacket edge
Issued:	1923-by 1946
Varieties:	HN 815, 826

Price:	U.S. $	Can. $	U.K. £
	1,000.00	1,350.00	500.00

HN 815
'Bonzo' Character Dog
Style Four - red buttons

Model No.:	393
Designer:	Charles Noke
Height:	2", 5.1 cm
Colour:	Cream-yellow with red buttons and jacket edge
Issued:	1923-by 1946
Varieties:	HN 814, 826

Price:	U.S. $	Can.. $	U.K. £
	1,000.00	1,350.00	500.00

*

HN 818
'Ooloo' Character Cat
Black

Model No.:	400
Designer:	Charles Noke
Height:	3", 7.6 cm
Colour:	Black with white face
Issued:	1923-1932
Varieties:	HN 819, 827, 828, 829; Also called "Lucky" K-12

Price:	U.S. $	Can. $	U.K. £
	950.00	1,275.00	425.00

HN 819
'Ooloo' Character Cat
White

Model No.:	400
Designer:	Charles Noke
Height:	3", 7.6 cm
Colour:	White
Issued:	1923-1932
Varieties:	HN 818, 827, 828, 829; Also called "Lucky" K-12

Price:	U.S. $	Can. $	U.K. £
	950.00	1,275.00	425.00

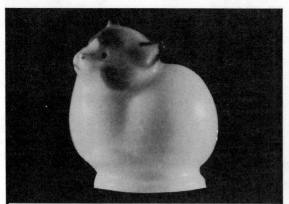

HN 820
Character Kitten
Curled - Style One - ginger head

Model No.:	397
Designer:	Unknown
Height:	1", 2.5 cm
Colour:	White body, ginger head
Issued:	1923-1936
Varieties:	HN 821, 822
Derivitive:	Onyx pin tray (Model No. 397A)

Price: *U.S. $*   *Can. $*   *U.K. £*
                                    Rare

HN 821
Character Kitten
Curled - Style One - brown head

Model No.:	397
Designer:	Unknown
Height:	1", 2.5 cm
Colour:	White front, brown back and head
Issued:	1923-1936
Varieties:	HN 820, 822
Derivitive:	Onyx pin tray (Model No. 397A)

Price: *U.S. $*   *Can. $*   *U.K. £*
                                    Rare

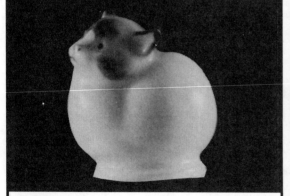

HN 822
Character Kitten
Curled - Style One - black head

Model No.:	397
Designer:	Unknown
Height:	1", 2.5 cm
Colour:	White body and black head
Issued:	1923-1936
Varieties:	HN 820, 821
Derivitive:	Onyx pin tray (Model No. 397A)

Price: *U.S. $*   *Can. $*   *U.K. £*
                                    Rare

HN 823
Character Kitten
Curled - Style Two - white

Model No.:	398
Designer:	Unknown
Height:	1 1/4", 3.2 cm
Colour:	White body and brown head
Issued:	1923-1936
Varieties:	HN 824, 825; Chinese Jade

Price: *U.S. $*   *Can. $*   *U.K. £*
                                    Rare

HN 824
Character Kitten
Curled - Style Two - black

Model No.: 398
Designer: Unknown
Height: 1 1/4", 3.2 cm
Colour: Black body
Issued: 1923-1936
Varieties: HN 823, 825; Chinese Jade

Price:	*U.S. $*	*Can. $*	*U.K. £*
		Rare	

HN 825
Character Kitten
Curled - Style Two - ginger

Model No.: 398
Designer: Unknown
Height: 1 1/4", 3.2 cm
Colour: White and ginger body
Issued: 1923-1936
Varieties: HN 823, 824; Chinese Jade

Price:	*U.S. $*	*Can. $*	*U.K. £*
		Rare	

HN 826
'Bonzo' Character Dog
Style Four - red

Model No.: 393
Designer: Charles Noke
Height: 2", 5.1 cm
Colour: Red
Issued: 1923-1936
Varieties: HN 814, 815

Price:	*U.S. $*	*Can. $*	*U.K. £*
	1,000.00	1,350.00	500.00

HN 827
'Ooloo' Character Cat
Ginger

Model No.: 400
Designer: Charles Noke
Height: 3", 7.6 cm
Colour: Ginger
Issued: 1923-1932
Varieties: HN 818, 819, 828, 829; Also called
"Lucky" K-12

Price:	*U.S. $*	*Can. $*	*U.K. £*
	950.00	1,275.00	425.00

HN 828
'Ooloo' Character Cat
Tabby

Model No.:	400
Designer:	Charles Noke
Height:	3", 7.6 cm
Colour:	Tabby
Issued:	1923-1932
Varieties:	HN 818, 819, 827, 829; Also called "Lucky" K-12

Price:	*U.S. $*	*Can. $*	*U.K. £*
	950.00	1,275.00	425.00

HN 829
'Ooloo' Character Cat
Black / white

Model No.:	400
Designer:	Charles Noke
Height:	3", 7.6 cm
Colour:	Black and white
Issued:	1923-1932
Varieties:	HN 818, 819, 827, 828; Also called "Lucky" K-12

Price:	*U.S. $*	*Can. $*	*U.K. £*
	950.00	1,275.00	425.00

*

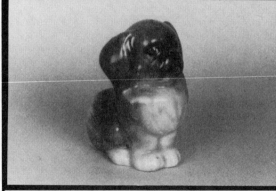

HN 831
Beagle Puppy

Model No.:	407
Designer:	Unknown
Height:	2 1/4", 5.7 cm
Colour:	White with light and dark brown patches
Issued:	1923-by 1946
Derivitives:	Onyx calendar; Sterling silver place card holder

Price:	*U.S. $*	*Can. $*	*U.K. £*
	1,000.00	*1,350.00*	*650.00*

HN 832
Pekinese Puppy
Seated

Model No.:	406
Designer:	Unknown
Height:	2 1/2", 6.4 cm
Colour:	Golden brown with black face, light tan tail
Issued:	1923-by 1946
Varieties:	Chinese Jade, Flambé
Derivitives:	Trinket boxes; Onyx calendars

Price:	*U.S. $*	*Can. $*	*U.K. £*
	900.00	1,200.00	600.00

HN 833
Pekinese Puppy
Standing

Model No.:	405
Designer:	Unknown
Height:	2", 5.1 cm
Colour:	Brown with black face, light tan tail and feet
Issued:	1923-by 1946
Varieties:	Chinese Jade, Flambé
Derivitives:	Trinket boxes

Price:	U.S. $	Can. $	U.K. £
	900.00	1,200.00	600.00

HN 834
Pekinese Puppy
Curled

Model No.:	403
Designer:	Unknown
Height:	1", 2.5 cm
Colour:	Pale brown with dark brown nose and tips of ears
Issued:	1923-by 1946
Varieties:	HN 835, 836
Derivitive:	Ashtray

Price:	U.S. $	Can. $	U.K. £
	700.00	950.00	300.00

HN 835
Pekinese Puppy
Curled - light brown

Model No.:	403
Designer:	Unknown
Height:	1", 2.5 cm
Colour:	Light brown
Issued:	1923-by 1946
Varieties:	HN 834, 836
Derivitive:	Ashtray

Price:	U.S. $	Can. $	U.K. £
	700.00	950.00	300.00

HN 836
Pekinese Puppy
Curled - pale brown

Model No.:	403
Designer:	Unknown
Height:	1", 2.5 cm
Colour:	Pale brown
Issued:	1923-by 1946
Varieties:	HN 834, 835
Derivitive:	Ashtray

Price:	U.S. $	Can. $	U.K. £
	700.00	950.00	300.00

HN 837
Pomeranian
Curled - brown

Model No.:	402
Designer:	Unknown
Height:	1", 2.5 cm
Colour:	Brown
Issued:	1923-by 1946
Varieties:	HN 838, 839

Price:	*U.S. $*	*Can. $*	*U.K. £*
	Very Rare		

HN 838
Pomeranian
Curled - light brown

Model No.:	402
Designer:	Unknown
Height:	1", 2.5 cm
Colour:	Light brown
Issued:	1923-by 1946
Varieties:	HN 837, 839

Price:	*U.S. $*	*Can. $*	*U.K. £*
	Very Rare		

HN 839
Pomeranian
Curled - white / grey

Model No.:	402
Designer:	Unknown
Height:	1", 2.5 cm
Colour:	White and grey
Issued:	1923-by 1946
Varieties:	HN 837, 838

Price:	*U.S. $*	*Can. $*	*U.K. £*
	Very Rare		

HN 840
Character Duck
Style One - Large - yellow / white

Model No.:	415
Designer:	Unknown
Height:	3", 7.6 cm
Size:	Large
Colour:	Pale yellow body, white head
Issued:	1924-by 1946
Varieties:	HN 842, 844

Price:	*U.S. $*	*Can. $*	*U.K. £*
	500.00	675.00	325.00

HN 841
Character Duck
Style One - Small - yellow / black

Model No.:	415A
Designer:	Unknown
Height:	Unknown
Size:	Small
Colour:	Pale yellow body, black wings, white head
Issued:	1924-by 1946
Varieties:	HN 843, 845
Derivitive:	Onyx pin tray (square and oblong bases)

Price:	U.S. $	Can. $	U.K. £
	375.00	525.00	250.00

HN 842
Character Duck
Style One - Large - yellow / brown

Model No.:	415
Designer:	Unknown
Height:	3", 7.6 cm
Size:	Large
Colour:	Yellow body, black wings, brown head
Issued:	1924-by 1946
Varieties:	HN 840, 844

Price:	U.S. $	Can. $	U.K. £
	500.00	675.00	325.00

HN 843
Character Duck
Style One - Small - yellow / brown

Model No.:	415A
Designer:	Unknown
Height:	Unknown
Size:	Small
Colour:	Yellow body with brown highlights
Issued:	1924-by 1946
Varieties:	HN 841, 845
Derivitive:	Onyx pin tray (square and oblong bases)

Price:	U.S. $	Can. $	U.K. £
	375.00	525.00	250.00

HN 844
Character Duck
Style One - Large - orange / black

Model No.:	415
Designer:	Unknown
Height:	3", 7.6 cm
Size:	Large
Colour:	Orange body, black and brown highlights
Issued:	1924-by 1946
Varieties:	HN 840, 842

Price:	U.S. $	Can. $	U.K. £
	500.00	675.00	325.00

HN 845
Character Duck
Style One - Small - orange / black

Model No.:	415A
Designer:	Unknown
Height:	Unknown
Size:	Small
Colour:	Orange body, black and brown highlights
Issued:	1924-by 1946
Varieties:	HN 841, 843
Derivitive:	Onyx pin tray (square and oblong bases)

Price:	*U.S. $*	*Can. $*	*U.K. £*
	375.00	525.00	250.00

HN 846
Toucan on Tree Stump (flower holder)

Model No.:	432
Designer:	Unknown
Height:	Unknown
Colour:	Unknown
Issued:	1924-1936

Price:	*U.S. $*	*Can. $*	*U.K. £*
		Very Rare	

HN 847
Bird on Tree Stump (flower holder)

Model No.:	430
Designer:	Unknown
Height:	Unknown
Colour:	Yellow and orange
Issued:	1924-1936

Price:	*U.S. $*	*Can. $*	*U.K. £*
		Very Rare	

HN 848
Heron on Grass Perch (flower holder)

Model No.:	437
Designer:	Unknown
Height:	Unknown
Colour:	Grey with black highlights, green base
Issued:	1924-1936

Price:	*U.S. $*	*Can. $*	*U.K. £*
		Very Rare	

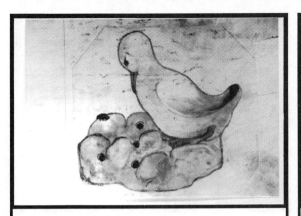

HN 849
Duck and Ladybird (flower holder)

Model No.:	435
Designer:	Unknown
Height:	4 1/2", 11.4 cm
Colour:	White duck, green base
Issued:	1924-1936

Price: *U.S. $*   *Can. $*   *U.K. £*
Very Rare

HN 850
Duckling on a Rock (flower holder)

Model No.:	438
Designer:	Unknown
Height:	Unknown
Colour:	Yellow with brown wing tips, brown white and green base
Issued:	1924-1936

Price: *U.S. $*   *Can. $*   *U.K. £*
Very Rare

HN 851
Robin on Tree Stump (flower holder)

Model No.:	Unknown
Designer:	Unknown
Height:	Unknown
Colour:	Red and brown robin, black base
Issued:	1924-1936
Varieties:	HN 860

Price: *U.S. $*   *Can. $*   *U.K. £*
Very Rare

HN 852A
Penguin on Rocks (flower holder)

Model No.:	441
Designer:	Unknown
Height:	6 1/2", 16.5 cm
Colour:	Black and white penguin, blue rocks
Issued:	1924-1936
Varieties:	HN 852B, 856

Price: *U.S. $*   *Can. $*   *U.K. £*
Very Rare

HN 852B
Penguin on Rocks (flower holder)

Model No.:	441
Designer:	Unknown
Height:	6 1/2", 16.5 cm
Colour:	Pearl glaze
Issued:	1924-1936
Varieties:	HN 852A, 856

Price: *U.S. $*   *Can. $*   *U.K. £*
                          Very Rare

HN 853
Mallard Drake on Rocks (flower holder)

Model No.:	436
Designer:	Unknown
Height:	Unknown
Colour:	Unknown
Issued:	1924-1936

Price: *U.S. $*   *Can. $*   *U.K. £*
                          Very Rare

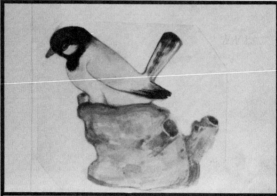

HN 854
Budgerigar on Branch (flower holder)

Model No.:	429
Designer:	Unknown
Height:	4", 10.1 cm
Colour:	Green and yellow budgerigar, green base
Issued:	1924-1936

Price: *U.S. $*   *Can. $*   *U.K. £*
                          Very Rare

HN 855
Wren on Tree Stump (flower holder)

Model No.:	431
Designer:	Unknown
Height:	Unknown
Colour:	Blue, green and grey bird on brown base
Issued:	1924-1936

Price: *U.S. $*   *Can. $*   *U.K. £*
                          Very Rare

HN 856
Penguin on Rocks (flower holder)

Model No.: 441
Designer: Unknown
Height: 6 1/2", 16.5 cm
Colour: Black and white penguin on brown and green rocks
Issued: 1924-1936
Varieties: HN 852A, 852B

Price: *U.S. $*   *Can. $*   *U.K. £*
                 Very Rare

HN 857
Cormorant Nesting on Tree Stump (flower holder)

Model No.: 439
Designer: Unknown
Height: Unknown
Colour: White bird on brown base
Issued: 1924-1936

Price: *U.S. $*   *Can. $*   *U.K. £*
                 Very Rare

HN 858
Kingfisher on Tree Stump (flower holder)
Style Two

Model No.: 227
Designer: Unknown
Height: 3", 7.6 cm
Colour: Green and blue bird on brown tree stump
Issued: 1924-1936
Varieties: HN 165, Flambé

Price: *U.S. $*   *Can. $*   *U.K. £*
             750.00   850.00   500.00

HN 859
Tortoise on Rocks (flower holder)

Model No.: 434
Designer: Unknown
Height: Unknown
Colour: Green and white
Issued: 1924-by 1946

Price: *U.S. $*   *Can. $*   *U.K. £*
                 Very Rare

HN 860
Robin on Tree Stump (flower holder)

Model No.:	Unknown
Designer:	Unknown
Height:	Unknown
Colour:	Black and green with yellow highlights
Issued:	1924-by 1946
Varieties:	HN 851

Price:	*U.S. $*	*Can. $*	*U.K. £*
	Very Rare		

HN 861
Polar Bear
Standing - Style One

Model No.:	433
Designer:	Unknown
Height:	4 1/2 ", 11.4 cm
Colour:	White
Issued:	1924-by 1946

Price:	*U.S. $*	*Can. $*	*U.K. £*
	700.00	850.00	450.00

HN 862A
Kingfisher on Stand with Primroses

Model No.:	44A
Designer:	Unknown
Height:	4 1/2", 11.4 cm
Colour:	Green, malachite blue and orange bird; yellow flowers
Issued:	1924-1936
Varieties:	HN 862B with kingcup flowers

Price:	*U.S. $*	*Can. $*	*U.K. £*
	400.00	475.00	225.00

HN 862B
Kingfisher on Stand with Kingcups

Model No.	44B
Designer:	Unknown
Height:	4 1/2", 11.4 cm
Colour:	Green, malachite blue and orange bird; yellow flowers
Issued:	1924-1936
Varieties:	HN 862A with primrose flowers

Price:	*U.S. $*	*Can. $*	*U.K. £*
	400.00	475.00	225.00

HN 863
Character Duck
Style Two - yellow / white

Model No.: 425
Designer: Unknown
Height: 2 1/2", 6.4 cm
Colour: Yellow body, white head
Issued: 1924-by 1946
Varieties: HN 864, 865

Price: *U.S. $*   *Can. $*   *U.K. £*
                  375.00   475.00   225.00

HN 864
Character Duck
Style Two - yellow / brown

Model No.: 425
Designer: Unknown
Height: 2 1/2", 6.4 cm
Colour: Yellow body, brown head
Issued: 1924-by 1946
Varieties: HN 863, 865

Price: *U.S. $*   *Can. $*   *U.K. £*
                  375.00   475.00   225.00

HN 865
Character Duck
Style Two - brown

Model No.: 425
Designer: Unknown
Height: 2 1/2", 6.4 cm
Colour: Brown body and head
Issued: 1924-by 1946
Varieties: HN 863, 864

Price: *U.S. $*   *Can. $*   *U.K. £*
                  375.00   475.00   225.00

HN 866
Character Fox

Model No.: 442
Designer: Unknown
Height: Unknown
Colour: Light brown with dark brown highlights
Issued: 1924-by 1946
Derivitives: Onyx pin tray

Price: *U.S. $*   *Can. $*   *U.K. £*
                               Rare

HN 871 Aero Animal Brown &
Yellow.

Match Green &
Aero Animal Brown
HN 872

Aero Kingfisher Blue
HN 573   Orange

Aero 1693 Blue
& 903 Green

76

HN 867
Miniature Bird
Grey / brown

Model No.:	396
Designer:	Unknown
Height:	Unknown
Colour:	Grey back and wings, brown head
Issued:	1924-by 1946
Varieties:	HN 813, 868, 869, 870, 871, 872, 873, 874

Price:	*U.S. $*	*Can. $*	*U.K. £*
		Rare	

HN 868
Miniature Bird
Green

Model No.:	396
Designer:	Unknown
Height:	Unknown
Colour:	Green back and head
Issued:	1924-by 1946
Varieties:	HN 813, 867, 869, 870, 871, 872, 873, 874

Price:	*U.S. $*	*Can. $*	*U.K. £*
		Rare	

HN 869
Miniature Bird
Green / yellow

Model No.:	396
Designer:	Unknown
Height:	Unknown
Colour:	Green-black back and head, yellow breast
Issued:	1924-by 1946
Varieties:	HN 813, 867, 868, 870, 871, 872, 873, 874

Price:	*U.S. $*	*Can. $*	*U.K. £*
		Rare	

HN 870
Miniature Bird
Green / grey

Model No.:	396
Designer:	Unknown
Height:	Unknown
Colour:	Green-black head, grey wings, yellow breast
Issued:	1924-by 1946
Varieties:	HN 813, 867, 868, 869, 871, 872, 873, 874

Price:	*U.S. $*	*Can. $*	*U.K. £*
		Rare	

HN 871
Miniature Bird
Brown

Model No.:	396
Designer:	Unknown
Height:	Unknown
Colour:	Brown back and wings
Issued:	1924-by 1946
Varieties:	HN 813, 867, 868, 869, 870, 872, 873, 874

Price:	*U.S. $*	*Can. $*	*U.K. £*
		Rare	

HN 872
Miniature Bird
Green / red

Model No.:	396
Designer:	Unknown
Height:	Unknown
Colour:	Green back, red head
Issued:	1924-by 1946
Varieties:	HN 813, 867, 868, 869, 870, 871, 873, 874

Price:	*U.S. $*	*Can. $*	*U.K. £*
		Rare	

HN 873
Miniature Bird
Blue

Model No.:	396
Designer:	Unknown
Height:	Unknown
Colour:	Blue back
Issued:	1924-by 1946
Varieties:	HN 813, 867, 868, 869, 870, 871, 872, 874

Price:	*U.S. $*	*Can. $*	*U.K. £*
		Rare	

HN 874
Miniature Bird
Green / mauve

Model No.:	396
Designer:	Unknown
Height:	Unknown
Colour:	Green back, mauve breast, blue head
Issued:	1924-by 1946
Varieties:	HN 813, 867, 868, 869, 870, 871, 872, 873

Price:	*U.S. $*	*Can. $*	*U.K. £*
		Rare	

For illustration of the Miniature Birds see page no. 76

HN 875
Kingfisher on Tree Stump (flower holder)
Style Three

Model No.: 446
Designer: Unknown
Height: 4", 10.1 cm
Colour: Blue
Issued: 1924-1936

Price:　　　　*U.S. $*　　*Can. $*　　*U.K. £*
　　　　　　　　　　　　　　Rare

HN 876
Tiger on a Rock
Style One

Model No.: 106
Designer: Charles Noke
Height: 3 1/2" x 9", 8.9 x 22.9 cm
Colour: Brown with dark brown stripes, black base
Issued: 1924-by 1946
Varieties: Flambé

Price:　　　　*U.S. $*　　*Can. $*　　*U.K. £*
　　　　　　　1,500.00　　1,750.00　　950.00

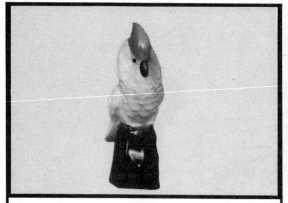

HN 877
Cockatoo on Rock

Model No.: 68
Designer: Leslie Harradine
Height: 6", 15.2 cm
Colour: Blue and orange
Issued: 1924-1936
Varieties: HN 185, 191, 192, 200, Flambé
Derivitive: Onyx pin tray

Price:　　　　*U.S. $*　　*Can. $*　　*U.K. £*
　　　　　　　400.00　　550.00　　275.00

HN 878
Cockerel
Seated - Style Two - white

Model No.: 451
Designer: Unknown
Height: 4", 10.1 cm
Colour: White
Issued: 1924-1936
Varieties: HN 879, 880

Price:　　　　*U.S. $*　　*Can. $*　　*U.K. £*
　　　　　　　325.00　　450.00　　145.00

HN 879
Cockerel
Seated - Style Two - blue

Model No.:	451
Designer:	Unknown
Height:	4". 10.1 cm
Colour:	Blue and green
Issued:	1924-1936
Varieties:	HN 878, 880

Price:	U.S. $	Can. $	U.K. £
	325.00	450.00	145.00

HN 880
Cockerel - Style Two - yellow

Model No.:	451
Designer:	Unknown
Height:	4", 10.1 cm
Colour:	Yellow, black and red
Issued:	1924-1936
Varieties:	HN 878, 879

Price:	U.S. $	Can. $	U.K. £
	325.00	450.00	145.00

HN 881A
Bulldog
Seated - Style Three

Model No.:	122
Designer:	Unknown
Height:	2 3/4", 7.0 cm
Size:	Small
Colour:	Cream with dark brown patches, black collar
Issued:	1938-by 1946
Varieties:	HN 881B; Chinese Jade, Flambé;
	On lid of lustre bowl HN 987

Price:	U.S. $	Can. $	U.K. £
	1,400.00	1,900.00	975.00

HN 881B
Bulldog
Seated - Style Three

Model No.:	122
Designer:	Unknown
Height:	2 3/4", 7.0 cm
Size:	Small
Colour:	Brindle
Issued:	1938-by 1946
Varieties:	HN 881A; Chinese Jade, Flambé;
	On lid of lustre bowl HN 987

Price:	U.S. $	Can. $	U.K. £
	1,400.00	1,900.00	975.00

HN 882
Penguin
Style Two

Model No.:	459
Designer:	Unknown
Height:	6 3/4', 17.2 cm
Colour:	Green head
Issued:	1925-by 1946
Varieties:	Flambé

Price: *U.S. $*   *Can. $*   *U.K. £*

                 Rare

HN 883
Apes

Model No.:	1
Designer:	Leslie Harradine
Height:	2 1/2", 6.4 cm
Colour:	Brown with black highlights
Issued:	1925-1936
Varieties:	Flambé

Price: *U.S. $*   *Can. $*   *U.K. £*

                 Rare

HN 884
Character Parrot on Pillar
Style One

Model No.:	465
Designer:	Unknown
Height:	Unknown
Colour:	Blue and orange
Issued:	1925-1936

Price: *U.S. $*   *Can. $*   *U.K. £*

                 Very Rare

Character Parrot on Pillar
Style Two

Model No.: 466
Designer: Unknown
Height: Unknown

HN 885

Colour: Pink, purple and orange
Issued: 1925-1936
Varieties: HN 886, 888

HN 886

Colour: Red, blue and orange
Issued: 1925-1936
Varieties: HN 885, 888

HN 888

Colour: Pale blue and yellow
Issued: 1925-1936
Varieties: HN 885, 886

Price:	U.S. $	Can. $	U.K. £
HN 885		Very Rare	
HN 886		Very Rare	
HN 888		Very Rare	

* HN 887 Cockatoo Not Issued

HN 889
Greyhound
Seated - black

Model No.: 80
Designer: Charles Noke
Height: 5", 12.7 cm
Colour: Black and white
Issued: 1925-by 1946
Varieties: HN 890, Flambé. First produced in the 1890's as part of a vellum piece.

Price:	U.S. $	Can. $	U.K. £
	1,350.00	1,800.00	600.00

HN 890
Greyhound
Seated - brown

Model No.: 80
Designer: Charles Noke
Height: 5", 12.7 cm
Colour: Brown and cream
Issued: 1925-by 1946
Varieties: HN 889, Flambé. First produced in the 1890's as part of a vellum piece.

Price:	U.S. $	Can. $	U.K. £
	1,350.00	1,800.00	600.00

HN 891A
Elephant
Trunk in salute - Style One - medium

Model No.:	489A
Designer:	Charles Noke
Height:	6", 15.2 cm
Size:	Medium
Colour:	Olive-grey, white tusks (earthenware)
Issued:	1926-1943
Varieties:	Flambé, Sung

Price:	U.S. $	Can. $	U.K. £
	600.00	800.00	450.00

HN 891B
Elephant
Trunk in salute - Style One - small

Model No.:	489B
Designer:	Charles Noke
Height:	4 1/2", 11.4 cm
Size:	Small
Colour:	Silver grey, white tusks (china)
Issued:	1926-1943
Varieties:	HN 941, 2644, Flambé, Sung

Price:	U.S. $	Can. $	U.K. £
	500.00	700.00	325.00

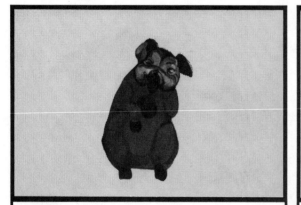

HN 892
Character Pig
Style One - red

Model No.:	494
Designer:	Unknown
Height:	Unknown
Colour:	Red with black spots
Issued:	1926-by 1946
Varieties:	HN 893

Price:	U.S. $	Can. $	U.K. £
		Rare	

HN 893
Character Pig
Style One

Model No.:	494
Designer:	Unknown
Height:	Unknown
Colour:	Green with black spots
Issued:	1926-by 1946
Varieties:	HN 892

Price:	U.S. $	Can. $	U.K. £
		Rare	

Photograph
Not Available
at Press Time

HN 894
Character Pig
Style Two

Model No.:	Unknown
Designer:	Unknown
Height:	Unknown
Colour:	Unknown
Issued:	1926-by 1946

Price:	***U.S. $***	***Can. $***	***U.K. £***
		Rare	

Photograph
Not Available
at Press Time

HN 895
Character Pig
Style Three

Model No.:	Unknown
Designer:	Unknown
Height:	Unknown
Colour:	Unknown
Issued:	1926-by 1946

Price:	***U.S. $***	***Can. $***	***U.K. £***
		Rare	

Photograph
Not Available
at Press Time

HN 896
Character Pig
Style Four

Model No.:	Unknown
Designer:	Unknown
Height:	Unknown
Colour:	Unknown
Issued:	1926-by 1946

Price:	***U.S. $***	***Can. $***	***U.K. £***
		Rare	

Photograph
Not Available
at Press Time

HN 897
Character Pig
Style Five

Model No.:	Unknown
Designer:	Unknown
Height:	Unknown
Colour:	Unknown
Issued:	1926-1936

Price:	***U.S. $***	***Can. $***	***U.K. £***
		Rare	

HN 898
Alsatian's Head
Pencil Holder
Model No.:   509
Designer: Unknown
Height: 3", 7.6 cm
Colour: Brown
Issued: 1926-1936
Derivitives: Onyx pin tray

Price: U.S. $ Can. $ U.K. £
            900.00   1,250.00   600.00

HN 899
Alsatian
Seated, with collar
Model No.:   497
Designer: Unknown
Height: 3 3/4", 9.5 cm
Colour: Dark brown coat, light brown underbody
Issued: 1926-by 1946
Varieties: Flambé, On lid of lustre bowl HN 986
Derivitive: Onyx calender, Onyx pin tray

Price: U.S. $ Can. $ U.K. £
            800.00   1,100.00   395.00

HN 900
Fox Terrier
Seated - Style One
Model No.:   511
Designer: Unknown
Height: 3 1/2", 8.9 cm
Colour: White, brown and ginger
Issued: 1926-by 1946
Varieties: HN 901
Derivitives: Onyx pin tray

Price: U.S. $ Can. $ U.K. £
                    Very Rare

HN 901
Fox Terrier
Seated - Style One
Model No.:   511
Designer: Unknown
Height: 3 1/2", 8.9 cm
Colour: White, black and brown
Issued: 1926-by 1946
Varieties: HN 900
Derivitives: Onyx pin tray

Price: U.S. $ Can. $ U.K. £
                    Very Rare

HN 902
Character Pig
Style Six - black

Model No.:   510
Designer: Unknown
Height: Unknown
Colour: White with black patches
Issued: 1926-1936
Varieties: HN 903

Price: *U.S. $*   *Can. $*   *U.K. £*
                              Rare

HN 903
Character Pig
Style Six - brown

Model No.:   510
Designer: Unknown
Height: Unknown
Colour: White with brown patches
Issued: 1926-1936
Varieties: HN 902

Price: *U.S. $*   *Can. $*   *U.K. £*
                              Rare

HN 904
Terrier Puppy
Begging - Style One

Model No.:   515
Designer: Unknown
Height: 3 1/4", 8.3 cm
Colour: White with black and brown patches
Issued: 1926-by 1946
Derivitive: Marble ashtray

Price: *U.S. $*   *Can. $*   *U.K. £*
                              Very Rare

HN 905
Frog
Style Two

Model No.:   516
Designer: Unknown
Height: 1 1/2", 3.8 cm
Colour: Green with ivory throat
Issued: 1926-1936

Price: *U.S. $*   *Can. $*   *U.K. £*
                              Rare

HN 906
Spaniel Puppy - Dark Brown Patches

Model No.: 514
Designer: Unknown
Height: Unknown
Colour: White with dark brown patches
Issued: 1926-1936
Varieties: HN 907

Price:	*U.S. $*	*Can. $*	*U.K. £*
	900.00	1,250.00	600.00

HN 907
Spaniel Puppy - Light Brown Patches

Model No.: 514
Designer: Unknown
Height: Unknown
Colour: White with light brown patches
Issued: 1926-1936
Varieties: HN 906

Price:	*U.S. $*	*Can. $*	*U.K. £*
	900.00	1,250.00	600.00

HN 908A
Spaniel Puppy's Head
Pencil Holder - Blue Roan

Model No.: 520
Designer: Unknown
Height: 3", 7.6 cm
Colour: Blue roan
Issued: 1926-1936
Varieties: HN 908B

Price:	*U.S. $*	*Can. $*	*U.K. £*
		Rare	

HN 908B
Spaniel Puppy's Head
Pencil Holder - Liver and White

Model No.: 520
Designer: Unknown
Height: 3", 7.6 cm
Colour: Liver and white
Issued: 1926-1936
Varieties: HN 908A

Price:	*U.S. $*	*Can. $*	*U.K. £*
		Rare	

HN 909
Fox Terrier
Standing - Style One

Model No.:	554
Designer:	Unknown
Height:	4", 10.1 cm
Size:	Medium
Colour:	White with dark brown patches
Issued:	1927-by 1946
Varieties:	HN 923

Price:	*U.S. $*	*Can. $*	*U.K. £*
	450.00	600.00	225.00

HN 910
Fox Terrier
Seated- Style Two

Model No.:	553
Designer:	Unknown
Height:	5 1/4", 13.3 cm
Size:	Medium
Colour:	White with black and dark brown patches
Issued:	1927-by 1946
Varieties:	HN 924, Flambé

Price:	*U.S. $*	*Can. $*	*U.K. £*
	400.00	550.00	275.00

HN 911
Tiger
(Lying)

Model No.:	533
Designer:	Charles Noke
Height:	2 1/2" x 7 1/2", 6.4 cm x 19.1 cm
Colour:	Brown with dark brown stripes
Issued:	1927-by 1946
Varieties:	Flambé

Price:	*U.S. $*	*Can. $*	*U.K. £*
	650.00	750.00	475.00

HN 912
Tiger
Seated

Model No.:	530
Designer:	Charles Noke
Height:	6 1/4", 15.9 cm
Colour:	Golden brown with dark brown stripes
Issued:	1927-1940
Varieties:	Flambé

Price:	*U.S. $*	*Can. $*	*U.K. £*
	650.00	750.00	475.00

Model No. 530 was also used to produced HN 919 Leopard

HN 913
Character Toucan With Hat
Style One

Model No.:   548
Designer: Unknown
Height: Unknown
Colour: Green and black body, yellow beak, red and yellow hat
Issued: 1927-by 1946

Price: *U.S. $*   *Can. $*   *U.K. £*
                             Rare

HN 914
Character Toucan With Hat
Style Two

Model No.:   546
Designer: Unknown
Height: Unknown
Colour: Green and black body, red and yellow hat
Issued: 1927-by 1946

Price: *U.S. $*   *Can. $*   *U.K. £*
                             Rare

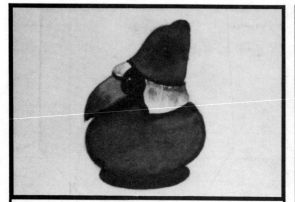

HN 915
Character Toucan With Hat
Style Three

Model No.:   549
Designer: Unknown
Height: Unknown
Colour: Turquoise body, red hat
Issued: 1927-by 1946

Price: *U.S. $*   *Can. $*   *U.K. £*
                             Rare

HN 916
Character Toucan With Hat
Style Four

Model No.:   550
Designer: Unknown
Height: Unknown
Colour: Black and orange body, brown hat
Issued: 1927-by 1946

Price: *U.S. $*   *Can. $*   *U.K. £*
                             Rare

HN 917
Character Toucan With Hat
Style Five

Model No.: 551
Designer: Unknown
Height: Unknown
Colour: Blue body, red and yellow hat
Issued: 1927-by 1946

Price: *U.S. $*   *Can. $*   *U.K. £*
                         Rare

HN 918
Character Toucan With Hat
Style Six

Model No.: 547
Designer: Unknown
Height: Unknown
Colour: Purple and black body, yellow beak,
                   red hat, green tassle
Issued: 1927-by 1946

Price: *U.S. $*   *Can. $*   *U.K. £*
                         Rare

HN 919
Leopard
Seated

Model No.: 530
Designer: Unknown
Height: 6 1/2", 16.5 cm
Colour: Brown with black spots
Issued: 1927-1940

Price: *U.S. $*   *Can. $*   *U.K. £*
          1,000.00   1,250.00   650.00

Model No. 530 was also used to produce HN 912 Tiger

HN 920
Foxes
Curled - Style Two

Model No.: 528
Designer: Unknown
Height: 3" x 6", 7.6 x 15.2 cm
Colour: Brown, with black highlights
Issued: 1927-by 1946
Varieties: HN 925, Flambé

Price: *U.S. $*   *Can. $*   *U.K. £*
          Very Rare

HN 921
Alsatian
Seated, without collar

Model No.:	525		
Designer:	Unknown		
Height:	7", 17.8 cm		
Colour:	Light and dark brown		
Issued:	1927-by 1946		
Varieties:	Flambé		

Price:	*U.S. $*	*Can. $*	*U.K. £*
	1,350.00	1,500.00	750.00

HN 922
Wilfred the Rabbit

Model No.:	559		
Designer:	Charles Noke		
Height:	4", 10.1 cm		
Colour:	Light brown and white rabbit; yellow trumpet		
Issued:	1927-1936		

Price:	*U.S. $*	*Can. $*	*U.K. £*
	600.00	700.00	295.00

HN 923
Fox Terrier
Standing - Style One

Model No.:	554		
Designer:	Unknown		
Height:	4", 10.1 cm		
Size:	Medium		
Colour:	White with light brown patches		
Issued:	1927-by 1946		
Varieties:	HN 909		

Price:	*U.S. $*	*Can. $*	*U.K. £*
	550.00	700.00	225.00

HN 924
Fox Terrier
Seated - Style Two

Designer:	553		
Height:	5 1/4", 13.3 cm		
Size:	Medium		
Colour:	White with light brown patches		
Issued:	1927-by 1946		
Varieties:	HN 910, Flambé		

Price:	*U.S. $*	*Can. $*	*U.K. £*
	550.00	700.00	325.00

HN 925
Foxes
Curled - Style Two

Model No.:	528
Designer:	Unknown
Height:	3" x 6", 7.6 x 15.2 cm
Colour:	Grey and brown
Issued:	1927-by 1946
Varieties:	HN 920, Flambé

Price: *U.S. $*   *Can. $*   *U.K. £*
                    Very Rare

HN926
Foxes
Curled - Style Three

Model No.:	545
Designer:	Unknown
Height:	1 3/4", 5.1 cm
Size:	Miniature
Colour:	Brown with black highlights
Issued:	1927-by 1946
Varieties:	Flambé

Price: *U.S. $*   *Can. $*   *U.K. £*
        400.00   550.00   225.00

HN 927
Pekinese (two)

Model No.:	544
Designer:	Unknown
Height:	2 1/2" x 4 1/2", 6.4 cm x 11.4 cm
Colour:	Golden brown and grey-blue with black markings and white chests
Issued:	1927-by 1946
Varieties:	Chinese Jade, Flambé

Price: *U.S. $*   *Can. $*   *U.K. £*
        800.00   950.00   500.00

HN 928
Ousel Bowl

Model No.:	Unknown
Designer:	Unknown
Height:	7", 17.8 cm
Colour:	Green, blue, brown and orange
Issued:	1927-by 1946

Price: *U.S. $*   *Can. $*   *U.K. £*
               Very Rare

(Bird comes apart to make bowl)

HN 929
Fox Terrier Puppy
Seated

Model No.:	570
Designer:	Unknown
Height:	Unknown
Colour:	White with black patches
Issued:	1927-by 1946
Varieties:	HN 931

Price: *U.S. $*   *Can. $*   *U.K. £*
                              Very Rare

HN 930
Alsatian Puppy

Model No.:	568
Designer:	Unknown
Height:	Unknown
Colour:	Brown
Issued:	1927-by 1946

Price: *U.S. $*   *Can. $*   *U.K. £*
                              Very Rare

HN 931
Fox Terrier Puppy
Seated

Model No.:	570
Designer:	Unknown
Height:	Unknown
Colour:	Brown
Issued:	1927-by 1946
Varieties:	HN 929

Price: *U.S. $*   *Can. $*   *U.K. £*
                              Very Rare

HN 932
Scottish Terrier
Seated - Style One - steel grey

Model No.:	569
Designer:	Unknown
Height:	Unknown
Colour:	Steel grey
Issued:	1927-by 1946
Varieties:	HN 933, 934

Price: *U.S. $*   *Can. $*   *U.K. £*
                              Very Rare

HN 933
Scottish Terrier
Seated - Style One - black

Model No.:	569
Designer:	Unknown
Height:	Unknown
Colour:	Black
Issued:	1927-by 1946
Varieties:	HN 932, 934

Price:	*U.S. $*	*Can. $*	*U.K. £*
		Very Rare	

Steel grey

HN 934
Scottish Terrier
Seated - Style One - brown

Model No.:	569
Designer:	Unknown
Height:	Unknown
Colour:	Brown
Issued:	1927-by 1946
Varieties:	HN 932, 933

Price:	*U.S. $*	*Can. $*	*U.K. £*
		Very Rare	

HN 935
Pip, Squeak and Wilfred Tray

Model No.:	564
Designer:	Charles Noke
Height:	4", 10.1 cm
Colour:	Brown, black and white; cream ashtray
Issued:	1927-1936

Price:	*U.S. $*	*Can. $*	*U.K. £*
	650.00	750.00	375.00

Note: On base "Daily Mirror"

HN 936
Teal Duck

Model No.:	Unknown
Designer:	Unknown
Height:	Unknown
Colour:	Unknown
Issued:	1927-by 1946

Price:	*U.S. $*	*Can. $*	*U.K. £*
		Rare	

HN 937
Alsatian
Standing on plinth
Model No.: 572
Designer: Unknown
Height: Unknown
Colour: Brown
Issued: 1927-by 1946

Price: *U.S. $*   *Can. $*   *U.K. £*
                Extremely Rare

HN 938
Alsatian
Lying on plinth
Model No.: 571
Designer: Unknown
Height: Unknown
Colour: Brown
Issued: 1927-by 1946

Price: *U.S. $*   *Can. $*   *U.K. £*
                Extremely Rare

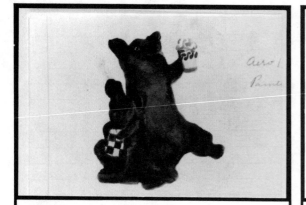

HN 939
Bears Drinking - Dark Brown
Model No.: 561
Designer: Unknown
Height: 3", 7.6 cm
Colour: Dark brown
Issued: 1927-1936
Varieties: HN 940

Price: *U.S. $*   *Can. $*   *U.K. £*
                Extremely Rare

HN 940
Bears Drinking - Light Brown
Model No.: 561
Designer: Unknown
Height: 3", 7.6 cm
Colour: Light brown
Issued: 1927-1936
Varieties: HN 939

Price: *U.S. $*   *Can. $*   *U.K. £*
                Extremely Rare

HN 941
Elephant
Trunk in salute - Style One

Model No.:	489A
Designer:	Charles Noke
Height:	4 1/2", 11.4 cm
Size:	Small
Colour:	Black with white tusks
Issued:	1927-by 1946
Varieties:	HN 891B, 2644, Flambé, Sung

Price:	*U.S. $*	*Can. $*	*U.K. £*
		Rare	

HN 942
Fox Terrier
Standing - Style Three

Model No.:	581
Designer:	Unknown
Height:	6", 15.2 cm
Colour:	White with light brown patches
Issued:	1927-1936
Varieties:	HN 944

Price:	*U.S. $*	*Can. $*	*U.K. £*
	550.00	675.00	325.00

HN 943
Fox Terrier
Standing - Style Two

Model No.:	580
Designer:	Unknown
Height:	5 1/2', 14.0 cm
Colour:	White with light brown patches
Issued:	1927-1940
Varieties:	HN 945, Flambé

Price:	*U.S. $*	*Can. $*	*U.K. £*
	550.00	675.00	325.00

HN 944
Fox Terrier
Standing - Style Three

Model No.:	581
Designer:	Unknown
Height:	6", 15.2 cm
Size:	Large
Colour:	White with dark brown patches
Issued:	1927-1936
Varieties:	HN 942

Price:	*U.S. $*	*Can. $*	*U.K. £*
	550.00	675.00	325.00

HN 945
Fox Terrier
Standing - Style Two
Model No.:   580
Designer: Unknown
Height: 5 1/2", 14.0 cm
Colour: White with black-brown patches
Issued: 1927-1940
Varieties: HN 943, Flambé

Price:	U.S. $	Can. $	U.K. £
	550.00	675.00	325.00

HN 946
Peruvian Penguin
Model No.:   585
Designer: Unknown
Height: 7 3/4", 19.7 cm
Size: Small
Colour: Black and white
Issued: 1927-by 1946
Varieties: HN 1190, Flambé

Price:	U.S. $	Can. $	U.K. £
	850.00	1,000.00	575.00

HN 947
King Penguin
Model No.:   591
Designer: Unknown
Height: 7 1/2", 19.0 cm
Colour: Silver grey
Issued: 1927-by 1946
Varieties: HN 1189, Flambé

Price:	U.S. $	Can. $	U.K. £
	700.00	875.00	275.00

HN 948
Bulldog
Seated - Style Four
Model No.:   135
Designer: Unknown
Height: 6", 15.2 cm
Colour: Dark brown
Issued: 1927-by 1946
Varieties: HN 129, Flambé

Price:	U.S. $	Can. $	U.K. £
	1,500.00	1,500.00	650.00

CHARACTER ELEPHANT

	Designer:	Unknown
	Height:	Unknown
	Issued:	1928-by 1946

	HN 949 Style One	HN 950 Style Two	HN 951 Style Two	HN 952 Style One
Model No.:	596	595	595	596
Colour:	Orange	Yellow	Brown and blue	Pink
Varieties:	HN 952	HN 951	HN 950	HN 949
Price:	HN 949	HN 950	HN 951	HN952
U.S. $				
Can. $	Rare	Rare	Rare	Rare
U.K. £				

Terrier Puppy
Seated

HN 953

Model No.: 597
Designer: Unknown
Height: Unknown
Colour: Black, brown and white
Issued: 1928-by 1946
Varieties: HN 954

HN 954

Model No.: 597
Designer: Unknown
Height: Unknown
Colour: Black, dark brown and white
Issued: 1928-by 1946
Varieties: HN 953

Price:	*U.S. $*	*Can. $*	*U.K. £*
HN 953		Rare	
HN 954		Rare	

HN 955
Brown Bear
Style One

Model No.: 592
Designer: Unknown
Height: 5", 12.7 cm
Colour: Brown
Issued: 1928-by 1946
Varieties: Flambé

Price:	*U.S. $*	*Can. $*	*U.K. £*
	600.00	750.00	400.00

HN 956
Mallard Drake
Standing

Model No.: 137
Designer: Unknown
Height: 5 1/2", 14.0 cm
Size: Medium
Colour: Unknown
Issued: 1928-by 1946
Varieties: HN 114, 115, 116, 1191, 2555, 2647, Flambé

Price:	*U.S. $*	*Can. $*	*U.K. £*
	400.00	550.00	250.00

HN 957
King Charles Spaniel
Model No.:   532
Designer: Unknown
Height: 4 3/4" 12.1 cm
Colour: Liver and white
Issued: 1928-by 1946
Varieties: HN 958

Price: *U.S. $*   *Can. $*   *U.K. £*
        Very Rare

HN 958
King Charles Spaniel
Model No.:   532
Designer: Unknown
Height: 4 3/4", 12.1 cm
Colour: Black and white
Issued: 1928-by 1946
Varieties: HN 957

Price: *U.S. $*   *Can. $*   *U.K. £*
        Very Rare

*

HN 960
Character Ape with Book
Eyes open
Model No.:   604
Designer: Charles Noke
Height: 4", 10.1 cm
Colour: Brown
Issued: 1928-1936

Price: *U.S. $*   *Can. $*   *U.K. £*
        1,000.00   1,250.00   650.00

HN 961
Character Ape with Book
Eyes closed
Model No.:   604
Designer: Charles Noke
Height: 4", 10.1 cm
Colour: Brown
Issued: 1928-1936

Price: *U.S. $*   *Can. $*   *U.K. £*
        1,000.00   1,250.00   650.00

HN 962
Great Dane's Head
Pencil Holder

Model No.:	529
Designer:	Unknown
Height:	3", 7.6 cm
Colour:	Grey and white
Issued:	1928-1936
Derivitive:	Onyx calendar

Price:	*U.S. $*	*Can. $*	*U.K. £*
		Very Rare	

HN 963
Fox
Seated - Style Four

Model No.:	599
Designer:	Unknown
Height:	5 1/2", 14.0 cm
Size:	Medium
Colour:	Brown with black ear tips
Issued:	1928-by 1946

Price:	*U.S. $*	*Can. $*	*U.K. £*
	400.00	550.00	250.00

HN 964
Scottish Terrier
Standing - Style One - black

Model No.:	78
Designer:	Unknown
Height:	4", 10.1 cm
Colour:	Black
Issued:	1928-by 1946
Varieties:	HN 965, Flambé

Price:	*U.S. $*	*Can. $*	*U.K. £*
	850.00	1,150.00	500.00

HN 965
Scottish Terrier
Standing - Style One -brown

Model No.:	78
Designer:	Unknown
Height:	4", 10.1 cm
Colour:	Brown
Issued:	1928-by 1946
Varieties:	HN 964, Flambé

Price:	*U.S. $*	*Can. $*	*U.K. £*
	850.00	1,150.00	500.00

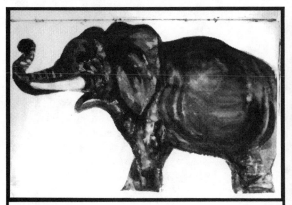

HN 966
Elephant
Trunk in salute

Model No.:	489
Designer:	Charles Noke
Height:	7 ", 17.8 cm
Size:	Large
Colour:	Brown and grey
Issued:	1928-by 1946
Varieties:	Flambé

Price:	U.S. $	Can. $	U.K. £
		Very Rare	

HN 967
Cat
Seated - Style One

Model No.:	9
Designer:	Charles Noke
Height:	4 1/2", 11.4 cm
Colour:	Brown and white
Issued:	1928-by 1946
Varieties:	HN 109, 120, Flambé, Sung

Price:	U.S. $	Can. $	U.K. £
	600.00	800.00	350.00

HN 968A
Pig
Snorting - large

Model No.:	72
Designer:	Unknown
Height:	2 1/2" x 5 1/2", 6.4 x 14.0 cm
Size:	Large
Colour:	Black and white
Issued:	1928-1936
Varieties:	Flambé

Price:	U.S. $	Can. $	U.K. £
	700.00	800.00	375.00

HN 968B
Pig
Snorting - small

Model No.:	72A
Designer:	Unknown
Height:	Unknown
Size:	Small
Colour:	Black and white
Issued:	1928-1936
Varieties:	Flambé

Price:	U.S. $	Can. $	U.K. £
	550.00	675.00	325.00

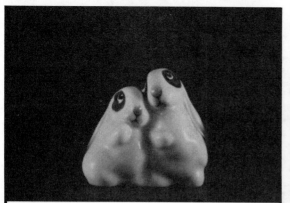

HN 969
Rabbits

Model No.:	249
Designer:	Unknown
Height:	3 1/2", 8.9 cm
Colour:	White with brown patches
Issued:	1928-by 1946
Varieties:	HN 209, 217, 218, 219, Flambé

Price:	*U.S. $*	*Can. $*	*U.K. £*
	850.00	1,000.00	500.00

HN 970
Dachshund
Standing - Style One

Model No.:	36
Designer:	Unknown
Height:	4 1/2" x 6 1/2", 11.4 x 6.5 cm
Colour:	Brown
Issued:	1928-by 1946
Varieties:	Flambé

Price:	*U.S. $*	*Can. $*	*U.K. £*
		Rare	

HN 971
'Ooloo' Character Cat
Ashtray

Model No.:	400
Designer:	Unknown
Height:	3", 7.6 cm
Colour:	Black and white cat, yellow tray
Issued:	1928-by 1946

Price:	*U.S. $*	*Can. $*	*U.K. £*
		Rare	

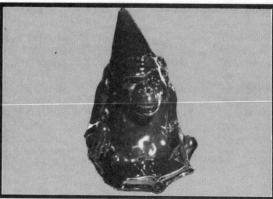

HN 972
Character Ape in Dunce's Cap with Book

Model No.:	640
Designer:	Charles Noke
Height:	5 1/2", 14.0 cm
Colour:	Dark brown ape wearing white dunce's cap, elaborately decorated book pages
Issued:	1928-1936
Varieties:	Flambé (illustrated)

Price:	*U.S. $*	*Can. $*	*U.K. £*
	1,700.00	2,000.00	950.00

HN 973
Character Duck
Style Three

Model No.:	647
Designer:	Unknown
Height:	6", 15.2 cm
Colour:	Yellow to yellowish- brown head, black wings and feet
Issued:	1930-by 1946
Varieties:	HN 974, Flambé

Price:	*U.S. $*	*Can. $*	*U.K. £*
	1,000.00	1,250.00	600.00

HN 974
Character Duck
Style Three

Model No.:	647
Designer:	Unknown
Height:	6", 15.2 cm
Colour:	Lemon-yellow
Issued:	1930-by 1946
Varieties:	HN 973, Flambé

Price:	*U.S. $*	*Can. $*	*U.K. £*
	1,000.00	1,250.00	600.00

HN 975
English Setter with Collar

Model No.:	646
Designer:	Unknown
Height:	6", 15.2 cm
Colour:	Black and white
Issued:	1930-by 1946
Varieties:	Also called "Red Setter with Collar", HN 976

Price:	*U.S. $*	*Can. $*	*U.K. £*
		Very Rare	

HN 976
Red Setter with Collar

Model No.:	646
Designer:	Unknown
Height:	6", 15.2 cm
Colour:	Light brown
Issued:	1930-by 1946
Varieties:	Also called "English Setter with Collar", HN 975

Price:	*U.S. $*	*Can. $*	*U.K. £*
		Very Rare	

HN 977
Drake
Resting
Model No.:   654
Designer: Unknown
Height: 3 1/2", 8.9 cm
Size: Large
Colour: Green and white feathers, brown head
    and breast
Issued: 1930-by 1946
Varieties: HN 1192, Flambé

Price:	*U.S. $*	*Can. $*	*U.K. £*
	350.00	425.00	225.00

Blown Animal Brown

HN 978
Fox
Curled - Style Two
Model No.:   653
Designer: Unknown
Height: Unknown
Colour: Brown
Issued: 1930-by 1946
Varieties: Flambé

Price:	*U.S. $*	*Can. $*	*U.K. £*
		Very Rare	

HN 979
Hare
Lying, legs stretched behind
Model No.:   656
Designer: Unknown
Height: 3" x 7 1/2", 7.6 x 19.1 cm
Size: Large
Colour: Light brown and white, black ear tips
Issued: 1930-by 1946
Varieties: HN 984, 985, 1071, 2593, Flambé

Price:	*U.S. $*	*Can. $*	*U.K. £*
	325.00	400.00	200.00

HN 980
Aberdeen Terrier - black
Model No.:   657
Designer: Unknown
Height: 3" x 5", 7.6 x 12.7 cm
Colour: Black
Issued: 1930-by 1946
Varieties: HN 981

Price:	*U.S. $*	*Can. $*	*U.K. £*
	850.00	1,100.00	450.00

HN 981
Aberdeen Terrier - grey

Model No.: 657
Designer: Unknown
Height: 3" x 5", 7.6 x 12.7 cm
Colour: Grey with brown highlights
Issued: 1930-by 1946
Varieties: HN 980

Price:	*U.S. $*	*Can. $*	*U.K. £*
	850.00	1,100.00	450.00

HN 982A
Sealyham
Standing - Style One - black patches

Model No.: 658
Designer: Unknown
Height: 3", 7.6 cm
Colour: White with black patches over ears
and eyes
Issued: 1930-1936
Varieties: HN 982B, 982C, 983, Flambé

Price:	*U.S. $*	*Can. $*	*U.K. £*
	850.00	1,150.00	475.00

HN 982B
Sealyham
Standing - Style One - brown and black patches

Model No.: 658
Designer: Unknown
Height: 3", 7.6 cm
Colour: White with brown and black patches
over ears and eyes
Issued: 1930-1936
Varieties: HN 982A, 982C, 983, Flambé

Price:	*U.S. $*	*Can. $*	*U.K. £*
	850.00	1,150.00	475.00

HN 982C
Sealyham
Standing - Style One - light tan

Model No.: 658
Designer: Unknown
Height: 3", 7.6 cm
Colour: Light tan
Issued: 1930-1936
Varieties: HN 982A, 982B, 983, Flambé

Price:	*U.S. $*	*Can. $*	*U.K. £*
	850.00	1,150.00	475.00

HN 983
Sealyham
Standing - Style One - light brown patches

Model No.: 658
Designer: Unknown
Height: 3", 7.6 cm
Colour: White with light brown patches on face and body
Issued: 1930-1936
Varieties: HN 982A, 982B, 982C, Flambé

Price:	U.S. $	Can. $	U.K. £
	850.00	1,150.00	475.00

HN 984
Hare
Lying, legs stretched behind - white

Model No.: 656
Designer: Unknown
Height: 3" x 7 1/2", 7.6 x 19.1 cm
Size: Large
Colour: White
Issued: 1930-by 1946
Varieties: HN 979, 985, 1071, 2593, Flambé

Price:	U.S. $	Can. $	U.K. £
	325.00	400.00	200.00

HN 985
Hare
Lying, legs stretched behind - grey

Model No.: 656
Designer: Unknown
Height: 3" x 7 1/2", 7.6 x 19.1 cm
Size: Large
Colour: Grey
Issued: 1930-by 1946
Varieties: HN 979, 984, 1071, 2593, Flambé

Price:	U.S. $	Can. $	U.K. £
	325.00	400.00	200.00

HN 986
Alsatian Seated on Lid of a Lustre Bowl

Model No.: 497A
Designer: Unknown
Height: 5", 12.7 cm (includes bowl)
Colour: Brown dog on mother of pearl bowl
Issued: 1930-by 1946
Varieties: HN 899 (without bowl)

Price:	U.S. $	Can. $	U.K. £
	Very Rare		

HN 987
Bulldog Seated on Lid of Lustre Bowl

Model No.:	122
Designer:	Unknown
Height:	4", 10.1 cm (includes bowl)
Colour:	White bulldog with dark brown patches, mother of pearl bowl
Issued:	1930-by 1946
Varieties:	HN 881 (without bowl)

Price:	U.S. $	Can. $	U.K. £
		Very Rare	

HN 988
Airedale Terrier
Standing

Model No.:	685
Designer:	Unknown
Height:	8" x 8", 20.3 x 20.3 cm
Size:	Large
Colour:	Light brown
Issued:	1930-1936
Varieties:	HN 996

Price:	U.S. $	Can. $	U.K. £
	900.00	1,100.00	500.00

HN 989
Scottish Terrier
Standing - Style Two

Model No.:	Unknown
Designer:	Unknown
Height:	3 1/2" x 6 3/4", 8.9 x 17.1 cm
Colour:	Black with grey highlights
Issued:	1930-1936
Varieties:	HN 992

Price:	U.S. $	Can. $	U.K. £
	1,000.00	1,250.00	650.00

NOTE ON PRICING

This is a first edition and for the first time a complete list of Doulton animals is being priced. These prices have been arrived at by concensus among knowledgeable dealers. They are not to be considered the final word. An animal figure that is common, appears more often that not in every dealer's inventory and is easy to price. However, when a figure is seldom (if ever) seen its scarcity becomes a problem in establishing its value.

We have used two methods to record prices:
1. Rarity classifications
2. Italicized prices

The rarity classification provides a price range. This simply means that the item should sell in the range given. Italicized prices zero in a little closer than the price range. Italicized prices are the level of the last known sale and serve as a basis for the possible current price. However, it still is an indication only and the next transaction may be higher or lower depending on market demand. When dealing with rare animal figures you always need two willing parties, a willing buyer and a willing seller.

Popularity of a series will exert market pressure that will cause price increases for rare figures. An extremely rare character bird cannot and should not be compared with an extremely rare dog in price level due to the popularity of the dog series. Italicized prices and rarity classifications are interchangeable to a certain degree.

Rarity Classification	Rare	Very Rare	Extremely Rare
U.S. $	1,000./1,500.	1,500./2,000.	2,000./3,000.
Can. $	1,500./2,000.	2,000./3,000.	3,000./4,500.
U.K. £	750./1,000.	1,000./1,500.	1,500./2,250.

N/A (not available) in the pricing table indicates that the item was not available in that particular market.

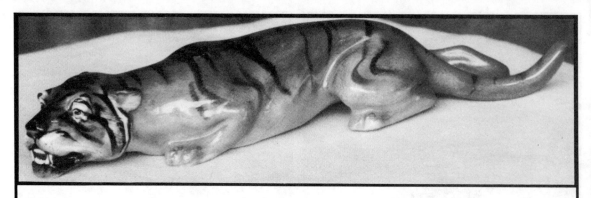

Tiger
Stalking - Style One

	HN 990	HN 991A	HN 991B
Designer:	Charles Noke		
Colour:	Brown		
Issued:	1930-by 1946		
Model No.:	680	680A	680B
Size:	Large	Medium	Small
Length:	7 1/2", 19.1 cm	5 1/2", 14.0 cm	Unknown
Price:	*Large*	*Medium*	*Small*
U.S. $	500.00	425.00	350.00
Can. $	675.00	575.00	475.00
U.K. £	325.00	275.00	225.00

HN 992
Scottish Terrier
Standing - Style Two

Model No.:	Unknown
Designer:	Unknown
Height:	3 1/2" x 6 3/4", 8.9 x 17.1 cm
Colour:	Brown and black
Issued:	1930-by 1946
Varieties:	HN 989

Price:	*U.S. $*	*Can. $*	*U.K. £*
	1,000.00	1,250.00	670.00

HN 993
Cat Asleep on Cushion

Model No.:	24
Designer:	Unknown
Height:	1 3/4", 4.4 cm
Colour:	Black and blue
Issued:	1930-1936

Price:	*U.S. $*	*Can. $*	*U.K. £*
	Very Rare		

HN 994
Fox on Pedestal
Model No.:	21
Designer:	Unknown
Height:	6", 15.2 cm
Colour:	Brown
Issued:	1930-1936
Varieties:	Flambé

Price:	*U.S. $*	*Can. $*	*U.K. £*
	1,000.00	1,250.00	450.00

HN 995
Pekinese
Standing
Model No.:	689
Designer:	Unknown
Height:	3 1/2" x 5", 8.9 x 12.7 cm
Colour:	Brown with black highlights
Issued:	1930-1937
Varieties:	HN 1003, Chinese Jade

Price:	*U.S. $*	*Can. $*	*U.K. £*
	1,150.00	1,350.00	650.00

HN 996
Airedale Terrier
Standing
Model No.:	685
Designer:	Unknown
Height:	8" x 8", 20.3 x 20.3 cm
Size:	Large
Colour:	Light brown with black highlights
Issued:	1930-1936
Varieties:	HN 988

Price:	*U.S. $*	*Can. $*	*U.K. £*
	900.00	1,100.00	500.00

HN 997
Airedale Terrier
Seated
Model No.:	686
Designer:	Unknown
Height:	5", 12.7 cm
Colour:	White with black and dark brown patches on ears, eyes and body
Issued:	1930-by 1946

Price:	*U.S. $*	*Can. $*	*U.K. £*
	Rare		

HN 998
King Penguin and Chick
Model No.: 239
Designer: Unknown
Height: 5 1/2", 14.0 cm
Colour: Green head, yellow neck
Issued: 1930-by 1946
Varieties: HN 198, 297; Flambé

Price: *U.S. $*   *Can. $*   *U.K. £*
              850.00   1,150.00   475.00

HN 999
Persian Cat
Seated - Style One
Model No.: 690
Designer: Unknown
Height: 5", 12.7 cm
Colour: Black and white
Issued: 1930-1985
Varieties: HN 2539A, 2539B

Price: *U.S. $*   *Can. $*   *U.K. £*
              150.00   200.00   85.00

HN 1000
Cocker Spaniel Ch. 'Lucky Star of Ware'
Model No.: 709
Designer: Frederick Daws
Height: 6 1/2", 16.5 cm
Size: Large
Colour: Black with grey highlights
Issued: 1931-1960
Varieties: HN 1002, 1108, 1134, 1186; also called
           "Lucky Pride of Ware"

Price: *U.S. $*   *Can. $*   *U.K. £*
              575.00   700.00   325.00

HN 1001
Cocker Spaniel with Pheasant
Model No.: 714
Designer: Unknown
Height: 6 1/2" x 7 3/4", 16.5 x 19.7 cm
Size: Large
Colour: White with brown markings, reddish-
          brown and green pheasant
Issued: 1931-1968
Varieties: HN 1137

Price: *U.S. $*   *Can. $*   *U.K. £*
              550.00   700.00   375.00

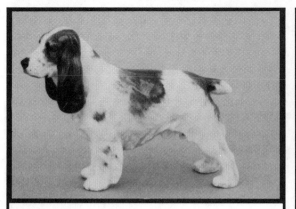

HN 1002
Cocker Spaniel

Model No.:	709
Designer:	Frederick Daws
Height:	6 1/2", 16.5 cm
Size:	Large
Colour:	Liver and white
Issued:	1931-1960
Varieties:	HN 1000, 1108, 1134, 1186; Also called "Lucky Star of Ware" and "Lucky Pride of Ware"

Price:	U.S. $	Can. $	U.K. £
	650.00	750.00	325.00

HN 1003
Pekinese
Standing

Model No.:	689
Designer:	Unknown
Height:	3 1/2" x 5", 8.9 x 12.7 cm
Colour:	Dark brown
Issued:	1931-1937
Varieties:	HN 995, Chinese Jade

Price:	U.S. $	Can. $	U.K. £
	1,150.00	1,350.00	750.00

HN 1004
Blue Tit and Blossom

Model No.:	721
Designer:	Unknown
Height:	Unknown
Colour:	Blue and yellow
Issued:	1931-1937

Price:	U.S. $	Can. $	U.K. £
		Rare	

HN 1005
Thrush and Blossom

Model No.:	716
Designer:	Unknown
Height:	Unknown
Colour:	Brown
Issued:	1931-1937

Price:	U.S. $	Can. $	U.K. £
		Rare	

*

HN 1007
Rough Haired Terrier Ch. 'Crackley Startler'

Model No.:	725
Designer:	Frederick Daws
Height:	7 1/2", 19.1 cm
Size:	Large
Colour:	White with black and brown markings
Issued:	1931-1955
Varieties:	Also known as "Crackley Hunter"

Price:	*U.S. $*	*Can. $*	*U.K. £*
	800.00	1,000.00	475.00

HN 1008
Scottish Terrier Ch. 'Albourne Arthur'

Model No.:	720
Designer:	Frederick Daws
Height:	7", 17.8 cm
Size:	Large
Colour:	Black
Issued:	1931-1955

Price:	*U.S. $*	*Can. $*	*U.K. £*
	1,000.00	*1,300.00*	*600.00*

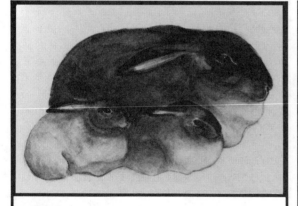

HN 1009
Hare and Leverets

Model No.:	731
Designer:	Unknown
Length:	5", 12.7 cm
Colour:	Brown
Issued:	1931-1937

Price:	*U.S. $*	*Can. $*	*U.K. £*
		Very Rare	

NOTE ON PRICING

This is a first edition and for the first time a complete list of Doulton animals is being priced. These prices have been arrived at by concensus among knowledgeable dealers. They are not to be considered the final word. An animal figure that is common, appears more often that not in every dealer's inventory and is easy to price. However, when a figure is seldom (if ever) seen its scarcity becomes a problem in establishing its value.

We have used two methods to record prices:
1. Rarity classifications
2. Italicized prices

The rarity classification provides a price range. This simply means that the item should sell in the range given. Italicized prices zero in a little closer than the price range. Italicized prices are the level of the last known sale and serve as a basis for the possible current price. However, it still is an indication only and the next transaction may be higher or lower depending on market demand. When dealing with rare animal figures you always need two willing parties, a willing buyer and a willing seller.

Popularity of a series will exert market pressure that will cause price increases for rare figures. An extremely rare character bird cannot and should not be compared with an extremely rare dog in price level due to the popularity of the dog series. Italicized prices and rarity classifications are interchangeable to a certain degree.

Rarity Classification	Rare	Very Rare	Extremely Rare
U.S. $	1,000./1,500.	1,500./2,000.	2,000./3,000.
Can. $	1,500./2,000.	2,000./3,000.	3,000./4,500.
U.K. £	750./1,000.	1,000./1,500.	1,500./2,250.

N/A (not available) in the pricing table indicates that the item was not available in that particular market.

PEKINESE CH. 'BIDDEE OF IFIELD'
Standing

Designer:	Frederick Daws		
Colour:	Golden brown with black highlights		

	HN 1010	**HN 1011**	**HN 1012**
Model No.:	734	734A	734B
Height:	7", 17.8 cm	6 1/2", 16.5 cm	3", 11.4 cm
Size:	Extra-large	Large	Small
Issued:	1931-1955	1931-1955	1931-1985
Price:	*Extra-Large*	*Large*	*Small*
U.S. $	*1,000.00*	800.00	150.00
Can. $	*1,250.00*	1,000.00	175.00
U.K. £	*550.00*	475.00	75.00

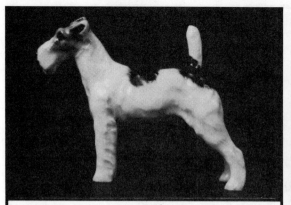

HN 1013
Rough-Haired Terrier Ch. 'Crackley Startler'

Model No.:	725A
Designer:	Frederick Daws
Height:	5 1/2", 17.8 cm
Size:	Medium
Colour:	White with black and brown markings
Issued:	1931-1960
Varieties:	Also called "Crackley Hunter"

Price:	*U.S. $*	*Can. $*	*U.K. £*
	400.00	500.00	225.00

HN 1014
Rough-Haired Terrier Ch. 'Crackley Startler'

Model No.:	725B
Designer:	Frederick Daws
Height:	3 3/4", 13.3 cm
Size:	Small
Colour:	White with black and brown markings
Issued:	1931-1985
Varieties:	Also called "Crackley Hunter"

Price:	*U.S. $*	*Can. $*	*U.K. £*
	250.00	325.00	150.00

HN 1015
Scottish Terrier Ch. 'Albourne Arthur'

Model No.:	720A
Designer:	Frederick Daws
Height:	5", 16.5 cm
Size:	Medium
Colour:	Black
Issued:	1931-1960

Price:	*U.S. $*	*Can. $*	*U.K. £*
	375.00	450.00	200.00

HN 1016
Scottish Terrier Ch. 'Albourne Arthur'

Model No.:	720B
Designer:	Frederick Daws
Height:	3 1/2", 12.7 cm
Size:	Small
Colour:	Black
Issued:	1931-1985

Price:	*U.S. $*	*Can. $*	*U.K. £*
	175.00	225.00	100.00

SCOTTISH TERRIER - Seated - Style Two

Designer: Unknown
Colour: Black

HN 1017

Model No.:   733
Height: 7", 17.8 cm
Size: Large
Issued: 1931-1946

Price:	U.S. $	Can. $	U.K. £
	1,000.00	1,250.00	650.00

HN 1018

Model No.:   733A
Height: 5", 12.7 cm
Size: Medium
Issued: 1931-by 1946

Price:	U.S. $	Can. $	U.K. £
	800.00	950.00	475.00

HN 1019

Model No.:   733B
Height: 3 1/2", 8.9 cm
Size: Small
Issued: 1931-by 1946

Price:	U.S. $	Can. $	U.K. £
	600.00	700.00	325.00

HN 1020
Cocker Spaniel Ch. 'Lucky Star of Ware'

Model No.:   709A
Designer: Frederick Daws
Height: 5", 17.8 cm
Size: Medium
Colour: Black with grey highlights
Issued: 1981-1985
Varieties: HN 1036, 1109, 1135, 1187, Flambé; Also
              called "Lucky Pride of Ware"

Price:	U.S. $	Can. $	U.K. £
	225.00	300.00	175.00

HN 1021
Cocker Spaniel Ch. 'Lucky Star of Ware'

Model No.:   709B
Designer: Frederick Daws
Height: 3 1/2", 8.9 cm
Size: Small
Colour: Black coat with grey markings
Issued: 1931-1968
Varieties: HN 1037, 1078, 1136, 1188; Also called
              "Lucky Pride of Ware"

Price:	U.S. $	Can. $	U.K. £
	150.00	200.00	125.00

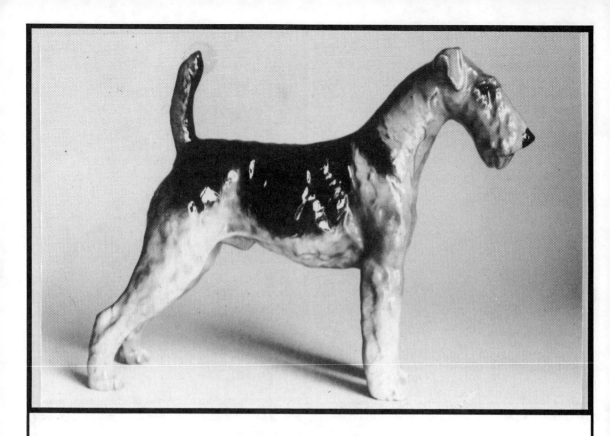

AIREDALE TERRIER CH. 'COTSFORD TOPSAIL'

Designer: Frederick Daws
Colour: Dark brown and black coat, light brown underbody

	HN 1022	HN 1023	HN 1024
Model No.:	738	783A	738B
Height:	8", 20.3 cm	5 1/4", 13.3 cm	4", 10.1 cm
Size:	Large	Medium	Small
Issued:	1931-1960	1931-1985	1931-1968
Varieties	Flambé	Flambé	

Price:	Large	Medium	Small
U.S. $	875.00	375.00	225.00
Can. $	975.00	475.00	325.00
U.K. £	450.00	225.00	165.00

ENGLISH FOXHOUND CH. 'TRING RATTLER'

Designer:	Frederick Daws		
Colour:	White, black and brown		

	HN 1025	**HN 1026**	**HN 1027**
Model No.:	740	740A	740B
Height:	8", 20.3 cm	5", 12.7 cm	4", 10.1 cm
Size:	Large	Medium	Small
Issued:	1931-1955	1931-1960	1931-1956
Price:	*Large*	*Medium*	*Small*
U.S. $	*1,200.00*	600.00	450.00
Can. $	*1,500.00*	750.00	600.00
U.K. £	*675.00*	350.00	295.00

COCKER SPANIEL WITH PHEASANT

Designer: Frederick Daws
Colour: White coat with dark brown markings;
red brown and green pheasant

HN 1028

Model No.: 714A
Height: 5 1/4", 13.3 cm
Size: Medium
Issued: 1931-1985
Varieties: HN 1138

HN 1029

Model No.: 714B
Height: 3 1/2", 8.9 cm
Size: Small
Issued: 1931-1968
Varieties: HN 1062, 2600

Price:	U.S. $	Can. $	U.K. £
HN 1028	275.00	350.00	160.00
HN 1029	225.00	275.00	145.00

SEALYHAM, CH. 'SCOTIA STYLIST '

Designer: Frederick Daws
Colour: White with light brown patches over
eyes and ears

HN 1030

Model No.: 748
Height: 5 1/2", 13.9 cm
Size: Large
Issued: 1931-1955
Varieties: Flambé

HN 1031

Model No.: 748A
Height: 4", 10.1 cm
Size: Medium
Issued: 1931-1955

HN 1032

Model No.: 748B
Height: 3", 12.7 cm
Size: Small
Issued: 1931-1960

Price:	U.S. $	Can. $	U.K. £
HN 1030	750.00	950.00	425.00
HN 1031	425.00	550.00	250.00
HN 1032	300.00	400.00	200.00

CAIRN CH. 'CHARMING EYES'

Designer: Frederick Daws
Colour: Grey with black markings

	HN 1033	**HN 1034**	**HN 1035**
Model No.:	750	750A	750B
Height:	7", 17.8 cm	4 1/2", 11.4 cm	3 1/4", 8.3 cm
Size:	Large	Medium	Small
Issued:	1931-1955	1931-1960	1931-1985
Varieties:	HN 1104	HN 1105	HN 1106
Price:	*Large*	*Medium*	*Small*
U.S. $	800.00	325.00	175.00
Can. $	975.00	425.00	200.00
U.K. £	475.00	195.00	95.00

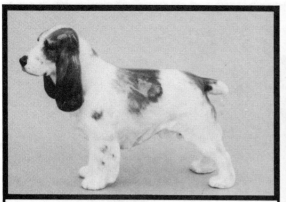

HN 1036
Cocker Spaniel

Model No.:	709A
Designer:	Frederick Daws
Height:	5 1/4", 13.3 cm
Size:	Medium
Colour:	White with light brown ears and eyes, brown patches on back
Issued:	1931-1985
Varieties:	HN 1020, 1109, 1135, 1187, Flambé, Also called 'Lucky Star of Ware'

Price:	*U.S. $*	*Can. $*	*U.K. £*
	200.00	250.00	125.00

HN 1037
Cocker Spaniel

Model No.:	709B
Designer:	Frederick Daws
Height:	3 1/2", 8.9 cm
Size:	Small
Colour:	White with light brown ears and eyes, brown patches on back
Issued:	1931-1968
Varieties:	HN 1021, 1078, 1136, 1188; Also called 'Lucky Star of Ware'

Price:	*U.S. $*	*Can. $*	*U.K. £*
	150.00	200.00	95.00

HN 1038
Scottish Terrier
Begging - Style One

Model No.:	Unknown
Designer:	Unknown
Height:	Unknown
Colour:	Unknown
Issued:	1931-by 1946

Price:	*U.S. $*	*Can. $*	*U.K. £*
		Extremely Rare	

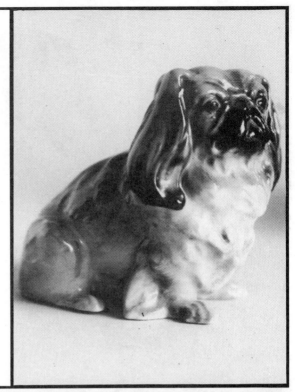

PEKINESE CH. 'BIDDEE OF IFIELD'
Seated

Designer: Frederick Daws
Colour: Butterscotch coat with black highlight

HN 1039

Model No.: 752
Height: 7", 17.8 cm
Size: Large
Issued: 1931-by 1946

HN 1040

Model No.: 752B
Height: 3", 7.6 cm
Size: Small
Issued: 1931-by 1946
Varieties: Flambé

Price:	U.S. $	Can. $	U.K. £
HN 1039	1,200.00	1,500.00	700.00
HN 1040	600.00	900.00	425.00

HN 1041
Sealyham Ch. 'Scotia Stylist - Lying - Style One

Model No.: 753
Designer: Frederick Daws
Height: Unknown
Size: Large
Colour: White with light browpatches over the ears and eyes
Issued: 1931-by 1946

Price:	U.S. $	Can. $	U.K. £
	1,800.00	2,250.00	1,200.00

BULLDOG
Standing

Designer: Frederick Daws
Colour: Brindle

	HN 1042	HN 1043	HN 1044
Model No.:	754	754A	754B
Height:	5 1/2", 14.0 cm	4 3/4", 12.1 cm	3 1/4", 8.3 cm
Size:	Large	Medium	Small
Issued:	1931-1960	1931-1960	1931-1968
Varieties:	HN 1045, 1072	HN 1046, 1073	HN 1047, 1074
Price:	*Large*	*Medium*	*Small*
U.S. $	850.00	550.00	300.00
Can. $	1,100.00	750.00	400.00
U.K. £	575.00	325.00	195.00

HN 1045
Bulldog
Standing

Model No.:	754
Designer:	Frederick Daws
Height:	5 1/4", 13.3 cm
Size:	Large
Colour:	Brindle
Issued:	1931-1960
Varieties:	HN 1042, 1072

Price:	*U.S. $*	*Can. $*	*U.K. £*
	850.00	1,100.00	575.00

HN 1046
Bulldog
Standing

Model No.:	754A
Designer:	Frederick Daws
Height:	4 3/4", 12.1 cm
Size:	Medium
Colour:	Brindle
Issued:	1931-1960
Varieties:	HN 1043, 1073

Price:	*U.S. $*	*Can. $*	*U.K. £*
	550.00	750.00	325.00

HN 1047
Bulldog
Standing

Model No.:	754B
Designer:	Frederick Daws
Height:	3 1/4", 8.3 cm
Size:	Small
Colour:	Brindle
Issued:	1931-1985
Varieties:	HN 1044, 1074

Price:	*U.S. $*	*Can. $*	*U.K. £*
	300.00	400.00	195.00

HN 1048
West Highland Terrier
Style One

Model No.:	756
Designer:	Unknown
Height:	6 1/2" x 9", 16.5 x 22.9 cm
Size:	Large
Colour:	White with brown highlights
Issued:	1931-1931

Price:	*U.S. $*	*Can. $*	*U.K. £*
	Extremely Rare.		
	Only three known to exist.		

ENGLISH SETTER CH. 'MAESYDD MUSTARD'

	Designer:	Frederick Daws	
	Colour:	Off white coat with black highlights	

	HN 1049	HN 1050	HN 1051
Model No.:	770	770A	770B
Height:	7 1/2", 19.0 cm	5 1/4", 13.3 cm	4", 10.1 cm
Size:	Large	Medium	Small
Issued:	1931-1960	1931-1985	1931-1968
Varieties:	Also called English Setter		
	HN 2620	HN 2621	HN 2622

Price:	Large	Medium	Small
U.S. $	650.00	200.00	200.00
Can. $	875.00	275.00	275.00
U.K. £	425.00	125.00	145.00

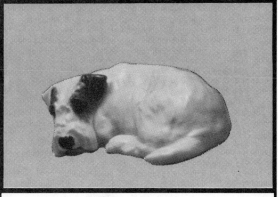

HN 1052
Sealyham Ch. 'Scotia Stylist'
Lying

Model No.:	753A
Designer:	Frederick Daws
Height:	Unknown
Size:	Medium
Colour:	White with light brown patches over ears and eyes
Issued:	1931-by 1946

Price:	*U.S. $*	*Can. $*	*U.K. £*
	1,400.00	1,800.00	900.00

HN 1053
Sealyham Ch. 'Scotia Stylist'
Lying

Model No.:	753B
Designer:	Frederick Daws
Height:	Unknown
Size:	Small
Colour:	White with light brown patches over ears and eyes
Issued:	1931-by 1946

Price:	*U.S. $*	*Can. $*	*U.K. £*
	1,000.00	1,300.00	700.00

IRISH SETTER CH. 'PAT O'MOY'

Designer: Frederick Daws
Colour: Reddish-brown

	HN 1054	**HN 1055**	**HN 1056**
Model No.:	770	770A	770B
Height:	7 1/2", 19.0 cm	5", 12.7 cm	4", 10.1 cm
Size:	Large	Medium	Small
Issued:	1931-1960	1931-1985	1931-1968
Price:	*Large*	*Medium*	*Small*
U.S. $	950.00	200.00	225.00
Can. $	1,200.00	275.00	300.00
U.K. £	600.00	125.00	150.00

COLLIE CH. 'ASHSTEAD APPLAUSE'

	Designer:	Frederick Daws
	Colour:	Dark and light brown coat, white chest, shoulders and feet

	HN 1057	**HN 1058**	**HN 1059**
Model No.:	779	779A	779B
Height:	7 1/2", 19.1 cm	5", 12.7 cm	3 1/2", 11.4 cm
Size:	Large	Medium	Small
Issued:	1931-1960	1931-1985	1931-1969
Price:	*Lareg*	*Medium*	*Small*
U.S. $	775.00	250.00	225.00
Can. $	1,000.00	325.00	275.00
U.K. £	475.00	150.00	125.00

*

HN 1062
Cocker Spaniel with Pheasant

Model No.:	714B
Designer:	Frederick Daws
Height:	3 1/2", 8.9 cm
Size:	Small
Colour:	White with black markings, reddish-brown pheasant
Issued:	1931-1968
Varieties:	HN 1029, 2600

Price:	*U.S. $*	*Can. $*	*U.K. £*
	225.00	300.00	165.00

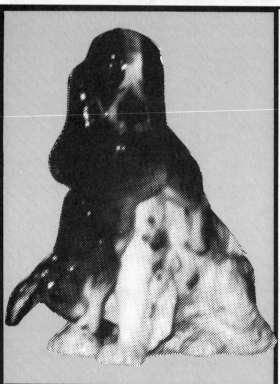

COCKER SPANIEL WITH HARE

Designer:	Unknown
Colour:	Brown and white dog, brown hare

HN 1063

Model No.:	784
Height:	5", 12.7 cm
Size:	Large
Issued:	1931-1935

HN 1064

Model No.:	784A
Height:	4", 10.1 cm
Size:	Small
Issued:	1931-1935

Price:	*U.S. $*	*Can. $*	*U.K. £*
HN 1063		Very Rare	
HN 1064		Very Rare	

GREYHOUND
Standing

Designer: Unknown
Colour: Golden brown with dark brown markings, cream chest and feet

	HN 1065	**HN 1066**	**HN 1067**
Model No.:	792	792A	792B
Height:	8 1/2", 21.6 cm	6", 15.2 cm	4 1/2", 11.4 cm
Size:	Large	Medium	Small
Issued:	1931-1955	1931-1955	1931-1960
Varieties:	HN 1075	HN 1076	HN 1077
Price:	*Large*	*Medium*	*Small*
U.S. $	*1,200.00*	750.00	550.00
Can. $	*1,500.00*	1,000.00	725.00
U.K. £	*750.00*	500.00	375.00

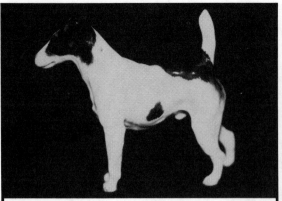

HN 1068
Smooth-Haired Terrier Ch. 'Chosen Don of Notts'

Model No.:	791
Designer:	Frederick Daws
Height:	8 1/2", 21.6 cm
Size:	Large
Colour:	White, black patches on eyes, ears and back
Issued:	1931-by 1952
Varieties:	HN 2512

Price:	*U.S. $*	*Can. $*	*U.K. £*
	1,950.00	2,500.00	1,250.00

HN 1069
Smooth-Haired Terrier Ch. 'Chosen Don of Notts'

Model No.:	791A
Designer:	Frederick Daws
Height:	6", 15.2 cm
Size:	Medium
Colour:	White, black patches on eyes, ears and back
Issued:	1932-1960
Varieties:	HN 2513

Price:	*U.S. $*	*Can. $*	*U.K. £*
	950.00	1,250.00	650.00

HN 1070
Smooth-Haired Terrier Ch. 'Chosen Don of Notts'

Model No.:	791B
Designer:	Frederick Daws
Height:	5", 12.7 cm
Size:	Small
Colour:	White, black patches on eyes, ears and back
Issued:	1931-1952
Varieties:	HN 2514

Price:	*U.S. $*	*Can. $*	*U.K. £*
	850.00	1,150.00	575.00

HN 1071
Hare
Lying, legs stretched behind

Model No.:	656
Designer:	Unknown
Height:	3" x 7" , 7.6 cm x 17.8 cm
Size:	Large
Colour:	Brown and white
Issued:	1932-1941
Varieties:	HN 979, 984, 985, 2593, Flambé

Price:	*U.S. $*	*Can. $*	*U.K. £*
	325.00	400.00	200.00

BULLDOG
Standing

Designer: Frederick Daws
Colour: White, brown collar, gold (tan) studs

	HN 1072	HN 1073	HN 1074
Model No.:	754	754A	754B
Height:	6", 15.2 cm	5", 12.7 cm	3 1/4", 8.2 cm
Size:	Large	Medium	Small
Issued:	1932-1960	1932-1960	1932-1985
Varieties:	HN 1042, 1045	HN 1043, 1046	HN 1044, 1047
Price:	*Large*	*Medium*	*Small*
U.S. $	*1,300.00*	*700.00*	*225.00*
Can. $	*1,750.00*	*950.00*	*300.00*
U.K. £	*850.00*	*425.00*	*150.00*

GREYHOUND
Standing

Designer: Unknown
Colour: White with dark brown patches on eyes, ears and back

	HN 1075	HN 1076	HN 1077
Model No.:	792	792A	792B
Height:	8 1/2", 21.6 cm	6", 15.2 cm	4 1/2", 11.4 cm
Size:	Large	Medium	Small
Issued:	1932-1955	1932-1955	1932-1955
Varieties:	HN 1065	HN 1066	HN 1067
Price:	*Large*	*Medium*	*Small*
U.S. $	1,250.00	750.00	550.00
Can. $	1,500.00	1,000.00	725.00
U.K. £	750.00	500.00	375.00

HN 1078
Cocker Spaniel
Model No.: 709B
Designer: Frederick Daws
Height: 3", 7.6 cm
Size: Small
Colour: White with black markings
Issued: 1932-1968
Varieties: HN 1021, 1037, 1136, 1188; Also called "Lucky Pride of Ware" and "Lucky Star of Ware"

Price:	U.S. $	Can. $	U.K. £
	225.00	300.00	125.00

HN 1079
Gordon Setter
Model No.: 770
Designer: Frederick Daws
Height: 8", 20.3 cm
Size: Large
Colour: Dark brown coat, light brown underbody
Issued: 1932-1955

Price:	U.S. $	Can. $	U.K. £
	2,200.00	2,500.00	1,300.00

HN 1080
Gordon Setter
Model No.: 770A
Designer: Frederick Daws
Height: 5", 12.7 cm
Size: Medium
Colour: Dark brown coat, light brown underbody
Issued: 1932-1955

Price:	U.S. $	Can. $	U.K. £
	700.00	900.00	475.00

HN 1081
Gordon Setter
Model No.: 770B
Designer: Frederick Daws
Height: 4", 10.1 cm
Size: Small
Colour: Dark brown coat, light brown underbody
Issued: 1932-1960

Price:	U.S. $	Can. $	U.K. £
	525.00	700.00	375.00

HN 1082
Tiger
Stalking - Style Two - large

Model No.:	809
Designer:	Charles Noke
Height:	5 3/4" x 13 1/4", 14.6 cm x 33.5 cm
Size:	Extra large
Colour:	Brown with dark brown stripes
Issued:	1933-by 1946
Varieties:	HN 2646, Flambé;
	Tiger on Alabaster Base HN 1125

Price:	U.S. $	Can. $	U.K. £
	1,500.00	1,750.00	850.00

HN 1083
Tiger
Stalking - Style Two - medium

Model No.:	809A
Designer:	Charles Noke
Height:	3 1/4" x 7", 8.3 x 17.8 cm
Size:	Medium
Colour:	Brown with dark brown stripes
Issued:	1933-by 1946

Price:	U.S. $	Can. $	U.K. £
	750.00	1,000.00	475.00

HN 1084
Tiger
Stalking - Style Two - small

Model No.:	809B
Designer:	Charles Noke
Height:	2", 5.1 cm
Size:	Small
Colour:	Brown with dark brown stripes
Issued:	1933-by 1946

Price:	U.S. $	Can. $	U.K. £
	500.00	600.00	295.00

Mould No. 809B was also used to produce HN 1094 Leopard

HN 1085
Lion
Standing - Style One - large

Model No.:	801
Designer:	Charles Noke
Height:	9" x 13", 22.9 cm x 33.0 cm
Size:	Large
Colour:	Brown coat, dark brown mane
Issued:	1933-by 1946
Varieties:	Lion on Alabaster Base HN 1125

Price:	U.S. $	Can. $	U.K. £
	1,500.00	1,750.00	900.00

HN 1086
Lion
Standing - Style One - small

Model No.:	801A
Designer:	Charles Noke
Height:	5", 12.7 cm
Size:	Small
Colour:	Brown coat, dark brown mane
Issued:	1931-by 1946

Price:	*U.S. $*	*Can. $*	*U.K. £*
	650.00	850.00	450.00

Photograph
Not Available
At Press Time

HN 1087
Drake on Ashtray

Model No.:	395
Designer:	Unknown
Height:	3 1/2", 8.9 cm
Colour:	Green drake, cream ashtray
Issued:	1934-by 1946

Price:	*U.S. $*	*Can. $*	*U.K. £*
HN 1087A Plain		Rare	
HN 1087B Fluted		Rare	

HN 1088
Duck on Ashtray

Model No.:	Unknown
Designer:	Unknown
Height:	3 1/2", 8.9 cm
Colour:	White duck, cream ashtray
Issued:	1934-by 1946

Price:	*U.S. $*	*Can. $*	*U.K. £*
HN 1088A Plain		Rare	
HN 1088B Fluted		Rare	

HN 1089
Robin on Ashtray

Model No.:	155
Designer:	Unknown
Height:	3", 7.6 cm
Colour:	Dark brown bird with red breast; cream ashtray
Issued:	1934-by 1946

Price:	*U.S. $*	*Can. $*	*U.K. £*
HN 1089A Plain	250.00	350.00	195 .00
HN 1089B Fluted	250.00	350.00	195 .00

HN 1090
Mouse on Ashtray

Model No.:   1164B
Designer: Unknown
Height: 3", 7.6 cm
Colour: Grey mouse on cream ashtray
Issued: 1934-by 1946

Price:	*U.S. $*	*Can. $*	*U.K. £*
HN 1090A Plain		Rare	
HN 1090B Fluted		Rare	

HN 1091
Lop-eared Rabbit on Ashtray

Model No.:   1165
Designer: Unknown
Height: 3 1/2", 8.9 cm
Colour: Brown and white rabbit on cream ashtray
Issued: 1934-by 1946

Price:	*U.S. $*	*Can. $*	*U.K. £*
HN 1091A Plain		Rare	
HN 1091B Fluted		Rare	

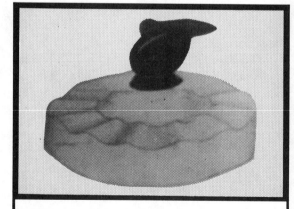

HN 1092A
Comical Bird on Ashtray

Model No.:   366
Designer: Unknown
Height: Unknown
Colour: Unknown
Issued: 1934-by 1946

Price:	*U.S. $*	*Can. $*	*U.K. £*
HN 1092A Plain		Rare	
HN 1092B Fluted		Rare	

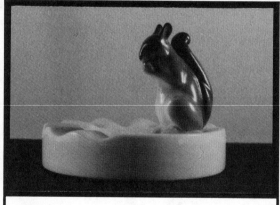

HN 1093
Squirrel on Ashtray

Model No.:   115
Designer: Unknown
Height: 3", 7.6 cm
Colour: Brown squirrel on cream ashtray
Issued: 1934-by 1946

Price:	*U.S. $*	*Can. $*	*U.K. £*
HN 1093A Plain		Rare	
HN 1093B Fluted		Rare	

HN 1094
Leopard
Standing

Model No.:	809B
Designer:	Charles Noke
Height:	2", 5.1 cm
Colour:	Brown
Issued:	1934-by 1946

Price:	U.S. $	Can. $	U.K. £
		Rare	

Mould No. 809B was also used to produce HN 1084 Tiger

HN 1095
Kingfisher on Ashtray

Model No.:	Unknown
Designer:	Unknown
Height:	3", 7.6 cm
Colour:	Unknown
Issued:	1934-by 1946
Varieties:	Fluted or plain ashtray

Price:	U.S. $	Can. $	U.K. £
HN 1095A Plain		Rare	
HN 1095B Fluted		Rare	

HN 1096
Character Fox with Stolen Goose

Model No.:	857
Designer:	Charles Noke
Height:	4 3/4", 12.1 cm
Colour:	Green cloak and hat, brown fox
Issued:	1934-by 1946
Varieties:	HN 1102

Price:	U.S. $	Can. $	U.K. £
		Very Rare	

HN 1097
Character Dog Running with Ball

Model No.:	853
Designer:	Unknown
Height:	2 ", 12.7 cm
Colour:	White with light brown patches over eyes and ears, light and dark brown patches on back, yellow and red striped ball
Issued:	1934-1985
Varieties:	Also known with plain ball

Price:	U.S. $	Can. $	U.K. £
Striped ball	100.00	125.00	65.00
Plain ball		Very Rare	

HN 1098
Character Dog Lying on Back

Model No.:	854
Designer:	Unknown
Height:	2", 11.4 cm
Colour:	White with brown and black patches over ears and eyes
Issued:	1934-1959

Price:	U.S. $	Can. $	U.K. £
	175.00	225.00	125.00

HN 1099
Character Dog Yawning

Model No.:	856
Designer:	Unknown
Height:	4", 10.1 cm
Colour:	White with brown patches over ears and eyes, black patches on back
Issued:	1934-1985

Price:	U.S. $	Can. $	U.K. £
	100.00	125.00	65.00

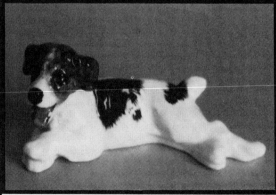

HN 1100
Bull Terrier
Standing - Style One

Model No.:	852
Designer:	Unknown
Height:	4", 10.1 cm
Colour:	White with brown patches over eyes and ears, black patches on back
Issued:	1934-1959

Price:	U.S. $	Can. $	U.K. £
	250.00	325.00	150.00

HN 1101
Character Dog Lying, Panting

Model No.:	866
Designer:	Unknown
Height:	2 1/4", 5.7 cm
Colour:	White with brown patches over ears and eyes, black patches on back
Issued:	1934-1959

Price:	U.S. $	Can. $	U.K. £
	150.00	200.00	125.00

HN 1102
Character Fox with Stolen Goose

Model No.:	857		
Designer:	Charles Noke		
Height:	4 3/4", 12.1 cm		
Colour:	Red cloak, black hat, grey chicken		
Issued:	1934-by 1946		
Varieties:	HN 1096		

Price:	*U.S. $*	*Can. $*	*U.K. £*
		Very Rare	

HN 1103
Character Dog with Ball

Model No.:	855
Designer:	Unknown
Height:	2 1/2", 10.2 cm
Colour:	White with light and dark brown patches; maroon ball
Issued:	1934-1985

Price:	*U.S. $*	*Can. $*	*U.K. £*
	100.00	125.00	65.00

HN 1104
Cairn
Standing - Style One

Model No.:	750
Designer:	Frederick Daws
Height:	7", 17.8 cm
Size:	Large
Colour:	Black
Issued:	1937-1955
Varieties:	Also called Cairn Ch. 'Charming Eyes' HN 1033

Price:	*U.S. $*	*Can. $*	*U.K. £*
	1,250.00	*1,500.00*	*850.00*

HN 1105
Cairn
Standing - Style One

Model No.:	750A
Designer:	Frederick Daws
Height:	4 1/2", 11.4 cm
Size:	Medium
Colour:	Black
Issued:	1937-1960
Varieties:	Also called Cairn Ch. 'Charming Eyes' HN 1034

Price:	*U.S. $*	*Can. $*	*U.K. £*
	700.00	950.00	450.00

HN 1106
Cairn
Standing - Style One

Model No.:	750B
Designer:	Frederick Daws
Height:	3", 7.6 cm
Size:	Small
Colour:	Black
Issued:	1937-1960
Varieties:	Also called Cairn Ch. 'Charming Eyes' HN 1035

Price:	*U.S. $*	*Can. $*	*U.K. £*
	500.00	675.00	350.00

HN 1107
Scottish Terrier
Standing - Style Three

Model No.:	Unknown
Designer:	Unknown
Height:	6 3/4" x 11", 17.2 x 27.9 cm
Size:	Large
Colour:	Black (earthenware)
Issued:	1934-by 1946

Price:	*U.S. $*	*Can. $*	*U.K. £*
		Very Rare	

HN 1108
Cocker Spaniel

Model No.:	709
Designer:	Frederick Daws
Height:	6 1/2", 16.5 cm
Size:	Large
Colour:	White with black markings
Issued:	1937-1960
Varieties:	HN 1000, 1002, 1134, 1186; Also called "Lucky Star of Ware" and "Lucky Pride of Ware"

Price:	*U.S. $*	*Can. $*	*U.K. £*
	575.00	750.00	350.00

HN 1109
Cocker Spaniel

Model No.:	709A
Designer:	Frederick Daws
Height:	5", 12.7 cm
Size:	Medium
Colour:	White with black markings
Issued:	1937-1985
Varieties:	HN 1020, 1036, 1135, 1187, Flambé; "Lucky Star of Ware", "Lucky Pride of Ware"

Price:	*U.S. $*	*Can. $*	*U.K. £*
	200.00	250.00	125.00
*			

HN 1110
Scottish Terrier
Standing - Style Four

Model No.:   873
Designer: Frederick Daws
Height: 7", 17.8 cm
Size: Large
Colour: Black (earthenware)
Issued: 1937-by 1946

Price:	*U.S. $*	*Can. $*	*U.K. £*
		Very Rare	

HN 1111
Dalmation Ch. 'Goworth Victor'

Model No.:   900
Designer: Frederick Daws
Height: 7 3/4", 19.7 cm
Size: Large
Colour: White with black spots, black ears
Issued: 1937-1955

Price:	*U.S. $*	*Can. $*	*U.K. £*
	1,600.00	2,000.00	1,000.00

HN 1112
Lion
Standing - Style Two

Model No.:   Unknown
Designer: Charles Noke
Height: 16", 40.6 cm (length)
Size: Large
Colour: Brown with dark brown mane (china)
Issued: 1937-1946
Varieties: HN 1119 Lion on the Rock

Price:	*U.S. $*	*Can. $*	*U.K. £*
	1,500.00	2,000.00	1,000.00

HN 1113
Dalmation Ch. 'Goworth Victor'

Model No.:   900A
Designer: Frederick Daws
Height: 5 1/2", 14.0 cm
Size: Medium
Colour: White with black spots, black ears
Issued: 1937-1985

Price:	*U.S. $*	*Can. $*	*U.K. £*
	250.00	325.00	150.00

HN 1114
Dalmation Ch. 'Goworth Victor'

Model No.:	900B
Designer:	Frederick Daws
Height:	4 1/4", 10.8 cm
Size:	Small
Colour:	White with black spots, black ears
Issued:	1937-1968

Price:	*U.S. $*	*Can. $*	*U.K. £*
	300.00	400.00	200.00

HN 1115
Alsatian Ch. 'Benign of Picardy'

Model No.:	925
Designer:	Frederick Daws
Height:	9", 22.9 cm
Size:	Large
Colour:	Dark brown coat with light brown underbody, black highlights
Issued:	1937-1960

Price:	*U.S. $*	*Can. $*	*U.K. £*
	850.00	1,100.00	575.00

HN 1116
Alsatian Ch. 'Benign of Picardy'

Model No.:	925A
Designer:	Frederick Daws
Height:	6", 15.2 cm
Size:	Medium
Colour:	Dark brown coat with light brown underbody, black highlights
Issued:	1937-1985

Price:	*U.S. $*	*Can. $*	*U.K. £*
	200.00	250.00	125.00

HN 1117
Alsatian Ch. 'Benign of Picardy'

Model No.:	925B
Designer:	Frederick Daws
Height:	4 1/2", 11.4 cm
Size:	Small
Colour:	Dark brown coat with light brown underbody, black highlights
Issued:	1937-1968

Price:	*U.S. $*	*Can. $*	*U.K. £*
	225.00	300.00	125.00

Photograph
Not Available
At Press Time

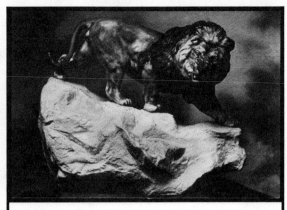

HN 1118
Tiger on the Rock
Style Two

Model No.:	809
Designer:	Charles Noke
Height:	12", 30.5 cm
Colour:	Brown and black (earthenware)
Issued:	1937-by 1946
Varieties:	HN 1082 without rock

Price:

	U.S. $	Can. $	U.K. £
	2000.00	2,500.00	1,250.00

HN 1119
Lion on the Rock
Style One

Model No.:	Unknown
Designer:	Charles Noke
Height:	11", 27.9 cm
Colour:	Tan, brown and black (earthenware)
Issued:	1937-by 1946
Varieties:	Lion (standing) HN 1112

Price:

	U.S. $	Can. $	U.K. £
	2000.00	2.500.00	1,250.00

HN 1120
Fighter Elephant

Model No.:	626
Designer:	Charles Noke
Height:	12" x 9", 30.5 x 22.9 cm
Size:	Large
Colour:	Matt grey with white tusks (earthenware)
Issued:	1937-by 1946
Varieties:	HN 2640; Flambé

Price:

	U.S. $	Can. $	U.K. £
	2,250.00	2,750.00	1,500.00

HN 1121
Elephant
Trunk down

Model No.:	600
Designer:	Charles Noke
Height:	13", 33.0 cm
Size:	Large
Colour:	Grey with white tusks (earthenware)
Issued:	1937-1960
Varieties:	Flambé, Sung

Price:

	U.S. $	Can. $	U.K. £
	3,000.00	3,750.00	1,800.00

*

HN 1125
Lion on Alabaster Base

Model No.:	801
Designer:	Charles Noke
Height:	7", 17.8 cm
Size:	Extra large
Colour:	Tan
Issued:	1937-by 1946
Varieties:	HN 1085 (without base)

Price:	*U.S. $*	*Can. $*	*U.K. £*
		Rare	

HN 1126
Tiger on Alabaster Base

Model No.:	809
Designer:	Charles Noke
Height:	5 3/4" x 13 1/4", 14.6 x 33.5 cm
Size:	Extra large
Colour:	Golden brown with dark brown stripes
Issued:	1937-by 1946
Varieties:	HN 1082, 2646; Flambé

Price:	*U.S. $*	*Can. $*	*U.K. £*
		Rare	

HN 1127
Dachshund Ch. 'Shrewd Saint'

Model No.:	938
Designer:	Frederick Daws
Height:	6", 15.2 cm
Size:	Large
Colour:	Dark brown, light brown feet and nose (earthenware)
Issued:	1937-1955
Varieties:	Also called Dachshund HN 1139; Flambé

Price:	*U.S. $*	*Can. $*	*U.K. £*
	650.00	800.00	375.00

HN 1128
Dachshund Ch. 'Shrewd Saint'

Model No.:	938A
Designer:	Frederick Daws
Height:	4", 10.1 cm
Size:	Medium
Colour:	Dark brown, light brown feet and nose
Issued:	1937-1985
Varieties:	Also called Dachshund 1140; Flambé

Price:	*U.S. $*	*Can. $*	*U.K. £*
	225.00	300.00	150.00

HN 1129
Dachshund Ch. 'Shrewd Saint'

Model No.: 938B
Designer: Frederick Daws
Height: 3", 7.6 cm
Size: Small
Colour: Dark brown, light brown feet and nose
Issued: 1937-1968
Varieties: Also called Dachshund HN 1141; Flambé

Price:	U.S. $	Can. $	U.K. £
	225.00	300.00	150.00

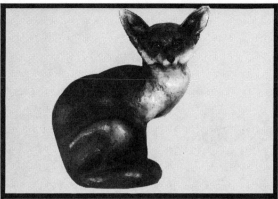

HN 1130
Fox
Seated - Style Five

Model No.: 978
Designer: Raoh Schorr
Height: 11", 27.9 cm
Size: Extra large
Colour: Brown and white
Issued: 1937-by 1946
Varieties: HN 2527

Price:	U.S. $	Can. $	U.K. £
	750.00	950.00	500.00

HN 1131
Staffordshire Bull Terrier
Style One

Model No.: 959
Designer: Frederick Daws
Height: 9", 22.9 cm
Size: Large
Colour: White
Issued: 1937-by 1946
Varieties: Also called Bull Terrier Ch. 'Bokos Brock' HN 1142

Price:	U.S. $	Can. $	U.K. £
	Extremely Rare		

HN 1132
Staffordshire Bull Terrier
Style One

Model No.: 959A
Designer: Frederick Daws
Height: 6 1/2", 16.5 cm
Size: Medium
Colour: White
Issued: 1937-1960
Varieties: Also called Bull Terrier Ch. 'Bokos Brock' HN 1143

Price:	U.S. $	Can. $	U.K. £
	800.00	950.00	450.00

HN 1133
Staffordshire Bull Terrier
Style One

Model No.:	959B
Designer:	Frederick Daws
Height:	4 1/2", 11.4 cm
Size:	Small
Colour:	White
Issued:	1937-by 1946
Varieties:	Also called Bull Terrier Ch. 'Bokos Brock' HN 1144

Price:	*U.S. $*	*Can. $*	*U.K. £*
	2,200.00	2,500.00	1,500.00

HN 1134
Cocker Spaniel

Model No.:	709
Designer:	Frederick Daws
Height:	6 1/2", 16.5 cm
Size:	Large
Colour:	Liver and white
Issued:	1937-by 1946
Varieties:	HN 1000, 1002, 1108, 1186; Also called "Lucky Star of Ware" and "Luck Pride of Ware"

Price:	*U.S. $*	*Can. $*	*U.K. £*
	550.00	700.00	325.00

HN 1135
Cocker Spaniel

Model No.:	709A
Designer:	Frederick Daws
Height:	5", 12.7 cm
Size:	Medium
Colour:	Liver and white
Issued:	1937-by 1946
Varieties:	HN 1020, 1036, 1109, 1187; Also called "Lucky Star of Ware" and "Lucky Pride of Ware"

Price:	*U.S. $*	*Can. $*	*U.K. £*
	200.00	250.00	125.00

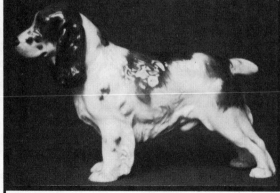

HN 1136
Cocker Spaniel

Model No.:	709B
Designer:	Frederick Daws
Height:	3", 7.6 cm
Size:	Small
Colour:	Liver and white
Issued:	1937-by 1946
Varieties:	HN 1021, 1037, 1078, 1188; Also called "Lucky Star of Ware" and "Lucky Pride of Ware"

Price:	*U.S. $*	*Can. $*	*U.K. £*
	200.00	250.00	125.00

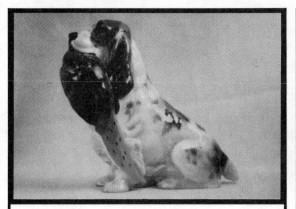

HN 1137
Cocker Spaniel with Pheasant

Model No.:	714
Designer:	Frederick Daws
Height:	6 1/2" x 7 3/4", 16.5 x 19.7 cm
Size:	Large
Colour:	Black and white
Issued:	1937-1968
Varieties:	HN 1001

Price:	*U.S. $*	*Can. $*	*U.K. £*
	550.00	700.00	295.00

HN 1138
Cocker Spaniel with Pheasant

Model No.:	714A
Designer:	Frederick Daws
Height:	5 1/4", 13.3 cm
Size:	Medium
Colour:	White coat with black markings; red-brown pheasant
Issued:	1937-1985
Varieties:	HN 1028

Price:	*U.S. $*	*Can. $*	*U.K. £*
	375.00	475.00	250.00

HN 1139
Dachshund
Standing - Style Two

Model No.:	938
Designer:	Frederick Daws
Height:	6", 15.2 cm
Size:	Large
Colour:	Brown
Issued:	1937-1955
Varieties:	Flambé; Also called Dachshund Ch. 'Shrewd Saint' HN 1127

Price:	*U.S. $*	*Can. $*	*U.K. £*
	650.00	800.00	350.00

HN 1140
Dachshund
Standing - Style Two

Model No.:	938A
Designer:	Frederick Daws
Height:	4", 10.1 cm
Size:	Medium
Colour:	Brown
Issued:	1937-1968
Varieties:	Flambé; Also called Dachshund Ch. 'Shrewd Saint' HN 1128

Price:	*U.S. $*	*Can. $*	*U.K. £*
	295.00	400.00	175.00

HN 1141
Dachshund
Standing - Style Two

Model No.:	938B
Designer:	Frederick Daws
Height:	2 3/4", 7.0 cm
Size:	Small
Colour:	Brown
Issued:	1937-1968
Varieties:	Flambé; Also called Dachshund Ch. 'Shrewd Saint' HN 1129

Price:	U.S. $	Can. $	U.K. £
	200.00	270.00	150.00

HN 1142
Bull Terrier Ch. 'Bokos Brock'

Model No.:	959
Designer:	Frederick Daws
Height:	9", 22.9 cm
Size:	Large
Colour:	Dark brown and white
Issued:	1937-by 1946
Varieties:	Also called Staffordshire Bull Terrier HN 1131

Price:	U.S. $	Can. $	U.K. £
	Extremely Rare		

HN 1143
Bull Terrier Ch. 'Bokos Brock'

Model No.:	959A
Designer:	Frederick Daws
Height:	6 1/2", 16.5 cm
Size:	Medium
Colour:	Dark brown and white
Issued:	1937-1960
Varieties:	Also called Staffordshire Bull Terrier HN 1132

Price:	U.S. $	Can. $	U.K. £
	1,200.00	1,500.00	775.00

HN 1144
Bull Terrier Ch. 'Bokos Brock'

Model No.:	959B
Designer:	Frederick Daws
Height:	4 1/2", 11.4 cm
Size:	Small
Colour:	Dark brown and white
Issued:	1937-by 1946
Varieties:	Also called Staffordshire Bull Terrier HN 1133

Price:	U.S. $	Can. $	U.K. £
	2,500.00	3,000.00	1,500.00

HN 1145
Moufflon
Style One

Model No.:	952
Designer:	Raoh Schorr
Height:	6", 15.2 cm
Colour:	Green bronze
Issued:	1937-1942
Varieties:	HN 1160, 1179

Price:	U.S. $	Can. $	U.K. £
	450.00	575.00	295.00

HN 1146
Calf
Style One

Model No.:	946
Designer:	Raoh Schorr
Height:	2" x 5 1/2", 5.1 x 14.0 cm
Colour:	Green Bronze
Issued:	1937-1942
Varieties:	HN 1161, 1173

Price:	U.S. $	Can. $	U.K. £
	450.00	575.00	325.00

HN 1147
Calf
Style Two

Model No.:	947
Designer:	Raoh Schorr
Height:	6" x 9", 15.2 x 22.9 cm
Colour:	Green Bronze
Issued:	1937-1942
Varieties:	HN 1162, 1174

Price:	U.S. $	Can. $	U.K. £
	450.00	575.00	295.00

HN 1148
Water Buffalo

Model No.:	948
Designer:	Raoh Schorr
Height:	7" x 12 1/2", 17.8 x 31.7 cm
Colour:	Green bronze
Issued:	1937-1942
Varieties:	HN 1163, 1175

Price:	U.S. $	Can. $	U.K. £
	600.00	700.00	395.00

HN 1149
Donkey
Style One

Model No.: 949
Designer: Raoh Schorr
Height: 6", 15.2 cm
Colour: Green Bronze
Issued: 1937-1942
Varieties: HN 1164, 1176

Price:	*U.S. $*	*Can. $*	*U.K. £*
	450.00	575.00	375.00

HN 1150
Young Doe

Model No.: 950
Designer: Raoh Schorr
Height: 4", 10.1 cm
Colour: Green Bronze
Issued: 1937-1942
Varieties: HN 1165, 1177

Price:	*U.S. $*	*Can. $*	*U.K. £*
	450.00	575.00	295.00

HN 1151
Swiss Goat

Model No.: 951
Designer: Raoh Schorr
Height: 5", 12.7 cm
Colour: Green-bronze
Issued: 1937-1942
Varieties: HN 1166, 1178

Price:	*U.S. $*	*Can. $*	*U.K. £*
	450.00	575.00	295.00

HN 1152
Horse
Prancing

Model No.: 953
Designer: Raoh Schorr
Height: 6 3/4", 17.2 cm
Colour: Green-bronze
Issued: 1937-1942
Varieties: HN 1167, 1180

Price:	*U.S. $*	*Can. $*	*U.K. £*
	600.00	700.00	350.00

HN 1153
Moufflon
Style Two

Model No.:	954
Designer:	Raoh Schorr
Height:	2", 5.1 cm
Colour:	Green-bronze
Issued:	1937-1942
Varieties:	HN 1168, 1181

Price:	*U.S. $*	*Can. $*	*U.K. £*
	450.00	575.00	325.00

HN 1154
Jumping Goat

Model No.:	955
Designer:	Raoh Schorr
Height:	6 3/4", 17.2 cm
Colour:	Green-bronze
Issued:	1937-1942
Varieties:	HN 1169, 1182

Price:	*U.S. $*	*Can. $*	*U.K. £*
	450.00	575.00	325.00

Photograph
Not Available
At Press Time

HN 1155
Donkey
Style Two

Model No.:	956
Designer:	Raoh Schorr
Height:	6", 15.2 cm
Colour:	Green-bronze
Issued:	1937-1942
Varieties:	HN 1170, 1183

Price:	*U.S. $*	*Can. $*	*U.K. £*
	450.00	575.00	325.00

HN 1156
'Suspicion'
Doe

Model No.:	957
Designer:	Raoh Schorr
Height:	8 1/4", 21.0 cm
Colour:	Green-bronze
Issued:	1937-1942
Varieties:	HN 1171, 1184

Price:	*U.S. $*	*Can. $*	*U.K. £*
	450.00	575.00	325.00

HN 1157
Antelope

Model No.:	958
Designer:	Raoh Schorr
Height:	6", 15.2 cm
Colour:	Green-bronze
Issued:	1937-1942
Varieties:	HN 1172, 1185

Price:	*U.S. $*	*Can. $*	*U.K. £*
	450.00	575.00	295.00

HN 1158
Character Dog with Plate

Model No.:	963
Designer:	Unknown
Height:	3 1/4", 12.7 cm
Colour:	White with black and light brown patches
Issued:	1937-1985

Price:	*U.S. $*	*Can. $*	*U.K. £*
	100.00	125.00	75.00

HN 1159
Character Dog with Bone

Model No.:	962
Designer:	Unknown
Height:	3 3/4", 9.5 cm
Colour:	White with black and light brown patches on back, light brown patch over left ear
Issued:	1937-1985

Price:	*U.S. $*	*Can. $*	*U.K. £*
	100.00	125.00	75.00

HN 1160
Moufflon
Style One

Model No.:	952
Designer:	Raoh Schorr
Height:	6", 15.2 cm
Colour:	Cream (matt)
Issued:	1937-1942
Varieties:	HN 1145, 1179

Price:	*U.S. $*	*Can. $*	*U.K. £*
	450.00	575.00	295.00

HN 1161
Calf
Style One

Model No.:	946
Designer:	Raoh Schorr
Height:	2" x 5 1/2", 5.1 x 14.0 cm
Colour:	Cream (matt)
Issued:	1937-1942
Varieties:	HN 1146, 1173

Price:	*U.S. $*	*Can. $*	*U.K. £*
	450.00	575.00	325.00

HN 1162
Calf
Style Two

Model No.:	947
Designer:	Raoh Schorr
Height:	6" x 9", 15.2 x 22.9 cm
Colour:	Cream (matt)
Issued:	1937-1942
Varieties:	HN 1147, 1174

Price:	*U.S. $*	*Can. $*	*U.K. £*
	450.00	575.00	295.00

HN 1163
Water Buffalo

Model No.:	948
Designer:	Raoh Schorr
Height:	7" x 12 1/2", 17.8 x 31.7 cm
Colour:	Cream (matt)
Issued:	1937-1942
Varieties:	HN 1148, 1175

Price:	*U.S. $*	*Can. $*	*U.K. £*
	600.00	700.00	350.00

HN 1164
Donkey
Style One

Model No.:	949
Designer:	Raoh Schorr
Height:	6", 15.2 cm
Colour:	Cream (matt)
Issued:	1937-1942
Varieties:	HN 1149, 1176

Price:	*U.S. $*	*Can. $*	*U.K. £*
	450.00	575.00	375.00

HN 1165
Young Doe

Model No.:	950
Designer:	Raoh Schorr
Height:	4", 10.1 cm
Colour:	Cream (matt)
Issued:	1937-1942
Varieties:	HN 1150, 1177

Price:	*U.S. $*	*Can. $*	*U.K. £*
	450.00	575.00	295.00

HN 1166
Swiss Goat

Model No.:	951
Designer:	Raoh Schorr
Height:	5", 12.7 cm
Colour:	Cream (matt)
Issued:	1937-1942
Varieties:	HN 1151, 1178

Price:	*U.S. $*	*Can. $*	*U.K. £*
	450.00	575.00	295.00

HN 1167
Horse
Prancing

Model No.:	953
Designer:	Raoh Schorr
Height:	6 3/4", 17.2 cm
Colour:	Cream (matt)
Issued:	1937-1942
Varieties:	HN 1152, 1180

Price:	*U.S. $*	*Can. $*	*U.K. £*
	600.00	700.00	350.00

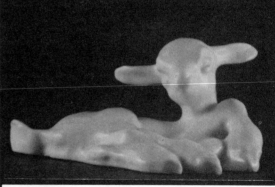

HN 1168
Moufflon
Style Two

Model No.:	954
Designer:	Raoh Schorr
Height:	2 1/2" x 5", 6.4 x 12.7 cm
Colour:	Cream (matt)
Issued:	1937-1942
Varieties:	HN 1153, 1181

Price:	*U.S. $*	*Can. $*	*U.K. £*
	450.00	575.00	325.00

Photograph
Not Available
At Press Time

HN 1169
Jumping Goat
Model No.: 955
Designer: Raoh Schorr
Height: 6 3/4", 17.2 cm
Colour: Cream(matt)
Issued: 1937-1942
Varieties: HN 1154, 1182

Price:	*U.S. $*	*Can. $*	*U.K. £*
	450.00	575.00	300.00

HN 1170
Donkey
Style Two
Model No.: 956
Designer: Raoh Schorr
Height: 6", 15.2 cm
Colour: Cream (matt)
Issued: 1937-1942
Varieties: HN 1155, 1183

Price:	*U.S. $*	*Can. $*	*U.K. £*
	450.00	575.00	325.00

HN 1171
'Suspicion'
Doe
Model No.: 957
Designer: Raoh Schorr
Height: 8 1/4", 21.0 cm
Colour: Cream (matt)
Issued: 1937-1942
Varieties: HN 1156, 1184

Price:	*U.S. $*	*Can. $*	*U.K. £*
	450.00	575.00	325.00

HN 1172
Antelope
Model No.: 958
Designer: Raoh Schorr
Height: 6", 15.2 cm
Colour: Cream (matt)
Issued: 1937-1942
Varieties: HN 1157, 1185

Price:	*U.S. $*	*Can. $*	*U.K. £*
	450.00	575.00	295.00

HN 1173
Calf
Style One

Model No.:	946
Designer:	Raoh Schorr
Height:	2" x 5 1/2", 5.1 x 14.0 cm
Colour:	Light brown
Issued:	1937-1942
Varieties:	HN 1146, 1161

Price:	*U.S. $*	*Can. $*	*U.K. £*
	450.00	575.00	325.00

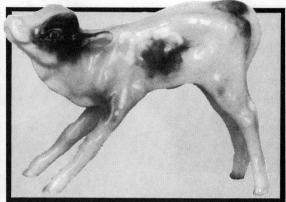

HN 1174
Calf
Style Two

Model No.:	947
Designer:	Raoh Schorr
Height:	6" x 9", 15.2 x 22.9 cm
Colour:	Natural colours
Issued:	1937-1942
Varieties:	HN 1147, 1162

Price:	*U.S. $*	*Can. $*	*U.K. £*
	450.00	575.00	295.00

HN 1175
Water Buffalo

Model No.:	948
Designer:	Raoh Schorr
Height:	7" x 12 1/2", 17.8 x 31.7 cm
Colour:	Brown with black highlights
Issued:	1937-1942
Varieties:	HN 1148, 1163

Price:	*U.S. $*	*Can. $*	*U.K. £*
	600.00	700.00	350.00

HN 1176
Donkey
Style One

Model No.:	949
Designer:	Raoh Schorr
Height:	6", 15.2 cm
Colour:	Natural colours
Issued:	1937-1942
Varieties:	HN 1149, 1164

Price:	*U.S. $*	*Can. $*	*U.K. £*
	450.00	575.00	375.00

HN 1177
Young Doe

Model No.:	950
Designer:	Raoh Schorr
Height:	4", 10.1 cm
Colour:	Natural colours
Issued:	1937-1942
Varieties:	HN 1150, 1165

Price:	U.S. $	Can. $	U.K. £
	450.00	575.00	295.00

HN 1178
Swiss Goat

Model No.:	951
Designer:	Raoh Schorr
Height:	5", 12.7 cm
Colour:	Natural colours
Issued:	1937-1942
Varieties:	HN 1151, 1166

Price:	U.S. $	Can. $	U.K. £
	450.00	575.00	295.00

HN 1179
Moufflon
Style One

Model No.:	952
Designer:	Raoh Schorr
Height:	6", 15.2 cm
Colour:	Natural colours
Issued:	1937-1942
Varieties:	HN 1145, 1160

Price:	U.S. $	Can. $	U.K. £
	450.00	575.00	295.00

HN 1180
Horse
Prancing

Model No.:	953
Designer:	Raoh Schorr
Height:	6 3/4", 17.2 cm
Colour:	White and brown body, grey mane
Issued:	1937-1942
Varieties:	HN 1152, 1167

Price:	U.S. $	Can. $	U.K. £
	600.00	700.00	350.00

HN 1181
Moufflon
Style Two

Model No.:	954
Designer:	Raoh Schorr
Height:	2", 5.1 cm
Colour:	Natural colours
Issued:	1937-1942
Varieties:	HN 1153, 1168

Price:	*U.S. $*	*Can. $*	*U.K. £*
	450.00	575.00	325.00

HN 1182
Jumping Goat

Model No.:	955
Designer:	Raoh Schorr
Height:	6 3/4", 17.2 cm
Colour:	Brown and white goat on grey base
Issued:	1937-1942
Varieties:	HN 1154, 1169

Price:	*U.S. $*	*Can. $*	*U.K. £*
	450.00	575.00	300.00

Photograph
Not Available
At Press Time

HN 1183
Donkey
Style Two

Model No.:	956
Designer:	Raoh Schorr
Height:	6", 15.2 cm
Colour:	Natural colours
Issued:	1937-1942
Varieties:	HN 1155, 1170

Price:	*U.S. $*	*Can. $*	*U.K. £*
	450.00	575.00	295.00

HN 1184
'Suspicion'
Doe

Model No.:	957
Designer:	Raoh Schorr
Height:	8 1/4", 21.0 cm
Colour:	Natural colours
Issued:	1937-1942
Varieties:	HN 1156, 1171

Price:	*U.S. $*	*Can. $*	*U.K. £*
	450.00	575.00	325.00

HN 1185
Antelope

Model No.:	958
Designer:	Raoh Schorr
Height:	6", 15.2 cm
Colour:	Brown with black highlights
Issued:	1937-1942
Varieties:	HN 1157, 1172

Price:	*U.S. $*	*Can. $*	*U.K. £*
	450.00	575.00	295.00

HN 1186
Cocker Spaniel

Model No.:	709
Designer:	Frederick Daws
Height:	6 1/4", 15.9 cm
Size:	Large
Colour:	Golden brown with dark brown highlights
Issued:	1937-1960
Varieties:	HN 1000, 1002, 1108, 1134; Also called "Lucky Pride of Ware" and "Lucky Star of Ware"

Price:	*U.S. $*	*Can. $*	*U.K. £*
	575.00	700.00	395.00

HN 1187
Cocker Spaniel

Model No.:	709A
Designer:	Frederick Daws
Height:	5", 12.7 cm
Size:	Medium
Colour:	Golden brown with dark brown highlights
Issued:	1937-1985
Varieties:	HN 1020, 1036, 1135, 1109, Flambé; Also called Lucky Pride of Ware" and "Lucky Star of Ware"

Price:	*U.S. $*	*Can. $*	*U.K. £*
	200.00	250.00	125.00

HN 1188
Cocker Spaniel

Model No.:	709B
Designer:	Frederick Daws
Height:	3 1/2", 8.9 cm
Size:	Small
Colour:	Golden brown with dark brown highlights
Issued:	1937-1969
Varieties:	HN 1021, 1037, 1078, 1136; Also called "Lucky Pride of Ware" and "Lucky Star of Ware"

Price:	*U.S. $*	*Can. $*	*U.K. £*
	200.00	250.00	125.00

HN 1189
King Penguin

Model No.:	591
Designer:	Unknown
Height:	7 1/2", 19.0 cm
Colour:	Black, white, with orange highlights
Issued:	1937-by 1946
Varieties:	HN 947; Flambé

Price:	U.S. $	Can. $	U.K. £
	550.00	675.00	325.00

HN 1190
Peruvian Penguin

Model No.:	585
Designer:	Unknown
Height:	7 3/4", 19.7 cm
Size:	Small
Colour:	Black and white
Issued:	1936-by 1946
Varieties:	HN 946; Flambé

Price:	U.S. $	Can. $	U.K. £
	600.00	750.00	375.00

HN 1191
Mallard Drake
Standing

Model No.:	137
Designer:	Unknown
Height:	5 1/2", 14.0 cm
Size:	Medium
Colour:	Green head, brown feathers and chest, white lower body
Issued:	1937-by 1960
Varieties:	HN 114, 115, 116, 956, 2555, 2647; Flambé

Price:	U.S. $	Can. $	U.K. £
	400.00	550.00	250.00

HN 1192
Drake
Resting

Model No.:	654
Designer:	Unknown
Height:	3 1/2", 8.9 cm
Colour:	White with black markings, green head orange bill
Issued:	1937-by 1946
Varieties:	HN 977; Flambé

Price:	U.S. $	Can. $	U.K. £
	350.00	425.00	200.00

HN 1193
Tern (male)

Model No.:	231
Designer:	Unknown
Height:	2 1/2" x 8 1/2", 6.4 x 21.6 cm
Colour:	White with black head and wing tips
Issued:	1937-by 1946
Varieties:	HN 168; Also called Tern (female) HN 16, 1194; Flambé

Price:	*U.S. $*	*Can. $*	*U.K. £*
	200.00	275.00	145.00

HN 1194
Tern (female)

Model No.:	231
Designer:	Unknown
Height:	2 1/2" x 8 1/2", 6.4 x 21.6 cm
Colour:	White head and breast, grey wings
Issued:	1937-by 1946
Varieties:	HN 167; Also called "Tern" (male) HN 168, 1193; Flambé

Price:	*U.S. $*	*Can. $*	*U.K. £*
	200.00	275.00	120.00

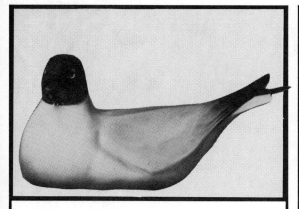

HN 1195
Black-Headed Seagull (male)

Model No.:	235
Designer:	Unknown
Height:	3 3/4", 9.5 cm
Colour:	White with black head and wing tips
Issued:	1937-by 1946
Varieties:	HN 212; Also called "Seagull" HN 211, 1196

Price:	*U.S. $*	*Can. $*	*U.K. £*
		Rare	

HN 1196
Seagull (female)

Model No.:	235
Designer:	Unknown
Height:	3 3/4", 9.5 cm
Colour:	White with grey wings and black tail feathers
Issued:	1937-by 1946
Varieties:	HN 211; Also called "Black-Headed" Gull HN 212, 1195

Price:	*U.S. $*	*Can. $*	*U.K. £*
		Rare	

HN 1197
Gannet

Model No.:	243
Designer:	Unknown
Height:	6 1/2", 16.5 cm
Colour:	Lemon and grey
Issued:	1937-by 1946
Varieties:	HN 195; Flambé

Price:	*U.S. $*	*Can. $*	*U.K. £*
	700.00	800.00	395.00

HN 1198
Drake
Standing

Model No.:	307
Designer:	Unknown
Height:	13", 33.0 cm
Size:	Large
Colour:	Unknown
Issued:	1937-by 1952
Varieties:	HN 248, 249, 252, 2635

Price:	*U.S. $*	*Can. $*	*U.K. £*
		Very Rare	

HN 1199
Penguin
Style Three

Model No.:	769
Designer:	Unknown
Height:	12", 30.1 cm
Size:	Large
Colour:	Black and white
Issued:	1937-by 1946
Varieties:	HN 2633

Price:	*U.S. $*	*Can. $*	*U.K. £*
	1, 500.00	1, 750.00	950.00

*

HN 1407
The Winner
Style One

Model No.:	Unknown
Designer:	G. D'Illiers
Height:	6 3/4", 17.2 cm
Colour:	Grey horse
Issued:	1930-1938

Price:	*U.S. $*	*Can. $*	*U.K. £*
		Very Rare	

*

HN 2500
Cerval

Model No.	966
Designer:	Raoh Schorr
Height:	5", 12.7 cm
Colour:	White (matt)
Issued:	1937-1937

Price:	*U.S. $*	*Can. $*	*U.K. £*
	250.00	350.00	225.00

HN 2501
Lynx

Model No.	966
Designer:	Raoh Schorr
Height:	4 1/2" x 7", 11.4 x17.8 cm
Colour:	White-cream (matt)
Issued:	1937-1937

Price:	*U.S. $*	*Can. $*	*U.K. £*
	250.00	350.00	225.00

HN 2502
Deer
Style One - green

Model No.	994
Designer:	Raoh Schorr
Height:	2 1/2", 6.4 cm
Colour:	Green (matt)
Issued:	1937-1937
Varieties:	HN 2503

Price:	*U.S. $*	*Can. $*	*U.K. £*
	250.00	350.00	225.00

HN 2503
Deer
Style One - white

Model No.:	994
Designer:	Raoh Schorr
Height:	2". 5.1 cm
Colour:	White (matt)
Issued:	1937-1937
Varieties:	HN 2502

Price:	*U.S. $*	*Can. $*	*U.K. £*
	250.00	350.00	225.00

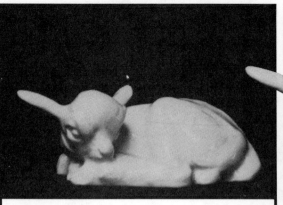

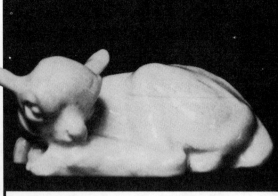

HN 2504
Lamb
Style One - green
Model No.:   995
Designer: Raoh Schorr
Height: 1 1/2", 3.8 cm
Colour: Green (matt)
Issued: 1937-1937
Varieties: HN 2505

Price:	*U.S. $*	*Can. $*	*U.K. £*
	200.00	300.00	195.00

HN 2505
Lamb
Style One - white
Model No.:   995
Designer: Raoh Schorr
Height: 1 1/2", 3.8 cm
Colour: White (matt)
Issued: 1937-1937
Varieties: HN 2504

Price:	*U.S. $*	*Can. $*	*U.K. £*
	200.00	300.00	195.00

HN 2506
Asiatic Elephant
Model No.:   993
Designer: Raoh Schorr
Height: 12", 30.5 cm
Colour: Green (matt)
Issued: 1937-1937

Price:	*U.S. $*	*Can. $*	*U.K. £*
	750.00	950.00	475.00

HN 2507
Zebu Cow
Model No.:   997
Designer: Raoh Schorr
Height: 11 1/2", 29.2 cm
Colour: Green (matt)
Issued: 1937-1937

Price:	*U.S. $*	*Can. $*	*U.K. £*
	500.00	650.00	300.00

HN 2508
Sealyham
Seated

Model No.:	986		
Designer:	Unknown		
Height:	3", 7.6 cm		
Colour:	White with brown patches over eyes and ears		
Issued:	1938-1959		

Price:	*U.S. $*	*Can. $*	*U.K. £*
	275.00	375.00	165.00

HN 2509
Sealyham
Standing - Style Two

Model No.:	985		
Designer:	Unknown		
Height:	2 1/2", 6.3 cm		
Colour:	White with light brown patches over eyes and ears		
Issued:	1938-1959		

Price:	*U.S. $*	*Can. $*	*U.K. £*
	295.00	375.00	165.00

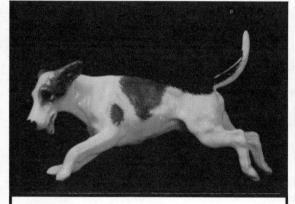

HN 2510
Character Dog Running

Model No.:	989		
Designer:	Unknown		
Height:	2 3/4", 7.0 cm		
Colour:	White with light brown patches over ears and eyes, black and brown patch on back		
Issued:	1938-1959		

Price:	*U.S. $*	*Can. $*	*U.K. £*
	400.00	500.00	225.00

HN 2511
Bull Terrier
Standing - Style Two

Model No.:	988		
Designer:	Unknown		
Height:	4", 10.1 cm		
Colour:	White with light and dark brown patches over eyes, ears and back		
Issued:	1938-1959		

Price:	*U.S. $*	*Can. $*	*U.K. £*
	450.00	550.00	275.00

SMOOTH-HAIRED TERRIER CH. 'CHOSEN DON OF NOTTS'

Designer: Frederick Davis
Colour: White with dark brown patches on ears

	HN 2512	HN 2513	HN 2514
Model No.:	791	791A	791B
Height:	8 1/2", 21.6 cm	6", 15.2 cm	4 1/2", 11.4 cm
Size:	Large	Medium	Small
Issued:	1938-1952	1938-1960	1938-1952
Varieties:	HN 1068	HN 1069	HN 1070
Price:	*Large*	*Medium*	*Small*
U.S. $	2,300.00	850.00	750.00
Can. $	2,750.00	1,100.00	1,000.00
U.K. £	1,500.00	500.00	475.00

HN 2515
Springer Spaniel Ch. 'Dry Toast'
Model No.: 1009
Designer: Frederick Daws
Height: 8", 20.3 cm
Size: Large
Colour: White coat with dark brown markings
Issued: 1938-1955

Price:

	U.S. $	Can. $	U.K. £
	975.00	1,250.00	600.00

HN 2516
Springer Spaniel Ch. 'Dry Toast'
Model No.: 1009A
Designer: Frederick Daws
Height: 5", 12.7 cm
Size: Medium
Colour: White coat with dark brown markings
Issued: 1938-1968

Price:

	U.S. $	Can. $	U.K. £
	425.00	550.00	275.00

HN 2517
Springer Spaniel Ch. 'Dry Toast'
Model No.: 1009B
Designer: Frederick Daws
Height: 3 3/4", 9.5 cm
Size: Small
Colour: White coat with dark brown markings
Issued: 1938-1985

Price:

	U.S. $	Can. $	U.K. £
	250.00	275.00	150.00

HN 2518
Pride of the Shires and Foal
Model No.: 1018
Designer: W. M. Chance
Height: 9 3/4", 24.8 cm
Size: Large
Colour: Brown mare, light brown foal
Issued: 1938-1960
Varieties: HN 2523, 2528

Price:

	U.S. $	Can. $	U.K. £
	650.00	875.00	425.00

HN 2519
Gude Grey Mare and Foal

Model No.:	1016
Designer:	W. M. Chance
Height:	7 1/2", 19.0 cm
Size:	Large
Colour:	White mare with grey markings on legs, light brown foal with white stockings,
Issued:	1938-1960

Price:	U.S. $	Can. $	U.K. £
	700.00	950.00	475.00

HN 2520
Farmer's Boy

Model No.:	1013
Designer:	W. M. Chance
Height:	8 1/2", 21.6 cm
Size:	Large
Colour:	White horse, rider in brown and green
Issued:	1938-1960

Price:	U.S. $	Can. $	U.K. £
	2,500.00	3,000.00	1,500.00

HN 2521
Dapple Grey and Rider

Model No.:	1017
Designer:	W. M. Chance
Height:	7 1/4", 18.4 cm
Size:	Large
Colour:	White horse, rider in red and brown
Issued:	1938-1960

Price:	U.S. $	Can. $	U.K. £
	3,000.00	4,000.00	1,500.00

HN 2522
Chestnut Mare and Foal

Model No.:	1020
Designer:	W. M. Chance
Height:	6 1/2", 16.5 cm
Size:	Large
Colour:	Chestnut mare with white stockings, fawn coloured foal with white stockings
Issued:	1938-1960

Price:	U.S. $	Can. $	U.K. £
	650.00	800.00	400.00

HN 2523
Pride of the Shires and Foal
Model No.:	1018
Designer:	W. M. Chance
Height:	9 3/4", 24.8 cm
Size:	Large
Colour:	White mare, grey markings on legs and hind quarters, light brown foal with white stockings
Issued:	1938-1960
Varieties:	HN 2518, 2528

Price:	U.S. $	Can. $	U.K. £
	650.00	800.00	400.00

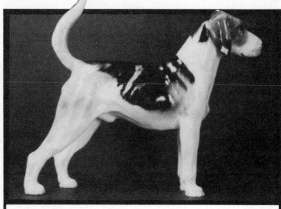

HN 2524
American Foxhound
Model No.:	1026
Designer:	Frederick Daws
Height:	8", 20.3 cm
Size:	Large
Colour:	White with black and brown markings
Issued:	1938-1955

Price:	U.S. $	Can. $	U.K. £
	1,600.00	2,000.00	950.00

HN 2525
American Foxhound
Model No.:	1026A
Designer:	Frederick Daws
Height:	5", 12.7 cm
Size:	Medium
Colour:	White with black and brown markings
Issued:	1938-1960

Price:	U.S. $	Can. $	U.K. £
	650.00	875.00	500.00

HN 2526
American Foxhound
Model No.:	1026B
Designer:	Frederick Daws
Height:	4", 10.1 cm
Size:	Small
Colour:	White with black and brown markings
Issued:	1938-1952

Price:	U.S. $	Can. $	U.K. £
	525.00	700.00	375.00

HN 2527
Fox
Seated - Style Five
Model No.: 978
Designer: Raoh Schorr
Height: 11", 27.9 cm
Size: Extra large
Colour: Brown and white
Issued: 1938-by 1946
Varieties: HN 1130

Price:	U.S. $	Can. $	U.K. £
	750.00	950.00	500.00

HN 2528
Pride of the Shires and Foal
Model No.: 1018
Designer: W. M. Chance
Height: 9 3/4" x 14", 24.8 x 35.5 cm
Size: Large
Colour: Brown mare, light fawn foal
Issued: 1939-1960
Varieties: HN 2518, 2523

Price:	U.S. $	Can. $	U.K. £
	650.00	875.00	425.00

HN 2529
English Setter with Pheasant
Model No.: 1028
Designer: Frederick Daws
Height: 8", 20.3 cm
Size: Large
Colour: Grey with black markings; red-brown pheasant; yellow-brown leaves on base
Issued: 1939-1985
Varieties: HN 2599

Price:	U.S. $	Can. $	U.K. £
	650.00	875.00	425.00

HN 2530
Merely a Minor
Model No.: 1039
Designer: Frederick Daws
Height: 12", 30.5 cm
Size: Large
Colour: Brown with white stockings and nose
Issued: 1939-1960
Varieties: HN 2531

Price:	U.S. $	Can. $	U.K. £
	600.00	800.00	375.00

HN 2531
Merely a Minor

Model No.:	1039
Designer:	Frederick Daws
Height:	12", 30.5 cm
Size:	Large
Colour:	Grey
Issued:	1939-1960
Varieties:	HN 2530

Price:	*U.S. $*	*Can. $*	*U.K. £*
	600.00	800.00	375.00

HN 2532
Gude Grey Mare and Foal

Model No.:	1016A
Designer:	W. M. Chance
Height:	5 1/2", 14.0 cm
Size:	Small
Colour:	White mare with grey markings on legs, light brown foal with white stockings
Issued:	1940-1967

Price:	*U.S. $*	*Can. $*	*U.K. £*
	600.00	800.00	400.00

HN 2533
Chestnut Mare and Foal

Model No.:	1020B
Designer:	W. M. Chance
Height:	5", 12.7 cm
Size:	Small
Colour:	Chestnut brown mare with white stockings, fawn coloured foal with white stockings
Issued:	1940-1960

Price:	*U.S. $*	*Can. $*	*U.K. £*
	500.00	650.00	300.00

HN 2534
Pride of the Shires and Foal

Model No.:	1018A
Designer:	W. M. Chance
Height:	6 1/2", 16.5 cm
Size:	Small
Colour:	Brown mare, light brown foal
Issued:	1940-1960
Varieties:	HN 2536

Price:	*U.S. $*	*Can. $*	*U.K. £*
	500.00	650.00	325.00

HN 2535
Tiger on a Rock
Style Three

Model No.:	1038	
Designer:	Charles Noke	
Height:	4" x 9", 10.1 x 22.9 cm	
Colour:	Browns; charcoal rock	
Issued:	1940-1960	

Price:	*U.S. $*	*Can. $*	*U.K. £*
	1,200.00	1,500.00	850.00

HN 2536
Pride of the Shires and Foal

Model No.:	1018A	
Designer:	W. M. Chance	
Height:	6 1/2", 16.5 cm	
Size:	Small	
Colour:	White mare, grey markings on legs and hind quarters, light brown foal white stockings	
Issued:	1940-1960	
Varieties:	HN 2534	

Price:	*U.S. $*	*Can. $*	*U.K. £*
	500.00	650.00	325.00

HN 2537
Merely a Minor

Model No.:	1039A
Designer:	Frederick Daws
Height:	9 1/4", 24.0 cm
Size:	Medium
Colour:	Brown with white stockings and nose
Issued:	1940-1960
Varieties:	HN 2538

Price:	*U.S. $*	*Can. $*	*U.K. £*
	500.00	650.00	300.00

HN 2538
Merely a Minor

Model No.:	1039A
Designer:	Frederick Daws
Height:	9 1/4", 24.0 cm
Size:	Medium
Colour:	White with dark grey markings on legs and neck
Issued:	1940-1960
Varieties:	HN 2537

Price:	*U.S. $*	*Can. $*	*U.K. £*
	500.00	650.00	300.00

HN 2539A
Persian Cat
Seated - Style One - white

Model No.:	690
Designer:	Unknown
Height:	5", 12.7 cm
Colour:	White
Issued:	1940-1968
Varieties:	HN 999, 2539B

Price:	U.S. $	Can. $	U.K. £
	300.00	375.00	165.00

HN 2539B
Persian Cat
Seated - Style One - dark grey

Model No.:	690
Designer:	Unknown
Height:	5", 12.7 cm
Colour:	Dark grey with white highlights
Issued:	1940-1960
Varieties:	HN 999, 2539A

Price:	U.S. $	Can. $	U.K. £
	300.00	375.00	165.00

HN 2540
Kingfisher on a Tree Stump
Large

Model No.:	1053
Designer:	Unknown
Height:	4 1/2", 11.4 cm
Size:	Large
Colour:	Sea-green and blue feathers, brown breast, green and grey base
Issued:	1940-1946

Price:	U.S. $	Can. $	U.K. £
	350.00	475.00	225.00

HN 2541
Kingfisher on a Tree Stump
Small

Model No.:	1053A
Designer:	Unknown
Height:	3 1/2", 8.9 cm
Size:	Small
Colour:	Sea-green and blue feathers, brown breast, green and grey base
Issued:	1940-1946
Varieties:	HN 2540

Price:	U.S. $	Can. $	U.K. £
	350.00	475.00	225.00

HN 2542A
Baltimore Oriole
Style One

Model No.:	1051
Designer:	Unknown
Height:	4 1/4", 10.8 cm
Colour:	Black and orange bird, brown base, white flowers
Issued:	1940-1946

Price:	*U.S. $*	*Can. $*	*U.K. £*
	325.00	450.00	175.00

HN 2542B
Baltimore Oriole
Style Two

Model No.:	1051
Designer:	Unknown
Height:	4 1/4", 10.8 cm
Colour:	Black and orange bird, brown base, white flowers
Issued:	1940-1946

Price:	*U.S. $*	*Can. $*	*U.K. £*
	325.00	450.00	175.00

HN 2543
Bluebird with Lupins
Style One

Model No.:	1062
Designer:	Unknown
Height:	6", 15.2 cm
Colour:	Blue and pink bird with mauve and green stump
Issued:	1941-1946

Price:	*U.S. $*	*Can. $*	*U.K. £*
	325.00	450.00	175.00

HN 2544
Mallard Drake with Spill Vase

Model No.:	1057
Designer:	Unknown
Height:	8", 20.3 cm
Colour:	Green head, brown and white feathers, green spill and reeds
Issued:	1941-1946

Price:	*U.S. $*	*Can. $*	*U.K. £*
	325.00	450.00	225.00

HN 2545
Cock Pheasant
Model No.: 1063
Designer: Unknown
Height: 7", 17.8 cm
Size: Small
Colour: Red brown plummage, blue-green head
Issued: 1941-1952
Varieties: HN 2632

Price:	U.S. $	Can. $	U.K. £
	475.00	575.00	275.00

HN 2546
Yellow-Throated Warbler
Style Two
Model No.: 1058
Designer: Unknown
Height: 4 3/4", 12.1 cm
Colour: Blue feathers, black wing tips, yellow throat
Issued: 1941-1946

Price:	U.S. $	Can. $	U.K. £
	325.00	450.00	225.00

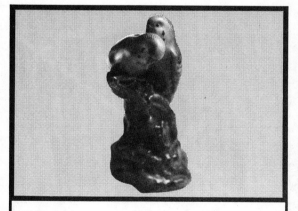

HN 2547
Budgerigars on a Tree Stump
Model No.: 1054
Designer: Unknown
Height: 6", 15.2 cm
Colour: Green and yellow birds with black markings, green and beige base
Issued: 1941-1946

Price:	U.S. $	Can. $	U.K. £
	425.00	575.00	275.00

HN 2548
Golden-Crested Wren
Style One
Model No.: 1052
Designer: Unknown
Height: 4 1/2", 11.4 cm
Colour: Green feathers with black markings, white flowers, brown base
Issued: 1941-1946

Price:	U.S. $	Can. $	U.K. £
	325.00	450.00	200.00

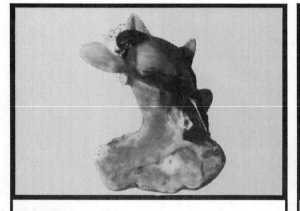

HN 2549
English Robin
Style One

Model No.:	1060
Designer:	Unknown
Height:	2 1/2", 6.4 cm
Colour:	Brown feathers, red breast, yellow
	flowers, green leaves, beige base
Issued:	1941-1946

Price:	*U.S. $*	*Can. $*	*U.K. £*
	325.00	450.00	200.00

HN 2550
Chaffinch
Style One

Model No.:	1066
Designer:	Unknown
Height:	2 1/2, 6.4 cm
Colour:	Brown with black, pink and blue wing
	tips, blue head, yellow flowers, green
	base
Issued:	1941-1946

Price:	*U.S. $*	*Can. $*	*U.K. £*
	325.00	450.00	200.00

HN 2551
Bullfinch
Style Two

Model No.:	1070
Designer:	Unknown
Height:	5 1/2", 14.0 cm
Colour:	Blue and pale blue feathers, red
	breast
Issued:	1941-1946

Price:	*U.S. $*	*Can. $*	*U.K. £*
	325.00	450.00	200.00

HN 2552
Thrush Chicks (two)

Model No.:	1071
Designer:	Unknown
Height:	3", 7.6 cm
Colour:	Brown feathers, brown breast with brown
	spots, yellow highlights, green base
Issued:	1941-1946
Varieties:	Flambé

Price:	*U.S. $*	*Can. $*	*U.K. £*
	325.00	450.00	225.00

HN 2553
Robin Chicks (two)
Model No.:   1069
Designer: Unknown
Height: 3", 7.6 cm
Colour: Brown feathers, red breast, green base
Issued: 1941-1946

Price: *U.S. $*   *Can. $*   *U.K. £*
                325.00   450.00   225.00

HN 2554
Cardinal
Style Two
Model No.:   1059
Designer: Unknown
Height: 6 3/4", 17.1 cm
Colour: Red feathers with black markings;
              green leaves and stump, white flowers
Issued: 1941-1946

Price: *U.S. $*   *Can. $*   *U.K. £*
                500.00   650.00   450.00

HN 2555
Mallard Drake
Standing
Model No.:   137
Designer: Unknown
Height: 5 1/2", 14.0 cm
Size: Medium
Colour: Green head, brown and white feathers
Issued: 1941-1946
Varieties: HN 114, 115, 116, 956, 1191, 2647, Flambé

Price: *U.S. $*   *Can. $*   *U.K. £*
                400.00   550.00   250.00

HN 2556
Duck
Head stretched forward
Model No.:   207
Designer: Unknown
Height: 4", 10.1 cm
Colour: Brown feathers, turquoise wing tips
Issued: 1941-1946
Varieties: HN 150, 229, Flambé

Price: *U.S. $*   *Can. $*   *U.K. £*
                375.00   450.00   225.00

HN 2557
Welsh Corgi Ch. 'Spring Robin'

Model No.:	1050
Designer:	Frederick Daws
Height:	8", 20.3 cm
Size:	Large
Colour:	Golden brown with white and brown underbody
Issued:	1941-1955

Price:	*U.S. $*	*Can. $*	*U.K. £*
	1,100.00	1,500.00	750.00

HN 2558
Welsh Corgi Ch. 'Spring Robin'

Model No.:	1050A
Designer:	Frederick Daws
Height:	5", 12.7 cm
Size:	Medium
Colour:	Golden brown with white and brown underbody
Issued:	1941-1968

Price:	*U.S. $*	*Can. $*	*U.K. £*
	450.00	600.00	300.00

HN 2559
Welsh Corgi Ch. 'Spring Robin'

Model No.:	1050B
Designer:	Frederick Daws
Height:	3 1/2", 8.9 cm
Size:	Small
Colour:	Golden brown with white and brown underbody
Issued:	1941-1985

Price:	*U.S. $*	*Can. $*	*U.K. £*
	250.00	325.00	165.00

HN 2560
Great Dane Ch. 'Rebeller of Ouborough'

Model No.:	1077
Designer:	Frederick Daws
Height:	8 1/2", 21.6 cm
Size:	Large
Colour:	Light brown
Issued:	1941-1955

Price:	*U.S. $*	*Can. $*	*U.K. £*
	1,600.00	2,000.00	900.00

HN 2561
Great Dane Ch. 'Rebeller of Ouborough'

Model No.:	1077A
Designer:	Frederick Daws
Height:	6", 15.2 cm
Size:	Medium
Colour:	Light brown
Issued:	1941-1960

Price:	U.S. $	Can. $	U.K. £
	850.00	975.00	450.00

HN 2562
Great Dane Ch. 'Rebeller of Ouborough'

Model No.:	1077B
Designer:	Frederick Daws
Height:	4 1/2", 11.3 cm
Size:	Small
Colour:	Light brown
Issued:	1941-1952

Price:	U.S. $	Can. $	U.K. £
	850.00	975.00	450.00

HN 2563
Pride of the Shires

Model No.:	1073
Designer:	W. M. Chance
Height:	9", 22.9 cm
Size:	Large
Colour:	Grey
Issued:	1941-1960

Price:	U.S. $	Can. $	U.K. £
	900.00	1,200.00	600.00

HN 2564
Pride of the Shires

Model No.:	1073A
Designer:	W. M. Chance
Height:	6 3/8", 16.5 cm
Size:	Small
Colour:	Light brown horse, black mane, tail and legs, white nose and feet, green-brown base
Issued:	1941-1960

Price:	U.S. $	Can. $	U.K. £
	550.00	700.00	350.00

HN 2565
Chestnut Mare - Large

Model No.:	1074
Designer:	W. M. Chance
Height:	6 1/2", 16.5 cm
Size:	Large
Colour:	Brown
Issued:	1941-1960

Price:	U.S. $	Can. $	U.K. £
	700.00	900.00	425.00

HN 2566
Chestnut Mare - Small

Model No.:	1074A
Designer:	W. M. Chance
Height:	5 1/4", 13.3 cm
Size:	Small
Colour:	Brown
Issued:	1941-1960

Price:	U.S. $	Can. $	U.K. £
	400.00	525.00	245.00

HN 2567
Merely a Minor

Model No.:	1039B
Designer:	Frederick Daws
Height:	6 1/2", 16.5 cm
Size:	Small
Colour:	White with grey markings on legs
Issued:	1941-1967
Varieties:	HN 2571

Price:	U.S. $	Can. $	U.K. £
	400.00	525.00	225.00

HN 2568
Gude Grey Mare - Large

Model No.:	1072
Designer:	W. M. Chance
Height:	8", 20.3 cm
Size:	Large
Colour:	White with grey markings on legs
Issued:	1941-1967

Price:	U.S. $	Can. $	U.K. £
	750.00	950.00	425.00

HN 2569
Gude Grey Mare - Medium
Model No.:   1072A
Designer: W. M. Chance
Height: 5", 12.7 cm
Size: Medium
Colour: White with grey markings on legs
Issued: 1941-1967

Price:	*U.S. $*	*Can. $*	*U.K. £*
	575.00	775.00	375.00

HN 2570
Gude Grey Mare - Small
Model No.:   1072B
Designer: W. M. Chance
Height: 3 3/4", 9.5 cm
Size: Small
Colour: White with grey markings on legs
Issued: 1941-1967

Price:	*U.S. $*	*Can. $*	*U.K. £*
	450.00	600.00	295.00

HN 2571
Merely a Minor
Model No.:   1039B
Designer: Frederick Daws
Height: 6 1/2", 16.5 cm
Size: Small
Colour: Light brown, white nose and feet, black tail
Issued: 1941-1967
Varieties: HN 2567

Price:	*U.S. $*	*Can. $*	*U.K. £*
	400.00	525.00	275.00

HN 2572
Mallard Drake
Resting
Model No.:   1102
Designer: Unknown
Height: 1 1/2" x 2 3/4" , 5.1 cm x 7.0 cm
Size: Small
Colour: Green head, brown wings, brown breast, white underbody white tail
Issued: 1941-1946

Price:	*U.S. $*	*Can. $*	*U.K. £*
	145.00	175.00	85.00

HN 2573
Kingfisher
Style Two

Model No.:	1103
Designer:	Unknown
Height:	2 1/2", 6.4 cm
Colour:	Turquoise, green and light brown feathers, black beak
Issued:	1941-1946

Price:	*U.S. $*	*Can. $*	*U.K. £*
	300.00	400.00	175.00

HN 2574
Seagull on Rock

Model No.:	1108
Designer:	Unknown
Height:	2 1/4", 5.7 cm
Colour:	White head and breast, grey wings with black tail feathers
Issued:	1941-1946

Price:	*U.S. $*	*Can. $*	*U.K. £*
	350.00	400.00	195.00

HN 2575
Swan

Model No.:	1105
Designer:	Unknown
Height:	2 1/4", 5.7 cm
Colour:	White, black and orange beak
Issued:	1941-1946

Price:	*U.S. $*	*Can. $*	*U.K. £*
	550.00	500.00	220.00

HN 2576
Pheasant

Model No.:	1107
Designer:	Unknown
Height:	2 1/2", 6.4 cm
Colour:	Red-brown feathers with green tail feathers, blue-green head, brown and green base
Issued:	1941-1946

Price:	*U.S. $*	*Can. $*	*U.K. £*
	400.00	500.00	225.00

HN 2577
Peacock

Model No.:	1106
Designer:	Unknown
Height:	2 3/4", 7.0 cm
Colour:	Dark turquoise breast; yellow, green and brown tail feathers
Issued:	1941-1946

Price:	*U.S. $*	*Can. $*	*U.K. £*
	400.00	500.00	225.00

HN 2578
Dapple Grey

Model No.:	1134
Designer:	W. M. Chance
Height:	7 1/2", 19.1 cm
Colour:	White with grey markings on legs
Issued:	1941-1960
Varieties:	Also called "Punch Peon", Chestnut Shire, HN 2623

Price:	*U.S. $*	*Can. $*	*U.K. £*
	650.00	800.00	375.00

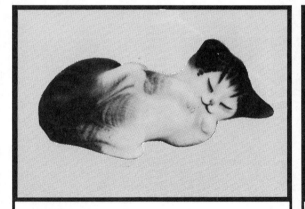

HN 2579
Character Kitten
Lying on back

Model No.:	1080
Designer:	Peggy Davies
Height:	1 1/2", 3.8 cm
Colour:	Brown and white
Issued:	1941-1985

Price:	*U.S. $*	*Can. $*	*U.K. £*
	75.00	100.00	65.00

HN 2580
Character Kitten
Licking hind paw

Model No.:	1079
Designer:	Peggy Davies
Height:	2 1/4", 5.7 cm
Colour:	Brown and white
Issued:	1941-1985

Price:	*U.S. $*	*Can. $*	*U.K. £*
	75.00	100.00	65.00

HN 2581
Character Kitten
Sleeping
Model No.:   1085
Designer: Peggy Davies
Height: 1 1/2", 3.8 cm
Colour: Brown and white
Issued: 1941-1985

Price:	*U.S. $*	*Can. $*	*U.K. £*
	75.00	100.00	65.00

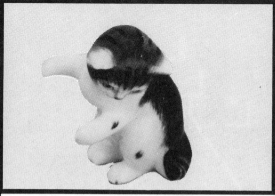

HN 2582
Character Kitten
On hind legs
Model No.:   1087
Designer: Peggy Davies
Height: 2 3/4", 7.0 cm
Colour: Light brown and black coat with
              white underbody
Issued: 1941-1985

Price:	*U.S. $*	*Can. $*	*U.K. £*
	75.00	100.00	65.00

HN 2583
Character Kitten
Licking front paw
Model No.:   1086
Designer: Peggy Davies
Height: 2", 5.1 cm
Colour: Tan and white
Issued: 1941-1985

Price:	*U.S. $*	*Can. $*	*U.K. £*
	75.00	100.00	65.00

HN 2584
Character Kitten
Looking up
Model No.:   1081
Designer: Peggy Davies
Height: 2", 5.1 cm
Colour: Tan and white
Issued: 1941-1985

Price:	*U.S. $*	*Can. $*	*U.K. £*
	75.00	100.00	65.00

HN 2585
Cocker Spaniel Lying in Basket
Model No.:   1155
Designer: Unknown
Height: 2", 5.1 cm
Colour: White with brown and black markings;
             light brown basket
Issued: 1941-1985

Price: U.S. $ Can. $ U.K. £
                   100.00   125.00   65.00

HN 2586
Cocker Spaniel Chewing Handle of Basket
Model No.:   1153
Designer: Unknown
Height: 2 3/4", 7.0 cm
Colour: White with dark brown ears and patches
             on back, light brown patches over eyes,
             light brown basket
Issued: 1941-1985

Price: U.S. $ Can. $ U.K. £
                   100.00   125.00   65.00

HN 2587
Terrier Sitting in Basket
Model No.:   1152
Designer: Unknown
Height: 3", 7.6 cm
Colour: White with brown markings; brown
             basket
Issued: 1941-1985

Price: U.S. $ Can. $ U.K. £
                   100.00   125.00   65.00

HN 2588
Terrier Puppies in a Basket
Model No.:   1154
Designer: Unknown
Height: 3", 7.6 cm
Colour: White with light and dark brown
             markings, brown basket
Issued: 1941-1985

Price: U.S. $ Can. $ U.K. £
                   125.00   150.00   75.00

HN 2589
Cairn Terrier
Begging

Model No.:   1131
Designer: Unknown
Height: 4", 10.1 cm
Colour: Beige with black highlights
Issued: 1941-1985

Price:	*U.S. $*	*Can. $*	*U.K. £*
	115.00	125.00	65.00

HN 2590
Cocker Spaniels Sleeping

Model No.:   1132
Designer: Unknown
Height: 1 3/4", 4.5 cm
Colour: White dog with brown markings and
              golden brown dog
Issued: 1941-1969

Price:	*U.S. $*	*Can. $*	*U.K. £*
	100.00	125.00	65.00

HN 2591
Duck
Standing

Model No.:   395
Designer: Unknown
Height: 2 1/2", 6.4 cm
Size: Small
Colour: Green head, white and brown feathers
              with black highlights
Issued: 1941-1968
Varieties: HN 806, 807; Flambé

Price:	*U.S. $*	*Can. $*	*U.K. £*
	150.00	200.00	85.00

HN 2592
Hare
Crouching - Style Three

Model No.:   1157
Designer: Unknown
Height: 2 3/4", 7.0 cm
Colour: Light brown with white markings
Issued: 1941-1968
Varieties: Flambé

Price:	*U.S $*	*Can. $*	*U.K. £*
	125.00	160.00	75.00

HN 2593
Hare
Lying, legs stretched behind

Model No.: 656
Designer: Unknown
Height: 3" x 7 1/2", 7.6 x 19.1 cm
Size: Large
Colour: Light brown with white markings
Issued: 1941-1968
Varieties: HN 979, 984, 985, 1071; Flambé

Price:	U.S $	Can. $	U.K. £
	150.00	200.00	165.00

HN 2594
Hare
Lying legs stretched behind

Model No.: 656A
Designer: Unknown
Height: 1 3/4" x 5 1/4", 4.45 cm x 13.3 cm
Size: Small
Colour: Light brown with white markings
Issued: 1941-1985
Varieties: Flambé

Price:	U.S $	Can. $	U.K. £
	100.00	125.00	75.00

HN 2595
Lamb
Style Two

Model No.: 1117
Designer: Peggy Davis
Height: Unknown
Colour: White
Issued: Modelled 1941

Price:	U.S $	Can. $	U.K. £
	Extremely Rare		

HN 2596
Lamb
Style Three

Model No.: 1112
Designer: Peggy Davis
Height: Unknown
Colour: White
Issued: Modelled 1941

Price:	U.S $	Can. $	U.K. £
	Extremely Rare		

HN 2597
Lamb
Style Four

Model No.:	1115
Designer:	Peggy Davis
Height:	3 1/4", 8.3 cm
Colour:	Black lamb on white base
Issued:	Modelled 1941

Price: *U.S $*   *Can. $*   *U.K. £*
          Extremely Rare

HN 2598
Lamb
Style Five

Model No.:	1116
Designer:	Peggy Davis
Height:	Unknown
Colour:	White
Issued:	Modelled 1941

Price: *U.S $*   *Can. $*   *U.K. £*
          Extremely Rare

HN 2599
English Setter with Pheasant

Model No.:	1028
Designer:	Frederick Daws
Height:	8 ", 20.3 cm
Colour:	Red-brown
Issued:	1941
Varieties:	HN 2529

Price: *U.S $*   *Can. $*   *U.K. £*
          Extremely Rare

HN 2600
Cocker Spaniel with Pheasant

Model No.:	714B
Designer:	Frederick Daws
Height:	3 1/2", 8.9 cm
Size:	Small
Colour:	Black
Issued:	1941
Varieties:	HN 1029, 1062

Price: *U.S $*   *Can. $*   *U.K. £*
          Extremely Rare

* Only one known.

AMERICAN GREAT DANE

Designer: Unknown
Colour: Light brown

	HN 2601	HN 2602	HN 2603
Model No.:	1171	1171A	1171B
Height:	8 1/2", 21.6 cm	6 1/2", 16.5 cm	4 1/2", 11.4 cm
Size:	Large	Medium	Small
Issued:	1941-1955	1941-1960	1941-1960
Price:	*Large*	*Medium*	*Small*
U.S $	*1,600.00*	*850.00*	*900.00*
Can. $	*1,800.00*	*1,000.00*	*1,000.00*
U.K. £	*850.00*	*475.00*	*475.00*

HN 2604
Peacock Butterfly

Model No.:	1178
Designer:	Unknown
Height:	2", 5.1 cm
Colour:	Unknown
Issued:	1941-by 1946

Price: *U.S $*   *Can. $*   *U.K. £*
           Very Rare

HN 2605
Camberwell Beauty Butterfly

Model No.:	1181
Designer:	Unknown
Height:	2", 5.1 cm
Colour:	Unknown
Issued:	1941-by 1946

Price: *U.S $*   *Can. $*   *U.K. £*
           Very Rare

HN 2606
Swallowtail Butterfly

Model No.:	1175
Designer:	Unknown
Height:	Unknown
Colour:	Unknown
Issued:	1941-by 1946

Price: *U.S $*   *Can. $*   *U.K. £*
           Very Rare

HN 2607
Red Admiral Butterfly

Model No.:	1179
Designer:	Unknown
Height:	2", 5.1 cm
Colour:	Unknown
Issued:	1941-by 1946

Price: *U.S $*   *Can. $*   *U.K. £*
           Very Rare

HN 2608
Copper Butterfly

Model No.:	1177
Designer:	Unknown
Height:	2", 5.1 cm
Colour:	Unknown
Issued:	1941-by 1946

Price:	*U.S $*	*Can. $*	*U.K. £*
		Very Rare	

HN 2609
Tortoiseshell Butterfly

Model No.:	1180
Designer:	Unknown
Height:	2", 5.1 cm
Colour:	Unknown
Issued:	1941-by 1946

Price:	*U.S $*	*Can. $*	*U.K. £*
		Very Rare	

HN 2610
Pheasant Hen

Model No.:	1195
Designer:	Unknown
Height:	6", 15.2 cm
Colour:	Light brown with dark brown markings, green base
Issued:	c.1945-1950

Price:	*U.S $*	*Can. $*	*U.K. £*
	350.00	475.00	225.00

HN 2611
Chaffinch
Style Two

Model No.:	1200
Designer:	Unknown
Height:	2", 5.1 cm
Colour:	Brown feathers, blue, yellow and black markings, green base
Issued:	c.1945-1950

Price:	*U.S $*	*Can. $*	*U.K. £*
	325.00	450.00	200.00

HN 2612
Baltimore Oriole
Style Three

Model No.:   1201
Designer: Unknown
Height: 4", 10.1 cm
Colour: Yellow with black head and wing tips,
              green base
Issued: c.1945-1950

Price: *U.S $*   *Can. $*   *U.K. £*
                      325.00   450.00   225.00

HN 2613
Golden-Crested Wren
Style Two

Model No.:   1202
Designer: Unknown
Height: 2 1/2", 6.4 cm
Colour: Green with black markings, yellow and
              white breast, brown base
Issued: c.1945-1950

Price: *U.S $*   *Can. $*   *U.K. £*
                      325.00   450.00   225.00

HN 2614
Blue Bird

Model No.:   1203
Designer: Unknown
Height: 5", 12.7 cm
Colour: Blue with pink and white breast,
              green base
Issued: c.1945-1950

Price: *U.S $*   *Can. $*   *U.K. £*
                      325.00   450.00   225.00

HN 2615
Cardinal
Style Three

Model No.:   1204
Designer: Unknown
Height: 4 1/2", 11.4 cm
Colour: Red feathers with black markings,
              green base
Issued: c.1945-1950

Price: *U.S $*   *Can. $*   *U.K. £*
                      325.00   450.00   225.00

HN 2616
Bullfinch
Style Three

Model No.:	1205
Designer:	Unknown
Height:	4", 10.1 cm
Colour:	Mauve and black feathers, pink breast, green base
Issued:	c.1945-1950

Price:	*U.S $*	*Can. $*	*U.K. £*
	325.00	450.00	225.00

HN 2617
Robin
Style Two

Model No.:	1206
Designer:	Unknown
Height:	2", 5.1 cm
Colour:	Brown feathers, red breast, green base
Issued:	c.1945-1950

Price:	*U.S $*	*Can. $*	*U.K. £*
	325.00	450.00	225.00

Photograph
Not Available
At Press Time

HN 2618
Yellow-Throated Warbler
Style Three

Model No.:	1207
Designer:	Unknown
Height:	4 1/2", 11.4 cm
Colour:	Blue feathers with black markings, yellow breast. green base
Issued:	c.1945-1950

Price:	*U.S $*	*Can. $*	*U.K. £*
	$325.00	450.00	225.00

HN 2619
Grouse

Model No.:	1161
Designer:	Unknown
Height:	Unknown
Colour:	Unknown
Issued:	Unknown

Price:	*U.S $*	*Can. $*	*U.K. £*
	Extremely Rare		

HN 2620
English Setter

Model No.: 770
Designer: Frederick Daws
Height: 7 1/2" x 12 1/4", 19.1 x 31.1 cm
Size: Large
Colour: White with liver highlights
Issued: 1950-c.1960
Varieties: Also called English Setter Ch. 'Maesydd Mustard', HN 1049

Price:	*U.S $*	*Can. $*	*U.K. £*
	Extremely Rare		

HN 2621
English Setter

Model No.: 770A
Designer: Frederick Daws
Height: 5 1/4", 13.3 cm
Size: Medium
Colour: Liver and white
Issued: 1950-c.1960
Varieties: Also called English Setter Ch. 'Maesydd Mustard', HN 1050

Price:	*U.S $*	*Can. $*	*U.K. £*
	1,750.00	2,250.00	1,000.00

HN 2622
English Setter

Model No.: 770B
Designer: Frederick Daws
Height: 3 3/4", 9.5 cm
Size: Small
Colour: Liver and white
Issued: 1950-c.1960
Varieties: Also called English Setter Ch. 'Maesydd Mustard', HN 1051

Price:	*U.S $*	*Can. $*	*U.K. £*
	1,500.00	2,000.00	1,000.00

HN 2623
Punch Peon, Chestnut Shire

Model No.: 1134
Designer: W. M. Chance
Height: 7 1/2", 19.1 cm
Colour: Brown with black mane and black and white markings on legs
Issued: 1950-1960
Varieties: Also called 'Dapple Grey', HN 2578

Price:	*U.S $*	*Can. $*	*U.K. £*
	1000.00	1,350.00	675.00

HN 2624
Pointer
Style One

Model No.: 1312
Designer: Peggy Davies
Height: 5 1/2" x 11 1/2", 14.0 cm x 29.2 cm
Colour: White with dark brown markings; yellow and green leaves, brown tree stump
Issued: 1952-1985

Price: *U.S $*   *Can. $*   *U.K. £*
             550.00   750.00   350.00

Photograph
Not Available
At Press Time

HN 2625
French Poodle

Model No.: 1212
Designer: Peggy Davies
Height: 9" x 10", 22.9 x 25.4 cm
Size: Large
Colour: White
Issued: Modelled 1952

Price: *U.S $*   *Can. $*   *U.K. £*
Only one known to exist.
On display at the American Kennel Club in New York
*

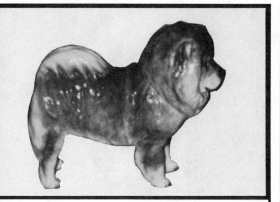

HN 2628
Chow Ch. 'T'Sioh of Kin-Shan'

Model No.: 1209
Designer: Unknown
Height: Unknown
Size: Large
Colour: Golden brown
Issued: Modelled 1952

Price: *U.S $*   *Can. $*   *U.K. £*
Extremely Rare.
Only one known to exist.

HN 2629
Chow Ch. 'T'Sioh of Kin-Shan'

Model No.: 1209A
Designer: Unknown
Height: Unknown
Size: Medium
Colour: Golden brown
Issued: Modelled 1952

Price: *U.S $*   *Can. $*   *U.K. £*
Not known to exist.

HN 2630
Chow Ch. 'T'Sioh of Kin-Shan'

Model No.:	1209B
Designer:	Unknown
Height:	Unknown
Size:	Small
Colour:	Golden brown
Issued:	Modelled 1952

Price:	*U.S $*	*Can. $*	*U.K. £*
	Not known to exist.		

HN 2631
French Poodle

Model No.:	1212A
Designer:	Peggy Davies
Height:	5 1/4", 13.3 cm
Size:	Medium
Colour:	White with pink, grey and black markings
Issued:	1952-1985

Price:	*U.S $*	*Can. $*	*U.K. £*
	225.00	300.00	140.00

HN 2632
Cock Pheasant

Model No.:	1063
Designer:	Unknown
Height:	6 3/4", 17.2 cm
Colour:	Red-brown feathers, dark blue markings, green-blue head, green-brown base (china)
Issued:	1952-1968
Varieties:	HN 2545
Series:	Prestige

Price:	*U.S $*	*Can. $*	*U.K. £*
	550.00	500.00	250.00

HN 2633
Peruvian Penguin

Model No.:	769
Designer:	Unknown
Height:	12", 30.1 cm
Size:	Large
Colour:	Black and white (china)
Issued:	1952-1973
Series:	Prestige
Varieties:	HN 1199

Price:	*U.S $*	*Can. $*	*U.K. £*
	1,500.00	*1,750.00*	*950.00*

HN 2634
Fox
Seated - Style Six

Model No.:	767
Designer:	Unknown
Height:	10 1/2", 26.7 cm
Colour:	Golden brown with black highlights (china)
Issued:	1952-1992
Series:	Prestige

Price:	*U.S $*	*Can. $*	*U.K. £*
	1,250.00	1,500.00	750.00

HN 2635
Drake
Standing

Model No.:	307
Designer:	Unknown
Height:	13 1/2", 34.3 cm
Size:	Large
Colour:	White with light brown shading (china)
Issued:	1952-1974
Series:	Prestige
Varieties:	HN 248, 249, 252, 1198

Price:	*U.S $*	*Can. $*	*U.K. £*
	2,000.00	2,000.00	950.00

HN 2636
Indian Runner Drake

Model No.:	1327
Designer:	Peggy Davies
Height:	18", 45.7 cm
Size:	Large
Colour:	Unknown
Issued:	1952-c.1960

Price:	*U.S $*	*Can. $*	*U.K. £*
		Extremely Rare	

HN 2637
Polar Bear and Cub on Base

Model No.:	613
Designer:	Unknown
Height:	15", 38.1 cm
Colour:	White bears on a green base (earthenware)
Issued:	1952-c.1960
Varieties:	Chang, Sung

Price:	*U.S $*	*Can. $*	*U.K. £*
	1,350.00	1,500.00	750.00

HN 2638
Leopard on Rock

Model No.:	1036
Designer:	Charles Noke
Height:	9" x 11 1/2", 22.9 x 29.2 cm
Colour:	Golden brown with dark brown spots; charcoal rock (earthenware)
Issued:	1952-1981
Series:	Prestige

Price:	*U.S $*	*Can. $*	*U.K. £*
	1,500.00	1,750.00	950.00

HN 2639
Tiger on a Rock
Style Four

Model No.:	1038
Designer:	Charles Noke
Height:	12" x 10 1/4", 30.5 x 26.0 cm
Colour:	Golden brown with dark brown stripes; charcoal rock (earthenware)
Issued:	1952-1992
Series:	Prestige

Price:	*U.S $*	*Can. $*	*U.K. £*
	1,500.00	1,750.00	950.00

HN 2640
Fighter Elephant

Model No.:	626
Designer:	Charles Noke
Height:	12" x 9", 30.5 x 22.9 cm
Size:	Large
Colour:	Grey elephant with white tusks (earthenware)
Issued:	1952-1992
Varieties:	HN 1120; Flambé
Series:	Prestige

Price:	*U.S $*	*Can. $*	*U.K. £*
	1,500.00	1,750.00	950.00

HN 2641
Lion on Rock
Style Two

Model No.:	1033
Designer:	Charles Noke
Height:	10 1/2", 26.7 cm
Colour:	Golden brown lion, charcoal rock (earthenware)
Issued:	1952-1992
Series:	Prestige

Price:	*U.S $*	*Can. $*	*U.K. £*
	1,500.00	1,750.00	950.00

HN 2642
Red Squirrel in a Pine Tree
Prototype

Model No.: 1292
Designer: Peggy Davies
Height: 8", 20.3 cm (length)
Colour: Nut brown
Issued: Modelled 1945

Price: *U.S $*   *Can. $*   *U.K. £*
               Prototype

HN 2643
Boxer Champion 'Warlord of Mazelaine'

Model No.: 1412A
Designer: Peggy Davies
Height: 6 1/2", 16.5 cm
Size: Medium
Colour: Golden brown coat with white bib
Issued: 1952-1985

Price: *U.S $*   *Can. $*   *U.K. £*
          200.00   275.00   125.00

HN 2644
Elephant
Trunk in salute

Model No.: 489A
Designer: Charles Noke
Height: 4 1/4", 10.8 cm
Size: Small
Colour: Grey with black markings,
          white tusks (china)
Issued: 1952-1985
Varieties: HN 891, 941; Flambé, Sung

Price: *U.S $*   *Can. $*   *U.K. £*
          200.00   250.00   125.00

HN 2645
Doberman Pinscher Ch. 'Rancho Dobe's Storm'

Model No.: 1508
Designer: Peggy Davies
Height: 6 1/4", 15.9 cm
Size: Medium
Colour: Black with brown feet and chin
Issued: 1955-1985
Varieties: Flambé

Price: *U.S $*   *Can. $*   *U.K. £*
          225.00   300.00   165.00

HN 2646
Tiger
Stalking - Style Two

Model No.: 809
Designer: Charles Noke
Height: 5 3/4" x 12 1/2", 14.6 x 31.7 cm
Colour: Golden brown with black stripes
Issued: 1955-1992
Varieties: HN 1082; Flambé; Also HN 1125 Tiger on alabaster base
Series: Prestige

Price:	*U.S $*	*Can. $*	*U.K. £*
	1,500.00	1,750.00	850.00

HN 2647
Drake
Standing

Model No.: 137
Designer: Unknown
Height: 5 1/2", 14.0 cm
Size: Medium
Colour: Green head, grey and brown body (china)
Issued: 1959-1962
Varieties: HN 114, 115, 116, 956, 1191, 2555, Flambé

Price:	*U.S $*	*Can. $*	*U.K. £*
	Rare		

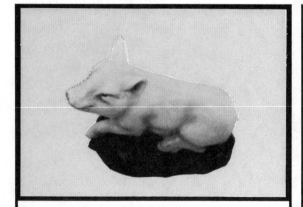

HN 2648
Piglet
Style One

Model No.: 1279
Designer: Peggy Davies
Height: 2", 5.1 cm
Colour: Pink piglet on green grassy mound
Issued: 1959-1967

Price:	*U.S $*	*Can. $*	*U.K. £*
	325.00	375.00	125.00

HN 2649
Piglet
Style Two

Model No.: 1275
Designer: Peggy Davies
Height: 2", 5.1 cm
Colour: Pink piglet on green grassy mound
Issued: 1959-1967

Price:	*U.S $*	*Can. $*	*U.K. £*
	325.00	375.00	125.00

HN 2650
Piglet
Style Three
Model No.:   1282
Designer: Peggy Davies
Height: 1", 2.5 cm
Colour: Pink piglet on green grassy mound
Issued: 1959-1967

Price: *U.S $*   *Can. $*   *U.K. £*
                     325.00   375.00   125.00

HN 2651
Piglet
Style Four
Model No.:   1280
Designer: Peggy Davies
Height: 1", 2.5 cm
Colour: Pink piglet on green grassy mound
Issued: 1959-1967

Price: *U.S $*   *Can. $*   *U.K. £*
                     325.00   375.00   125.00

HN 2652
Character Piglet
Style Five
Model No.:   1281
Designer: Peggy Davies
Height: 2", 5.1 cm
Colour: Pink piglet on green grassy mound
Issued: 1959-1967

Price: *U.S $*   *Can. $*   *U.K. £*
                     325.00   375.00   125.00

HN 2653
Character Piglet
Style Six
Model No.:   1278
Designer: Peggy Davies
Height: 2", 5.1 cm
Colour: Pink piglet on green grassy mound
Issued: 1959-1967

Price: *U.S $*   *Can. $*   *U.K. £*
                     325.00   375.00   125.00

HN 2654
Character Dog with Slipper

Model No.:	1673	
Designer:	Unknown	
Height:	3", 7.6 cm	
Colour:	White with black and brown patches, grey slipper	
Issued:	1959-1985	

Price:	*U.S $*	*Can. $*	*U.K. £*
	100.00	125.00	65.00

HN 2655
Siamese Cat
Seated - Style One

Model No.:	1672	
Designer:	Joseph Ledger	
Modeller:	Peggy Davies	
Height:	5 1/2", 14.0 cm	
Colour:	Cream with black markings	
Issued:	1960-1985	
Series:	Chatcull Range	

Price:	*U.S $*	*Can. $*	*U.K. £*
	175.00	235.00	100.00

HN 2656
Pine Marten

Model No.:	1689	
Designer:	Joseph Ledger	
Height:	4", 10.1 cm	
Colour:	Mushroom coat with black tail and paws	
Issued:	1960-1969	
Series:	Chatcull Range	
Varieties:	Flambé	

Price:	*U.S $*	*Can. $*	*U.K. £*
	400.00	500.00	225.00

HN 2657
Langur Monkey

Model No.:	1703	
Designer:	Joseph Ledger	
Height:	4 1/2", 11.4 cm	
Colour:	Long-haired brown and white coat	
Issued:	1960-1969	
Series:	Chatcull Range	

Price:	*U.S $*	*Can. $*	*U.K. £*
	325.00	450.00	225.00

HN 2658
White-Tailed Deer

Model No.:	1707
Designer:	Joseph Ledger
Height:	6", 15.2 cm
Colour:	Brown and grey
Issued:	1960-1969
Series:	Chatcull Range

Price:	*U.S $*	*Can. $*	*U.K. £*
	325.00	450.00	225.00

HN 2659
Brown Bear
Style Two

Model No.:	1688
Designer:	Joseph Ledger
Height:	4", 10.1 cm
Colour:	Brown with black highlights
Issued:	1960-1969
Series:	Chatcull Range
Varieties:	Mandarin

Price:	*U.S $*	*Can. $*	*U.K. £*
	325.00	400.00	195.00

HN 2660
Siamese Cat
Standing - Style One

Model No.:	1709
Designer:	Joseph Ledger
Modeller:	Peggy Davies
Height:	5", 12.7 cm
Colour:	Cream with black markings
Issued:	1960-1985
Series:	Chatcull Range

Price:	*U.S $*	*Can. $*	*U.K. £*
	175.00	235.00	100.00

HN 2661
Mountain Sheep

Model No.:	1692
Designer:	Joseph Ledger
Height:	5", 12.7 cm
Colour:	Brown with white highlights, green base
Issued:	1960-1969
Series:	Chatcull Range

Price:	*U.S $*	*Can. $*	*U.K. £*
	325.00	450.00	225.00

HN 2662
Siamese Cat
Lying - Style One
Model No.:   1710
Designer: Joseph Ledger
Modeller: Peggy Davies
Height: 3 3/4", 9.5 cm
Colour: Cream with black markings
Issued: 1960-1985
Series: Chatcull Range

Price: U.S $ Can. $ U.K. £
                  175.00   235.00   100.00

HN 2663
River Hog
Model No.:   1704
Designer: Joseph Ledger
Height: 3 1/2", 8.9 cm
Colour: Dark brown with light brown and white
               highlights
Issued: 1960-1969
Series: Chatcull Range

Price: U.S $ Can. $ U.K. £
                  300.00   400.00   175.00

HN 2664
Nyala Antelope
Model No.:   1705
Designer: Joseph Ledger
Height: 5 3/4", 14.6 cm
Colour: Mushroom coloured coat with black
               and brown highlights
Issued: 1960-1969
Series: Chatcull Range

Price: U. $ Can. $ U.K. £
                  375.00   450.00   225.00

HN 2665
Llama
Style Two
Model No.:   1687
Designer: Joseph Ledger
Height: 6 1/2", 16.5 cm
Colour: Brown with turquoise highlights
Issued: 1960-1969
Series: Chatcull Range

Price: U.S $ Can. $ U.K. £
                  375.00   450.00   225.00

HN 2666
Badger
Style One

Model No.:	1708
Designer:	Joseph Ledger
Height:	2 3/4", 7.0 cm
Colour:	Grey, black and white
Issued:	1960-1969
Series:	Chatcull Range
Varieties:	Mandarin

Price:	*U.S $*	*Can. $*	*U.K. £*
	325.00	375.00	175.00

HN 2667
Labrador Ch. 'Bumblikite of Mansergh'

Model No.:	1946
Designer:	John Bromley
Height:	5 1/4", 13.3 cm
Size:	Medium
Colour:	Black
Issued:	1967-1985

Price:	*U.S $*	*Can. $*	*U.K. £*
	200.00	275.00	125.00

HN 2668
Puffins

Model No.:	2289
Designer:	Robert Jefferson
Height:	9 3/4", 24.8 cm
Colour:	Dark grey and white birds with red, yellow and blue beaks
Issued:	1974 in a limited edition of 250
Series:	Jefferson Sculptures

Price:	*U.S $*	*Can. $*	*U.K. £*
	2,500.00	3,000.00	1,450.00

HN 2669
Snowy Owl (male)
Style One

Model No.:	2264
Designer:	Robert Jefferson
Height:	16", 40.1 cm
Colour:	White with grey markings
Issued:	1976 in a limited edition of 150
Series:	Jefferson Sculptures

Price:	*U.S $*	*Can. $*	*U.K. £*
	2,200.00	2,500.00	950.00

HN 2670
Snowy Owl (female)
Style Two

Model No.:   2389
Designer: Robert Jefferson
Height: 9 1/2", 24.0 cm
Colour: White with grey markings
Issued: 1976 in a limited edition of 150
Series: Jefferson Sculptures

Price: *U.S $*   *Can. $*   *U.K. £*
                    2,000.00   2,250.00   1,250.00

*

HN 3500
Black-Throated Loon

Model No.:   2268
Designer: Robert Jefferson
Height: 9 1/2" x 20", 24.0 x 50.8 cm
Colour: Green head, black and white wings,
              white underbody
Issued: 1974 in a limited edition of 150
Series: Jefferson Sculptures

Price: *U.S $*   *Can. $*   *U.K. £*
                    2,000.00   2,250.00   1,250.00

HN 3501
White-Winged Cross Bills

Model No.:   2208
Designer: Robert Jefferson
Height: 8", 20.3 cm
Colour: Red bird with white and brown wings;
              dull yellow bird with brown and white
              wings
Issued: 1974 in a limited edition of 250
Series: Jefferson Sculptures

Price: *U.S $*   *Can. $*   *U.K. £*
                    1,000.00   1,250.00   850.00

HN 3502
King Eider

Model No.:   2302
Designer: Robert Jefferson
Height: 10", 25.4 cm
Colour: Dark brown, grey head,
              red and yellow beak
Issued: 1974 in a limited edition of 150
Series: Jefferson Sculptures

Price: *U.S $*   *Can. $*   *U.K. £*
                    2,000.00   2,250.00   1,250.00

HN 3503
Roseate Terns

Model No.:	2319
Designer:	Robert Jefferson
Height:	11", 27.9 cm
Colour:	Grey and white large bird, light brown chicks
Issued:	1974 in a limited edition of 150
Series:	Jefferson Sculptures

Price:	*U.S $*	*Can. $*	*U.K. £*
	2,500.00	2,750.00	1,250.00

HN 3504
Golden-Crowned Kinglet

Model No.:	2406
Designer:	Robert Jefferson
Height:	8 1/4", 21.0 cm
Colour:	Brown branch and acorn, yellow, brown and red bird
Issued:	1974 in an unlimited number
Series:	Jefferson Sculptures

Price:	*U.S $*	*Can. $*	*U.K. £*
	750.00	950.00	500.00

HN 3505
Winter Wren

Model No.:	2405
Designer:	Robert Jefferson
Height:	5", 12.7 cm
Colour:	Brown with cream breast
Issued:	1974 in an unlimited number
Series:	Jefferson Sculptures

Price:	*U.S $*	*Can. $*	*U.K. £*
	750.00	950.00	650.00

HN 3506
Colorado Chipmunks

Model No.:	2404
Designer:	Robert Jefferson
Height:	13", 33.0 cm
Colour:	Brown with black patches
Issued:	1974 in a limited edition of 75
Series:	Jefferson Sculptures

Price:	*U.S $*	*Can. $*	*U.K. £*
	2,500.00	3,000.00	1,750.00

HN 3507
Harbour Seals

Model No.:	2434
Designer:	Robert Jefferson
Height:	8 1/2", 21.6 cm
Colour:	Greys and browns
Issued:	1975 in a limited edition of 75
Series:	Jefferson Sculptures

Price:	U.S $	Can. $	U.K. £
	2,000.00	2,500.00	1,250.00

HN 3508
Snowshoe Hares

Model No.:	2446
Designer:	Robert Jefferson
Height:	10 3/4", 27.3 cm
Colour:	Browns and white
Issued:	1975 in a limited edition of 75
Series:	Jefferson Sculptures

Price:	U.S $	Can. $	U.K. £
	3,500.00	3,000.00	1,250.00

HN 3509
Downy Woodpecker
Style One

Model No.:	2469
Designer:	Robert Jefferson
Height:	7 1/4", 18.4 cm
Colour:	Black and white bird; green leaves, blue flower
Issued:	1975 in an unlimited number
Series:	Jefferson Sculptures

Price:	U.S $	Can. $	U.K. £
	525.00	700.00	450.00

HN 3510
Eastern Bluebird Fledgling

Model No.:	2481
Designer:	Robert Jefferson
Height:	5 3/4", 14.6 cm
Colour:	Brown with light brown highlights, green leaves, purple flower; tan trowel
Issued:	1976 in a limited edition of 250
Series:	Jefferson Sculptures

Price:	U.S $	Can. $	U.K. £
	600.00	800.00	450.00

Royal Doulton News

Beatrix Potter Animals and Bunnykins appeal for spot in Animal Book

Want to appear in Seaway ad!

Santa Tiny - New for 1994

In what appears to be a very organized group protest, the animals in the Beatrix Potter collection have joined together with the Bunnys in the Bunnykins collection to appeal for recognition in the Royal Doulton animal book.

In their request to Seaway China to be included in their ad in the book, they state their importance and popularity as a Royal Doulton animal product.

Seaway China officials, who are known world-wide as specialists in Beatrix Potter and Bunnykins are considering their request. If the request is granted, their photo will be included along with a reminder that Seaway China always assists in the placement of members of these collections directly into collectors homes.

Arrangements can be made at 1-800-968-2424.

Second Santa Tiny Ready for 1994.

Marine City, USA

Seaway China of Marine City, Michigan have announced that their second Santa Claus Tiny character jug will be ready for the 1994 Christmas Season.

First in the series, the Tiny Santa Claus character jug, with a regular red handle is now over 80% Sold Out. Second in the series of three is Santa Claus with a red and white candy cane handle.

Seaway China is accepting orders for both character jugs at 1-800-968-2424.

Real Dog on Guard at Royal Doulton Store

"Mindy", a purebred Pomeranian, works at Seaway China Shop every day. When awake she serves as "guard dog" to the giant Seaway collection of Royal Doulton animals, character jugs and figurines. As international as Royal Doulton itself, Mindy is a native of Florida, lives in Canada and works in the Michigan, U.S.A. shop daily. Drop in and meet her.

Mindy has agreed to let her picture appear to represent all the real pets who serve as priceless companions to their masters who are Royal Doulton collectors.

Photograph
Not Available
At Press Time

HN 3511
Chipping Sparrow

Model No.:	2466
Designer:	Robert Jefferson
Height:	7 1/2", 19.1 cm
Colour:	Brown and yellow, red head
Issued:	1976 in a limited edition of 200
Series:	Jefferson Sculptures

Price:	*U.S $*	*Can. $*	*U.K. £*
	950.00	1,275.00	450.00

HN 3512
Mallard (male)

Model No.:	2614
Designer:	Harry Sales from Lem Ward originals
Height:	4", 10.1 cm
Colour:	Light and dark brown, green head, yellow beak
Issued:	1979-1985
Series:	Wildlife Decoys

Price:	*U.S $*	*Can. $*	*U.K. £*
	200.00	275.00	85.00

HN 3513
Pintail (male)

Model No.:	Unknown
Designer:	Harry Sales from Lem Ward originals
Height:	4", 10.1 cm
Colour:	Light and dark brown with cream markings
Issued:	1979-1985
Series:	Wildlife Decoys

Price:	*U.S $*	*Can. $*	*U.K. £*
	200.00	275.00	85.00

HN 3514
Greater Scaup (male)

Model No.:	2620
Designer:	Harry Sales from Lem Ward originals
Height:	3 3/4", 9.5 cm
Colour:	Dark green with light green and beige, blue bill
Issued:	1979-1985
Series:	Wildlife Decoys

Price:	*U.S $*	*Can. $*	*U.K. £*
	200.00	275.00	85.00

HN 3515
Mallard (female)
Model No.: 2603
Designer: Harry Sales from Lem Ward originals
Height: 4", 101. cm
Colour: Dark brown, orange-brown
Issued: 1979-1985
Series: Wildlife Decoys

Price:	*U.S $*	*Can. $*	*U.K. £*
	200.00	275.00	85.00

HN 3516
Pintail (female)
Model No.: 2612
Designer: Harry Sales from Lem Ward originals
Height: 4", 10.1 cm
Colour: Light brown, dark brown and cream
Issued: 1979-1985
Series: Wildlife Decoys

Price:	*U.S $*	*Can. $*	*U.K. £*
	200.00	275.00	£85.00

HN 3517
Greater Scaup (female)
Model No.: 2621
Designer: Harry Sales from Lem Ward originals
Height: 4", 10.1 cm
Colour: Dark brown, light brown, blue bill
Issued: 1979-1985
Series: Wildlife Decoys

Price:	*U.S $*	*Can. $*	*U.K. £*
	200.00	275.00	85.00

HN 3518
Merganser (male)
Model No.: Unknown
Designer: Harry Sales from Lem Ward originals
Height: 4", 10.1 cm
Colour: Charcoal, light brown and green
Issued: 1980-1985
Series: Wildlife Decoys

Price:	*U.S $*	*Can. $*	*U.K. £*
	200.00	275.00	85.00

HN 3519
Merganser (female)
Model No.:   2643
Designer: Harry Sales from Lem Ward originals
Height: 4", 10.1 cm
Colour: Brown, light brown and black
Issued: 1980-1985
Series: Wildlife Decoys

Price:	*U.S $*	*Can. $*	*U.K. £*
	200.00	275.00	85.00

HN 3520
Green Wing Teal (male)
Model No.:   2683
Designer: Harry Sales from Lem Ward originals
Height: 4", 10.1 cm
Colour: Brown, green and black
Issued: 1979-1986

Price:	*U.S. $*	*Can. $*	*U.K. £*
	200.00	275.00	85.00

HN 3521
Green Wing Teal (female)
Model No.:   2684
Designer: Harry Sales from Lem Ward originals
Height: 4", 10.1 cm
Colour: Beige, Brown and green
Issued: 1979-1986

Price:	*U.S. $*	*Can. $*	*U.K. £*
	200.00	275.00	85.00

HN 3522
'The Leap' Dolphin
Model No.:   2949
Designer: Adrian Hughes
Height: 9", 22.9 cm
Colour: White
Issued: 1982 to the present
Series: Images of Nature
Varieties: Flambé

Price:	*U.S. $*	*Can. $*	*U.K. £*
	175.00	185.00	65.00

HN 3523
'Capricorn' Mountain Goat

Model No.:	2959
Designer:	Adrian Hughes
Height:	9 3/4", 24.8 cm
Colour:	White
Issued:	1982-1988
Series:	Images of Nature
Varieties:	Flambé

Price:	*U.S. $*	*Can. $*	*U.K. £*
	125.00	175.00	95.00

HN 3524
'The Gift of Life' Mare and Foal

Model No.:	2923
Designer:	Russell Willis
Height:	8 1/4", 21.0 cm
Colour:	White
Issued:	1982 to the present
Series:	Images of Nature
Varieties:	HN 3536

Price:	*U.S. $*	*Can. $*	*U.K. £*
	700.00	750.00	235.00

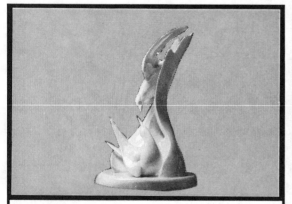

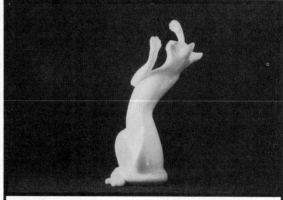

HN 3525
'Courtship' Terns

Model No.:	2930
Designer:	Russell Willis
Height:	14 1/4", 36.2 cm
Colour:	White
Issued:	1982 to the present
Series:	Images of Nature
Varieties:	HN 3535

Price:	*U.S. $*	*Can. $*	*U.K. £*
	815.00	1,000.00	299.00

HN 3526
'Shadow Play' Cat

Model No.:	2936
Designer:	Russell Willis
Height:	10", 25.4 cm
Colour:	White
Issued:	1982 to the present
Series:	Images of Nature
Varieties:	Flambé

Price:	*U.S. $*	*Can. $*	*U.K. £*
	170.00	185.00	65.00

HN 3527
'Going Home' Flying Geese

Model No.:	2925
Designer:	Adrian Hughes
Height:	6 1/4", 15.9 cm
Colour:	White
Issued:	1982 to the present
Series:	Images of Nature
Varieties:	HN 3564, Flambé

Price:	*U.S. $*	*Can. $*	*U.K. £*
	120.00	125.00	49.95

HN 3528
'Freedom' Otters

Model No.:	3058
Designer:	Robert Jefferson
Height:	8 1/2", 21.6 cm
Colour:	White
Issued:	1983-1986
Series:	Images of Nature

Price:	*U.S. $*	*Can. $*	*U.K. £*
	300.00	400.00	225.00

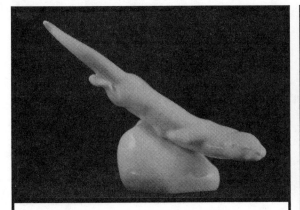

HN 3529
'Bright Water' Otter

Model No.:	3058A
Designer:	Robert Jefferson
Height:	7 1/2" x 11", 19.1 x 27.9 cm
Colour:	White
Issued:	1983-1986
Series:	Images of Nature

Price:	*U.S. $*	*Can. $*	*U.K. £*
	200.00	275.00	150.00

HN 3530
'Clear Water' Otter

Model No.:	3058B
Designer:	Robert Jefferson
Height:	8 1/4", 21.0 cm
Colour:	White
Issued:	1983-1986
Series:	Images of Nature

Price:	*U.S. $*	*Can. $*	*U.K. £*
	200.00	275.00	150.00

HN 3531
'Nestling Down' Swans

Model No.:	3198
Designer:	Adrian Hughes
Height:	8 1/2" x 12", 21.6 x 30.5 cm
Colour:	White
Issued:	1985 North America;
	1986 Worldwide to the present
Series:	Images of Nature
Varieties:	HN 3538

Price:	U.S. $	Can. $	U.K. £
	N/A	750.00	275.00

HN 3532
'The Homecoming' Doves

Model No.:	3304
Designer:	Russell Willis
Height:	14 3/4", 37.5 cm
Colour:	White
Issued:	1987 to the present
Series:	Images of Nature
Varieties:	HN 3539

Price:	U.S. $	Can. $	U.K. £
	700.00	825.00	299.00

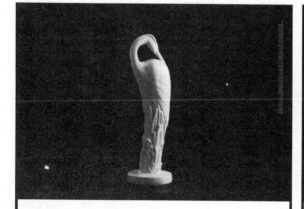

HN 3533
'Patience' Heron

Model No.:	3467
Designer:	Peter Gee
Height:	12 1/4", 31.1 cm
Colour:	White
Issued:	1987 to the present
Series:	Images of Nature

Price:	U.S. $	Can. $	U.K. £
	175.00	205.00	69.00

HN 3534
'Playful' Lion Cubs

Model No.:	3432
Designer:	Adrian Hughes
Height:	8", 20.3 cm
Colour:	White
Issued:	1987-1993
Series:	Images of Nature

Price:	U.S. $	Can. $	U.K. £
	150.00	200.00	95.00

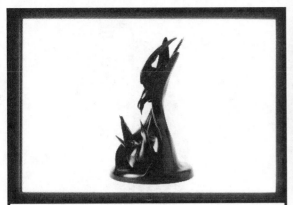

HN 3535
'Courtship' Terns

Model No.:	2930
Designer:	Russell Willis
Height:	15", 38.1 cm
Colour:	Flambé
Issued:	1987 to the present
Series:	Images of Fire
Varieties:	HN 3525

Price:	*U.S. $*	*Can. $*	*U.K. £*
	N/A	2,210.00	650.00

HN 3536
'The Gift of Life' Mare and Foal

Model No.:	2923
Designer:	Russell Willis
Height:	9", 22.9 cm
Colour:	Flambé
Issued:	1987 to the present
Series:	Images of Fire
Varieties:	HN 3524

Price:	*U.S. $*	*Can. $*	*U.K. £*
	N/A	1,630.00	525.00

*

HN 3538
'Nestling Down' Swans

Model No.:	3198
Designer:	Adrian Hughes
Height:	8 1/2" x 12", 21.6 x 30.5 cm
Colour:	Flambé
Issued:	1988 to the present
Series:	Images of Fire
Varieties:	HN 3531

Price:	*U.S. $*	*Can. $*	*U.K. £*
	N/A	1,630.00	550.00

HN 3539
'The Homecoming' Doves

Model No.:	3304
Designer:	Russell Willis
Height:	14 3/4", 37.5 cm
Colour:	Flambé
Issued:	1989 to the present
Series:	Images of Fire
Varieties:	HN 3532

Price:	*U.S. $*	*Can. $*	*U.K. £*
	N/A	2,210.00	599.00

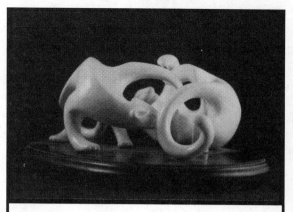

HN 3540
'Graceful' Panthers

Model No.:	3573
Designer:	John Ablitt
Height:	4 1/2" x 11", 11.4 x 27.9 cm
Colour:	White
Issued:	1989-1992
Series:	Images of Nature

Price:	*U.S. $*	*Can. $*	*U.K. £*
	450.00	500.00	225.00

HN 3541
Peregrine Falcon

Model No.:	3140
Designer:	Graham Tongue
Height:	11 1/2", 29.2 cm
Colour:	Dark brown and cream
Issued:	1990 in a limited edition of 2,500 (Lawley's By Post)
Series:	Artist's Signature Edition
Varieties:	DA 40

Price:	*U.S. $*	*Can. $*	*U.K. £*
	400.00	550.00	145.00

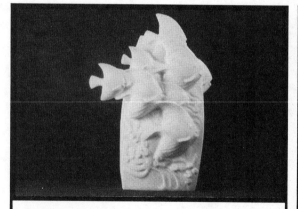

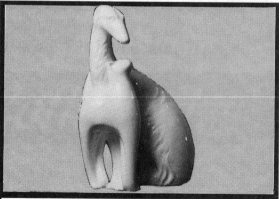

HN 3542
'Serenity' Tropical Shoal of Fish

Model No.:	3660
Designer:	John Ablitt
Height:	11", 27.9 cm
Colour:	White
Issued:	1990 to the present
Series:	Images of Nature

Price:	*U.S. $*	*Can. $*	*U.K. £*
	97.00	180.00	39.95

HN 3543
'Friendship' Borzoi Dog and Cat

Model No.:	3658
Designer:	John Ablitt
Height:	8 1/4", 21.0 cm
Colour:	White
Issued:	1990-1992
Series:	Images of Nature

Price:	*U.S. $*	*Can. $*	*U.K. £*
	175.00	200.00	100.00

HN 3544
'Playtime' Cat with Kitten

Model No.:	3864		
Designer:	John R. Ablitt		
Height:	8", 20.3 cm		
Colour:	White		
Issued:	1990-1992		
Series:	Images of Nature		

Price:	*U.S. $*	*Can. $*	*U.K. £*
	200.00	250.00	100.00

HN 3545
'Motherly Love' Swan and Two Cygnets

Model No.:	3901		
Designer:	Adrian Hughes		
Height:	6", 15.2 cm		
Colour:	White		
Issued:	1990 to the present		
Series:	Images of Nature		

Price:	*U.S. $*	*Can. $*	*U.K. £*
	N/A	245.00	69.00

HN 3546
'Going Home' Flying Geese

Model No.:	2925		
Designer:	Adrian Hughes		
Height:	6 1/4", 15.9 cm		
Colour:	White		
Issued:	1987 for Nabisco Foods Canada		
Varieties:	HN 3527, Flambé		

Price:	*U.S. $*	*Can. $*	*U.K. £*
	120.00	125.00	50.00

HN 3547
Pegasus

Model No.:	3187		
Designer:	Alan Maslankowski		
Height:	10", 25.4 cm		
Colour:	White		
Issued:	1990-1993 (Lawley's By Post)		

Price:	*U.S. $*	*Can. $*	*U.K. £*
	200.00	300.00	145.00

HN 3548
Elephant and Young

Model No.:	3789
Designer:	Eric Griffiths
Height:	3 1/4", 8.3 cm
Colour:	Flambé
Issued:	1990 to the present
Series:	Images of Fire

Price:	U.S. $	Can. $	U.K. £
	N/A	199.50	55.00

HN 3549
Unicorn

Model No.:	3927
Designer:	Alan Maslankowski
Height:	10", 25.4 cm
Colour:	White unicorn, gold horn
Issued:	1991-1993 (Lawley's By Post)

Price:	U.S. $	Can. $	U.K. £
	N/A	N/A	115.00

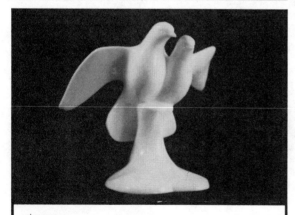

HN 3550
'Always and Forever' Doves

Model No.:	4188
Designer:	Adrian Hughes
Height:	4 1/2", 11.4 cm
Colour:	White
Issued:	1993 to the present
Series:	Images of Nature

Price:	U.S. $	Can. $	U.K. £
	55.00	125.00	29.95

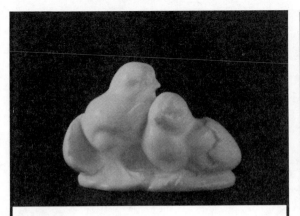

HN3551
'New Arrival' Chicks

Model No.:   4300
Designer: Alan Maslankowski
Height: 3", 7.6 cm
Colour: White
Issued: 1994 to the present
Series: Images of Nature

Price:	*U.S. $*	*Can. $*	*U.K. £*
	50.00	75.00	29.95

HN3552
Dragon

Model No.:   4315
Designer: Robert Tabbenor
Height: 5 1/4'", 13.3 cm
Colour: Flambé
Issued: 1993-1993
Series: R.D.I.C.C.

Price:	*U.S. $*	*Can. $*	*U.K. £*
	260.00	350.00	160.00

K SERIES

K1
Bulldog
Seated - Style Five
Model No.: 762
Designer: Unknown
Height: 2 1/2", 6.3 cm
Colour: Tan with dark brown patches over eye and back
Issued: 1931-1977

Price:	*U.S. $*	*Can. $*	*U.K. £*
	125.00	165.00	85.00

K2
Bulldog Puppy
Model No.: 763
Designer: Unknown
Height: 2", 5.1 cm
Colour: Tan with dark brown patches over eye and back
Issued: 1931-1977
Varieties: Two variations are known. The patch can be on either the left or right side of face.

Price:	*U.S. $*	*Can. $*	*U.K. £*
	100.00	125.00	65.00

K3
Sealyham
Begging
Model No.: 760
Designer: Unknown
Height: 2 3/4", 7.0 cm
Colour: White with light brown patches over the eyes and ears
Issued: 1931-1977

Price:	*U.S. $*	*Can. $*	*U.K. £*
	100.00	125.00	65.00

K4
Sealyham
Lying - Style Two
Model No.: 765
Designer: Unknown
Height: 1 1/2" x 3 1/4", 3.8 x 8.3 cm
Colour: White with light brown patches over eyes and ears
Issued: 1931-1959

Price:	*U.S. $*	*Can. $*	*U.K. £*
	325.00	400.00	165.00

K5
Airedale Terrier
Lying

Model No.:   757
Designer: Unknown
Height: 1 1/4" x 2 1/4", 3.1 x 5.7 cm
Colour: Dark brown coat, light brown head and
             underbody
Issued: 1931-1959

Price:	*U.S. $*	*Can. $*	*U.K. £*
	325.00	425.00	125.00

K6
Pekinese
Seated

Model No.:   758
Designer: Unknown
Height: 2", 5.1 cm
Colour: Golden brown with black markings on
             face and ears
Issued: 1931-1977

Price:	*U.S. $*	*Can. $*	*U.K. £*
	100.00	125.00	65.00

K7
Foxhound
Seated - Style Two

Model No.:   764
Designer: Unknown
Height: 2 1/2", 6.4 cm
Colour: White with dark brown and black patches
             over ears, eyes and back
Issued: 1931-1977

Price:	*U.S. $*	*Can. $*	*U.K. £*
	100.00	125.00	65.00

K8
Fox Terrier
Seated - Style Three

Model No.:   759
Designer: Unknown
Height: 2 1/2", 6.4 cm
Colour: White with black and brown patches over
             ears, eyes and back
Issued: 1931-1977

Price:	*U.S. $*	*Can. $*	*U.K. £*
	100.00	125.00	65.00

K9A
Cocker Spaniel
Seated - Style One

Model No.:	755
Designer:	Unknown
Height:	2 1/2", 6.4 cm
Colour:	Golden brown with black highlights
Issued:	1931-1977
Varieties:	K9B

Price:	*U.S. $*	*Can. $*	*U.K. £*
	125.00	165.00	65.00

K9B
Cocker Spaniel
Seated - Style One

Model No.:	755
Designer:	Unknown
Height:	2 1/2", 6.4 cm
Colour:	Black and brown
Issued:	1931-1977
Varieties:	K9A

Price:	*U.S. $*	*Can. $*	*U.K. £*
		Rare	

K10
Scottish Terrier
Begging - Style Two

Model No.:	761
Designer:	Unknown
Height:	2 3/4", 7.0 cm
Colour:	Grey with black highlights
Issued:	1931-1977

Price:	*U.S. $*	*Can. $*	*U.K. £*
	125.00	200.00	80.00

K11
Cairn Terrier
Seated

Model No.:	766
Designer:	Unknown
Height:	2 1/2", 6.4 cm
Colour:	Grey with black highlights
Issued:	1931-1977

Price:	*U.S. $*	*Can. $*	*U.K. £*
	100.00	125.00	65.00

K12
'Lucky' Black Cat
Model No.:   400
Designer: Charles Noke
Height: 2 3/4", 7.0 cm
Colour: Black with white face
Issued: 1932-1975
Varieties: Also called 'Ooloo' HN 818, 819,
               827, 828, 829

Price:	*U.S. $*	*Can. $*	*U.K. £*
	140.00	175.00	65.00

K13
Alsatian
Seated - Style One
Model No.:   787
Designer: Unknown
Height: 3", 7.6 cm
Colour: Dark brown body, light brown underbody
Issued: 1931-1977

Price:	*U.S. $*	*Can. $*	*U.K. £*
	100.00	125.00	75.00

K14
Bull Terrier
Lying
Model No.:   1093
Designer: Unknown
Height: 1 1/4" x 2 3/4", 3.2 x 7.0 cm
Colour: White
Issued: 1940-1959

Price:	*U.S. $*	*Can. $*	*U.K. £*
	400.00	500.00	165.00

K15
Chow (Shibu Ino)
Model No.:   1095
Designer: Unknown
Height: 2 1/2", 6.3 cm
Colour: Golden brown
Issued: 1940-1977

Price:	*U.S. $*	*Can. $*	*U.K. £*
	150.00	175.00	65.00

K16
Welsh Corgi

Model No.:	1094		
Designer:	Unknown		
Height:	2 1/2" x 2 1/4", 6.3 x 5.7 cm		
Colour:	Golden brown		
Issued:	1940-1977		

Price:	*U.S. $*	*Can. $*	*U.K. £*
	150.00	200.00	90.00

K17
Dachshund
Seated

Model No.:	1096
Designer:	Unknown
Height:	1 3/4" x 2 3/4", 4.4 x 7.0 cm
Colour:	Golden brown with dark brown markings
Issued:	1940-1977

Price:	*U.S. $*	*Can. $*	*U.K. £*
	100.00	125.00	65.00

K18
Scottish Terrier
Seated - Style Three

Model No.:	1092
Designer:	Unknown
Height:	2 1/4", x 2 3/4", 5.7 x 7.0 cm
Colour:	Black with grey highlights
Issued:	1940-1977

Price:	*U.S. $*	*Can. $*	*U.K. £*
	150.00	200.00	90.00

K19
St. Bernard
Lying

Model No.:	1097
Designer:	Unknown
Height:	1 1/2" x 2 1/2", 3.8 x 6.3 cm
Colour:	Brown and cream, black highlights
Issued:	1940-1977

Price:	*U.S. $*	*Can. $*	*U.K. £*
	100.00	125.00	65.00

K20
Penguin with Chick Under Wing
Model No.:   1084
Designer: Peggy Davies
Height: 2 1/4", 5.7 cm
Colour: Black and white
Issued: 1940-1968

Price:	*U.S. $*	*Can. $*	*U.K. £*
	325.00	425.00	165.00

K21
Penguin
Style four
Model No.:   1099
Designer: Peggy Davies
Height: 2", 5.1 cm
Colour: Black and white
Issued: 1940-1968

Price:	*U.S. $*	*Can. $*	*U.K. £*
	325.00	425.00	125.00

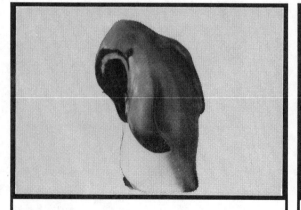

K22
Penguin
Style Five
Model No.:   1098
Designer: Peggy Davies
Height: 1 3/4", 5.1 cm
Colour: Grey and white with black tips
Issued: 1940-1968

Price:	*U.S. $*	*Can. $*	*U.K. £*
	325.00	425.00	110.00

K23
Penguin
Style Six
Model No.:   1101
Designer: Peggy Davies
Height: 1 1/2", 3.8 cm
Colour: Grey, white and black, green patches
              under eyes
Issued: 1940-1968

Price:	*U.S. $*	*Can. $*	*U.K. £*
	325.00	425.00	165.00

K24
Penguin
Style Seven

Model No.:	1100		
Designer:	Peggy Davies		
Height:	2", 5.1 cm		
Colour:	Black and white		
Issued:	1940-1968		

Price:	*U.S. $*	*Can. $*	*U.K. £*
	325.00	425.00	125.00

K25
Penguin
Style Eight

Model No.:	1083		
Designer:	Peggy Davies		
Height:	2 1/4", 5.7 cm		
Colour:	Grey, white and black		
Issued:	1940-1968		

Price:	*U.S. $*	*Can. $*	*U.K. £*
	325.00	425.00	120.00

K26
Mallard Duck

Model No.:	1133		
Designer:	Unknown		
Height:	1 1/2", 3.8 cm		
Colour:	Yellow with brown spots on green grass		
Issued:	1940-1946		

Price:	*U.S. $*	*Can. $*	*U.K. £*
	750.00	1,000.00	250.00

K27
Yellow-Throated Warbler
Style One

Model No.:	1128		
Designer:	Unknown		
Height:	2", 5.1 cm		
Colour:	Blue feathers with black markings, yellow breast; green base and leaves, pink and white flowers		
Issued:	1940-1946		

Price:	*U.S. $*	*Can. $*	*U.K. £*
	750.00	1,000.00	300.00

K28
Cardinal
Style One

Model No.: 1127
Designer: Unknown
Height: Unknown
Colour: Red feathers with black markings, green leaves and base, white flowers
Issued: 1940-1946

Price:	*U.S. $*	*Can. $*	*U.K. £*
	750.00	*1,000.00*	*300.00*

K29
Baltimore Oriole
Style Four

Model No.: 1130
Designer: Unknown
Height: 2 3/4", 7.0 cm
Colour: Orange with black head and wings, white flowers, green leaves, beige base
Issued: 1940-1946

Price:	*U.S. $*	*Can. $*	*U.K. £*
	750.00	*1,000.00*	*300.00*

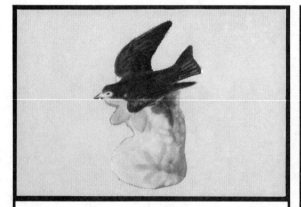

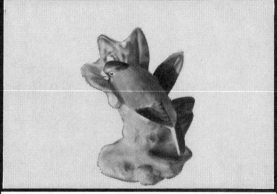

K30
Bluebird with Lupins
Style Two

Model No.: 1129
Designer: Unknown
Height: 2 1/2", 6.4 cm
Colour: Blue feathers with pink highlights, green leaves, pink-green base
Issued: 1940-1946

Price:	*U.S. $*	*Can. $*	*U.K. £*
	750.00	*1,000.00*	*300.00*

K31
Bullfinch
Style One

Model No.: 1126
Designer: Unknown
Height: 2 1/4", 5.7 cm
Colour: Blue feathers with black head and wing tips, red breast, pink flowers, green leaves and base
Issued: 1940-1946

Price:	*U.S. $*	*Can. $*	*U.K. £*
	750.00	*1,000.00*	*350.00*

K32
Budgerigar
Style One
Model No.: 1144
Designer: Unknown
Height: Unknown
Colour: Unknown
Issued: 1940-1946

Price: *U.S. $*   *Can. $*   *U.K. £*
                    Very Rare

K33
Golden-Crested Wren
Style Three
Model No.: 1135
Designer: Unknown
Height: Unknown
Colour: Unknown
Issued: 1940-1946

Price: *U.S. $*   *Can. $*   *U.K. £*
                    Very Rare

K34
Magpie
Model No.: 1151
Designer: Unknown
Height: Unknown
Colour: Unknown
Issued: 1940-1946

Price: *U.S. $*   *Can. $*   *U.K. £*
                    Very Rare

K35
Jay
Model No.: 1146
Designer: Unknown
Height: 2 1/4", 5.7 cm
Colour: Brown and white with blue wing
Issued: 1940-1946

Price: *U.S. $*   *Can. $*   *U.K. £*
        750.00   1,000.00   250.00

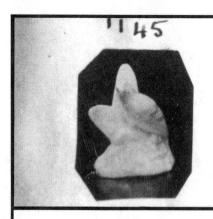

K36
Goldfinch
Style One

Model No.:   1145
Designer: Unknown
Height: Unknown
Colour: Unknown
Issued: 1940-1946

Price: *U.S. $*   *Can. $*   *U.K. £*
                              Very Rare

K37
Hare
Crouching - Style Two

Model No.:   1148
Designer: Unknown
Height: 1 1/2", 3.8 cm
Colour: Brown and white, with black highlights
Issued: 1940-1977

Price: *U.S. $*   *Can. $*   *U.K. £*
                      125.00   165.00   65.00

K38
Hare
Seated, ears down

Model No.:   1150
Designer: Unknown
Height: 2 1/2", 6.4 cm
Colour: Dark brown and white
Issued: 1940-1977

Price: *U.S. $*   *Can. $*   *U.K. £*
                      125.00   165S.00   75.00

K39
Hare
Seated, ears up

Model No.:   1149
Designer: Unknown
Height: 2 1/4", 5.7 cm
Colour: Light brown and white
Issued: 1940-1977

Price: *U.S. $*   *Can. $*   *U.K. £*
                      125.00   165.00   75.00

D SERIES

234

D 5772A
Owl Wall Pocket

Model No.:	Unknown
Designer:	Unknown
Height:	7 1/2", 19.0 cm
Colour:	Brown owl, green oak leaves, cream wall pocket
Issued:	1937

Price:	U.S. $	Can. $	U.K. £
	375.00	500.00	250.00

D 5772B
Crow Wall Pocket

Model No.:	Unknown
Designer:	Unknown
Height:	7 1/4", 18.4 cm
Colour:	Black crow, green oak leaves, cream wall pocket
Issued:	1937

Price:	U.S. $	Can. $	U.K. £
	375.00	500.00	250.00

D 5913A
Bulldog Draped in Union Jack

Model No.:	Unknown
Designer:	Charles Noke
Height:	6", 15.2 cm
Size:	Large
Colour:	Cream dog with black collar, red, white and blue Union Jack
Issued:	1941-1961

Price:	U.S. $	Can. $	U.K. £
	750.00	1,000.00	375.00

D 5913B
Bulldog Draped in Union Jack

Model No.:	Unknown
Designer:	Charles Noke
Height:	4" , 10.1 cm
Size:	Medium
Colour:	Cream dog, with black collar, red, white and blue Union Jack
Issued:	1941-1961

Price:	U.S. $	Can. $	U.K. £
	400.00	550.00	245.00

D 5913C
Bulldog Draped in Union Jack
Model No.: Unknown
Designer: Charles Noke
Height: 2 1/4", 5.7 cm
Size: Small
Colour: Cream dog with black collar, red, white and blue Union Jack
Issued: 1941

Price:	*U.S. $*	*Can. $*	*U.K. £*
	325.00	435.00	150.00

D 6178
Bulldog Draped in Union Jack with Derby Hat
Model No.: Unknown
Designer: Charles Noke
Height: 7 1/2", 19.1 cm
Size: Large
Colour: Cream dog, beige hat with brown band, blue spotted bow tie, brown cigar, Union Jack
Issued: 1941

Price:	*U.S. $*	*Can. $*	*U.K. £*
	3,500.00	4.725.00	1,250.00

D 6179
Bulldog Draped in Union Jack with Derby Hat
Model No.: Unknown
Designer: Charles Noke
Height: 5", 12.7 cm
Size: Medium
Colour: Cream dog, beige hat with brown band, blue spotted bow tie, brown cigar, Union Jack
Issued: 1941

Price:	*U.S. $*	*Can. $*	*U.K. £*
	1,700.00	2,300.00	950.00

D 6180
Bulldog Draped in Union Jack with Derby Hat
Model No.: Unknown
Designer: Charles Noke
Height: 3", 7.6 cm
Size: Small
Colour: Cream dog, beige hat with brown band, blue spotted bow tie, brown cigar, Union Jack
Issued: 1941

Price:	*U.S. $*	*Can. $*	*U.K. £*
	1,250.00	1,685.00	650.00

D 6181
Bulldog Draped in Union Jack With Trinity Cap

Model No.:	Unknown
Designer:	Charles Noke
Height:	7", 17.8 cm
Size:	Large
Colour:	Cream dog, navy cap, red, white and blue Union Jack
Issued:	1941

Price:	U.S. $	Can. $	U.K. £
	2,900.00	3,000.00	1,250.00

D 6182
Bulldog Draped in Union Jack With Trinity Cap

Model No.:	Unknown
Designer:	Charles Noke
Height:	5", 12.7 cm
Size:	Medium
Colour:	Cream dog, navy cap, red, white and blue Union Jack
Issued:	1941

Price:	U.S. $	Can. $	U.K. £
	1,400.00	1,500.00	950.00

D 6183
Bulldog Draped in Union Jack With Trinity Cap

Model No.:	Unknown
Designer:	Charles Noke
Height:	2 3/4", 6.9 cm
Size:	Small
Colour:	Cream dog, navy cap, red, white and blue Union Jack
Issued:	1941

Price:	U.S. $	Can. $	U.K. £
	1,250.00	1,500.00	750.00

D 6193A
Bulldog Wearing Sailor Suit and Hat

Model No.:	Unknown
Designer:	Charles Noke
Height:	6", 15.2 cm
Size:	Large
Colour:	Cream dog, navy and white sailor's suit and hat
Issued:	1941

Price:	U.S. $	Can. $	U.K. £
	3,500.00	4,000.00	1,500.00

D 6193B
Bulldog Wearing Sailor Suit and Hat

Model No.:	Unknown
Designer:	Charles Noke
Height:	5", 12.7 cm
Size:	Medium
Colour:	Cream dog, navy and white sailor's suit and hat
Issued:	1941

Price:	*U.S. $*	*Can. $*	*U.K. £*
	3,500.00	4, 000.00	1,500.00

D 6193C
Bulldog Wearing Sailor Suit and Hat

Model No.:	Unknown
Designer:	Charles Noke
Height:	2 3/4", 6.9 cm
Size:	Small
Colour:	Cream dog, navy and white sailor's suit and hat
Issued:	1941

Price:	*U.S. $*	*Can. $*	*U.K. £*
	2,000.00	2,000.00	1,000.00

D 6448
Huntsman Fox

Model No.:	Unknown
Designer:	Unknown
Height:	4 1/2", 11.4 cm
Colour:	Brown fox wearing a maroon jacket, white jodphurs, black hat and boots
Issued:	1956-1981

Price:	*U.S. $*	*Can. $*	*U.K. £*
	175.00	235.00	110.00

D 6449
Christmas Turkey

Model No.:	Unknown
Designer:	Graham Tongue
Height:	6 1/4", 15.9 cm
Colour:	White feathers, red head
Issued:	1990-1990
Varieties:	DA 161

Price:	*U.S. $*	*Can. $*	*U.K. £*
	75.00	125.00	50.00

Commissioned by Sir Bernard Matthews, Norfolk.
A turkey was given to each member of his staff.

ROYAL ADDERLEY
(BIRD STUDIES)

American Blue Bird

Height:	3 3/4", 9.5 cm
Colour:	Blue bird with orange breast; brown nest and white eggs
Issued:	1979-1983

Finish		*Price*	
	U.S. $	*Can. $*	*U.K. £*
Glossy	185.00	250.00	125.00

Baltimore Oriole
Style Five

Height:	4 1/2", 11.4 cm
Colour:	Orange feathers, black head; black and yellow wings and tail feathers
Issued:	1979-1983

Finish		*Price*	
	U.S. $	*Can. $*	*U.K. £*
Glossy	185.00	250.00	125.00

Black-Headed Gouldian Finch

Height:	4", 10.1 cm
Colour:	Black head, pink and yellow breast, green feathers, white and black tail feathers; blue & pink flowers
Issued:	1979-1982
Varieties:	Also called "Red-Headed Gouldian Finch"

Finish		*Price*	
	U.S. $	*Can. $*	*U.K. £*
Glossy	185.00	250.00	125.00

Blue Gnatcatcher

Height:	4", 10.1 cm
Colour:	Blue and pink feathers with black markings, yellow breast
Issued:	1979-1982

Finish		*Price*	
	U.S. $	*Can. $*	*U.K. £*
Glossy	150.00	200.00	100.00

Blue Jay
Style One

Height:	4 3/4", 12.1 cm
Colour:	Blue feathers with black markings, white throat; pink flower
Issued:	1979-1983

Finish		*Price*	
	U.S. $	*Can. $*	*U.K. £*
Glossy	185.00	250.00	125.00

Blue Tit
Style One

Height:	3 3/4", 9.5 cm
Colour:	Yellow feathers, blue head and wings with black and white markings; pink flower
Issued:	1979-1983
Varieties:	Also called "Chicadee, Style One"

Finish		*Price*	
	U.S. $	*Can. $*	*U.K. £*
Glossy	185.00	250.00	125.00

Blue Tit
Style Two

Height:	3 1/4", 9.5 cm
Colour:	Yellow feathers, blue head and wings with black and white markings; pink flower
Issued:	1979-1983
Varieties:	Also alled"Chicadee, Style Two"

Finish		*Price*	
	U.S. $	*Can. $*	*U.K. £*
Glossy	185.00	250.00	125.00

Blue Tit and Young

Height:	4 3/4", 12.1 cm
Colour:	Yellow breasts, brown and green feathers, blue heads with white markings
Issued:	1979-1983

Finish		*Price*	
	U.S. $	*Can. $*	*U.K. £*
Glossy	250.00	350.00	175.00

Blue Tits (two)
Style One

Height: 5 1/4", 13.3 cm
Colour: Yellow breasts, light blue heads and wings
            with white markings; pink flowers
Issued: 1979-1983
Varieties: Also called "Great Tits" and
            "Hudsonian Chicadees"

Finish		Price	
	U.S. $	Can. $	U.K. £
Glossy	200.00	300.00	150.00

Blue Tits (three)
Style Two

Height: 4 3/4", 12.1 cm
Colour: Yellow breasts, light blue heads and wings
            with white markings; pink flowers
Issued: 1979-1983
Varieties: Also called "Chicadees"

Finish		Price	
	U.S. $	Can. $	U.K. £
Glossy	225.00	325.00	150.00

Budgerigar
Style Two - large

Height: 5 1/4", 13.3 cm
Size: Large
Colour: Yellow head and tail feathers, green
          breast, green wings with black markings,
          blue tail feathers
Issued: 1979-1983

Finish		Price	
	U.S. $	Can. $	U.K. £
Glossy	185.00	250.00	125.00
Matt	185.00	250.00	125.00

Budgerigar
Style Two - medium

Height: 4 3/4", 12.1 cm
Size: Medium
Colour: White head, white wings with black
          markings, blue breast and tail feathers;
          yellow and pink flowers
Issued: 1979-1983

Finish		Price	
	U.S. $	Can. $	U.K. £
Glossy	185.00	250.00	125.00
Matt	185.00	250.00	125.00

Budgerigars

Height:	4 1/2", 11.4 cm
Colour:	Yellow and green feathers with black markings; blue and white feathers with black markings
Issued:	1979-1983

Finish	Price		
	U.S. $	Can. $	U.K. £
Glossy	225.00	325.00	150.00
Matt	225.00	325.00	150.00

Canary - orange

Height:	5 1/4", 13.3 cm
Colour:	Orange with black tail feathers, black and red head, red flowers
Issued:	1979-1983
Varieties:	Also called "Canary - yellow"

Finish	Price		
	U.S. $	Can. $	U.K. £
Glossy	185.00	250.00	125.00

Canary - yellow

Height:	5 1/4", 13.3 cm
Colour:	Yellow with black and red markings, white breast
Issued:	1979-1983
Varieties:	Also called "Canary - orange"

Finish	Price		
	U.S. $	Can. $	U.K. £
Glossy	185.00	250.00	125.00
Matt	185.00	250.00	125.00

NOTE ON PRICING

This is a first edition and for the first time a complete list of Doulton animals is being priced. These prices have been arrived at by concensus among knowledgeable dealers. They are not to be considered the final word. An animal figure that is common, appears more often that not in every dealer's inventory and is easy to price. However, when a figure is seldom (if ever) seen its scarcity becomes a problem in establishing its value.

We have used two methods to record prices:
1. Rarity classifications
2. Italicized prices

The rarity classification provides a price range. This simply means that the item should sell in the range given. Italicized prices zero in a little closer than the price range. Italicized prices are the level of the last known sale and serve as a basis for the possible current price. However, it still is an indication only and the next transaction may be higher or lower depending on market demand. When dealing with rare animal figures you always need two willing parties, a willing buyer and a willing seller.

Popularity of a series will exert market pressure that will cause price increases for rare figures. An extremely rare character bird cannot and should not be compared with an extremely rare dog in price level due to the popularity of the dog series. Italicized prices and rarity classifications are interchangeable to a certain degree.

Rarity Classification	Rare	Very Rare	Extremely Rare
U.S. $	1,000./1,500.	1,500./2,000.	2,000./3,000.
Can. $	1,500./2,000.	2,000./3,000.	3,000./4,500.
U.K. £	750./1,000.	1,000./1,500.	1,500./2,250.

N/A (not available) in the pricing table indicates that the item was not available in that particular market.

Cardinal (female)
Style Four

Colour: Yellow face and breast, red head and wings
Issued: 1979-1983
Varieties: Also called "Cardinal - male", "Red-Crested
            Cardinal" and "Virginia Cardinal"

Large
Height: 4 1/2", 11.4 cm

Medium
Height: 4", 10.1 cm

Small
Height: 3 1/2", 8.9 cm

Price	Large	Medium	Small
U.S. $	250.00	185.00	150.00
Can. $	325.00	250.00	200.00
U.K. £	150.00	1250.00	100.00

Cardinal (male)
Style Five

Colour: Red feathers with yellow highlights,
            yellow tail feathers, pink flower
Issued: 1979-1983
Varieties: Also called "Cardinal - female",
            "Red-Crested Cardinal" and
            "Virginia Cardinal"

Large
Height: 5", 12.7 cm

Medium
Height: 4 1/2", 11.4 cm

Small
Height: 3 1/2", 8.9 cm

	Large	Medium	Small
U.S. $	250.00	185.00	150.00
Can. $	325.00	250.00	200.00
U.K. £	150.00	125.00	100.00

Cardinals

Height:	5 1/4", 13.3 cm
Colour:	Red and yellow; purple flowers
Issued:	1979-1983

Finish		*Price*	
	U.S. $	*Can. $*	*U.K. £*
Glossy	250.00	350.00	175.00

Chaffinch
Style Three

Height:	4 1/4", 10.8 cm
Colour:	Yellow and pink breast, black head, white, yellow and pink wings with black markings, pink and yellow flowers
Issued:	1979-1983
Varieties:	Also called "Coppersmith Barbet"

Finish		*Price*	
	U.S. $	*Can. $*	*U.K. £*
Glossy	185.00	250.00	125.00

Chicadee
Style One

Height:	3 3/4", 9.5 cm
Colour:	Dark blue head, white breast, brown feathers with black markings, pink flowers
Issued:	1979-1983
Varieties:	Also called "Blue Tit - Style Two"

Finish		*Price*	
	U.S. $	*Can. $*	*U.K. £*
Glossy	185.00	250.00	125.00

Chicadee
Style Two

Height:	3 1/2', 8.9 cm
Colour:	Dark blue head, white breast, brown feathers with black markings, pink flowers
Issued:	1979-1983
Varieties:	Also called "Blue Tit - Style Two"

Finish		*Price*	
	U.S. $	*Can. $*	*U.K. £*
Glossy	185.00	250.00	125.00

Chicadees

Height:	4 3/4", 12.1 cm
Colour:	Dark blue head, white breast, brown feathers with white markings, pink and yellow flowers
Issued:	1979-1983
Varieties:	Also called "Blue Tits - Style Two"

Finish		Price	
	U.S. $	Can. $	U.K.£
Glossy	200.00	300.00	150.00

Coppersmith Barbet

Height:	4 1/2", 11.4 cm
Colour:	Red and black head, yellow breast with black markings, pink flowers
Issued:	1979-1983

Finish		Price	
	U.S. $	Can. $	U.K. £
Glossy	185.00	250.00	125.00

English Robin
Style Two

Height:	4 1/2", 11.4 cm
Colour:	Red breast, brown feathers, red flowers
Issued:	1979-1983
Varieties:	Also called "Pekin Robin"

Finish		Price	
	U.S. $	Can. $	U.K. £
Glossy	185.00	250.00	125.00
Matt	185.00	250.00	125.00

Photograph
Not Available
At Press Time

Goldfinch
Style Two

Height:	3 3/4", 9.5 cm
Colour:	Unknown
Issued:	1979-1983

Finish		Price	
	U.S. $	Can. $	U.K. £
Glossy	185.00	250.00	125.00

Great Tits

Height:	5 1/4". 13.3 cm
Colour:	Dark blue heads, yellow feathers, blue wings and tail feathers with black and white markings, pink flowers
Issued:	1979-1983
Varieties:	Also called "Blue Tits - Style One" and "Hudsonian Chicadees"

Finish	Price		
	U.S. $	Can. $	U.K. £
Glossy	200.00	300.00	150.00

Hudsonian Chicadees

Height:	5 1/4", 13.3 cm
Colour:	Red heads, yellow breasts, black and yellow wings and tail feathers, pink flowers
Issued:	1979-1983
Varieties:	Also called "Blue Tits - Style One" and "Great Tits"

Finish	Price		
	U.S. $	Can. $	U.K. £
Glossy	200.00	300.00	150.00

Photograph
Not Available
At Press Time

Humming Bird

Height:	3 3/4", 9.5 cm
Colour:	Blue and green feathers with black markings, black beak, pink flowers
Issued:	1979-1983

Finish	Price		
	U.S. $	Can. $	U.K. £
Glossy	185.00	250.00	125.00

Mallard - Landing

Height:	3 1/2", 8.9 cm
Colour:	Unknown
Issued:	1979-1983

Finish	Price		
	U.S. $	Can. $	U.K. £
Glossy	225.00	325.00	150.00

Painted Bunting
Height: 3", 7.6 cm
Colour: Blue head, red breast, green wings with
            black markings, maroon tail feathers,
            pink flowers
Issued: 1979-1983

Finish	Price		
	U.S. $	Can. $	U.K. £
Glossy	185.00	250.00	125.00
Matt	185.00	250.00	125.00

Parakeet
Height: 5", 12.7 cm
Colour: Green, red and blue, pink flowers
Issued: 1979-1982

Finish	Price		
	U.S. $	Can. $	U.K. £
Glossy	185.00	250.00	125.00

Parakeets
Height: 6", 15.2 cm
Colour: Blue, green, red and yellow,
            pink flowers
Issued: 1979-1982

Finish	Price		
	U.S. $	Can. $	U.K. £
Glossy	225.00	325.00	150.00

Pekin Robin
Height: 4 1/2", 11.5 cm
Colour: Red, yellow and brown, red flowers
Issued: 1979-1982
Varieties: Also called "English Robin - Style Two"

Finish	Price		
	U.S. $	Can. $	U.K. £
Glossy	185.00	250.00	125.00

Red Crested Cardinal

Colour:	Red head, grey-white body, grey wings and tail feathers with black markings
Issued:	1979-1983
Varieties:	Also called "Cardinal - female", "Cardinal - male" and "Virginia Cardinal"

Medium

Height:	4", 10.1 cm

Small

Height:	3 1/3", 8.9 cm

Price	Medium	Small
U.S. $	225.00	185.00
Can. $	325.00	250.00
U.K. £	150.00	125.00

Red-Headed Gouldian Finch

Height:	4", 10.1 cm
Colour:	Red and black head, green wings with black markings, pink and yellow breast
Issued:	1979-1983
Varieties:	Also called "Black-Headed Gouldian Finch"

Finish	Price		
	U.S. $	Can. $	U.K. £
Glossy	185.00	250.00	125.00

Robin with Can

Height:	4", 10.1 cm
Colour:	Brown, red, green and pink. White and yellow outer piece
Issued:	1979-1983

Finish	Price		
	U.S. $	Can. $	U.K. £
Glossy	300.00	400.00	200.00
Matt	300.00	400.00	200.00

Tanager

Height:	4", 10.1 cm
Colour:	Red head, yellow and black feathers
Issued:	1979-1983

Finish	Price		
	U.S. $	Can. $	U.K. £
Glossy	185.00	250.00	125.00

Warbler Tall

Height:	6 1/2", 16.5 cm
Colour:	Blue and yellow feathers with black markings; orange and yellow bird with black markings; purple flowers
Issued:	1979-1983

Finish	Price		
Glossy	185.00	250.00	125.00

Virginia Cardinal

Colour:	Red
Issued:	1979-1982
Varieties:	Also called "Cardinal - female", "Cardinal - male" and "Red-Crested Cardinal"

Large

Height:	5", 12.7 cm

Medium

Height:	4 1/2", 11.4 cm

Small

Height:	3 1/2", 8.9 cm

Price	Large	Medium	Small
U.S. $	225.00	185.00	150.00
Can. $	325.00	250.00	200.00
U.K. £	150.00	125.00	100.00

254

3000L
Golden Eagle
Style One

Designer:	Carter Jones		
Height:	11", 27.9 cm		
Size:	Large		
Colour:	Dark brown, white beak		
Issued:	1980 in a limited edition of 3,000		
Series:	Bronze Menagerie / Americana Collection		

Price:	*U.S. $*	*Can. $*	*U.K. £*
	200.00	250.00	100.00

3002M
Golden Eagle
Style Two

Designer:	Carter Jones		
Height:	4 3/4", 12.1 cm		
Size:	Medium		
Colour:	Dark brown, white beak		
Issued:	1980 in a limited edition of 9,500		
Series:	Bronze Menagerie / Americana Collection		

Price:	*U.S. $*	*Can. $*	*U.K. £*
	50.00	70.00	35.00

3004M
Cougar
Style One

Designer:	Carter Jones		
Height:	4 1/2", 11.4 cm		
Size:	Medium		
Colour:	Grey-brown, with brown stump		
Issued:	1980 in a limited edition of 9,500		
Series:	Bronze Menagerie / Americana Collection		

Price:	*U.S. $*	*Can. $*	*U.K. £*
	70.00	95.00	45.00

3006S
Golden Eagle
Style Three

Designer:	Carter Jones		
Height:	3 1/2", 8.9 cm		
Size:	Small		
Colour:	Dark browns		
Issued:	1980		
Series:	Bronze Menagerie / Americana Collection		

Price:	*U.S. $*	*Can. $*	*U.K. £*
	30.00	40.00	20.00

3008S
Buffalo

Designer:	Carter Jones
Height:	3", 7.6 cm
Size:	Small
Colour:	Dark brown and green
Issued:	1980
Series:	Bronze Menagerie / Americana Collection

Price:	*U.S. $*	*Can. $*	*U.K. £*
	30.00	40.00	20.00

3010S
Bighorned Mountain Sheep

Designer:	Carter Jones
Height:	3 1/2", 8.9 cm
Size:	Small
Colour:	Browns and grey
Issued:	1980
Series:	Bronze Menagerie / Americana Collection

Price:	*U.S. $*	*Can. $*	*U.K. £*
	30.00	40.00	20.00

3012S
Cottontail Rabbit

Designer:	Carter Jones
Height:	2", 5.1 cm
Size:	Small
Colour:	Green and brown
Issued:	1980
Series:	Bronze Menagerie / Americana Collection

Price:	*U.S. $*	*Can. $*	*U.K. £*
	30.00	40.00	20.00

3014S
Cougar
Style Two

Designer:	Carter Jones
Height:	2 1/2", 6.3 cm
Size:	Small
Colour:	Browns
Issued:	1980
Series:	Bronze Menagerie / Americana Collection

Price:	*U.S. $*	*Can. $*	*U.K. £*
	30.00	40.00	20.00

3016S
Northeastern Chipmunk

Designer:	Carter Jones		
Height:	2 3/4", 7.0 cm		
Size:	Small		
Colour:	Grey, dark brown and dark green		
Issued:	1980		
Series:	Bronze Menagerie / Americana Collection		

Price:	*U.S. $*	*Can. $*	*U.K. £*
	30.00	40.00	20.00

3018S
Armadillo

Designer:	Valerie Skidmore		
Height:	2 1/4", 5.7 cm		
Size:	Small		
Colour:	Brown and grey		
Issued:	1981		
Series:	Bronze Menagerie / Americana Collection		

Price:	*U.S. $*	*Can. $*	*U.K. £*
	30.00	40.00	20.00

3020S
Leopard Frog

Designer:	Jean William		
Height:	2 3/4", 7.0 cm		
Size:	Small		
Colour:	Greens, black and brown		
Issued:	1981		
Series:	Bronze Menagerie / Americana Collection		

Price:	*U.S. $*	*Can. $*	*U.K. £*
	30.00	40.00	20.00

3022S
Wild Burro

Designer:	Carter Jones		
Height:	2 3/4", 7.0 cm		
Size:	Small		
Colour:	Black and dark green		
Issued:	1981		
Series:	Bronze Menagerie / Americana Collection		

Price:	*U.S. $*	*Can. $*	*U.K. £*
	30.00	40.00	20.00

3024S
Great Grey Owl

Designer:	Jean Williams
Height:	3", 7.6 cm
Size:	Small
Colour:	Dark brown, grey and green
Issued:	1981
Series:	Bronze Menagerie / Americana Collection

Price:	U.S. $	Can. $	U.K. £
	30.00	40.00	20.00

3026S
Great Horned Owl

Designer:	Jean Williams
Height:	3 1/4", 8.3 cm
Size:	Small
Colour:	Dark brown and dark green
Issued:	1981
Series:	Bronze Menagerie / Americana Collection

Price:	U.S. $	Can. $	U.K. £
	30.00	40.00	20.00

3028S
Screech Owl

Designer:	Carter Jones
Height:	3 1/4", 8.3 cm
Size:	Small
Colour:	Red-brown and grey
Issued:	1981
Series:	Bronze Menagerie / Americana Collection

Price:	U.S. $	Can. $	U.K. £
	30.00	40.00	20.00

3030S
Snowy Owl
Style Three

Designer:	Carter Jones
Height:	3", 7.6 cm
Size:	Small
Colour:	Grey and brown
Issued:	1981
Series:	Bronze Menagerie / Americana Collection

Price:	U.S. $	Can. $	U.K. £
	30.00	40.00	20.00

3032S
Black Bear

Designer:	Carter Jones
Height:	2 3/4", 7.0 cm
Size:	Small
Colour:	Black and green
Issued:	1980
Series:	Bronze Menagerie / Americana Collection

| *Price:* | *U.S. $* | *Can. $* | *U.K. £* |
| | 30.00 | 40.00 | 20.00 |

3034S
Raccoon

Designer:	Carter Jones
Height:	2 1/4", 5.7 cm
Size:	Small
Colour:	Dark brown and dark green
Issued:	1980
Series:	Bronze Menagerie / Americana Collection

| *Price:* | *U.S. $* | *Can. $* | *U.K. £* |
| | 30.00 | 40.00 | 20.00 |

3036S
Snowshoe Hare

Designer:	Valerie Skidmore
Height:	3 1/4", 8.3 cm
Size:	Small
Colour:	Brown, grey and dark green
Issued:	1980
Series:	Bronze Menagerie / Americana Collection

| *Price:* | *U.S. $* | *Can. $* | *U.K. £* |
| | 30.00 | 40.00 | 20.00 |

3201L
African Elephant
Style One

Designer:	Carter Jones
Height:	8", 20.3 cm
Size:	Large
Colour:	Grey, slate and green
Issued:	1981 in a limited edition of 3,000
Series:	Bronze Menagerie / Safari Collection

| *Price:* | *U.S. $* | *Can. $* | *U.K. £* |
| | 350.00 | 400.00 | 200.00 |

3203M
African Elephant
Style Two

Designer:	Valerie Skidmore
Height:	4 3/4", 12.1 cm
Size:	Medium
Colour:	Grey, white, green and brown
Issued:	1981 in a limited edition of 3,000
Series:	Bronze Menagerie / Safari Collection

Price:	*U.S. $*	*Can. $*	*U.K. £*
	100.00	125.00	50.00

3205M
Lioness
Style One

Designer:	Carter Jones
Height:	4", 10.1 cm
Size:	Medium
Colour:	Browns
Issued:	1981
Series:	Bronze Menagerie / Safari Collection

Price:	*U.S. $*	*Can. $*	*U.K. £*
	75.00	95.00	40.00

3207S
Baboon

Designer:	Carter Jones
Height:	2 1/2" x 6.4 cm
Size:	Small
Colour:	Grey, slate and green
Issued:	1981
Series:	Bronze Menagerie / Safari Collection

Price:	*U.S. $*	*Can. $*	*U.K. £*
	30.00	40.00	20.00

3209S
Cheetah

Designer:	Carter Jones
Height:	3", 7.6 cm
Size:	Small
Colour:	Browns and green
Issued:	1981
Series:	Bronze Menagerie / Safari Collection

Price:	*U.S. $*	*Can. $*	*U.K. £*
	30.00	40.00	20.00

3211S
Hippopotamus

Designer:	Carter Jones
Height:	2 1/4", 5.7 cm
Size:	Small
Colour:	Dark grey and dark green
Issued:	1981
Series:	Bronze Menagerie / Safari Collection

Price:	U.S. $	Can. $	U.K. £
	30.00	40.00	20.00

3213S
Kudu

Designer:	Valerie Skidmore
Height:	2 3/4", 7.0 cm
Size:	Small
Colour:	Brown, white, grey, green grass
Issued:	1980
Series:	Bronze Menagerie / Safari Collection

Price:	U.S. $	Can. $	U.K. £
	30.00	40.00	20.00

3215S
Lioness
Style Two

Designer:	Carter Jones
Height:	2 1/4", 5.7 cm
Size:	Small
Colour:	Light brown, green grass, brown tree stump
Issued:	1981
Series:	Bronze Menagerie / Safari Collection

Price:	U.S. $	Can. $	U.K. £
	30.00	40.00	20.00

3217S
Markhor Goat

Designer:	Valerie Skidmore
Height:	3 1/2", 8.9 cm
Size:	Small
Colour:	Grey, greyish brown, slate rocks
Issued:	1981
Series:	Bronze Menagerie / Safari Collection

Price:	U.S. $	Can. $	U.K. £
	30.00	40.00	20.00

3219S
Tiger Preying

Designer:	Carter Jones		
Height:	3 1/2", 8.9 cm		
Colour:	Browns and dark green		
Issued:	1981		
Series:	Bronze Menagerie / Safari Collection		

Price:	*U.S. $*	*Can. $*	*U.K. £*
	30.00	40.00	20.00

3221S
Elephant Calf

Designer:	Valerie Skidmore
Height:	3 1/2", 8.9 cm
Size:	Small
Colour:	Grey, Grey rocks
Issued:	1981
Series:	Bronze Menagerie / Safari Collection

Price:	*U.S. $*	*Can. $*	*U.K. £*
	30.00	40.00	20.00

3301S
Pig and Piglets

Designer:	Valerie Skidmore
Height:	2 1/4", 5.7 cm
Size:	Small
Colour:	Light grey, brown ground
Issued:	1982
Series:	Bronze Menagerie / Country Collection

Price:	*U.S. $*	*Can> $*	*U.K. £*
	30.00	40.00	20.00

3302S
Turkeys

Designer:	Valerie Skidmore
Height:	3", 7.6 cm
Size:	Small
Colour	Grey, red, brown, white and green
Issued:	1982
Series:	Bronze Menagerie / Country Collection

Price:	*U.S. $*	*Can. $*	*U.K. £*
	30.00	40.00	20.00

3303S
Chickens

Designer:	Valerie Skidmore
Height:	Unknown
Size:	Unknown
Colour:	Red, maroon, grey, brown basket
Issued:	1982
Series:	Bronze Menagerie / Country Collection

Price:	*U.S. $*	*Can. $*	*U.K. £*
	30.00	40.00	20.00

3304S
Cows

Designer:	Valerie Skidmore
Height:	2 1/2", 6.4 cm
Size:	Small
Colour:	White and black with green grass
Issued:	1982
Series:	Bronze Menagerie / Country Collection

Price:	*U.S. $*	*Can. $*	*U.K. £*
	30.00	40.00	20.00

3305S
Rooster
Style Two

Designer:	Valerie Skidmore
Height:	3 1/4", 8.3 cm
Size:	Small
Colour:	Red, yellow, reddish brown
Issued:	1982
Series:	Bronze Menagerie / Country Collection

Price:	*U.S. $*	*Can. $*	*U.K. £*
	30.00	40.00	20.00

3306S
Ducks

Designer:	Valerie Skidmore
Height:	2 1/4", 5.7 cm
Size:	Small
Colour:	Green and brown
Issued:	1982
Series:	Bronze Menagerie / Country Collection

Price:	*U.S. $*	*Can. $*	*U.K. £*
	30.00	40.00	20.00

3307S
Collies

Designer:	Valerie Skidmore
Height:	2 1/4", 5.7 cm
Size:	Small
Colour:	Light brown, white
Issued:	1982
Series:	Bronze Menagerie / Country Collection

Price:	*U.S. $*	*Can. $*	*U.K. £*
	30.00	40.00	20.00

3400M
Deer
Style Two

Model No.:	Unknown
Designer:	Valerie Skidmore
Height:	4", 10.1 cm
Size:	Medium
Colour:	Browns and dark green
Issued:	1981
Series:	Bronze Menagerie / Family Collection

Price:	*U.S. $*	*Can. $*	*U.K. £*
	80.00	100.00	50.00

3402M
Giraffes
Style One

Designer:	Valerie Skidmore
Height:	5 1/2", 14.0 cm
Size:	Medium
Colour:	Red-brown, grey and green
Issued:	1981
Series:	Bronze Menagerie / Family Collection

Price:	*U.S. $*	*Can. $*	*U.K. £*
	95.00	125.00	75.00

3404M
Mare and Colt

Designer:	Valerie Skidmore
Height:	5 1/2", 14.0 cm
Size:	Medium
Colour:	Brown, black, white and green
Issued:	1981
Series:	Bronze Menagerie / Family Collection

Price:	*U.S. $*	*Can. $*	*U.K. £*
	135.00	150.00	75.00

3406S
Chimpanzees

Designer:	Jean Williams
Height:	3", 7.6 cm
Size:	Small
Colour:	Browns and dark green
Issued:	1980
Series:	Bronze Menagerie / Family Collection

Price:	*U.S. $*	*Can. $*	*U.K. £*
	30.00	40.00	20.00

3408S
Deer
Style Three

Designer:	Valerie Skidmore
Height:	2", 5.1 cm
Size:	Small
Colour:	Brown, grey and dark green
Issued:	1981
Series:	Bronze Menagerie / Family Collection

Price:	*U.S. $*	*Can. $*	*U.K. £*
	30.00	40.00	20.00

3410S
Giant Pandas

Designer:	Valerie Skidmore
Height:	3", 7.6 cm
Size:	Small
Colour:	Black, white and dark brown
Issued:	1981
Series:	Bronze Menagerie / Family Collection

Price:	*U.S. $*	*Can. $*	*U.K. £*
	30.00	40.00	20.00

3412S
Giraffes
Style Two

Designer:	Valerie Skidmore
Height:	3 1/2", 8.9 cm
Size:	Small
Colour:	Red-brown, white and dark green
Issued:	1981
Series:	Bronze Menagerie / Family Collection

Price:	*U.S. $*	*Can. $*	*U.K. £*
	30.00	40.00	20.00

3414S
Harvest Mice

Designer:	Valerie Skidmore
Height:	2 3/4", 7.0 cm
Size:	Small
Colour:	Browns, grey and green
Issued:	1980
Series:	Bronze Menagerie / Family Collection

Price:	*U.S. $*	*Can. $*	*U.K. £*
	30.00	40.00	20.00

3416S
Kangaroos

Designer:	Valerie Skidmore
Height:	3 1/2", 8.9 cm
Size:	Small
Colour:	Brown, grey and green
Issued:	1980
Series:	Bronze Menagerie / Family Collection

Price:	*U.S. $*	*Can. $*	*U.K. £*
	30.00	40.00	20.00

3418S
Koala Bears

Designer:	Valerie Skidmore
Height:	3 1/4", 8.2 cm
Size:	Small
Colour:	Browns, grey and green
Issued:	1980
Series:	Bronze Menagerie / Family Collection

Price:	*U.S. $*	*Can. $*	*U.K. £*
	30.00	40.00	20.00

3420S
Pinto Mare and Colt

Designer:	Valerie Skidmore
Height:	3 1/4", 8.3 cm
Size:	Small
Colour:	Brown and white horses
Issued:	1981
Series:	Bronze Menagerie / Family Collection

Price:	*U.S. $*	*Can. $*	*U.K. £*
	30.00	40.00	20.00

3422S
Orang-Utans

Designer:	Valerie Skidmore
Height:	3", 7.6 cm
Size:	Small
Colour:	Dark brown, dark green
Issued:	1981
Series:	Bronze Menagerie / Family Collection

Price:	U.S. $	Can. $	U.K. £
	30.00	40.00	20.00

3424S
Shaggy Dogs

Designer:	Valerie Skidmore
Height:	2", 5.1 cm
Size:	Small
Colour:	White, brown with green grass
Issued:	1981
Series:	Bronze Menagerie / Family Collection

Price:	U.S. $	Can. $	U.K
	30.00	40.00	20.00

3426S
River Otters

Designer:	Valerie Skidmore
Height:	3 1/2", 8.9 cm
Size:	Small
Colour:	Dark brown, grey and blue
Issued:	1980
Series:	Bronze Menagerie / Family Collection

Price:	U.S. $	Can. $	U.K. £
	30.00	40.00	20.00

3601M
Baby Sittin'

Designer:	Jeam William
Height:	3", 7.6 cm
Size:	Medium
Colour:	Brown, black, white, multi-coloured cushion
Issued:	1980 limited edition of 10,000
Series:	Bronze Menagerie / Playmates Collection

Price:	U.S. $	Can. $	U.K. £
	50.00	75.00	40.00

3603M
Kissin' Cousins

Designer:	Jean Williams
Height:	3", 7.6 cm
Size:	Medium
Colour:	Brown, gray, red and black
Issued:	1980 limited edition of 10,000
Series:	Bronze Menagerie / Playmates Collection

Price:	*U.S. $*	*Can. $*	*U.K. £*
	50.00	75.00	40.00

3605M
Lickin' Good

Designer:	Jean Williams
Height:	3 12/", 8.9 cm
Size:	Medium
Colour:	Black and white, brown, multi-coloured rug
Issued:	1980 limited edition of 10,000
Series:	Bronze Menagerie / Playmates Collection

Price:	*U.S. $*	*Can. $*	*U.K. £*
	50.00	75.00	40.00

3606M
Snoozin'

Designer:	Jean Williams
Height:	2 1/4", 5.7 cm
Size:	Medium
Colour:	Brown, white, grey, green cushion
Issued:	1982 limited edition of 10,000
Series:	Bronze Menagerie / Playmates Collection

Price:	*U.S. $*	*Can. $*	*U.K. £*
	50.00	75.00	40.00

3607S
Wakin'

Designer:	Valerie Skidmore
Height:	1 1/2", 5.1 cm
Size:	Small
Colour:	Brown, tan, blue-green pillow
Issued:	1982
Series:	Bronze Menagerie / Playmates Collection

Price:	*U.S. $*	*Can. $*	*U.K. £*
	50.00	75.00	40.00

3608S
Hidin'

Designer:	Valerie Skidmore
Height:	2", 5.1 cm
Size:	Small
Colour:	Light brown, grey, tan hat and red
Issued:	1982
Series:	Bronze Menagerie / Playmates Collection

Price:	*U.S. $*	*Can. $*	*U.K. £*
	50.00	75.00	40.00

3609S
Shooin'

Designer:	Valerie Skidmore
Height:	3", 7.6 cm
Size:	Medium
Colour:	Grey, white with red cushion
Issued:	1982
Series:	Bronze Menagerie / Playmates Collection

Price:	*U.S. $*	*Can. $*	*U.K. £*
	50.00	75.00	40.00

Photograph
Not Available
At Press Time

3610S
Tuggin'

Designer:	Valerie Skidmore
Height:	1 1/2", 5.1 cm
Size:	Small
Colour:	White, brown, brown and blue mat
Issued:	1982
Series:	Bronze Menagerie / Playmates Collection

Price:	*U.S. $*	*Can. $*	*U.K. £*
	50.00	75.00	40.00

3611S
Cuddlin'

Designer:	Valerie Skidmore
Height:	2 1/2", 6.4 cm
Size:	Small
Colour:	White, black and brown
Issued:	1982
Series:	Bronze Menagerie / Playmates Collection

Price:	*U.S. $*	*Can. $*	*U.K. £*
	50.00	75.00	40.00

3612S
Huggin'

Designer:	Valerie Skidmore
Height:	2 3/4", 7.0 cm
Size:	Small
Colour:	Black, brown, green blanket
Issued:	1982
Series:	Bronze Menagerie / Playmates Collection

Price:

	U.S. $	Can. $	U.K. £
	50.00	75.00	40.00

Photograph
Not Available
At Press Time

4000
Barred Owl

Designer:	Unknown
Height:	Unknown
Colour:	Unknown
Issued:	Unknown
Series:	Bronze Menagerie / Fine Feathers Collection / Birds of Prey

Price:

	U.S. $	Can. $	U.K. £
	75.00	100.00	50.00

Photograph
Not Available
At Press Time

4002
Golden Eagle
Style Four

Designer:	Unknown
Height:	Unknown
Colour:	Unknown
Issued:	Unknown
Series:	Bronze Menagerie / Fine Feathers Collection / Birds of Prey

Price:

	U.S. $	Can. $	U.K. £
	95.00	125.00	50.00

Photograph
Not Available
At Press Time

4201
Belted Kingfisher

Designer:	Unknown
Height:	Unknown
Colour:	Unknown
Issued:	Unknown
Series:	Bronze Menagerie / Fine Feathers Collection / Songbirds

Price:

	U.S. $	Can. $	U.K. £
	95.00	125.00	50.00

Photograph
Not Available
At Press Time

4203
Blue Jay
Style Two

Designer: Unknown
Height: Unknown
Colour: Unknown
Issued: Unknown
Series: Bronze Menagerie / Fine Feathers
               Collection / Songbirds

Price:	*U.S. $*	*Can. $*	*U.K. £*
	95.00	125.00	50.00

Photograph
Not Available
At Press Time

4205
Cedar Waxwing

Designer: Unknown
Height: Unknown
Colour: Unknown
Issued: Unknown
Series: Bronze Menagerie / Fine Feathers
               Collection / Songbirds

Price:	*U.S. $*	*Can. $*	*U.K. £*
	95.00	125.00	50.00

Photograph
Not Available
At Press Time

4207
Downy Woodpecker
Style Two

Designer: Unknown
Height: Unknown
Colour: Unknown
Issued: Unknown
Series: Bronze Menagerie / Fine Feathers
               Collection / Songbirds

Price:	*U.S. $*	*Can. $*	*U.K. £*
	95.00	125.00	50.00

Photograph
Not Available
At Press Time

4209
Marsh Wren

Designer: Unknown
Height: Unknown
Colour: Unknown
Issued: Unknown
Series: Bronze Menagerie / Fine Feathers
               Collection / Songbirds

Price:	*U.S. $*	*Can. $*	*U.K. £*
	95.00	125.00	50.00

4211
Mockingbird

Designer:	Unknown
Height:	Unknown
Colour:	Unknown
Issued:	Unknown
Series:	Bronze Menagerie / Fine Feathers Collection / Songbirds

Price:	*U.S. $*	*Can. $*	*U.K. £*
	95.00	125.00	50.00

4213
White Breasted Nuthatch

Designer:	Unknown
Height:	Unknown
Colour:	Unknown
Issued:	Bronze Menagerie / Fine Feathers Collection / Songbirds

Price:	*U.S. $*	*Can. $*	*U.K. £*
	95.00	125.00	50.00

4215
American Redstart

Designer:	Unknown
Height:	Unknown
Colour:	Unknown
Issued:	Unknown
Series:	Bronze Menagerie / Fine Feathers Collection / Songbirds

Price:	*U.S. $*	*Can. $*	*U.K. £*
	95.00	125.00	50.00

4217
Tufted Titmouse

Designer:	Unknown
Height:	Unknown
Colour:	Unknown
Issued:	Unknown
Series:	Bronze Menagerie / Fine Feathers Collection / Songbirds

Price:	*U.S. $*	*Can. $*	*U.K. £*
	95.00	125.00	50.00

4400
Canada Goose

Designer:	Unknown
Height:	Unknown
Colour:	Unknown
Issued:	Unknown
Series:	Bronze Menagerie / Fine Feathers Collection / Waterfowl

Price:	U.S. $	Can. $	U.K. £
	125.00	150.00	50.00

4402
Common Mallard

Designer:	Unknown
Height:	Unknown
Colour:	Unknown
Issued:	Unknown
Series:	Bronze Menagerie / Fine Feathers Collection / Waterfowl

Price:	U.S. $	Can. $	U.K. £
	125.00	150.00	50.00

4404
Whistling Swan

Designer:	Unknown
Height:	Unknown
Colour:	Unknown
Issued:	Unknown
Series:	Bronze Menagerie / Fine Feathers Collection / Waterfowl

Price:	U.S. $	Can. $	U.K. £
	125.00	150.00	50.00

4406
Wood Duck

Designer:	Unknown
Height:	Unknown
Colour:	Unknown
Issued:	Unknown
Series:	Bronze Menagerie / Fine Feathers Collection / Waterfowl

Price:	U.S. $	Can. $	U.K. £
	125.00	150.00	50.00

DA SERIES

Spirit of the Wild

12"/30cm

DA 1
Barn Owl (Tyto Alba)
Style Two

Model No.: Unknown
Designer: Graham Tongue
Height: 11", 27.9 cm
Colour: Golden feathers with dark brown markings
Issued: 1989 to the present
Series: Wildlife Collection / Connoisseur

Price:	U.S. $	Can. $	U.K. £
	1,645.00	N/A	499.00

DA 2
Robin on Branch

Model No.: Unknown
Designer: Graham Tongue
Height: 6 1/4", 15.9 cm
Colour: Red breast, red-brown feathers with black highlights
Issued: 1989-1992
Series: Garden Birds

Price:	U.S. $	Can. $	U.K. £
	196.00	225.00	60.00

DA 3
Suspended Blue Tit

Model No.: Unknown
Designer: Martyn C. R. Alcock
Height: 5", 12.7 cm
Colour: Yellow breast, blue feathers with black markings
Issued: 1989-1992
Series: Garden Birds

Price:	U.S. $	Can. $	U.K. £
	196.00	225.00	75.00

DA 4
Wren
Style Two

Model No.: Unknown
Designer: Martyn C. R. Alcock
Height: 5 1/4", 13.3 cm
Colour: Light brown feathers with dark brown markings
Issued: 1989-1992
Series: Garden Birds

Price:	U.S. $	Can. $	U.K. £
	196.00	225.00	75.00

DA 5
Chaffinch
Style Four

Model No.:	Unknown		
Designer:	Warren Platt		
Height:	6", 15.2 cm		
Colour:	Reddish-brown with yellow and black highlights		
Issued:	1989-1992		
Series:	Garden Birds		

Price:	*U.S. $*	*Can. $*	*U.K. £*
	196.00	225.00	75.00

DA 6
Hare
Standing - Style Two

Model No.:	Unknown
Designer:	Warren Platt
Height:	8 1/2", 21.6 cm
Colour:	Golden brown hare with white highlights
Issued:	1989-1992
Series:	Wildlife Collection

Price:	*U.S. $*	*Can. $*	*U.K. £*
	298.00	350.00	125.00

DA 7
Otter

Model No.:	Unknown
Designer:	Amanda Hughes-Lubeck
Height:	9", 22.9 cm
Colour:	Black and white
Issued:	1989-1992
Series:	Wildlife Collection

Price:	*U.S. $*	*Can. $*	*U.K. £*
	298.00	350.00	125.00

DA 8
Badger
Style Two

Model No.:	Unknown
Designer:	Amanda Hughes-Lubeck
Height:	5 1/2", 14.0 cm
Colour:	Black with black and white striped face
Issued:	1989-1992
Series:	Wildlife Collection

Price:	*U.S. $*	*Can. $*	*U.K. £*
	298.00	350.00	100.00

DA 9
Fox
Standing

Model No.:	Unknown
Designer:	Warren Platt
Height:	7 1/2", 19.1 cm
Colour:	Brown fox with dark brown highlights, white neck and tail end
Issued:	1989-1992
Series:	Wildlife Collection

Price:	U.S. $	Can. $	U.K. £
	298.00	350.00	125.00

DA 10
Fox with Cub

Model No.:	Unknown
Designer:	Warren Platt
Height:	6 1/2", 16.5 cm
Colour:	Brown
Issued:	1989-1992
Series:	Wildlife Collection

Price:	U.S. $	Can. $	U.K. £
	175.00	200.00	75.00

DA 11
Wood Mice

Model No.:	Unknown
Designer:	Amanda Hughes-Lubeck
Height:	7 1/2", 19.1 cm
Colour:	Brown mice, cream mushroom
Issued:	1989-1992
Series:	Wildlife Collection

Price:	U.S. $	Can. $	U.K. £
	250.00	275.00	125.00

DA 12
Robin on Apple

Model No.:	Unknown
Designer:	Graham Tongue
Height:	6 1/4", 15.9 cm
Colour:	Red breast, red-brown feathers with black markings; yellow apple
Issued:	1989-1992
Series:	Garden Birds

Price:	U.S. $	Can. $	U.K. £
	175.00	200.00	75.00

DA 13
Blue Tit with Matches

Model No.:	Unknown
Designer:	Martyn C. R. Alcock
Height:	6 3/4", 17.2 cm
Colour:	Blue and yellow bird, brown and cream box of matches
Issued:	1989-1992
Series:	Garden Birds

Price:	U.S. $	Can. $	U.K. £
	196.00	225.00	100.00

DA 14
Arab Colt 'Xayal'

Beswick No.:	1265
Designer:	Arthur Gredington
Height:	7 1/4", 18.4 cm
Colour:	Dark brown (matt)
Issued:	1989-1990
Series:	Connoisseur Horses

Price:	U.S. $	Can. $	U.K. £
	275.00	375.00	175.00

DA 15
'Arkle'
Style One

Beswick No.:	2065
Designer:	Arthur Gredington
Height:	12", 30.5 cm
Colour:	Bay (matt)
Issued:	1989 to the present
Series:	Connoisseur Horses

Price:	U.S. $	Can. $	U.K. £
	350.00	N/A	149.00

DA 16
'Nijinsky'

Beswick No.:	2345
Designer:	Albert Hallam
Height:	11", 27.9 cm
Colour:	Bay (matt)
Issued:	1989 to the present
Series:	Connoisseur Horses

Price:	U.S. $	Can. $	U.K. £
	350.00	N/A	149.00

DA 17A
Black Beauty and Foal

Beswick No.:	2466/2536
Designer:	Graham Tongue
Height:	8", 20.3 cm
Colour:	Black (matt)
Issued:	1989 to the present
Series:	Connoisseur Horses
Varieties:	DA 17B

Price:	*U.S. $*	*Can. $*	*U.K. £*
	N/A	268.00	79.95

DA 17B
Black Beauty and Foal

Beswick No.:	2466/2536
Designer:	Graham Tongue
Height:	8", 20.3 cm
Colour:	Black (glossy)
Issued:	1989-1990
Series:	Connoisseur Horses
Varieties:	DA 17A

Price:	*U.S. $*	*Can. $*	*U.K. £*
	175.00	250.00	100.00

Available only from catalogue firm.

DA 18
'Red Rum'
Style One

Beswick No.:	2510
Designer:	Graham Tongue
Height:	12 1/2", 31.7 cm
Colour:	Bay (matt)
Issued:	1989 to the present
Series:	Connoisseur Horses

Price:	*U.S. $*	*Can. $*	*U.K. £*
	N/A	N/A	149.00

DA 19
Hereford Bull

Beswick No:	2542
Designer:	Graham Tongue
Height:	7 1/2" x 11", 19.1 x 27.9 cm
Colour:	Brown and cream (matt)
Issued:	1989 to the present
Series:	Connoisseur Cattle

Price:	*U.S. $*	*Can. $*	*U.K. £*
	N/A	N/A	129.00

DA 20
'Grundy'

Beswick No.:	2558
Designer:	Graham Tongue
Height:	11 1/4", 28.9 cm
Colour:	Chestnut (matt)
Issued:	1989 to the present
Series:	Connoisseur Horses

Price:	*U.S. $*	*Can. $*	*U.K. £*
	520.00	N/A	149.00

DA 21
Polled Hereford Bull

Beswick No.:	2574
Designer:	Graham Tongue
Height:	7 1/2", 19.1 cm
Colour:	Brown and white (matt)
Issued:	1989 to the present
Series:	Connoisseur Cattle

Price:	*U.S. $*	*Can. $*	*U.K. £*
	N/A	N/A	129.00

DA 22
Life Guard

Beswick No.:	2562
Designer:	Graham Tongue
Height:	14 1/2", 36.8 cm
Colour:	Black horse, Guardsman wears scarlet
	silver, white and black uniform (matt)
Issued:	1989 to the present
Series:	Connoisseur Horses
Varieties:	Also called "Blues and Royals" DA 25

Price:	*U.S. $*	*Can. $*	*U.K. £*
	N/A	N/A	365.00

DA 22A
British Bull Dog

Model No.:	Unknown
Designer:	Denise Andrews
Modeller:	Amanda Hughes-Lubeck
Height:	4 1/2" x 5 1/2", 11.3 x 14.0 cm
Colour:	White dog, black hat and jacket
Issued:	1994 in a limited edition of 1,000
Varieties:	DA 22B

Price:	*U.S. $*	*Can. $*	*U.K. £*
	165.00	150.00	65.00

DA 22B
British Bull Dog

Model No.:	Unknown
Designer:	Denise Andrews
Modeller:	Amanda Hughes-Lubeck
Height:	4 1/2" x 5 1/2", 11.3 x 14.0 cm
Colour:	Tan dog, white hat and jacket
Issued:	1994 in a limited edition of 1,000
Varieties:	DA 22A

Price:	U.S. $	Can. $	U.K. £
	165.00	150.00	65.00

DA 23
Friesian Bull

Beswick No.:	2580
Designer:	Graham Tongue
Height:	7" x 11 1/2", 17.8 x 29.2 cm
Colour:	Black and white (matt)
Issued:	1989 to the present
Series:	Connoisseur Cattle

Price:	U.S. $	Can. $	U.K. £
	N/A	N/A	129.00

DA 24
Collie
Standing

Beswick No.:	2587
Designer:	Graham Tongue
Height:	8 1/4", 21.0 cm
Colour:	Brown and white (matt)
Issued:	1989 to the present
Series:	Connoisseur Dogs

Price:	U.S. $	Can. $	U.K. £
	N/A	N/A	75.00

DA 25
Blues and Royals

Beswick No.:	2562
Designer:	Graham Tongue
Height:	14 1/2", 36.8 cm
Colour:	Black horse, Guardsman wears blue, silver, white and red uniform (matt)
Issued:	1989 to the present
Series:	Connoisseur Horses
Varieties:	Also called "Life Guard" DA 22

Price:	U.S. $	Can. $	U.K. £
	N/A	N/A	365.00

DA 26
Alsatian
Standing - Style One

Beswick No.: 2581
Designer: Graham Tongue
Height: 9", 22.9 cm
Colour: Dark and light brown (matt)
Issued: 1989 to the present
Series: Connoisseur Dogs

Price:	U.S. $	Can. $	U.K. £
	215.00	N/A	75.00

DA 27
Charolais Bull

Beswick No.: 2600
Designer: Graham Tongue
Height: 7 1/2" x 12", 19.1 x 30.5 cm
Colour: Light golden brown
Issued: 1989 to the present
Series: Connoisseur Cattle

Price:	U.S. $	Can. $	U.K. £
	N/A	478.00	129.00

DA 28
Morgan Horse

Beswick No.: 2605
Designer: Graham Tongue
Height: 11 1/2", 29.2 cm
Colour: Black (matt)
Issued: 1989 to the present
Series: Connoisseur Horses

Price:	U.S. $	Can. $	U.K. £
	370.00	478.00	129.00

DA 29
Friesian Cow

Beswick No.: 2607
Designer: Graham Tongue
Height: 7 1/2", 19.1 cm
Colour: Black and white (matt)
Issued: 1989 to the present
Series: Connoisseur Cattle

Price:	U.S. $	Can. $	U.K. £
	N/A	N/A	129.00

DA 30
Friesian Cow and Calf

Beswick No.: 2607
Designer: Graham Tongue
Height: 7 1/2", 19.1 cm
Colour: Black and white (matt)
Issued: 1989 to the present
Series: Connoisseur Cattle

Price:	*U.S. $*	*Can. $*	*U.K. £*
	N/A	N/A	149.00

DA 31
'The Minstrel'

Beswick No.: 2608
Designer: Graham Tongue
Height: 13 1/4", 33.5 cm
Colour: Chestnut (matt)
Issued: 1989 to the present
Series: Connoisseur Horses

Price:	*U.S. $*	*Can. $*	*U.K. £*
	N/A	N/A	149.00

DA 32
Majestic Stag

Beswick No.: 2629
Designer: Graham Tongue
Height: 13 1/2", 34.3 cm
Colour: Golden brown (matt)
Issued: 1989 to the present
Series: Connoisseur

Price:	*U.S. $*	*Can. $*	*U.K. £*
	N/A	N/A	155.00

DA 33
Charolais Cow and Calf

Beswick No.: 2648
Designer: Graham Tongue
Height: 7 1/4", 18.4 cm
Colour: Cream (matt)
Issued: 1989 to the present
Series: Connoisseur Cattle

Price:	*U.S. $*	*Can. $*	*U.K. £*
	N/A	N/A	149.00

DA 34
Hereford Cow and Calf

Beswick No.: 2667\2669
Designer: Graham Tongue
Height: 7", 17.8 cm
Colour: Brown and white (matt)
Issued: 1989 to the present
Series: Connoisseur Cattle

Price:	U.S. $	Can. $	U.K. £
	N/A	525.00	149.00

DA 35A
'Champion'

Designer: Graham Tongue
Height: 11 1/4", 28.9 cm
Colour: Chestnut (matt)
Issued: 1989 to the present
Series: Connoisseur Horses
Varieties: Also called "Moonlight" DA 35B,
               "Sunburst" DA 36

Price:	U.S. $	Can. $	U.K. £
	N/A	N/A	155.00

DA 35B
'Moonlight'

Beswick No.: 2671
Designer: Graham Tongue
Height: 11 1/4", 28.9 cm
Colour: Grey (matt)
Issued: 1989 to the present
Series: Connoisseur Horses
Varieties: Also called "Champion", DA 35A,
               "Sunburst" DA 36

Price:	U.S. $	Can. $	U.K. £
	298.00	N/A	115.00

DA 36
'Sunburst' Palomino Horse

Beswick No.: 2671
Designer: Graham Tongue
Height: 11 1/4", 28.9 cm
Colour: Light brown, white main and tail (matt)
Issued: 1989 to the present
Series: Connoisseur Horses
Varieties: Also called "Champion", DA 35A,
               "Moonlight" DA 35B

Price:	U.S. $	Can. $	U.K. £
	N/A	N/A	115.00

DA 37
'Troy'
Model No.: 2674
Designer: Graham Tongue
Height: 11 3/4", 29.8 cm
Colour: Bay (matt)
Issued: 1989 to the present
Series: Connoisseur Horses

Price:	U.S. $	Can. $	U.K. £
	N/A	N/A	149.00

DA 38
"Open Ground" (Pheasant)
Model No.: 2760
Designer: Graham Tongue
Height: 11 1/2", 29.2 cm
Colour: Golden brown with black and red head (matt)
Issued: 1989 to the present
Series: Connoisseur

Price:	U.S. $	Can. $	U.K. £
	N/A	N/A	249.00

DA 39
"The Watering Hole" (Leopard)
Model No.: Unknown
Designer: Graham Tongue
Height: 6 1/2", 16.5 cm
Colour: Pale brown with dark brown spots
Issued: 1989 to the present
Series: Connoisseur

Price:	U.S. $	Can. $	U.K. £
	N/A	N/A	155.00

DA 40
Peregrine Falcon
Model No.: 3140
Designer: Graham Tongue
Height: 11", 27.9 cm
Colour: Browns and creams
Issued: 1989 to the present
Series: Connoisseur
Varieties: HN 3541

Price:	U.S. $	Can. $	U.K. £
	315.00	N/A	155.00

DA 41A
Prancing Horse (rearing horse)

Beswick No.: 1014
Designer: Arthur Gredington
Height: 10 1/4", 26.0 cm
Colour: Brown (glossy)
Issued: 1989-1990
Varieties: DA 41B

Price:	*U.S. $*	*Can. $*	*U.K. £*
	175.00	250.00	100.00

DA 41B
Prancing Horse (rearing horse)

Beswick No.: 1014
Designer: Arthur Gredington
Height: 10 1/4", 26.0 cm
Colour: Black (glossy and matt)
Issued: 1994 Special commission for Lloyds Bank
Varieties: DA 41A

Price:	*U.S. $*	*Can. $*	*U.K. £*
Black (glossy)	N/A	N/A	125.00
Black (matt)	N/A	N/A	125.00

DA 42
'Bois Roussel' Race Horse

Beswick No.: 701
Designer: Arthur Gredington
Height: 8", 20.3 cm
Colour: See below (glossy and matt)
Issued: 1989 to the present

Price:	*U.S. $*	*Can. $*	*U.K. £*
Brown (glossy)	57.00	82.00	25.00
Brown (matt)	N/A	N/A	29.95
Dapple Grey (glossy)	N/A	116.50	27.00

DA 43
Shire Mare

Beswick No.: 818
Designer: Arthur Gredington
Height: 8 1/2", 21.6 cm
Colour: Brown with white feet (glossy and matt)
Issued: 1989 to the present

Price:	*U.S. $*	*Can. $*	*U.K. £*
Brown (glossy)	N/A	N/A	29.95
Brown (matt)	N/A	N/A	29.95

DA 44
Horse
Stocky, jogging mare

Beswick No.: 855
Designer: Arthur Gredington
Height: 6", 15.2 cm
Colour: Brown (glossy)
Issued: 1989 to the present

Price:	*U.S. $*	*Can. $*	*U.K. £*
	57.00	77.00	25.00

DA 45
Trotting Horse (cantering shire)

Beswick No.: 975
Designer: Arthur Gredington
Height: 8 3/4", 22.2 cm
Colour: Brown (glossy)
Issued: 1989 to the present
Varieties: Flambé prototype

Price:	*U.S. $*	*Can. $*	*U.K. £*
	125.00	116.50	35.00

DA 46
Mare (facing left)

Beswick No.: 976
Designer: Arthur Gredington
Height: 6 3/4", 17.2 cm
Colour: See below (glossy and matt)
Issued: 1989 to the present

Price:	*U.S. $*	*Can. $*	*U.K. £*
Brown (glossy)	52.00	77.00	25.00
Brown (matt)	N/A	N/A	29.95
Dapple Grey (glossy)	N/A	N/A	27.00

DA 47
Shetland Pony (woolly Shetland mare)
Style One

Beswick No.: 1033
Designer: Arthur Gredington
Height: 5 3/4", 14.6 cm
Colour: Brown (glossy)
Issued: 1989 to the present

Price:	*U.S. $*	*Can. $*	*U.K. £*
	57.00	70.50	19.95

DA 48
Horse (swish tail)

Beswick No:	1182
Designer:	Arthur Gredington
Height:	8 3/4", 22.2 cm
Colour:	Brown (matt and glossy)
Issued:	1989 to the present

	U.S. $	Can. $	U.K. £
Brown (matt)	N/A	N/A	35.00
Brown (glossy)	N/A	N/A	29.95

DA 49
Palomino Horse (prancing Arab type)

Beswick No.:	1261
Designer:	Arthur Gredington
Height:	6 3/4", 17.2 cm
Colour:	See below (glossy and matt)
Issued:	1989 to the present

Price:	U.S. $	Can. $	U.K. £
Brown (glossy)	57.00	77.00	25.00
Brown (matt)	N/A	N/A	29.95
Dapple Grey (glossy)	N/A	N/A	27.00
Palomino (glossy)	57.00	77.00	25.00

DA 50
Arab Horse 'Xayal'

Beswick No.:	1265
Designer:	Arthur Gredington
Height:	6 1/4", 15.9 cm
Colour:	See below (glossy)
Issued:	1989 to the present

Price:	U.S. $	Can. $	U.K. £
Brown	N/A	77.00	25.00
Dapple Grey	N/A	105.00	27.00
Palomino	N/A	99.00	25.00

DA 51
Horse (head tucked, leg up)

Beswick No.:	1549
Designer:	Pal Zalmen
Height:	7 1/2", 19.1 cm
Colour:	Brown (glossy)
Issued:	1989 to the present

Price:	U.S. $	Can. $	U.K. £
	57.00	77.00	25.00

DA 52
Arab Horse

Beswick No.: 1771
Designer: Arthur Gredington
Height: 7 1/2", 19.1 cm
Colour: Brown (glossy and matt)
Issued: 1989 to the present

Price:	*U.S. $*	*Can. $*	*U.K. £*
Brown (glossy)	N/A	77.00	25.00
Brown (matt)	N/A	N/A	29.95

DA 53
Thoroughbred Horse

Beswick No.: 1772
Designer: Arthur Gredington
Height: 8", 20.3 cm
Colour: See below (glossy)
Issued: 1989 to the present
Varieties: Also called "Appaloosa", DA 68

Price:	*U.S. $*	*Can. $*	*U.K. £*
Brown (glossy)	N/A	77.00	25.00
Dapple Grey (glossy)	N/A	116.50	27.00

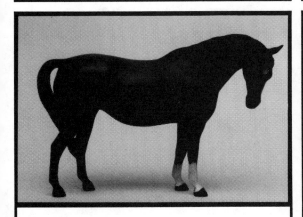

DA 54
Mare (facing right)

Beswick No.: 1812
Designer: Arthur Gredington
Height: 5 3/4", 14.6 cm
Colour: Brown (glossy)
Issued: 1989-1989

Price:	*U.S. $*	*Can. $*	*U.K. £*
	50.00	75.00	30.00

DA 55
Mare (small, facing right)

Beswick No.: 1991
Designer: Arthur Gredington
Height: 5 1/2", 14.0 cm
Colour: See below (glossy and matt)
Issued: 1989 to the present

Price:	*U.S. $*	*Can. $*	*U.K. £*
Brown (glossy)	40.00	50.00	18.95
Brown (matt)	N/A	0.00	21.00
Dapple Grey (glossy)	N/A	59.00	19.95
Palomino (glossy)	N/A	52.50	18.95

DA 56
Horse (small thoroughbred stallion)

Beswick No.:	1992		
Designer:	Arthur Gredington		
Height:	5 1/2", 14.0 cm		
Colour:	See below (glossy and matt)		
Issued:	1989 to the present		

Price:	*U.S. $*	*Can. $*	*U.K. £*
Brown (glossy)	40.00	50.00	18.95
Brown (matt)	N/A	N/A	21.00
Dapple Grey (glossy)	48.00	59.00	19.95

DA 57A
'Spirit of the Wind' (not on plinth)

Beswick No.:	2688		
Designer:	Graham Tongue		
Height:	8", 20.3 cm		
Colour:	Brown (glossy and matt)		
Issued:	1989 to the present		
Series:	Spirited Horses		

Price:	*U.S. $*	*Can. $*	*U.K. £*
Brown (glossy)	N/A	105.00	37.00
Brown (matt)	N/A	N/A	45.00

DA 57B
Spirit of the Wind (on plinth)

Beswick No.:	2688		
Designer:	Graham Tongue		
Height:	9", 22.9 cm		
Colour:	See below (matt)		
Issued:	See below		
Series:	Spirited Horses		

Price -	*U.S. $*	*Can. $*	*U.K. £*
White (1989-current)	N/A	N/A	47.00
Brown (1989-current)	N/A	N/A	49.95
Black (1989-1990)	150.00	180.00	49.95

DA 58A
Spirit of Freedom (not on plinth)

Beswick No.:	2689		
Designer:	Graham Tongue		
Height:	7", 17.8 cm		
Colour:	Brown (glossy and matt)		
Issued:	1989 to the present		
Series:	Spirited Horses		

Price:	*U.S. $*	*Can. $*	*U.K. £*
Brown (glossy)	N/A	N/A	37.00
Brown (matt)	89.00	N/A	45.00

DA 58B
Spirit of Freedom (on plinth)

Beswick No.: 2689
Designer: Graham Tongue
Height: 8", 20.3 cm
Colour: See below (matt)
Issued: See below
Series: Spirited Horses

Price;	U.S. $	Can. $	U.K. £
White (1989-current)	115.00	152.50	47.00
Brown (1989-current)	N/A	N/A	49.95
Black (1989-1993)	125.00	160.00	60.00

DA 59A
Spirit of Youth (not on plinth)

Beswick No.: 2703
Designer: Graham Tongue
Height: 7", 17.8 cm
Colour: Brown (glossy and matt)
Issued: 1989 to the present
Series: Spirited Horses

Price:	U.S. $	Can. $	U.K. £
Brown (glossy)	N/A	105.00	37.00
Brown (matt)	N/A	N/A	45.00

DA 59B
Spirit of Youth (on wooden plinth)

Beswick No.: 2703
Designer: Graham Tongue
Height: 8", 20.3 cm
Colour: See below (matt)
Issued: See below
Series: Spirited Horses

Price:	U.S. $	Can. $	U.K. £
White (1989-current)	N/A	152.50	47.00
Brown (1989-current)	N/A	210.00	49.95
Black (1989-1993)	162.00	175.00	75.00

DA 60A
Spirit of Fire (not on plinth)

Beswick No.: 2829
Designer: Graham Tongue
Height: 8", 20.3 cm
Colour: See below
Issued: 1989 to the present
Varieties: Spirited Horses

Price:	U.S. $	Can. $	U.K. £
Brown (glossy)	N/A	N/A	37.00
Brown (matt)	N/A	N/A	45.00

DA 60B
Spirit of Fire (on plinth)

Beswick No.:   2829
Designer: Graham Tongue
Height: 9", 22.9 cm
Colour: See below (matt)
Issued: See below
Series: Spirited Horses

Price:	U.S. $	Can. $	U.K. £
White (1989-current)	N/A	N/A	47.00
Brown (1989-current)	162.00	N/A	49.95
Black (1989-1993)	125.00	160.00	60.00

DA 61A
Spirit of Earth (not on plinth)

Beswick No.:   2914
Designer: Graham Tongue
Height: 7 1/2", 19.1 cm
Colour: Brown (glossy and matt)
Issued: 1989-1993

Price:	U.S. $	Can. $	U.K. £
Brown (glossy)	85.00	125.00	50.00
Brown (matt)	85.00	125.00	50.00

DA 61B
Spirit of Earth (on plinth)

Beswick No.:   2914
Designer: Graham Tongue
Height: 8 1/2", 21.6 cm
Colour: See below (matt)
Issued: 1989-1993
Series: Spirited Horses

Price:	U.S. $	Can. $	U.K. £
White	150.00	145.00	40.00
Brown	150.00	200.00	50.00
Black	150.00	200.00	50.00

DA 62A
Shire Horse (not on plinth)

Beswick No.:   2578
Designer: Alan Maslankowski
Height: 8 1/4", 21.0 cm
Colour: Brown (matt)
Issued: 1989 to the present
Series: Connoiseur Horses

Price:	U.S. $	Can. $	U.K. £
	142.00	N/A	75.00

DA 62B
Shire Horse (on wooden plinth)

Beswick No.: 2578
Designer: Alan Maslankowski
Height: 8 1/4", 21.0 cm
Colour: Brown (matt)
Issued: 1994 to the present
Series: Connoisseur Horses

Price:	*U.S. $*	*Can. $*	*U.K. £*
	150.00	N/A	75.00

DA 63A
Spirit of Peace (not on plinth)

Beswick No.: 2916
Designer: Graham Tongue
Height: 4 3/4", 12.1 cm
Colour: Brown (matt)
Issued: 1989 to the present

Price:	*U.S. $*	*Can. $*	*U.K. £*
	N/A	N/A	45.00

DA 63B
Spirit of Peace (on wooden plinth)

Beswick No.: 2916
Designer: Graham Tongue
Height: 5 3/4", 14.6 cm
Colour: See below (matt)
Issued: 1989 to the present
Series: Spirited Horses

Price:	*U.S. $*	*Can. $*	*U.K. £*
White (matt)	N/A	152.50	47.00
Brown (matt)	162.00	210.00	49.95

DA 64A
Spirit of Affection (not on plinth)

Beswick No.: 2353 / 2689
Designer: Graham Tongue
Height: 7", 17.8 cm
Colour: Brown (matt)
Issued: 1989 to the present
Series: Spirited Horses

Price:	*U.S. $*	*Can. $*	*U.K. £*
	N/A	N/A	75.00

DA 64B
Spirit of Affection (on wooden plinth)

Beswick No.: 2353 / 2689
Designer: Graham Tongue
Height: 8", 20.3 cm
Colour: See below (matt)
Issued: 1989 to the present
Series: Spirited Horses

Price:	*U.S. $*	*Can. $*	*U.K. £*
Brown	162.00	N/A	65.00
White	N/A	210.00	65.00

DA 65
Black Beauty

Beswick No.: 2466
Designer: Graham Tongue
Height: 7", 17.8 cm
Colour: Black (matt)
Issued: 1989 to the present

Price:	*U.S. $*	*Can. $*	*U.K. £*
	115.00	128.00	39.95

DA 66
Black Beauty as a Foal

Beswick No.: 2536
Designer: Graham Tongue
Height: 5 3/4", 14.6 cm
Colour: Black (matt)
Issued: 1989 to the present

Price:	*U.S. $*	*Can. $*	*U.K. £*
	52.00	64.00	17.95

DA 67
Pinto Pony

Beswick No.: 1373
Designer: Arthur Gredington
Height: 6 1/2", 16.5 cm
Colour: See below (glossy and matt)
Issued: 1989-1990

Price:	*U.S. $*	*Can. $*	*U.K. £*
Skewbald (glossy)	125.00	175.00	75.00
Skewbald (matt)	125.00	175.00	75.00
Piebald (glossy)	125.00	175.00	75.00
Piebald (matt)	125.00	175.00	75.00

DA 68
Appaloosa

Beswick No.: 1772
Designer: Arthur Gredington
Height: 8", 20.3 cm
Colour: See below (glossy)
Issued: 1989 to the present
Varieties: Also called "Thoroughbred Horse" DA 53

Price:	U.S. $	Can. $	U.K. £
Brown	134.00	170.00	49.95
Black	134.00	N/A	49.95
White	134.00	170.00	49.95

DA 69A
Springtime (not on plinth)

Beswick No.: 2837
Designer: Graham Tongue
Height: 4 1/2", 11.4 cm
Colour: Brown (glossy)
Issued: 1989 to the present
Series: Spirited Foals

Price:	U.S. $	Can. $	U.K. £
	48.00	N/A	16.95

DA 69B
Springtime (on wooden plinth)

Beswick No.: 2837
Designer: Graham Tongue
Height: 5 1/2", 14.0 cm
Colour: See below (matt)
Issued: 1989 to the present
Series: Spirited Foals

Price:	U.S. $	Can. $	U.K. £
White	N/A	63.00	19.95
Brown	60.00	84.00	23.00

DA 70A
Young Spirit (not on plinth)

Beswick No.: 2839
Designer: Graham Tongue
Height: 3 1/2", 8.9 cm
Colour: Brown (glossy)
Issued: 1989-1993
Series: Spirited Foals

Price:	U.S. $	Can. $	U.K. £
	48.00	N/A	16.95

DA 70B
Young Spirit (on wooden plinth)

Beswick No.:	2839		
Designer:	Graham Tongue		
Height:	4 1/4", 10.7 cm		
Colour:	See below (matt)		
Issued:	1989 to the present		
Series:	Spirited Foals		

Price:	*U.S. $*	*Can. $*	*U.K. £*
White	N/A	N/A	19.95
Brown	60.00	N/A	23.00
Black	60.00	N/A	19.95

DA 71A
Sunlight (not on plinth)

Beswick No.:	2875		
Designer:	Graham Tongue		
Height:	3 1/2", 8.9 cm		
Colour:	Brown (glossy)		
Issued:	1989 to the present		
Series:	Spirited Foals		

Price:	*U.S. $*	*Can. $*	*U.K. £*
	48.00	N/A	16.95

DA 71B
Sunlight (on wooden plinth)

Beswick No.:	2875		
Designer:	Graham Tongue		
Height:	4 1/4", 10.7 cm		
Colour:	See below (matt)		
Issued:	1989 to the present		
Series:	Spirited Foals		

Price:	*U.S. $*	*Can. $*	*U.K. £*
White	46.00	63.00	19.95
Brown	55.00	84.00	23.00
Black	N/A	N/A	19.95

DA 72A
Adventure (not on plinth)

Beswick No.:	2876		
Designer:	Graham Tongue		
Height:	4 1/2", 11.4 cm		
Colour:	Brown (glossy)		
Issued:	1989 to the present		
Series:	Spirited Foals		

Price:	*U.S. $*	*Can. $*	*U.K. £*
	48.00	N/A	16.95

DA 72B
Adventure (on plinth)

Beswick No.:	2876		
Designer:	Graham Tongue		
Height:	5 1/2", 14.0 cm		
Colour:	See below (matt)		
Issued:	1989 to the present		
Series:	Spirited Foals		

Price:	*U.S. $*	*Can. $*	*U.K. £*
White (matt)	N/A	63.00	19.95
Brown (matt)	55.00	84.00	23.00

DA 73
Spirit of Nature (on wooden plinth)

Beswick No.:			
Designer:	Graham Tongue		
Height:	6 1/4", 15.9 cm		
Colour:	Brown (matt)		
Issued:	1989 to the present		
Series:	Spirited Horses		

Price:	*U.S. $*	*Can. $*	*U.K. £*
	N/A	N/A	49.95

DA 74
Foal (small, stretched, facing right)

Beswick No:	815		
Designer:	Arthur Gredington		
Height:	3 1/4", 8.3 cm		
Colour:	See below		
Issued:	1989 to the present		

Price:	*U.S. $*	*Can. $*	*U.K. £*
Brown (glossy)	33.00	29.50	8.95
Brown (matt)	N/A	0.00	9.95
Dapple Grey (glossy)	32.00	35.00	8.95

DA 75
Foal (lying)

Beswick No:	915		
Designer:	Arthur Gredington		
Height:	3 1/4", 8.3 cm		
Colour:	See below (glossy and matt)		
Issued:	1989 to the present		

Price:	*U.S. $*	*Can. $*	*U.K. £*
Brown (glossy)	42.00	43.00	9.95
Brown (matt)	N/A	N/A	14.95
Dapple Grey (glossy)	42.00	52.50	9.95

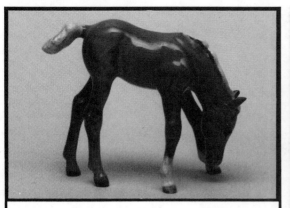

DA 76
Foal (grazing)

Beswick No.: 946
Designer: Arthur Gredington
Height: 3 1/4", 8.3 cm
Colour: See below (glossy and matt)
Issued: 1989 to the present

Price:	U.S. $	Can. $	U.K. £
Brown (glossy)	42.00	40.00	9.95
Brown (matt)	N/A	N/A	12.95
Dapple Grey (glossy)	42.00	N/A	9.95
Palomino (glossy)	N/A	N/A	9.95

DA 77
Foal (large, head down)

Beswick No.: 947
Designer: Arthur Gredington
Height: 4 1/2", 11.4 cm
Colour: Brown (glossy and matt)
Issued: 1989 to the present

Price:	U.S. $	Can. $	U.K. £
Brown (glossy)	42.00	52.50	12.95
Brown (matt)	N/A	N/A	16.95

DA 78
Foal (small, stretched, facing left)

Beswick No.: 997
Designer: Arthur Gredington
Height: 3 1/4", 8.3 cm
Colour: See below (glossy and matt)
Issued: 1989 to the present

Price:	U.S. $	Can. $	U.K. £
Brown (glossy)	N/A	29.50	8.95
Brown (matt)	N/A	N/A	9.95
Dapple Grey (glossy)	N/A	35.00	8.95

DA 79
Shetland Foal

Beswick No.: 1034
Designer: Arthur Gredington
Height: 3 3/4", 9.5 cm
Colour: Brown (glossy and matt)
Issued: 1989 to the present

Price:	U.S. $	Can. $	U.K. £
Brown (glossy)	33.00	N/A	9.95
Brown (matt)	N/A	N/A	12.95

DA 80
Foal (Arab type)

Beswick No.: 1407
Designer: Arthur Gredington
Height: 4 1/2", 11.4 cm
Colour: See below (glossy and matt)
Issued: 1989 to the present

Price:	U.S. $	Can. $	U.K. £
Brown (glossy)	N/A	40.00	9.95
Brown (matt)	N/A	N/A	12.95
Dapple Grey (glossy)	37.00	43.00	9.95
Palomino (glossy)	38.00	N/A	9.95

DA 81
Foal (larger, thoroughbred type)

Beswick No.: 1813
Designer: Arthur Gredington
Height: 4 1/2", 11.4 cm
Colour: Brown (glossy and matt)
Issued: 1989 to the present

Price:	U.S. $	Can. $	U.K. £
Brown (glossy)	42.00	40.00	9.95
Brown (matt)	N/A	N/A	12.95

DA 82
Foal (smaller, thoroughbred type, facing left)

Beswick No.: 1816
Designer: Arthur Gredington
Height: 3 1/2", 8.9 cm
Colour: See below
Issued: 1989 to the present

Price:	U.S. $	Can. $	U.K. £
Brown (glossy)	37.00	35.00	9.95
Brown (matt)	N/A	N/A	12.95
Palomino (glossy)	N/A	N/A	9.95

DA 83
Siamese Cat
Seated - Style Two

Beswick No.: 2139
Designer: Mr. Garbet
Height: 13 3/4", 34.9 cm
Colour: Cream and black
Issued: 1989 to the present
Series: Fireside Models

Price:	U.S. $	Can. $	U.K. £
	170.00	228.00	58.00

DA 84
Old English Sheepdog
Seated

Beswick No.: 2232
Designer: Albert Hallan
Height: 11 1/2", 29.2 cm
Colour: Grey and white
Issued: 1989 to the present
Series: Fireside Models

Price:	*U.S. $*	*Can. $*	*U.K. £*
	230.00	289.00	75.00

DA 85
Dalmation

Beswick No.: 2271
Designer: Graham Tongue
Height: 13 3/4", 34.9 cm
Colour: White with black spots
Issued: 1989 to the present
Series: Fireside Models

Price:	*U.S. $*	*Can. $*	*U.K. £*
	225.00	289.00	85.00

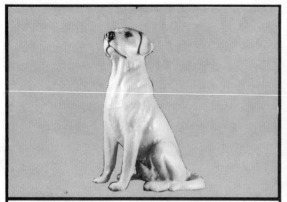

DA 86
Labrador (seated)

Beswick No.: 2314
Designer: Graham Tongue
Height: 13 1/4", 33.6 cm
Colour: See below (glossy)
Issued: 1989 to the present
Series: Fireside Models
Varieties: HN 86B, "Black Labrador"

Price:	*U.S. $*	*Can. $*	*U.K. £*
Golden (Glossy)	230.00	289.00	85.00
Black (Glossy)	230.00	289.00	85.00

DA 87
Yorkshire Terrier
Seated - Style One

Beswick No.: 2377
Designer: Graham Tongue
Height: 10 1/4", 26.0 cm
Colour: Dark and light brown (glossy)
Issued: 1989 to the present
Series: Fireside Models

Price:	*U.S. $*	*Can. $*	*U.K. £*
	188.00	228.00	58.00

DA 88
Alsatian
Seated - Style Two

Beswick No.:   2410
Designer: Graham Tongue
Height: 14", 35.5 cm
Colour: Dark and light brown (glossy)
Issued: 1989 to the present
Series: Fireside Models

Price:	U.S. $	Can. $	U.K. £
	230.00	289.00	79.95

OLD ENGLISH DOGS (facing pairs)

Designer: Unknown
Colour: White and gold (glossy)
Issued: 1989 to the present
Series: Traditional Staffordshire dogs

	DA 89 - 90	DA 91 - 92	DA 93 - 94	DA 95 - 96	DA 97 - 98
Beswick No.:	M1378 / 3	M1378 / 4	M1378 / 5	M1378 / 6	M1378 / 7
Height:	10", 25.4 cm	9", 22.9 cm	7 1/2", 19.1 cm	5 1/2", 14.0 cm	3 1/2", 8.9 cm
Price:	DA 89 - 90	DA91 - 92	DA 93 - 94	DA 95 -96	DA 97 -98
U.S. $	N/A	N/A	N/A	45.00	N/A
Can. $	N/A	N/A	N/A	N/A	N/A
U.K. £	55.00	35.00	26.00	18.50	11.00

DA 99
Rottweiler

Beswick No.:	3055		
Designer:	Alan Maslankowski		
Height:	5 1/4", 13.3 cm		
Colour:	Brown and black		
Issued:	1990 to the present		

Price:	*U.S. $*	*Can. $*	*U.K. £*
Glossy	80.00	100.00	27.95
Matt	80.00	N/A	27.95

DA 100
Old English Sheepdog (standing)

Beswick No.:	3058		
Designer:	Warren Platt		
Height:	5 1/2", 14.0 cm		
Colour:	Grey and white		
Issued:	1990 to the present		

Price:	*U.S. $*	*Can. $*	*U.K. £*
Glossy	80.00	100.00	27.95
Matt	80.00	N/A	27.95

DA 101
Staffordshire Bull Terrier - Style Two

Beswick No.:	3060		
Designer:	Alan Maslankowski		
Height:	4", 10.1 cm		
Colour:	See below		
Issued:	1990 to the present		

Price:	*U.S. $*	*Can. $*	*U.K. £*
White/Tan (glossy)	80.00	100.00	27.95
White/Tan (matt)	80.00	N/A	27.95
Brindle (glossy)	80.00	100.00	27.95
Brindle (matt)	80.00	N/A	27.95

DA 102
Afghan Hound

Beswick No.:	3070		
Designer:	Alan Maslankowski		
Height:	5 1/2", 14.0 cm		
Colour:	Cream		
Issued:	1990 to the present		

Price:	*U.S. $*	*Can. $*	*U.K. £*
Glossy	N/A	100.00	27.95
Matt	80.00	N/A	27.95

DA 103
Alsatian
Standing - Style Two

Beswick No.: 3073
Designer: Alan Maslankowski
Height: 5 3/4", 14.6 cm
Colour: Dark and light brown
Issued: 1990 to the present

Price:	U.S. $	Can. $	U.K. £
Glossy	78.00	100.00	27.95
Matt	80.00	N/A	27.95

DA 104
Boxer

Beswick No.: 3081
Designer: Alan Maslankowski
Height: 5 1/2", 14.0 cm
Colour: Golden brown and white
Issued: 1990 to the present

Price:	U.S. $	Can. $	U.K. £
Glossy	80.00	100.00	27.95
Matt	N/A	N/A	27.95

DA 105
Doberman

Beswick No.: 3121
Designer: Alan Maslankowski
Height: 5 1/4", 13.3 cm
Colour: Dark brown
Issued: 1990 to the present

Price:	U.S. $	Can. $	U.K. £
Glossy	N/A	100.00	27.95
Matt	N/A	N/A	27.95

DA 106
Rough Collie

Beswick No.: 3129
Designer: Warren Platt
Height: 5 1/2", 14.0 cm
Colour: Golden brown and white
Issued: 1990 to the present

Price:	U.S. $	Can. $	U.K. £
Glossy	80.00	100.00	27.95
Matt	80.00	N/A	27.95

DA 107
Springer Spaniel

Beswick No.: 3135
Designer: Amanda Hughes-Lubeck
Height: 5", 12.7 cm
Colour: Dark brown and white
Issued: 1990 to the present

Price:	U.S. $	Can. $	U.K. £
Glossy	84.00	100.00	27.95
Matt	80.00	N/A	27.95

DA 108
The Spaniel (on ceramic plinth)

Beswick No.: 2980
Designer: Alan Maslankowski
Height: 8 1/4", 21.0 cm
Colour: See below (matt)
Issued: 1990 to the present
Series: Spirited Dogs

Price:	U.S. $	Can. $	U.K. £
Black/white	150.00	N/A	59.00
Golden	N/A	N/A	59.00
Orange/white	N/A	N/A	59.00

DA 109
The Setter (on ceramic plinth)

Beswick No.: 2986
Designer: Graham Tongue
Height: 8 1/2", 21.6 cm
Colour: See below
Issued: 1990 to the present
Series: Spirited Dogs

Price:	U.S. $	Can. $	U.K. £
English (matt)	150.00	N/A	59.00
Red (matt)	150.00	N/A	59.00
Gordon (matt)	156.00	N/A	59.00

DA 110
The Pointer (on ceramic plinth)
Style Two

Beswick No.: 3011
Designer: Graham Tongue
Height: 8 1/2", 21.6 cm
Colour: White with dark brown patches
Issued: 1990 to the present
Series: Spirited Dogs

Price:	U.S. $	Can. $	U.K. £
Matt	150.00	N/A	59.00

DA 111
The Labrador (on ceramic plinth)
Standing - Style One

Beswick No.:	3062		
Designer:	Alan Maslankowski		
Height:	7 1/2", 19.1 cm		
Colour:	See below		
Issued:	1990 to the present		
Series:	Spirited Dogs		

Price:	*U.S. $*	*Can. $*	*U.K. £*
Golden (matt)	150.00	N/A	49.95
Black (matt)	150.00	N/A	49.95

DA 112
The Retriever (on ceramic plinth)
Style One

Beswick No.:	3066		
Designer:	Graham Tongue		
Height:	7 1/2", 19.1 cm		
Colour:	Golden brown		
Issued:	1990 to the present		
Series:	Spirited Dogs		

Price:	*U.S. $*	*Can. $*	*U.K. £*
Matt	167.00	N/A	59.00

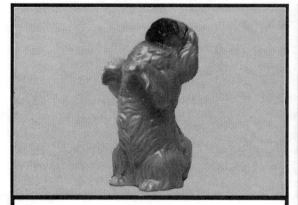

DA 113
Pekinese
Begging

Beswick No.:	2982		
Designer:	Alan Maslankowski		
Height:	5 1/2", 14.0 cm		
Colour:	Cream		
Issued:	1990 to the present		
Series:	Good Companions		

Price:	*U.S. $*	*Can. $*	*U.K. £*
Glossy	62.00	67.50	19.95
Matt	50.00	N/A	19.95

DA 114
Norfolk Terrier

Beswick No.:	2984		
Designer:	Alan Maslankowski		
Height:	4", 10.1 cm		
Colour:	Dark brown		
Issued:	1990 to the present		
Series:	Good Companions		

Price:	*U.S. $*	*Can. $*	*U.K. £*
Glossy	50.00	67.50	19.95
Matt	60.00	N/A	19.95

DA 115
Poodle on Blue Cushion

Beswick No.: 2985
Designer: Alan Maslankowski
Height: 5", 12.7 cm
Colour: White poodle, blue cushion
Issued: 1990 to the present
Series: Good Companions

Price:	U.S. $	Can. $	U.K. £
Glossy	62.00	84.00	27.95
Matt	62.00	N/A	27.95

DA 116
Dachshund
Standing - Style Three

Beswick No.: 3013
Designer: Alan Maslankowski
Height: 4 1/2", 11.4 cm
Colour: See below (glossy and matt)
Issued: 1990 to the present
Series: Good Companions

Price:	U.S. $	Can. $	U.K. £
Tan	62.00	67.50	19.95
Black/Tan	50.00	57.95	19.95

DA 117
Shetland Sheepdog

Beswick No.: 3080
Designer: Alan Maslankowski
Height: 5", 12.7 cm
Colour: Brown and white
Issued: 1990 to the present
Series: Good Companions

Price:	U.S. $	Can. $	U.K. £
Glossy	54.00	67.50	25.00
Matt	57.00	N/A	25.00

DA 118
Cairn Terrier
Standing - Style Two

Beswick No.: 3082
Designer: Warren Platt
Height: 4 1/2", 11.4 cm
Colour: Pale brown
Issued: 1990 to the present
Series: Good Companions

Price:	U.S. $	Can. $	U.K. £
Glossy	50.00	67.50	19.95
Matt	50.00	N/A	19.95

DA 119
Yorkshire Terrier
Seated - Style Two

Beswick No.: 3083
Designer: Warren Platt
Height: 5", 12.7 cm
Colour: Light brown and cream
Issued: 1990 to the present
Series: Good Companions

Price:	*U.S. $*	*Can. $*	*U.K. £*
Glossy	62.00	67.50	19.95
Matt	50.00	N/A	19.95

DA 120
West Highland Terrier
Style Two

Beswick No.: 3149
Designer: Martyn C. R. Alcock
Height: 5", 12.7 cm
Colour: White
Issued: 1990 to the present
Series: Good Companions

Price:	*U.S. $*	*Can. $*	*U.K. £*
Glossy	62.00	67.50	19.95
Matt	62.00	N/A	19.95

DA 121
Cavalier King Charles Spaniel - Style Two

Beswick No.: 3155
Designer: Warren Platt
Height: 5", 12.7 cm
Colour: See below (glossy and matt)
Issued: 1990 to the present
Series: Good Companions

Price:	*U.S. $*	*Can. $*	*U.K. £*
Tan/white	62.00	67.50	33.00
Black/tan/white	62.00	67.50	33.00

DA 122
Siamese Kittens

Beswick No.: 1296
Designer: Miss Granoska
Height: 2 3/4", 7.0 cm
Colour: Cream and black
Issued: 1990 to the present

Price:	*U.S. $*	*Can. $*	*U.K. £*
Glossy	37.00	N/A	9.95

DA 123
Kitten

Beswick No.: 1436
Designer: Colin Melbourne
Height: 3 1/4", 8.3 cm
Colour: See below
Issued: 1990 to the present

Price:	U.S. $	Can. $	U.K. £
White (glossy)	19.00	N/A	6.50
Grey (glossy)	19.00	N/A	6.95
Ginger (glossy)	19.00	N/A	6.95

DA 124
Siamese Cat
Lying - Style Two

Beswick No.: 1558
Designer: Pal Zalmen
Height: 7 1/4", 18.4 cm (length)
Colour: Cream and black
Issued: 1990 to the present

Price:	U.S. $	Can. $	U.K. £
Glossy	62.00	N/A	14.95

DA 125
Siamese Cat
Lying - Style Three

Beswick No.: 1558
Designer: Pal Zalmen
Height: 7 1/4", 18.4 cm (length)
Colour: Cream and black
Issued: 1990 to the present

Price:	U.S. $	Can. $	U.K. £
Glossy	62.00	N/A	14.95

DA 126
Persian Cat (seated)
Style Two

Beswick No.: 1867
Designer: Albert Hallam
Height: 6 1/4", 15.9 cm
Colour: See below
Issued: 1990 to the present

Price:	U.S. $	Can. $	U.K. £
White (glossy)	67.00	N/A	23.00
Grey (glossy)	78.00	N/A	25.00
Ginger (glossy)	78.00	N/A	25.00

DA 127
Siamese Cat
Seated - Style Three

Beswick No.: 1882
Designer: Albert Hallam
Height: 9", 22.9 cm
Size: Large
Colour: Cream and black
Issued: 1990 to the present

Price:	U.S. $	Can. $	U.K. £
Glossy	75.00	N/A	27.95

DA 128
Persian Kitten
Style Two

Beswick No.: 1886
Designer: Albert Hallam
Height: 4", 10.1 cm
Colour: See below
Issued: 1990 to the present

Price:	U.S. $	Can. $	U.K. £
White (glossy)	24.00	N/A	8.50
Grey (glossy)	37.00	N/A	9.50
Ginger (glossy)	N/A	N/A	9.50

DA 129
Siamese Cat
Seated - Style Four

Beswick No.: 1887
Designer: Albert Hallam
Height: 4", 10.1 cm
Size: Small
Colour: Cream and black
Issued: 1990 to the present

Price:	U.S. $	Can. $	U.K. £
Glossy	24.00	N/A	8.95

DA 130
Siamese Cat (standing)
Style Two

Beswick No.: 1897
Designer: Albert Hallam
Height: 6 1/2", 16.5 cm
Colour: Cream and black
Issued: 1990 to the present

Price:	U.S. $	Can. $	U.K. £
Glossy	56.00	N/A	19.95

DA 131
Black Cat

Beswick No.:	1897		
Designer:	Albert Hallam		
Height:	6 1/2", 16.5 cm		
Colour:	Black		
Issued:	1990 to the present		

Price:	*U.S. $*	*Can. $*	*U.K. £*
Glossy	56.00	N/A	19.95

DA 132
Persian Cat (standing)

Beswick No.:	1898		
Designer:	Albert Hallam		
Height:	5", 12.7 cm		
Colour:	See below		
Issued:	1990 to the present		

Price:	*U.S. $*	*Can. $*	*U.K. £*
White (glossy)	42.00	N/A	14.50
Grey (glossy)	56.00	N/A	19.95
Ginger (glossy)	56.00	N/A	19.95

DA 134
Desert Orchid
Style One

Model No.:	Unknown
Designer:	Graham Tongue
Height:	12" x 14", 30.5 x 35.5 cm
Colour:	Light grey
Issued:	1990 in a limited edition of 7,500
	Lawleys By Post

Price:	*U.S. $*	*Can. $*	*U.K. £*
Ceramic Base	N/A	N/A	395.00
Wooden Base	N/A	N/A	395.00

DA 137
The Barn Owl
Style Three

Model No.:	Unknown
Designer:	Amanda Hughes-Lubeck
Height:	7 1/2", 19.1 cm
Colour:	Browns and cream
Issued:	1990-1992
Series:	Wildlife

Price:	*U.S. $*	*Can. $*	*U.K. £*
	200.00	225.00	95.00

DA 138
Kingfisher (on plinth)
Style Three

Model No.:	Unknown
Designer:	Warren Platt
Height:	8 3/4", 22.2 cm
Colour:	Blue and orange-red, cream and brown
Issued:	1990-1992
Series:	Nature Sculptures

Price:	U.S. $	Can. $	U.K. £
	200.00	225.00	95.00

DA 139
Osprey (on plinth)

Model No.:	Unknown
Designer:	Unknown
Height:	7 3/4", 19.7 cm
Colour:	Browns and white
Issued:	1990-1992
Series:	Wildlife

Price:	U.S. $	Can. $	U.K. £
	200.00	225.00	95.00

DA 141
Cocker Spaniel
Seated - Style Two

Model No.:	Unknown
Designer:	Martyn C. R. Alcock
Height:	4 1/4", 10.8 cm
Colour:	See below (glossy and matt)
Issued:	1990 to the present

Price:	U.S. $	Can. $	U.K. £
Golden	80.00	100.00	27.95
Liver/white	80.00	N/A	27.95

DA 142
Golden Retriever

Model No.:	Unknown
Designer:	Amanda Hughes-Lubeck
Height:	5", 12.7 cm
Colour:	Golden brown (glossy and matt)
Issued:	1990 to the present

Price:	U.S. $	Can. $	U.K. £
Glossy	80.00	100.00	27.95
Matt	80.00	N/A	27.95

DA 143
Border Collie

Model No.:	Unknown
Designer:	Amanda Hughes-Lubeck
Height:	4", 10.1 cm
Colour:	See below (glossy and matt)
Issued:	1990 to the present

Price:	U.S. $	Can. $	U.K. £
Tan/black/white	80.00	N/A	27.95
Black/white	80.00	N/A	27.95

DA 144
Kestrel (on plinth)
Style One

Model No.:	Unknown
Designer:	Graham Tongue
Height:	12 1/4", 31.1 cm
Colour:	Golden brown bird with black markings; pink bone china flowers
Issued:	1991 in a limited edition of 950
Series:	Artist's Signature Edition/Wildlife

Price:	U.S. $	Can. $	U.K. £
	1,200.00	N/A	595.00

DA 145
Labrador
Standing - Style Two

Model No.:	Unknown
Designer:	Warren Platt
Height:	5", 12.7 cm
Colour:	See below (glossy and matt)
Issued:	1990 to the present
Varieties:	DA 145B, 145C

Price:	U.S. $	Can. $	U.K. £
Golden	80.00	100.00	27.95
Chocolate	N/A	85.00	27.95
Black	80.00	100.00	27.95

DA 148
Cat
Walking

Model No.:	Unknown
Designer:	Alan Maslankowski
Height:	5 1/2", 14.0 cm
Colour:	See below (glossy)
Issued:	1992 to the present

Price:	U.S. $	Can. $	U.K. £
Black with white	47.00	64.00	16.95
White with black	47.00	64.00	16.95

DA 149
Cat
Stalking

Model No.:	Unknown
Designer:	Alan Maslankowski
Height:	5 1/2", 14.0 cm
Colour:	See below
Issued:	1992 to the present

Price:	U.S. $	Can. $	U.K. £
White (Glossy)	47.00	64.00	16.95
Grey (Glossy)	47.00	64.00	16.95

DA 150A
Panda (not on plinth)

Model No.:	Unknown
Designer:	Warren Platt
Height:	5 1/2", 14.0 cm
Colour:	White
Issued:	Black and white panda, green and brown base
Issued:	1991-1992
Series:	Endangered Species

Price:	U.S. $	Can. $	U.K. £
	72.00	125.00	50.00

DA 150B
Panda (on plinth)

Model No.:	Unknown
Designer:	Warren Platt
Height:	5 ", 12.7 cm
Colour:	Black and white panda, green and brown base
Issued:	1991 in a limited edition of 2,500 for Lawleys By Post
Series:	Artist's Signature Edition

Price:	U.S. $	Can. $	U.K. £
	75.00	125.00	50.00

DA 154A
Spirit of Life (on wooden plinth)

Model No.:	Unknown
Designer:	Amanda Hughes-Lubeck
Height:	7 1/2", 19.1 cm
Colour:	White (matt)
Issued:	1991 to the present
Varieties:	DA 154B "The Winner"
Series:	Spirited Horses

Price:	U.S. $	Can. $	U.K. £
	N/A	N/A	47.00

DA 154B
The Winner (on wooden plinth) - Style Two

Model No.:	Unknown
Designer:	Amanda Hughes-Lubeck
Height:	7 1/2", 19.1 cm
Colour:	Brown with black mane and tail
Issued:	1991 to the present
Varieties:	DA 154A "The Spirit of Life"
Series:	Connoisseur Horses

Price:	U.S. $	Can. $	U.K. £
Glossy	N/A	N/A	65.00
Matt	N/A	N/A	65.00

DA 155A
Polar Bear (standing) (not on plinth)
Style Two

Model No.:	Unknown
Designer:	Amanda Hughes-Lubeck
Height:	4 3/4", 12.1 cm
Colour:	White, grey base
Issued:	1991-1992
Series:	Endangered Species
Varieties:	DA 155B

Price:	U.S. $	Can. $	U.K. £
	72.00	125.00	50.00

DA 155B
Polar Bear (standing) (on wooden plinth)
Style Two

Model No.:	Unknown
Designer:	Amanda Hughes-Lubeck
Height:	4 3/4", 12.1 cm
Colour:	White, grey base
Issued:	1991 in a limited edition of 2,500 for Lawleys By Post
Series:	Artist's Signature Edition
Varieties:	DA 155A

Price:	U.S. $	Can. $	U.K. £
	75.00	125.00	50.00

DA 156A
The Tawny Owl (on plinth)

Model No.:	Unknown
Designer:	Graham Tongue
Height:	9 3/4", 24.8 cm
Colour:	Light and golden brown
Issued:	1991 to the present
Series:	Connoisseur Birds

Price:	U.S. $	Can. $	U.K. £
	N/A	N/A	155.00

DA 156B
The Tawny Owl (on plinth)

Model No.:	Unknown
Designer:	Graham Tongue
Height:	9 3/4", 24.8 cm
Colour:	Light and golden brown
Issued:	1991 in a limited edition of 2,500 for Lawleys By Post
Series:	Artist's Signature Edition

Price:	U.S. $	Can. $	U.K. £
	225.00	300.00	150.00

DA 158
The Christmas Robin (on plinth)

Model No.:	Unknown
Designer:	Graham Tongue
Height:	5 1/4", 13.3 cm
Colour:	Red breast, brown feathers; green holly on snowy bough
Issued:	1990-1992

Price:	U.S. $	Can. $	U.K. £
	75.00	125.00	50.00

DA 159A
African Elephant (not on plinth)
Style Two

Model No.:	Unknown
Designer:	Martyn C. R. Alcock
Height:	6", 15.2 cm
Colour:	Grey
Issued:	1991-1992
Varieties:	DA 159B
Series:	Endangered Species

Price:	U.S. $	Can. $	U.K. £
	72.00	125.00	50.00

DA 159B
African Elephant (on plinth)
Style Two

Model No.:	Unknown
Designer:	Martyn C. R. Alcock
Height:	6", 15.2 cm
Colour:	Grey
Issued:	1991 in a limited edition of 2,500 for Lawleys By Post
Series:	Artist's Signature Edition
Varieties:	DA 159A

Price:	U.S. $	Can. $	U.K. £
	75.00	125.00	50.00

DA 161
Christmas Turkey

Model No.:	Unknown		
Designer:	Graham Tongue		
Height:	6 1/4", 15.9 cm		
Colour:	White feathers, red head		
Issued:	1990-1990		
Varieties:	D 6449		

Price:	*U.S. $*	*Can. $*	*U.K. £*
	75.00	125.00	50.00

*

DA 163A
Quarter Horse (without plinth)

Model No.:	Unknown		
Designer:	Graham Tongue		
Height:	7 1/2", 19.1 cm		
Colour:	Brown (glossy)		
Issued:	1991 to the present		
Series:	Nature Sculptures		

Price:	*U.S. $*	*Can. $*	*U.K. £*
	N/A	N/A	45.00

DA 163B
Quarter Horse (on wooden plinth)

Model No.:	Unknown		
Designer:	Graham Tongue		
Height:	8 1/2", 21.6 cm		
Colour:	Bay (matt)		
Issued:	1991 to the present		
Series:	Connoisseur Horses		

Price:	*U.S. $*	*Can. $*	*U.K. £*
	130.00	N/A	55.00

DA 164
Welsh Mountain Pony

Model No.:	Unknown		
Designer:	Amanda Hughes-Lubeck		
Height:	6 1/4", 15.9 cm		
Colour:	Dapple grey (glossy)		
Issued:	1991 to the present		

Price:	*U.S. $*	*Can. $*	*U.K. £*
	N/A	N/A	35.00

DA 165
Poodle

Model No.:	Unknown		
Designer:	Warren Platt		
Height:	5 1/2", 14.0 cm		
Colour:	See below		
Issued:	1993-1993		

Price:	U.S. $	Can. $	U.K. £
Black	45.00	65.00	30.00
White	0.00	65.00	30.00

*

DA 168
Labrador and Pup

Model No.:	Unknown		
Designer:	Warren Platt		
Height:	7", 17.8 cm (length)		
Colour:	Golden brown (glossy)		
Issued:	1992 to the present		
Series:	Dogs and Puppies		

Price:	U.S. $	Can. $	U.K. £
	84.00	84.00	29.95

*

DA 172
Leaping Trout (on wooden plinth)

Model No.:	Unknown		
Designer:	Graham Tongue		
Height:	11", 27.9 cm		
Colour:	Brown and cream trout on blue-grey base, yellow flowers, green reeds		
Issued:	1994 to the present		
Series:	Connoiseur		

Price:	U.S. $	Can. $	U.K. £
	N/A	N/A	199.95

DA 173
Retriever and Pup

Model No.:	Unknown		
Designer:	Warren Platt		
Height:	6", 15.2 cm (length)		
Colour:	Golden brown (glossy)		
Issued:	1992 to the present		
Series:	Dogs and Puppies		

Price:	U.S. $	Can. $	U.K. £
	84.00	N/A	29.95

DA 174
Spaniel and Pup

Model No.:	Unknown		
Designer:	Warren Platt		
Height:	5 1/2", 14.0 cm (length)		
Colour:	See below (glossy)		
Issued:	1992 to the present		
Series:	Dogs and Puppies		

Price:	U.S. $	Can. $	U.K. £
Golden	84.00	N/A	29.95
Liver and white	84.00	N/A	29.95

*

DA 176
Sheepdog and Pup

Model No.:	Unknown		
Designer:	Warren Platt		
Height:	4 1/2", 11.4 cm		
Colour:	Grey and white (glossy)		
Issued:	1992 to the present		
Series:	Dogs and Puppies		

Price:	U.S. $	Can. $	U.K. £
	84.00	N/A	29.95

*

DA 179
Black Bess

Model No.:	Unknown		
Designer:	Graham Tongue		
Height:	7 3/4", 19.7 cm		
Colour:	Black (matt)		
Issued:	1992 to the present		
Series:	Connoisseur Horses		

Price:	U.S. $	Can. $	U.K. £
	N/A	N/A	69.95

*

DA 182
First Born (on wooden plinth)

Model No.:	Unknown		
Designer:	Amanda Hughes-Lubeck		
Height:	7", 17.8 cm		
Colour:	Chestnut mare and foal		
Issued:	1992 to the present		
Series:	Connoisseur Horses		

Price:	U.S. $	Can. $	U.K. £
	N/A	N/A	69.95

Combination of DA 180 and DA 181

DA 183
Spirit of the Wild (on wooden plinth)

Model No.:	Unknown
Designer:	Warren Platt
Height:	12", 30.5 cm
Colour:	See below (matt)
Issued:	1993 to the present
Series:	Spirited Horses

Price:	*U.S. $*	*Can. $*	*U.K. £*
White	N/A	N/A	49.95
Black	N/A	N/A	59.95
Brown	N/A	N/A	75.00

DA 184
Desert Orchid (on wooden plinth)
Style Two

Model No.:	Unknown
Designer:	Warren Platt
Height:	7 3/4" 19.7 cm
Colour:	Light grey (matt)
Issued:	1994 to the present
Series:	Connoisseur Horses

Price:	*U.S. $*	*Can. $*	*U.K. £*
	N/A	N/A	69.95

DA 185
Shetland Pony
Style Two

Model No.:	Unknown
Designer:	Amanda Hughes-Lubeck
Height:	5 1/4", 13.3 cm
Colour:	Dapple grey (glossy)
Issued:	1992 to the present

Price:	*U.S. $*	*Can. $*	*U.K. £*
	N/A	N/A	23.00

*

DA 188
Mr. Frisk (on plinth)
Style One

Model No.:	Unknown
Designer:	Graham Tongue
Height:	12 1/4" x 14", 31.1 x35.5 cm
Colour:	Chestnut (matt)
Issued:	1992 in a limited edition of 7,500 for Lawleys By Post

Price:	*U.S. $*	*Can. $*	*U.K. £*
	N/A	N/A	395.00

DA 189
Vietnamese Pot Bellied Pig

Model No.:	Unknown		
Designer:	Amanda Hughes-Lubeck		
Height:	6", 15.2 cm (length)		
Colour:	Dark brown		
Issued:	1992 to the present		
Series:	Connoisseur		

Price:	*U.S. $*	*Can. $*	*U.K. £*
	57.00	82.00	19.95

DA 190
Mr. Frisk (on wooden plinth)
Style Two

Model No.:	Unknown		
Designer:	Warren Platt		
Height:	7 1/2", 19.1 cm		
Colour:	Chestnut (matt)		
Issued:	1992 to the present		
Series:	Connoiseur Horses		

Price:	*U.S. $*	*Can. $*	*U.K. £*
	N/A	N/A	69.00

*

DA 193A
Horse of the Year 1992

Model No.:	Unknown		
Designer:	Amanda Hughes-Lubeck		
Height:	8 1/4", 21.0 cm		
Colour:	Chestnut (matt)		
Issued:	1992-1992		
Varieties:	Also called "My First Horse" DA 193B Available through Lawleys By Post and British Horse Society in 1992.		

Price:	*U.S. $*	*Can. $*	*U.K. £*
	100.00	125.00	60.00

DA 193B
My First Horse (on wooden plinth)

Model No.:	Unknown		
Designer:	Amanda Hughes-Lubeck		
Height:	8 1/4", 21.0 cm		
Colour:	Chestnut		
Issued:	1994 to the present		
Varieties:	Also called "Horse of the Year 1992" DA 193A		

Price:	*U.S. $*	*Can. $*	*U.K. £*
Glossy	N/A	N/A	49.95

DA 194
Cat
Seated - Style Three

Model No.:	Unknown		
Designer:	Martyn C. R. Alcock		
Height:	3 3/4", 9.5 cm		
Colour:	See below		
Issued:	1992 to the present		

Price:	*U.S. $*	*Can. $*	*U.K. £*
Black with white	33.00	41.00	11.95
Ginger	33.00	41.00	11.95

DA 195
Cat with Bandaged Paw

Model No.:	Unknown		
Designer:	Martyn C. R. Alcock		
Height:	3 1/2, 8.9 cm		
Colour:	Grey cat, white bandage		
Issued:	1992 to the present		

Price:	*U.S. $*	*Can. $*	*U.K. £*
Glossy	33.00	41.00	11.95

DA 196
Give Me A Home, Dog

Beswick No.:	3376		
Designer:	Martyn C. R. Alcock		
Height:	5 3/4", 14.6 cm		
Colour:	Brown and white		
Issued:	1994 to the present		

Price:	*U.S. $*	*Can. $*	*U.K. £*
Glossy	42.99	100.00	27.95

*

DA 205
Kestrel
Style Two

Model No.:	Unknown		
Designer:	Graham Tongue		
Height:	10", 24.5 cm		
Colour:	Light and dark brown		
Issued:	1992 in a limited editon of 2,500 for Lawleys By Post		
Series:	Artist's Signature Edition		

Price:	*U.S. $*	*Can. $*	*U.K. £*
	N/A	N/A	158.00

*

DA 213
Vietnamese Pot-Bellied Piglet

Model No.:	Unknown		
Designer:	Warren Platt		
Height:	3", 7.6 cm (length)		
Colour:	Grey		
Issued:	1993 to the present		

Price:	*U.S. $*	*Can. $*	*U.K. £*
	30.00	N/A	8.95

DA 214
Mick the Miller (Greyhound) (on wooden base)

Model No.:	Unknown		
Designer:	Graham Tongue		
Height:	9 1/2", 24.1 cm		
Colour:	Pale brown and white		
Issued:	1993 in a limited edition of 7,500 for Lawleys By Post		

Price:	*U.S. $*	*Can. $*	*U.K. £*
	N/A	N/A	95.00

DA 215
Tamworth Pig

Model No.:	Unknown		
Designer:	Amanda Hughes-Lubeck		
Height:	6", 15.2 cm		
Colour:	Brown		
Issued:	1994 to the present		

Price:	*U.S. $*	*Can. $*	*U.K. £*
	57.00	N/A	19.95

*

DA 218
Red Rum
Style Two

Model No.:	Unknown		
Designer:	Graham Tongue		
Height:	12", 30.5 cm		
Colour:	Bay (matt)		
Issued:	1993 in a limited edition of 7,500 for Lawleys by Post		

Price:	*U.S. $*	*Can. $*	*U.K. £*
Ceramic Base	N/A	N/A	395.00
Wooden plinth	N/A	N/A	395.00

*

DA 222
Bulldog
Style Five

Model No.:	Unknown		
Designer:	Warren Platt		
Height:	5", 12.7 cm		
Colour:	White with light brown patches over ears		
Issued:	1993 to the present		

Price:	*U.S. $*	*Can. $*	*U.K. £*
	37.00	100.00	19.95

DA 223
Nigerian Pot-Bellied Pygmy Goat

Model No.:	Unknown		
Designer:	Amanda Hughes-Lubeck		
Height:	5 1/4", 14.0 cm		
Colour:	White with black patches		
Issued:	1993 to the present		

Price:	*U.S. $*	*Can. $*	*U.K. £*
	N/A	75.00	19.95

*

DA 225
Spirit of Love, Horses (on wooden plinth)

Model No.:	Unknown		
Designer:	Alan Maslankowski		
Height:	6 1/2", 16.5 cm		
Colour:	Bay (matt)		
Issued:	1994 to the present		
Series:	Spirited Horses		

Price:	*U.S. $*	*Can. $*	*U.K. £*
	185.00	210.00	69.95

*

DA 227
Arkle
Style Two

Model No.:	Unknown		
Designer:	Graham Tongue		
Height:	12", 30.5 cm		
Colour:	Bay		
Issued:	1994 for Lawleys By Post		

Price:	*U.S. $*	*Can. $*	*U.K. £*
	N/A	N/A	N/A

CHINESE JADE
FLAMBÉ
SUNG

ANIMALS

NAME	MODEL No.	PAGE No.
Airedale Terrier (Ch, 'Cotsfold Tiosail') - Medium	738A	335
Airedale Terrier (Ch, 'Cotsfold Topsail') - Large	738	335
Alsatian (Seated, with collar)	497	335
Alsatian (Seated, without collar)	525	335
Apes (cuddling)	1	331
Badger (Style One)	1708	331
Bison (Style Three)	184	332
Bison (Style Two)	1693	332
Bloodhound	48	336
Brown bear (Style One)	592	332
Brown bear (Style Two - Chatcull series)	1688	332
Bull (Style One)	612	333
Bull (Style Two)	Unknown	333
Bulldog (seated - Style Four)	135A	337
Bulldog (seated - Style One)	38	336
Bulldog (seated - Style Two)	120	336
Bulldog - (seated - Style Three)	122	336
Cat (lying)	70	333
Cat (seated - Style One)	9	333
Cat (seated - Style Two)	2269	334
Cat with Mouse on Tail	216	334
Cavalier King Charles Spaniel (Style One)	82	337
Character Ape (dunce's cap and book)	640	331
Character Kitten (curled - Style Two)	398	334
Character Monkey	213	353
Cocker Spaniel Champion	709A	337
Collie (seated)	47	337
Comic Brown Bear	58	331
Dachshund (standing - Style One)	36	338
Dachshund Ch, 'Shrewd Saint' - Large	938	338
Dachshund Ch, 'Shrewd Saint' - Medium	938A	338
Dachshund Ch, 'Shrewd Saint' - Small	938B	338
Doberman Pinscher Ch, 'Rancho Dobe's Storm	1508	339
Elephant (stylized)	633	345
Elephant (trunk down, curled - Large) 13"	600	343
Elephant (trunk down, curled - Medium) 6 1/2"	Unknown	343
Elephant (trunk down, curled - Small) 4"	65	343
Elephant (trunk in salute - Large)	489	344
Elephant (trunk in salute - Medium)	489A	344
Elephant (trunk in salute - Small)	489B	344
Elephant (trunk stretching)	Unknown	344
Elephant and Young	3789	345
English St. Bernard	262	339
Fighter Elephant - Large	626	345
Fighter Elephant - Small	624	345
Fox (bowl)	20	349
Fox (curled - Style One)	15	346
Fox (curled - Style Two)	653	346
Fox (seated - Style One - Medium)	12	347
Fox (seated - Style One - Small)	12A	347
Fox (seated - Style Three)	102	348
Fox (seated - Style Two - Medium)	14A	347
Fox (seated - Style Two - Small)	14	348
Fox (seated - Style Two)	653	346
Fox (stalking - Large)	29A	348
Fox (stalking - Medium)	29	348
Fox (stalking - Small)	29B	349
Fox on Pedestal	21	349
Fox Terrier (seated - Style Two)	553	339
Fox Terrier (standing - Style Two)	580	339
Foxes (curled - Style One)	6	346
Foxes (curled - Style Two)	528	346

Apes
Model No.: 1
Designer: Leslie Harradine
Height: 2 1/2", 6.4 cm
Glaze: Flambé
Issued: c.1913-1936
Varieties: HN 883

Price:	U.S. $	Can. $	U.K. £
Flambé	900.00	1,250.00	600.00

Character Ape in Dunce's Cap with Book
Model No.: 640
Designer: Charles Noke
Height: 5 1/2", 14.0 cm
Glaze: Flambé
Issued: c.1929-1937
Varieties: HN 972

Price:	U.S. $	Can. $	U.K. £
Flambé	1,800.00	2,000.00	1,000.00

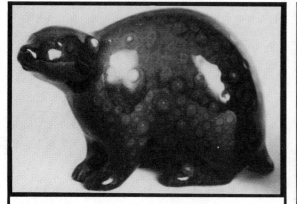

Badger
Style One
Model No.: 1708
Designer: Joseph Ledger
Height: 2 3/4", 7.0 cm
Glaze: Mandarin
Issued: c.1960
Series: Chatcull Range
Varieties: HN 2666

Price:	U.S. $	Can. $	U.K. £
Mandarin		Very Rare	

Comic Brown Bear
Model No.: 58
Designer: Unknown
Height: 5", 12.7 cm
Glaze: Flambé
Issued: c.1918-1936
Varieties: HN 170, 270

Price:	U.S. $	Can. $	U.K. £
Flambé	650.00	900.00	450.00

For illustration of
model no. 592 in
naturalistic colours
see page no. 98

For illustration of model no. 592 in naturalistic colours see page no. 98

Brown Bear
Style One

Model No.:	592
Designer:	Unknown
Height:	5", 12.7 cm
Glaze:	Flambé
Issued:	c.1928
Varieties:	HN 955

Price:	*U.S. $*	*Can. $*	*U.K. £*
Flambé	900.00	1,250.00	600.00

Brown Bear
Style Two - Chatcull Series

Model No.:	1688
Designer:	Joseph Ledger
Height:	4", 10.1 cm
Glaze:	Mandarin
Issued:	c.1960
Varieties:	HN 2659

Price:	*U.S. $*	*Can. $*	*U.K. £*
Mandarin		Very Rare	

Photograph
Not Available
at Press Time

Bison
Style Two

Model No.:	1799
Designer:	Joseph Ledger
Height:	5 1/2", 14.0 cm
Size:	Medium
Glaze:	Flambé
Issued:	c.1960

Price:	*U.S. $*	*Can. $*	*U.K. £*
Flambé		Very Rare	

Bison
Style Three

Model No.:	1847
Designer:	Unknown
Height:	3", 7.6 cm
Size:	Small
Glaze:	Flambé
Issued:	c.1963

Price:	*U.S. $*	*Can. $*	*U.K. £*
Flambé		Very Rare	

Bull
Style One

Model No.:	612
Designer:	Unknown
Height:	7" x 10 3/4", 17.8 x 27.3 cm
Glaze:	Flambé
Issued:	c.1928

Price:	U.S. $	Can. $	U.K. £
Flambé		Extremely Rare	

Bull
Style Two

Model No.:	Unknown
Designer:	Eric Griffiths
Height:	10 1/2", 26.7 cm
Glaze:	Flambé
Issued:	c.1927

Price:	U.S. $	Can. $	U.K. £
Flambé		Prototype	

Cat
Seated - Style One

Model No.:	9
Designer:	Charles Noke
Height:	4 1/2", 11.4 cm
Glaze:	See below
Issued:	1920 to the present
Varieties:	HN 109, 120. 967, Sung

Price:	U.S. $	Can. $	U.K. £
Flambé	125.00	170.00	35.00
Sung	600.00	750.00	350.00

Cat
Lying

Model No.:	70
Designer:	Unknown
Height:	3 1/2", 8.9 cm
Glaze:	Flambé
Issued:	c.1920-1936
Varieties:	HN 233

Price:	U.S. $	Can. $	U.K. £
Flambé		Very Rare	

Cat with Mouse on Tail

Model No.:	216		
Designer:	Unknown		
Height:	4 1/2", 11.4 cm		
Glaze:	See below		
Issued:	c.1920		
Varieties:	HN 201, 202		

Price:	*U.S. $*	*Can. $*	*U.K. £*
Flambé	1,000.00	1,300.00	650.00
Sung	1,200.00	1,500.00	750.00

Persian Kitten
Style One

Model No.:	242		
Designer:	Unknown		
Height:	5", 12.7 cm		
Glaze:	Sung		
Issued:	c.1920		
Varieties:	HN 204, 221		

Price:	*U.S. $*	*Can. $*	*U.K. £*
Sung		Very Rare	

Character Kitten
Curled - Style Two

Model No.:	398		
Designer:	Unknown		
Height:	1 1/4", 3.2 cm		
Glaze:	Chinese Jade		
Issued:	c.1930		
Varieties:	HN 823, 824, 825		

Price:	*U.S. $*	*Can. $*	*U.K. £*
Chinese Jade		Very Rare	

Cat
Seated - Style Two

Model No.:	2269		
Designer:	Alan Maslankowski		
Height:	11 1/2", 29.2 cm		
Glaze:	Flambé		
Issued:	1977 to the present		

Price:	*U.S. $*	*Can. $*	*U.K. £*
Flambé	500.00	700.00	160.00

Airedale Terrier, Ch. 'Cotsfold Topsail' - Large

Model No.: 738
Designer: Frederick Daws
Height: 7 1/2", 19.1 cm
Size: Large
Glaze: Flambé
Issued: c.1931
Varieties: HN 1022

Price:	*U.S. $*	*Can. $*	*U.K. £*
Flambé	1,100.00	1,400.00	650.00

Airedale Terrier Ch, 'Cotsfold Topsail' - Medium

Model No.: 738A
Designer: Frederick Daws
Height: 5 1/2", 14.0 cm
Size: Medium
Glaze: Flambé
Issued: c.1931
Varieties: HN 1023

Price:	*U.S. $*	*Can. $*	*U.K. £*
Flambé	800.00	1,000.00	550.00

Alsatian
Seated, with collar

Model No.: 497
Designer: Unknown
Height: 3 3/4", 9.5 cm
Glaze: Flambé
Issued: c.1926-by 1946
Varieties: HN 899; On lid of lustre bowl HN 986

Price:	*U.S. $*	*Can. $*	*U.K. £*
Flambé	700.00	900.00	375.00

For illustration of
model no. 525
in naturalistic colours
see page no. 90

Alsatian
Seated, without collar

Model No.: 525
Designer: Unknown
Height: 7", 17.8 cm
Glaze: Flambé
Issued: c.1927
Varieties: HN 921

Price:	*U.S. $*	*Can. $*	*U.K. £*
Flambé	1,250.00	1,600.00	850.00

Bloodhound

Model No.: 48
Designer: Unknown
Height: 5 3/4", 14.6 cm
Glaze: Flambé
Issued: c.1926
Varieties: HN 176

Price:	U.S. $	Can. $	U.K. £
Flambé	1,200.00	1,500.00	750.00

Bulldog
Seated - Style One

Model No.: 38
Designer: Unknown
Height: 4", 10.1 cm
Glaze: Flambé
Issued: 1912-1936

Price:	U.S. $	Can. $	U.K. £
Flambé		Extremely Rare	

Bulldog
Seated - Style Two

Model No.: 120
Designer: Unknown
Height: 3", 7.6 cm
Glaze: Flambé
Issued: c.1913

Price:	U.S. $	Can. $	U.K. £
Flambé	800.00	1,100.00	500.00

For illustration of
model no. 122
in naturalistic colours
see page no. 79

Bulldog
Seated - Style Three

Model No.: 122
Designer: Unknown
Height: 2 3/4", 7.0 cm
Glaze: See below
Issued: c.1913-by 1946
Varieties: HN 881A, 881B;
On lid of Lustre Bowl HN 987

Price:	U.S. $	Can. $	U.K. £
Chinese Jade		Very Rare	
Flambé		Very Rare	

Bulldog
Seated - Style Four
Model No.:   135A
Designer: Unknown
Height: 6", 15.2 cm
Glaze: Flambé
Issued: c.1913
Varieties: HN 129. 948

Price:	U.S. $	Can. $	U.K. £
Flambé	1,000.00	1,300.00	600.00

Cavalier King Charles Spaniel
Style One
Model No.:   82
Designer: Charles Noke
Height: 3 1/2", 8.9 cm
Glaze: See below
Issued: 1920-1936
Varieties: HN 127

Price:	U.S. $	Can. $	U.K. £
Chinese Jade	1,500.00	1,750.00	750.00
Flambé	800.00	1,000.00	500.00

Cocker Spaniel, Ch. 'Lucky Star of Ware'
Model No.:   709A
Designer: Frederick Daws
Height: 5 1/4" x 6 3/4", 13.3 x 17.2 cm
Glaze: Flambé
Issued: c.1937
Varieties: HN 1020, 1036, 1109, 1187

Price:	U.S. $	Can. $	U.K. £
Flambé	900.00	1,200.00	500.00

Collie
Seated
Model No.:   47
Designer: Unknown
Height: 7 1/2", 19.1 cm
Glaze: Flambé
Issued: c.1912
Varieties: HN 105, 106, 112

Price:	U.S. $	Can. $	U.K. £
Flambé	950.00	1,200.00	500.00

Dachshund
Standing - Style One
Model No.:   36
Designer: Unknown
Height: 4 1/2" x 6 1/2", 11.4 x 16.5 cm
Glaze: Flambé
Issued: c.1912
Varieties: HN 970

Price:	*U.S. $*	*Can. $*	*U.K. £*
Flambé	750.00	950.00	450.00

For illustration of
model no. 938
in naturalistic colours
see page no. 144

Dachshund Ch, 'Shrewd Saint' - Large
Model No.:   938
Designer: Frederick Daws
Height: 6", 15.2 cm
Size: Large
Glaze: Flambé
Issued: c.1937
Varieties: HN 1127, 1139

Price:	*U.S. $*	*Can. $*	*U.K. £*
Flambé	950.00	1,250.00	500.00

For illustration of
model no. 938A
in naturalistic colours
see page no. 144

Dachshund, Ch, 'Shrewd Saint' - Medium
Model No.:   938A
Designer: Frederick Daws
Height: 4", 10.1 cm
Size: Medium
Glaze: Flambé
Issued: c.1937
Varieties: HN 1128, 1140

Price:	*U.S. $*	*Can. $*	*U.K. £*
Flambé	600.00	775.00	375.00

For illustration of
model no. 938B
in naturalistic colours
see page no. 145

Dachshund Ch, 'Shrewd Saint' - Small
Model No.:   938B
Designer: Frederick Daws
Height: 3" x 4 1/2", 7.6 x 11.4 cm
Size: Small
Glaze: Flambé
Issued: c.1937
Varieties: HN 1129, 1141

Price:	*U.S. $*	*Can. $*	*U.K. £*
Flambé	450.00	600.00	300.00

For illustration of
model no. 1508
in naturalistic colours
see page no. 199

Doberman Pinscher, Ch. 'Rancho Dobe's Storm'

Model No.:	1508
Designer:	Frederick Daws
Height:	6 1/4" x 6 1/2", 15.9 x 16.5 cm
Glaze:	Flambé
Issued:	c.1955
Varieties:	HN 2645

Price:	U.S. $	Can. $	U.K. £
Flambé		Extremely Rare	

English St. Bernard

Model No.:	262
Designer:	Unknown
Height:	7 3/4", 19.7 cm
Glaze:	Flambé
Issued:	c.1919
Varieties:	HN 231

Price:	U.S. $	Can. $	U.K. £
Flambé	950.00	1,200.00	650.00

Fox Terrier
Seated - Style Two

Model No.:	553
Designer:	Unknown
Height:	4 1/2", 11.4 cm
Glaze:	Flambé
Issued:	c.1927
Varieties:	HN 910, 924

Price:	U.S. $	Can. $	U.K. £
Flambé	700.00	900.00	375.00

Fox Terrier
Standing - Style Two

Model No.:	580
Designer:	Frederick Daws
Height:	5 1/2", 14.0 cm
Glaze:	Flambé
Issued:	c.1927-by 1946
Varieties:	HN 943, 945

Price:	U.S. $	Can. $	U.K. £
Chinese Jade	950.00	1,300.00	600.00
Flambé	750.00	1,000.00	500.00

Foxhound
Seated - Style One

Model No.:	209		
Designer:	Unknown		
Height:	3", 7.6 cm		
Glaze:	Flambé		
Issued:	c.1917		
Varieties:	HN 166		

Price:	*U.S. $*	*Can. $*	*U.K. £*
Flambé		Very Rare	

Greyhound
Seated

Model No.:	80		
Designer:	Charles Noke		
Height:	5", 12.7 cm		
Glaze:	Flambé		
Issued:	c.1913-by 1946		
Varieties:	HN 889, 890		

Price:	*U.S. $*	*Can. $*	*U.K. £*
Flambé	650.00	800.00	400.00

For illustration of
model no. 405
in naturalistic colours
see page no. 67

For illustration of
model no. 406
in naturalistic colours
see page no. 66

Pekinese Puppy
Standing

Model No.:	405		
Designer:	Unknown		
Height:	2", 5.1 cm		
Glaze:	See below		
Issued:	c.1923		
Varieties:	HN 833		

Price:	*U.S. $*	*Can. $*	*U.K. £*
Chinese Jade		Very Rare	
Flambé		Very Rare	

Pekinese Puppy
Seated

Model No.:	406		
Designer:	Unknown		
Height:	2 1/2", 6.4 cm		
Glaze:	See below		
Issued:	c.1923		
Varieties:	HN 832		

Price:	*U.S. $*	*Can. $*	*U.K. £*
Chinese Jade		Very Rare	
Flambé		Very Rare	

For illustration of
model no. 544
in naturalistic colours
see page no. 91

Pekinese (two)

Model No.: 544
Designer: Unknown
Height: 2 1/2" x 4 1/2". 6.4 x 11.4 cm
Glaze: See below
Issued: c.1927
Varieties: HN 927

Price:	*U.S. $*	*Can. $*	*U.K. £*
Chinese Jade		Very Rare	
Flambé		Very Rare	

**Pekinese
Standing**

Model No.: 689
Designer: Unknown
Height: 3 1/2" x 5", 8.9 x 12.7 cm
Glaze: Chinese Jade
Issued: c.1930
Varieties: HN 995, 1003

Price:	*U.S. $*	*Can. $*	*U.K. £*
Chinese Jade	1,500.00	1,800.00	900.00

**Pekinese, Ch. 'Biddee of Ifield'
Seated**

Model No.: 752B
Designer: Frederick Daws
Height: 3", 7.6 cm
Glaze: Flambé
Issued: c.1931
Varieties: HN 1040

Price:	*U.S. $*	*Can. $*	*U.K. £*
Flambé		Very Rare	

**Puppy
Seated**

Model No.: 116
Designer: Unknown
Height: 4", 10.1 cm
Glaze: See below
Issued: c.1913
Varieties: HN 128
Derivitive: Onyx pin tray

Price:	*U.S. $*	*Can. $*	*U.K. £*
Flambé	400.00	500.00	250.00
Sung	750.00	900.00	425.00

For illustration of
model no. 118
in naturalistic colours
see page no. 40

Puppy with Bone
Model No.:   118
Designer: Unknown
Height: 4", 10.1 cm
Glaze: Flambé
Issued: c.1913
Varieties: HN 232

Price: *U.S. $*   *Can. $*   *U.K. £*
Flambé   Extremely Rare

Scottish Terrier
Standing - Style One
Model No.:   78
Designer: Unknown
Height: 3" x 5", 7.6 x 12.7 cm
Glaze: Flambé
Issued: c.1913
Varieties: HN 964, 965

Price: *U.S. $*   *Can. $*   *U.K. £*
Flambé   Very Rare

For illustration of
model no. 658
in naturalistic colours
see page no. 105

Sealyham
Standing - Style One
Model No.:   658
Designer: Unknown
Height: 3", 7.6 cm
Glaze: Flambé
Issued: c.1930
Varieties: HN 982A, 982B, 982C, 983

Price: *U.S. $*   *Can. $*   *U.K. £*
Flambé   Very Rare

Sealyham Ch, 'Scotia Stylist'
Model No.:   748
Designer: Frederick Daws
Height: 5 1/2" x 9", 14.0 x 22.9 cm
Size: Large
Glaze: Flambé
Issued: c.1931
Varieties: HN 1030

Price: *U.S. $*   *Can. $*   *U.K. £*
Flambé   1,600.00   2,000.00   950.00

For illustration of
model no. 121
in naturalistic colours
see page no. 31

Terrier Puppy
Lying

Model No.:	121
Designer:	Unknown
Height:	3" x 7 3/4", 7.6 x 19.7 cm
Glaze:	Flambé
Issued:	c.1913
Varieties:	HN 194

Price:	U.S. $	Can. $	U.K. £
Flambé		Very Rare	

Elephant
Trunk down, curled - large

Model No.:	600
Designer:	Charles Noke
Height:	13", 33.0 cm
Size:	Large
Glaze:	See below
Issued:	c.1938-1968
Varieties:	HN 1121

Price:	U.S. $	Can. $	U.K. £
Flambé	4,000.00	5,000.00	2,500.00
Sung	4,000.00	5,000.00	2,500.00

Elephant
Trunk down, curled - medium

Model No.:	Unknown
Designer:	Unknown
Height:	6 1/2", 16.5 cm
Size:	Medium
Glaze:	Flambé
Issued:	Unknown

Price:	U.S. $	Can. $	U.K. £
Flambé	450.00	600.00	300.00

Elephant
Trunk down, curled - small

Model No.:	65
Designer:	Charles Noke
Height:	4", 10.1 cm
Size:	Small
Glaze:	See below
Issued:	c.1913-by 1946
Varieties:	HN 181, 186

Price:	U.S. $	Can. $	U.K. £
Flambé	350.00	500.00	250.00
Sung	475.00	650.00	350.00

Elephant
Trunk in salute - large

Model No.:	489		
Designer:	Charles Noke		
Height:	7", 17.8 cm		
Size:	Large		
Glaze:	See below		
Issued:	c.1926-1962		
Varieties:	HN 966		

Price:	U.S. $	Can. $	U.K. £
Chinese Jade	750.00	1,000.00	500.00
Flambé	300.00	425.00	200.00

Elephant
Trunk in salute - medium

Model No.:	489A		
Designer:	Charles Noke		
Height:	5 1/4", 13.3 cm		
Size:	Medium		
Glaze:	See below		
Issued:	Originally introduced c.1926-1950		
	Re-introduced in 1962 to the present		
Varieties:	HN 891A		

Price:	U.S. $	Can. $	U.K. £
Flambé original	150.00	200.00	100.00
Flambé current	192.00	250.00	55.00

For illustration of
model no. 489B
in naturalistic colours
see page no. 82

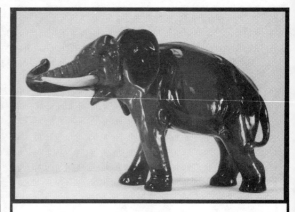

Elephant
Trunk in salute - small

Model No.:	489B		
Designer:	Charles Noke		
Height:	4 1/2", 11.4 cm		
Size:	Small		
Glaze:	See below		
Issued:	c.1926-1962		
Varieties:	HN 891B, 964, 2644		

Price:	U.S. $	Can. $	U.K. £
Flambé	150.00	200.00	100.00

Elephant
Trunk stretching

Model No.:	Unknown		
Designer:	Charles Noke		
Height:	12" x 18", 30.5 x 45.7 cm		
Glaze:	See below		
Issued:	c.1930		

Price:	U.S. $	Can. $	U.K. £
Flambé	3,500.00	5,000.00	2,000.00
Sung	3,500.00	5,000.00	2,000.00

Fighter Elephant - large

Model No.: 626
Designer: Charles Noke
Height: 12" x 9", 30.5 x 22.9 cm
Size: Large
Glaze: Flambé
Issued: c.1929
Varieties: HN 1120, 2640

Price:	U.S. $	Can. $	U.K. £
Flambé	4,000.00	5,000.00	2,500.00

Fighter Elephant - Small

Model No.: 624
Designer: Charles Noke
Height: 4", 10.1 cm
Size: Small
Glaze: See below
Issued: c.1929

Price:	U.S. $	Can. $	U.K. £
Flambé	450.00	600.00	300.00
Chinese Jade	800.00	1,200.00	600.00

Elephant and Young (HN 3548)

Model No.: 3789
Designer: Eric Griffiths
Height: 3 1/2", 8.3 cm
Glaze: Flambé
Issued: 1990 to the present
Series: Images of Fire

Price:	U.S. $	Can. $	U.K. £
Flambé	N/A	199.50	55.00

Elephant
Stylized

Model No.: 633
Designer: Unknown
Height: 3", 7.6 cm
Glaze: Chinese Jade
Issued: c.1929

Price:	U.S. $	Can. $	U.K. £
Chinese Jade		Extremely Rare	

For illustration of
model no. 15
in naturalistic colours
see page no. 19

For illustration of
model no. 653
in naturalistic colours
see page no. 104

Fox
Curled - Style One

Model No.:	15
Designer:	Unknown
Height:	4 3/4". 12.1 cm
Glaze:	See below
Issued:	c.1912
Varieties:	HN 147D

Price:	U.S. $	Can. $	U.K. £
Flambé	450.00	500.00	250.00
Matt Red Glaze	450.00	500.00	250.00
Treacle Glaze	450.00	500.00	250.00

Fox
Curled - Style Two

Model No.:	653
Designer:	Unknown
Height:	Unknown
Size:	Medium
Glaze:	Flambé
Issued:	c.1929
Varieties:	HN 978

Price:	U.S. $	Can. $	U.K. £
		Very Rare	

For illustration of
model no. 6
in naturalistic colours
see page no. 7

For illustration of
model no. 528
in naturalistic colours
see page no. 89

Foxes
Curled - Style One

Model No.:	6
Designer:	Unknown
Height:	3 1/2", 8.9 cm
Glaze:	See below
Issued:	c.1912
Varieties:	HN 117, 179

Price:	U.S. $	Can. $	U.K. £
Flambé	750.00	850.00	350.00
Sung	950.00	1,000.00	450.00
Treacle Glaze	500.00	600.00	275.00

Foxes
Curled - Style Two

Model No.:	528
Designer:	Unknown
Height:	3" x 6", 7.6 x 15.2 cm
Glaze:	See below
Issued:	c.1926
Varieties:	HN 920, 925

Price:	U.S. $	Can. $	U.K. £
Flambé	750.00	850.00	550.00
Matt Red Glaze	500.00	600.00	165.00

<table>
<tr><td colspan="2">

For illustration of
model no. 545
in naturalistic colours
see page no. 91

</td><td colspan="2">

For illustration of
model no. 12
in naturalistic colours
see page no. 18

</td></tr>
</table>

Foxes
Curled - Style Three

Model No.:	545		
Designer:	Unknown		
Height:	1 3/4", 5.1 cm		
Size:	Miniature		
Glaze:	Flambé		
Issued:	c.1927		
Varieties:	HN 926		

Price:	U.S. $	Can. $	U.K. £
Flambé	500.00	600.00	225.00

Fox
Seated - Style One - Medium

Model No.:	12		
Designer:	Unknown		
Height:	4 3/4", 12.1 cm		
Size:	Medium		
Glaze:	See below		
Issued:	c.1912-1946		
Varieties:	HN 147C		

Price:	U.S. $	Can. $	U.K. £
Flambé	350.00	400.00	175.00
Sung	450.00	500.00	225.00

Fox
Seated - Style One - Small

Model No.:	12A		
Designer:	Unknown		
Height:	3", 7.6 cm		
Size:	Small		
Glaze:	Flambé		
Issued:	1912-1938		
Varieties:	HN 147C-1		

Price:	U.S. $	Can. $	U.K. £
Flambé	350.00	400.00	175.00

Fox
Seated - Style Two - Medium

Model No.:	14A		
Designer:	Unknown		
Height:	5 1/2", 14.0 cm		
Size:	Medium		
Glaze:	Flambé		
Issued:	c.1912		

Price:	U.S. $	Can. $	U.K. £
Flambé	350.00	400.00	225.00

Fox
Seated - Style Two - Small

Model No.:	14
Designer:	Unknown
Height:	4 1/2", 11.4 cm
Size:	Small
Glaze:	See below
Issued:	Flambé: 1912 to the present
	Sung: c.1920
Varieties:	HN 147B

Price:	U.S. $	Can. $	U.K. £
Flambé	125.00	160.00	35.00
Sung	350.00	400.00	200.00

Fox
Seated - Style Three

Model No.:	102
Designer:	Charles Noke
Height:	9 1/4", 23.5 cm
Size:	Large
Glaze:	Flambé
Issued:	1913 - 1962
Varieties:	HN 130

Price:	U.S. $	Can. $	U.K. £
Flambé	850.00	1,000.00	295.00

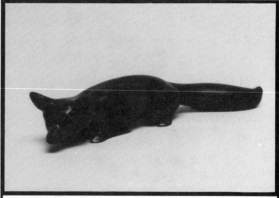

Fox
Stalking -Large

Model No.:	29A
Designer:	Unknown
Height:	2 3/4" x 13", 7.0 x 33.0 cm
Size:	Large
Glaze:	Flambé
Issued:	c.1912-1962
Varieties:	HN 147A

Price:	U.S. $	Can. $	U.K. £
Flambé	450.00	500.00	225.00

Fox
Stalking - Medium

Model No.	29
Designer:	Unknown
Height:	1 3/4" x 9 1/4", 4.4 x 23.5 cm
Size:	Medium
Glaze:	Flambé
Issued:	c.1912-1962
Varieties:	HN 147E

Price:	U.S. $	Can. $	U.K. £
Flambé	250.00	300.00	150.00

Fox
Stalking - Small

Model No.:	29B
Designer:	Unknown
Height:	1" x 5 1/4", 2.5 x 13.3 cm
Size:	Small
Glaze:	See below
Issued:	c.1912 to the present (Flambé)
Varieties:	HN 147A-1

Price:	U.S. $	Can. $	U.K. £
Chinese Jade	200.00	300.00	175.00
Flambé	N/A	118.00	24.95
Sung	200.00	250.00	150.00

Photograph
Not Available
at Press Time

Fox Bowl

Model No.:	20
Designer:	Unknown
Length:	2 1/2" x 12 1/2", 6.4 x 31.7 cm
Glaze:	Flambé
Issued:	c.1912-1936

Price:	U.S. $	Can. $	U.K. £
Flambé	375.00	450.00	250.00

For illustration of
model no. 21
in naturalistic colours
see page no. 109

Fox on Pedestal

Model No.:	21
Designer:	Unknown
Height:	5 1/4", 13.3 cm
Glaze:	Flambé
Issued:	c.1912-1936
Varieties:	HN 994

Price:	U.S. $	Can. $	U.K. £
Flambé	1,350.00	1,500.00	650.00

Photograph
Not Available
at Press Time

Hare
Standing - Style One

Model No.:	86
Designer:	Unknown
Height:	5 3/4", 14.6 cm
Glaze:	Flambé
Issued:	c.1912-1936

Price:	U.S. $	Can. $	U.K. £
Flambé		Rare	

Hare
Crouching - Style One
Model No.: 119
Designer: Unknown
Height: 2" x 4 1/2", 5.1 x 11.4 cm
Glaze: Flambé
Issued: 1913-by 1946
Varieties: HN 107, 126, 142, 273, 803

Price:	U.S. $	Can. $	U.K. £
Flambé	325.00	375.00	175.00
Sung	400.00	450.00	225.00

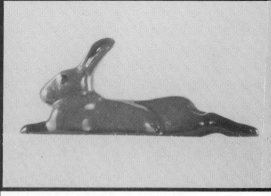

Hare
Lying, legs stretched behind - Large
Model No.: 656
Designer: Unknown
Height: 3" x 7 1/2", 7.6 x 19.1 cm
Size: Large
Glaze: Flambé
Issued: 1929-1962
Varieties: HN 979, 984, 985, 1071, 2593

Price:	U.S. $	Can. $	U.K. £
Flambé	350.00	400.00	175.00

Hare
Lying, legs stretched behind - Small
Model No.: 656A
Designer: Unknown
Height: 1 3/4" x 5 1/4", 4.4 x 13.3 cm
Size: Small
Glaze: Flambé
Issued: 1929 to the present
Varieties: HN 2594

Price:	U.S. $	Can. $	U.K. £
Flambé	N/A	118.00	24.95

Hare
Crouching - Style Three
Model No.: 1157
Designer: Unknown
Height: 2 3/4", 7.0 cm
Glaze: Flambé
Issued: 1945 to the present
Varieties: HN 2592

Price:	U.S. $	Can. $	U.K. £
Flambé	120.00	170.00	35.00

Photograph
Not Available
at Press Time

Horse

Model No.: 882
Designer: Unknown
Height: Unknown
Glaze: Chinese Jade
Issued: c.1934
Derivitive: Lamp

Price:	*U.S. $*	*Can. $*	*U.K. £*
Chinese Jade		Extremely Rare	

'Gift of Life' Mare and Foal (HN 3536)

Model No.: 2923
Designer: Russell Willis
Height: 9", 22.9 cm
Glaze: Flambé
Issued: 1987 to the present
Series; Images of Fire
Varieties: HN 3524

Price:	*U.S. $*	*Can. $*	*U.K. £*
Flambé	N/A	1,630.00	525.00

Lion
Seated

Model No.: 59
Designer: Unknown
Height: 6 1/2", 16.5 cm
Glaze: See below
Issued: c.1912
Varieties: HN 223

Price:	*U.S. $*	*Can. $*	*U.K. £*
Flambé		Rare	
Treacle Glaze		Rare	

Photograph
Not Available
at Press Time

Lion
Lying

Model No.: 64
Designer: Unknown
Height: 2 1/2" x 7", 6.4 x 17.8 cm
Glaze: Flambé
Issued: c.1918-1936

Price:	*U.S. $*	*Can. $*	*U.K. £*
Flambé	1,100.00	1,300.00	575.00

Llama
Style One
Model No.: 827
Designer: Unknown
Height: 6", 15.2 cm
Glaze: See below
Issued: c.1933
Derivitive: Lamp

Price:	U.S. $	Can. $	U.K. £
Chinese Jade		Very Rare	
Flambé		Very Rare	

For illustration of
model no. 16
in naturalistic colours
see page no. 22

Monkey
Hand to ear
Model No.: 16
Designer: Unknown
Height: 3 1/2", 8.9 cm
Glaze: See below
Issued: c.1912
Varieties: HN 156

Price:	U.S. $	Can. $	U.K. £
Flambé	450.00	550.00	300.00

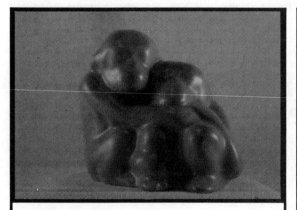

Monkies (Mother and Baby)
Model No.: 52
Designer: Leslie Harradine
Height: 3", 7.6 cm
Glaze: See below
Issued: c.1912-1962
Varieties: HN 254

Price:	U.S. $	Can. $	U.K. £
Flambé	450.00	500.00	225.00
Sung	450.00	500.00	225.00
Yellow/gold matt	475.00	350.00	250.00

Monkey
Seated, arms folded
Model No.: 53
Designer: Unknown
Height: 3", 7.6 cm
Glaze: See below
Issued: c.1912-by 1946
Varieties: HN 118, 253

Price:	U.S. $	Can. $	U.K. £
Flambé	400.00	450.00	225.00
Titanian		Rare	

Character Monkey

Model No.:	213		
Designer:	Charles Noke		
Height:	7", 17.8 cm		
Glaze:	Flambé		
Issued:	c.1920		
Varieties:	HN 182, 183		

Price:	*U.S. $*	*Can. $*	*U.K. £*
Flambé		Very Rare	

Mountain Goat, 'Capricorn'

Model No.:	882		
Designer:	Adrien Hughes		
Height:	9 3/4", 24.8 cm		
Glaze:	Flambé		
Issued:	1983-1983		
Varieties:	HN 3523		

Price:	*U.S. $*	*Can. $*	*U.K. £*
Flambé	250.00	300.00	150.00

For illustration of
model no. 1164
in naturalistic colours
see page no. 46

Photograph
Not Available
at Press Time

Mouse on a Cube

Model No.:	1164		
Designer:	Charles Noke		
Height:	2 1/2", 6.4 cm		
Glaze:	Flambé		
Issued:	c.1912-by 1946		
Varieties:	HN 255		

Price:	*U.S. $*	*Can. $*	*U.K. £*
Flambé	500.00	500.00	250.00

Mouse with a Nut

Model No.:	1164A		
Designer:	Unknown		
Height:	2 1/4", 5.7 cm		
Glaze:	Flambé		
Issued:	c.1912		
Varieties:			

Price:	*U.S. $*	*Can. $*	*U.K. £*
Flambé	500.00	500.00	250.00

Mouse
Crouching

Photograph
Not Available
at Press Time

Model No.:	1164B
Designer:	Unknown
Height:	Unknown
Glaze:	Flambé
Issued:	c.1912
Varieties:	HN 1090B on Fluted Ashtray
	HN 1090A on Plain Ashtray

Price:	U.S. $	Can. $	U.K. £
Flambé	500.00	500.00	250.00

Panther

Model No.:	111
Designer:	Unknown
Height:	8 1/2" x 9", 21.6 x 22.9 cm
Glaze:	Flambé
Issued:	c.1912

Price:	U.S. $	Can. $	U.K. £
Flambé	750.00	800.00	550.00

Model No. 111 was also used to produce the Flambé Tiger

Pig
Snorting - Large

Model No.:	72
Designer:	Unknown
Height:	2 1/2" x 5 1/2", 6.4 x 14.0 cm
Glaze:	Flambé
Issued:	c.1912-1936
Varieties:	HN 968A

Price:	U.S. $	Can. $	U.K. £
Flambé	575.00	750.00	350.00

For illustration of
model no. 72A
in naturalistic colours
see page no. 101

Pig
Snorting - Small

Model No.:	72A
Designer:	Unknown
Height:	Unknown
Size:	Small
Glaze:	Flambé
Issued:	c.1928-1936
Varieties:	HN 968B

Price:	U.S. $	Can. $	U.K. £
Flambé	550.00	675.00	325.00

Pig
Snoozing - Large
Model No.:	110		
Designer:	Unknown		
Height:	2" x 4 1/2", 5.1 x 11.4 cm		
Size:	Large		
Glaze:	See below		
Issued:	c.1912		
Varieties:	HN 800		

Price:	*U.S. $*	*Can. $*	*U.K. £*
Flambé	575.00	650.00	350.00
Sung	350.00	400.00	225.00

Pig
Snoozing - Medium
Model No.:	110A		
Designer:	Unknown		
Height:	Unknown		
Size:	Medium		
Glaze:	See below		
Issued:	c.1912		
Varieties:	HN 801A		

Price:	*U.S. $*	*Can. $*	*U.K. £*
Flambé	550.00	600.00	300.00
Sung	350.00	400.00	225.00

Photograph
Not Available
at Press Time

Pig
Standing Squealing
Model No.:	114
Designer:	Unknown
Height:	2 1/2", 6.4 cm
Glaze:	Flambé
Issued:	c.1912

Price:	*U.S. $*	*Can. $*	*U.K. £*
Flambé		Extremely Rare	

Pigs
Snoozing - Ears Down
Model No.:	61
Designer:	Unknown
Height:	4", 10.1 cm
Glaze:	Flambé
Issued:	1912-1936
Varieties:	HN 213, 238, 802

Price:	*U.S. $*	*Can. $*	*U.K. £*
Flambé	600.00	700.00	350.00

For illustration of
model no. 62
in naturalistic colours
see page no. 36

Pigs
Snoozing - Ears Up

Model No.:	62		
Designer:	Charles Noke		
Height:	2" x 3 3/4", 5.1 x 9.5 cm		
Glaze:	Flambé		
Issued:	1912-1936		

Price:	*U.S. $*	*Can. $*	*U.K. £*
Flambé	600.00	700.00	350.00

Pigs at a Trough

Model No.:	81		
Designer:	Unknown		
Height:	2 1/2" x 4", 6.4 x 10.1 cm		
Glaze:	Flambé		
Issued:	c.1931-1936		

Price:	*U.S. $*	*Can. $*	*U.K. £*
Flambé	550.00	600.00	300.00

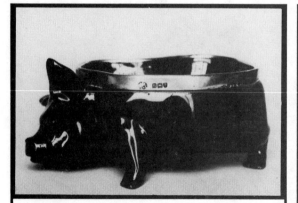

Pig Bowl
Style One

Model No.:	Unknown		
Designer:	Unknown		
Height:	2 1/2" x 5 1/2", 6.4 x 14.0 cm		
Glaze:	See below (Sterling silver rim)		
Issued:	c.1920		
Varieties:	HN 243		

Price:	*U.S. $*	*Can. $*	*U.K. £*
Flambé	750.00	800.00	400.00
Titanian (1934)		Very Rare	

Pig Bowl
Style Two

Model No.:	Unknown		
Designer:	Unknown		
Height:	1 3/4" x 3 1/2", 4.4 x 8.9 cm		
Glaze:	Flambé with Sterling silver rim		
Issued:	c.1922		

Price:	*U.S. $*	*Can. $*	*U.K. £*
Flambé		Very Rare	

For illustration of
model no. 1689
in naturalistic colours
see page no. 202

Pine Martin

Model No.:	1689		
Designer:	Joseph Ledger		
Height:	4", 10.1 cm		
Glaze:	Flambé		
Issued:	c.1960		
Varieties:	HN 2656		

Price:	*U.S. $*	*Can. $*	*U.K. £*
Flambé		Rare	

**Polar Bear
Seated**

Model No.:	39		
Designer:	Unknown		
Height:	3 1/2", 8.9 cm		
Glaze:	Flambé		
Issued:	c.1912 - 1936		
Varieties:	HN 121		

Price:	*U.S. $*	*Can. $*	*U.K. £*
Flambé	675.00	800.00	400.00

Polar Bear on Dish

Model No.:	40		
Designer:	Unknown		
Height:	5", 12.7 cm		
Glaze:	Flambé		
Issued:	c.1912-1936		

Price:	*U.S. $*	*Can. $*	*U.K. £*
Flambé	750.00	800.00	400.00

Polar Bears on Ice Floe

Model No.:	54		
Designer:	Unknown		
Height:	3 1/2", 8.9 cm		
Glaze:	See below		
Issued:	c.1912-1936		

Price:	*U.S. $*	*Can. $*	*U.K. £*
Flambé	1,200.00	1,300.00	650.00

For illustration of
model no. 67
in naturalistic colours
see page no. 8

For illustration of
model no. 613
in naturalistic colours
see page no. 197

Polar Bear on Cube

Model No.:	67
Designer:	Leslie Harradine
Height:	4", 10.1 cm
Glaze:	Flambé
Issued:	c.1936
Varieties:	HN 119

Price:	*U.S. $*	*Can. $*	*U.K. £*
Flambé	1,100.00	1,100.00	275.00

Polar Bear and Cub - Large

Model No.:	613
Designer:	Charles Noke
Height:	15", 38.1 cm
Size:	Large
Glaze:	See below
Issued:	c.1929
Varieties:	HN 2637

Price:	*U.S. $*	*Can. $*	*U.K. £*
Chang		Extremely Rare	
Sung		Extremely Rare	

Photograph
Not Available
at Press Time

Polar Bear and Cub - Small

Model No.:	617
Designer:	Unknown
Height:	8" x 10", 20.3 x 25.4 cm
Size:	Small
Glaze:	See below
Issued:	c.1929

Price:	*U.S. $*	*Can. $*	*U.K. £*
Chang		Very Rare	
Sung		Very Rare	

Lop-Eared Rabbit

Model No.:	113
Designer:	Unknown
Height:	2 1/2", 6.4 cm
Glaze:	Flambé
Issued:	1913 to the present
Varieties:	HN 108, 151, 276
	HN 1091A on Plain Ashtray
	HN 1091B on Fluted Ashtray

Price:	*U.S. $*	*Can. $*	*U.K. £*
Flambé	135.00	170.00	35.00
Matt Red Glaze	100.00	150.00	35.00

Rabbit
Crouching - Style One
Model No.:	1165A
Designer:	Unknown
Height:	3 1/2", 8.9 cm
Glaze:	Flambé
Issued:	c.1912-by 1946

Price:	*U.S. $*	*Can. $*	*U.K. £*
Flambé		Very Rare	

Rabbit
Crouching - Style Two
Model No.:	1165B
Designer:	Unknown
Height:	4", 10.1 cm
Glaze:	Sung
Issued:	c.1912-by 1946

Price:	*U.S. $*	*Can. $*	*U.K. £*
Sung		Very Rare	

Rabbits
Model No.:	249
Designer:	Unknown
Height:	3 1/2", 8.9 cm
Glaze:	Flambé
Issued:	c.1919
Varieties:	HN 209, 217, 218, 219, 969

Price:	*U.S. $*	*Can. $*	*U.K. £*
Flambé		Very Rare	

Rhinoceros
Standing
Model No.:	107
Designer:	Unknown
Height:	3 1/2" x 7", 8.9 x 17.8 cm
Glaze:	See below
Issued:	c.1912
Varieties:	HN 141

Price:	*U.S. $*	*Can. $*	*U.K. £*
Light Brown	300.00	350.00	150.00
Orange-brown	300.00	350.00	150.00
(Experimental Glazes)			

Rhinoceros
Lying

Model No.: 615
Designer: Leslie Harradine
Height: 9 1/2", 24.1 cm (length)
Glaze: See below
Issued: c.1973 to the present

Price:	U.S. $	Can. $	U.K. £
Flambé	1,100.00	1,600.00	360.00

For illustration of
model no. 115
in naturalistic colours
see page no. 13

Squirrel

Model No.: 115
Designer: Unknown
Height: 2 1/4", 5.7 cm
Glaze: Flambé
Issued: c.1912-by 1946
Varieties: HN 138; HN 1093B Fluted Ashtray
HN 1093A Plain Ashtray

Price:	U.S. $	Can. $	U.K. £
Flambé	300.00	400.00	225.00

For illustration of
model no. 106
in naturalistic colours
see page no. 78

Tiger on a Rock
Style One

Model No.: 106
Designer: Charles Noke
Height: 3 1/2" x 9", 8.9 x 22.9 cm
Glaze: Flambé
Issued: c.1913
Varieties: HN 876

Price:	U.S. $	Can. $	U.K. £
Flambé	1,200.00	1,300.00	575.00

Tiger
Crouching

Model No.: 111
Designer: Charles Noke
Height: 2" x 9 1/2", 5.1 x 24.0 cm
Glaze: Flambé
Issued: c.1912-1968
Varieties: HN 225

Price:	U.S. $	Can. $	U.K. £
Flambé	600.00	700.00	350.00

Mould No. 111 was also used to produce flambé Panther

<table>
<tr><td>

Tiger
Seated

Model No.: 530
Designer: Charles Noke
Height: 6 1/4", 15.9 cm
Glaze: Flambé
Issued: c,1926-1940
Varieties: HN 912

Price:	*U.S. $*	*Can. $*	*U.K. £*
Flambé		Rare	

</td><td>

Tiger
Lying

Model No.: 533
Designer: Charles Noke
Height: 2 1/2" x 7 1/2", 6.4 x 19.1 cm
Glaze: Flambé
Issued: c.1926
Varieties: HN 911

Price:	*U.S. $*	*Can. $*	*U.K. £*
Flambé		Rare	

</td></tr>
</table>

For illustration of model no. 530 in naturalistic colours see page no. 87

For illustration of model no. 533 in naturalistic colours see page no. 87

Tiger
Stalking - Style Two

Model No.: 809
Designer: Charles Noke
Height: 6" x 13 1/2", 15.3 x 34.3 cm
Glaze: Flambé
Issued: 1950 to the present
Varieties: HN 1082, 2646;
HN 1125 Tiger on alabaster base

Price:	*U.S. $*	*Can. $*	*U.K. £*
Flambé	950.00	1,000.00	475.00

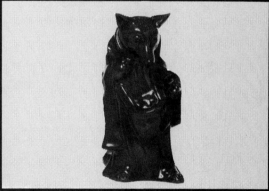

Wolf (Pedlar)

Model No.: 76
Designer: Charles Noke
Height: 5 1/2". 14.0 cm
Glaze: Flambé
Issued: c.1913-1983
Varieties: HN 7

Price:	*U.S. $*	*Can. $*	*U.K. £*
Flambé		Very Rare	

BIRDS

Budgerigar on Tree Stump
Model No.:   221
Designer: Unknown
Height: 7", 17.8 cm
Glaze: Flambé
Issued: c.1918-1936
Varieties: HN 163A, 163B, 199

Price:	U.S. $	Can. $	U.K. £
Flambé	400.00	500.00	250.00
Sung	500.00	600.00	300.00

Chicks (three)
Model No.:   1163
Designer: Charles Noke
Height: 2 1/4" x 3 1/2", 5.7 x 8.9 cm
Glaze: Flambé
Issued: c.1908

Price:	U.S. $	Can. $	U.K. £
Flambé	245.00	375.00	195.00

Chicks (two)
Model No.:   1163A
Designer: Charles Noke
Height: 2", 5.1 cm
Glaze: See below
Issued: c.1908-by 1946
Varieties: HN 236

Price:	U.S. $	Can. $	U.K. £
Flambé	425.00	500.00	200.00
Sung	475.00	550.00	225.00

Chick
Model No.:   1163B
Designer: Charles Noke
Height: 2 1/2", 6.3 cm
Glaze: Flambé
Issued: c.1908
Varieties: HN 274, 282

Price:	U.S. $	Can. $	U.K. £
Flambé	195.00	250.00	125.00

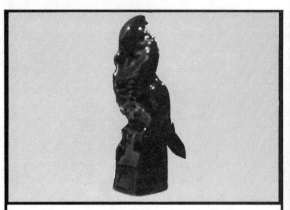

Cockatoo on a Rock

Model No.: 68
Designer: Unknown
Height: 6 1/2", 16.5 cm
Glaze: Flambé
Issued: c.1912-1936
Varieties: HN 185, 191, 192, 200, 877

Price:	*U.S. $*	*Can. $*	*U.K. £*
Flambé	600.00	700.00	350.00

Cockatoos

Model No.: 630
Designer: Charles Noke
Height: 4 1/2", 11.4 cm
Glaze: Chinese Jade
Issued: c.1929

Price:	*U.S. $*	*Can. $*	*U.K. £*
Chinese Jade		Very rare	

For illustration of
model no. 25
in naturalistic colours
see page no. 6

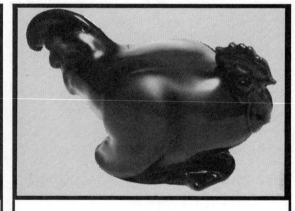

Cockerel
Crowing

Model No.: 25
Designer: Unknown
Height: 3 1/4", 8.3 cm
Glaze: Flambé
Issued: c.1912-1936
Varieties: HN 111

Price:	*U.S. $*	*Can. $*	*U.K. £*
Flambé		Rare	

Cockerel
Crouching

Model No.: 30
Designer: Unknown
Height: 3 1/4", 8.3 cm
Glaze: Flambé
Issued: c.1912
Varieties: HN 124, 178, 180, 267

Price:	*U.S. $*	*Can. $*	*U.K. £*
Flambé		Rare	

Cockerel Bowl

Model No.: Unknown
Designer: Unknown
Height: 3 1/4", 8.3 cm
Glaze: Flambé with sterling silver rim
Issued: Unknown

Price:	*U.S. $*	*Can. $*	*U.K. £*
Flambé		Rare	

'The Homecoming' (Doves - HN 3539)

Model No.: 3304
Designer: Russell Willis
Height: 14 3/4", 37.5 cm
Glaze: Flambé
Issued: 1989 to the present
Series: Images of Fire
Varieties: HN 3532

Price:	*U.S. $*	*Can. $*	*U.K. £*
	N/A	2,210.00	599.00

Drake
Standing - medium

Model No.: 137
Designer: Unknown
Height: 6 1/2", 16.5 cm
Size: Medium
Glaze: Flambé
Issued: 1913 to the present
Varieties: HN 114, 115, 116, 956, 1191, 2555, 2647

Price:	*U.S. $*	*Can. $*	*U.K. £*
Flambé	155.00	190.00	175.00

Drake
Standing - small

Model No.: 395
Designer: Unknown
Height: 2 3/4", 7.0 cm
Size: Small
Glaze: Flambé
Issued: 1922 to the present
Varieties: HN 806, 807, 2591

Price:	*U.S. $*	*Can. $*	*U.K. £*
Flambé	N/A	118.00	24.95

For illustration
of model no. 2
in naturalistic colours
see page no. 41

Duck
Preening - Style One

Model No.:	2		
Designer:	Unknown		
Height:	2 1/2", 6.4 cm		
Glaze:	Flambé		
Issued:	c.1912-1936		
Varieties:	HN 235, 298		

Price:	*U.S. $*	*Can. $*	*U.K. £*
Flambé	400.00	450.00	200.00

Duck
Resting - large

Model No.:	654		
Designer:	Unknown		
Height:	3 3/4" x 7 1/4", 9.5 x 18.4 cm		
Glaze:	Flambé		
Issued:	c.1929-1961		
Varieties:	HN 977, 1192		

Price:	*U.S. $*	*Can. $*	*U.K. £*
Flambé	400.00	450.00	200.00

For illustration
of model no. 207
in naturalistic colours
see page no. 20

Duck
Resting - small

Model No.:	112		
Designer:	Unknown		
Height:	2", 5.1 cm		
Glaze:	Flambé		
Issued:	1912 to the present		
Varieties:	HN 148B		

Price:	*U.S. $*	*Can. $*	*U.K. £*
Flambé	N/A	118.00	24.95

Duck
Head stretched forward

Model No.:	207		
Designer:	Unknown		
Height:	4", 10.1 cm		
Glaze:	Flambé		
Issued:	c.1917		
Varieties:	HN 150, 229, 2556		

Price:	*U.S. $*	*Can. $*	*U.K. £*
Flambé		Rare	

Duckling
New born

Model No.:	3
Designer:	Unknown
Height:	3", 7.6 cm
Glaze:	Flambé
Issued:	c.1912
Varieties:	HN 188, 189, 190

Price:	*U.S. $*	*Can. $*	*U.K. £*
Flambé		Rare	

For illustration of
model no. 97
in naturalistic colours
see page no. 42

Ducklings
Resting

Model No.:	97
Designer:	Unknown
Height:	1 3/4" x 5 1/2", 4.5 x 14.0 cm
Glaze:	See below
Issued:	c.1913
Varieties:	HN 239

Price:	*U.S. $*	*Can. $*	*U.K. £*
Flambé		Rare	

For illustration of
model no. 247
in naturalistic colours
see page no. 34

Ducklings
Standing

Model No.:	247
Designer:	Unknown
Height:	2 3/4", 6.4 cm
Glaze:	Flambé
Issued:	c.1919
Varieties:	HN 205, 206, 275

Price:	*U.S. $*	*Can. $*	*U. K. £*
Flambé		Very rare	

For illustration of
model no. 138
in naturalistic colours
see page no. 11

Drake on Rock

Model No.:	138
Designer:	Unknown
Height:	3 1/2", 8.9 cm
Glaze:	Flambé
Issued:	c.1913-1936
Varieties:	HN 132; Chinese jade pin tray

Price:	*U.S. $*	*Can. $*	*U.K. £*
Flambé	400.00	450.00	175.00

For illustration of
model no. 647
in naturalistic colours
see page no. 103

Character Duck
Style Three

Model No.: 647
Designer: Unknown
Height: 6", 15.2 cm
Glaze: Flambé
Issued: c.1930
Varieties: HN 973, 974

Price: *U.S. $*   *Can. $*   *U.K. £*
Flambé   Very rare

Eagle on Rock

Model No.: 145
Designer: Unknown
Height: 9", 22.9 cm
Glaze: Brown Titanian
Issued: c.1913-1936
Varieties: HN 139

Price: *U.S. $*   *Can. $*   *U.K. £*
Titanian   Extremely Rare

For illustration of
model no. 264
in naturalistic colours
see page no. 54

Photograph
Not Available
at Press Time

Finches (three)

Model No.: 264
Designer: Charles Noke
Height: 2" x 3 3/4", 5.1 x 9.5 cm
Glaze: Flambé
Issued: c.1913
Varieties: HN 280

Price: *U.S. $*   *Can. $*   *U.K. £*
Flambé   Rare

Finches (two)

Model No.: 263
Designer: Unknown
Height: 2 1/2" 6.4 cm
Glaze: Flambé
Issued: c.1922
Varieties: HN 278

Price: *U.S. $*   *Can. $*   *U.K. £*
Flambé   Rare

For illustration of
model no. 1236
in naturalistic colours
see page no. 15

Fledgling
Style One

Model No.: 1236
Designer: Unknown
Height: 2", 5.1 cm
Glaze: Flambé
Issued: c.1908-by 1946
Varieties: HN145A, 145B

Price:	*U.S. $*	*Can. $*	*U.K. £*
Flambé	300.00	400.00	175.00

For illustration of
model no. 1238
in naturalistic colours
see page no. 13

Fledgling
Style Two

Model No.: 1238
Designer: Unknown
Height: 2", 5.1 cm
Glaze: Flambé
Issued: c.1908
Varieties: HN 137C, 137D

Price:	*U.S. $*	*Can. $*	*U.K. £*
Flambé	300.00	400.00	175.00

For illustration of
model no. 98
in naturalistic colours
see page no. 14

Fledgling
Style Three

Model No.: 98
Designer: Unknown
Height: 2", 5.1 cm
Glaze: Flambé
Issued: c.1912
Varieties: HN 143A, 143B

Price:	*U.S. $*	*Can. $*	*U.K. £*
Flambé	300.00	400.00	175.00

For illustration of
model no. 99
in naturalistic colours
see page no. 12

Fledgling
Style Four

Model No.: 99
Designer: Unknown
Height: 2", 5.1 cm
Glaze: Flambé
Issued: c.1912-by 1946
Varieties: HN 137A, 137B

Price:	*U.S. $*	*Can. $*	*U.K. £*
Flambé	300.00	400.00	175.00

For illustration of
model no. 139
in naturalistic colours
see page no. 16

For illustration of
model no. 243
in naturalistic colours
see page no. 31

Fledgling on Rock
Style One
Model No.: 139
Designer: Unknown
Height: 3 3/4", 9.5 cm
Glaze: Flambé
Issued: c.1913
Varieties: HN 145C, 145D, 145E, 145F

Price:	*U.S. $*	*Can. $*	*U.K. £*
Flambé	350.00	450.00	225.00

Gannet
Model No.: 243
Designer: Unknown
Height: 6 1/2", 16.5 cm
Glaze: Flambé
Issued: c.1919
Varieties: HN 195, 1197

Price:	*U.S. $*	*Can. $*	*U.K. £*
Flambé		Very rare	

Guinea Fowl
Model No.: 69
Designer: Unknown
Height: 3 1/4" x 5 1/4", 8.3 x 13.3 cm
Glaze: Flambé
Issued: 1912-1967
Varieties: HN 125

Price:	*U.S. $*	*Can. $*	*U.K. £*
Flambé	350.00	400.00	175.00

Kingfisher
Style One
Model No.: 91
Designer: Unknown
Height: 2 1/2", 6.4 cm
Glaze: Flambé
Issued: c.1912
Varieties: HN 268

Price:	*U.S. $*	*Can. $*	*U.K. £*
Flambé	300.00	350.00	150.00

For illustration of
model no. 227
in naturalistic colours
see page no. 24

Kingfisher on a Rock
Style One

Model No.: 44
Designer: Unknown
Height: 4", 10.1 cm
Glaze: Flambé
Issued: c.1913-by 1946
Varieties: HN 131, 152

Price:	*U.S. $*	*Can. $*	*U.K. £*
Flambé	350.00	400.00	175.00

Kingfisher on Tree Stump
Style One

Model No.: 227
Designer: Unknown
Height: 3", 7.6 cm
Glaze: Flambé
Issued: c.1918-1936
Varieties: HN 165, 858

Price:	*U.S. $*	*Can. $*	*U.K. £*
Flambé		Very rare	

Owl in a Crescent Moon-Shaped Dish

Model No.: 37
Designer: Unknown
Height: 4", 10.1 cm
Glaze: Flambé
Issued: c.1912
Varieties: HN 222

Price:	*U.S. $*	*Can. $*	*U.K. £*
Flambé		Very rare	

Owl with Owlet Under Wing

Model No.: 71
Designer: Unknown
Height: 4 3/4", 12.1 cm
Glaze: Flambé
Issued: c.1912-1936
Varieties: HN 160
Derivatives: Onyx Pin Tray

Price:	*U.S. $*	*Can. $*	*U.K. £*
Flambé	900.00	1,000.00	475.00

Owl (Barn)
Style One
Model No.:   148
Designer: Harry Tittensor
Height: 3", 7.6 cm
Glaze: Flambé
Issued: c.1913
Varieties: HN 169

Price:	*U.S. $*	*Can. $*	*U.K. £*
Flambé	500.00	600.00	275.00

Owl
Style Two
Model No.:   2249
Designer: Alan Maslankowski
Height: 12", 30.5 cm
Glaze: Flambé
Issued: 1973 to the present

Price:	*U.S. $*	*Can. $*	*U.K. £*
Flambé	510.00	700.00	225.00

Photograph
Not Available
at Press Time

For illustration of
model no. 270
in naturalistic colours
see page no. 44

Parrot on Pillar
Model No.:   45
Designer: Unknown
Height: 6 1/2", 16.5 cm
Glaze: Flambé
Issued: c.1913-1936

Price:	*U.S. $*	*Can. $*	*U.K. £*
Flambé	850.00	1,000.00	475.00

Peahen
Model No.:   270
Designer: Unknown
Height: 4 1/2", 11.4 cm
Glaze: Flambé
Issued: c.1920
Varieties: HN 247

Price:	*U.S. $*	*Can. $*	*U.K. £*
Flambé		Very rare	

For illustration of
model no. 109
in naturalistic colours
see page no. 9

For illustration of
model no. 125
in naturalistic colours
see page no. 57

Pelican
Beak Up

Model No.:	109
Designer:	Unknown
Height:	4", 10.1 cm
Glaze:	Flambé
Issued:	c.1913-1936
Varieties:	HN 123

Price:	*U.S. $*	*Can. $*	*U.K. £*
Flambé		Very rare	

Pelican
Beak Down

Model No.:	125
Designer:	Unknown
Height:	6 1/4", 15.9 cm
Glaze:	Flambé
Issued:	c.1920
Varieties:	HN 295A, 295B

Price:	*U.S. $*	*Can. $*	*U.K. £*
Flambé		Very rare	

For illustration
of model no. 591
in naturalistic colours
see page no. 96

Emperor Penguin

Model No.:	84
Designer:	Unknown
Height:	6", 15.2 cm
Glaze:	Flambé
Issued:	1913 to the present
Varieties:	HN 113, 296

Price:	*U.S. $*	*Can. $*	*U.K. £*
Flambé	N/A	200.00	43.00

King Penguin

Model No.:	591
Designer:	Unknown
Height:	7 1/2", 19.0 cm
Glaze:	Flambé
Issued:	c.1927
Varieties:	HN 947, 1189

Price:	*U.S. $*	*Can. $*	*U.K. £*
Flambé	850.00	950.00	475.00

King Penguin and Chick

Model No.:	239
Designer:	Unknown
Height:	5 3/4", 14.6 cm
Glaze:	Flambé
Issued:	c.1918-1961
Varieties:	HN 198, 297, 998

Price:	*U.S. $*	*Can. $*	*U.K. £*
Flambé	650.00	700.00	325.00

Penguin
Style One

Model No.:	85
Designer:	Unknown
Height:	4 1/4", 10.8 cm
Glaze:	Flambé
Issued:	1913-by 1946
Varieties:	HN 104, 134

Price:	*U.S. $*	*Can. $*	*U.K. £*
Flambé	350.00	400.00	175.00

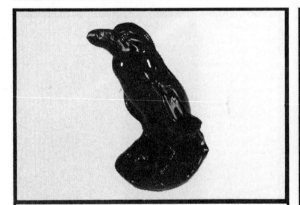

Penguin
Style Two

Model No.:	459
Designer:	Unknown
Height:	7", 17.8 cm
Glaze:	Flambé
Issued:	c.1925-1961
Varieties:	HN 882

Price:	*U.S. $*	*Can. $*	*U.K. £*
Flambé	750.00	850.00	425.00

For illustration
of model no. 1287
in naturalistic colours
see page no. 162

Penguin
Style Three

Model No.:	1287
Designer:	Charles Noke
Height:	5 1/2", 14.0 cm or 7" ??
Glaze:	Flambé
Issued:	c.1946-1962
Varieties:	HN 1199

Price:	*U.S. $*	*Can. $*	*U.K. £*
Flambé	500.00	600.00	325.00

For illustration
of model no. 585
in naturalistic colours
see page no. 96

Penguins

Model No.:   103
Designer: Unknown
Height: 6", 15.2 cm
Glaze: Flambé
Issued: c.1913-by 1946
Varieties: HN 103, 133

Price:	U.S. $	Can. $	U.K. £
Flambé	650.00	750.00	375.00

Peruvian Penguin

Model No.:   585
Designer: Charles Noke
Height: 7 3/4" x 9", 19.7 x 22.9 cm
Glaze: Flambé
Issued: c.1936-1961
Varieties: HN 946, 1190

Price:	U.S. $	Can. $	U.K. £
Flambé	850.00	950.00	475.00

Fantail Pigeons

Model No.:   46
Designer: Unknown
Height: 3 3/4", 9.5 cm
Glaze: Flambé
Issued: c.1912-by 1946
Varieties: HN 122

Price:	U.S. $	Can. $	U.K. £
Flambé		Rare	

Raven

Model No.:   43
Designer: Unknown
Height: 3" x 5 1/4", 7.6 x 13.3 cm
Glaze: Flambé
Issued: c.1912
Varieties: HN 135

Price:	U.S. $	Can. $	U.K. £
Flambé	700.00	800.00	425.00

Robin
Style One

Model No.:	104
Designer:	Unknown
Height:	2", 5.1 cm
Glaze:	Flambé
Issued:	c.1913-by 1946
Varieties:	HN 144, 277;
	HN 1089B on Fluted Ashtray
	HN 1089A on Plain Ashtray

Price:	*U.S. $*	*Can. $*	*U.K. £*
Flambé	300.00	350.00	150.00

'Nestling Down' (Swans HN 3538)

Model No.:	3198
Designer:	Adrian Hughes
Height:	8 1/2" x 12", 21.6 x 30.5 cm
Glaze:	Flambé
Issued:	1988 to the present
Series:	Images of Fire
Varieties:	HN 3531

Price:	*U.S. $*	*Can. $*	*U.K. £*
Flambé	N/A	1,630.00	550.00

Tern

Model No.:	231
Designer:	Unknown
Height:	2 1/2" x 8 1/2", 6.4 x 21.6 cm
Glaze:	Flambé
Issued:	c.1912
Varieties:	HN 167, 168, 1193, 1194

Price:	*U.S. $*	*Can. $*	*U.K. £*
Flambé		Very rare	

'Courtship' (Terns HN 3535)

Model No.:	2930
Designer:	Russell Willis
Height:	15", 38.1 cm
Glaze:	Flambé
Issued:	1987 to the present
Series:	Images of Fire
Varieties	HN 3525

Price:	*U.S. $*	*Can. $*	*U.K. £*
Flambé	N/A	2,210.00	650.00

For illustration
of model no. 208
in naturalistic colours
see page no. 23

For illustration
of model no. 1071
in naturalistic colours
see page no. 176

Thrush Chicks (four)

Model No.:	208
Designer:	Unknown
Height:	2" x 5 1/2", 5.1 x 14.0 cm
Glaze:	Flambé
Issued:	c.1912
Varieties:	HN 161, 171; Also called "Four Fledglings"

Price:	U.S. $	Can. $	U.K. £
Flambé		Very rare	

Thrush Chicks (two)

Model No.:	1071
Designer:	Unknown
Height:	3", 7.6 cm
Glaze:	Flambé
Issued:	c.1941
Varieties:	HN 2552

Price:	U.S. $	Can. $	U.K. £
Flambé		Very rare	

MISCELLANEOUS

Name	Model No.	Page No.
Butterfly	142A	379
Crab	42	379
Dog of Fo	2957	381
"Dolphin" (The Leap)	2949	381
Dragon	2085	382
Dragon (HN 3552)	4315	382
Fish	625	380
Fish (Shoal of Fish)	632	380
Leaping Salmon	666	380
Frog (Style One - Large)	1162	380
Frog (Style One - Medium)	1162A	381
Frog (Style One - Small)	1162B	381
Tortoise	101	379
Tortoise	101A	379

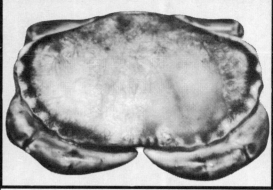

Butterfly

Model No.:	142A
Designer:	Unknown
Height:	2" x 4 1/2", 5.1 x 11.4 cm
Glaze:	Flambé
Issued:	c.1912

Price:	*U.S. $*	*Can. $*	*U.K. £*
Flambé		Rare	

Crab

Model No.:	42
Designer:	Unknown
Height:	2" x 4 1/2", 5.1 x 11.4 cm
Glaze:	See below
Issued:	c.1936

Price:	*U.S. $*	*Can. $*	*U.K. £*
Crystalline		Very rare	
Flambé		Very rare	

For illustration
of model no. 101
in naturalistic colours
see page no. 31

Photograph
Not Available
at Press Time

Tortoise

Model No.:	101
Designer:	Unknown
Height:	2" x 4 3/4", 5.1 x 12.1 cm
Size:	Large
Glaze:	See below
Issued:	c.1912
Varieties:	HN 193

Price:	*U.S. $*	*Can. $*	*U.K. £*
Flambé	450.00	500.00	275.00
Sung	500.00	600.00	325.00

Tortoise

Model No.:	101A
Designer:	Unknown
Height:	1" x 3", 2.5 x 7.6 cm
Size:	Small
Glaze:	See below
Issued:	c.1912-by 1946

Price:	*U.S. $*	*Can. $*	*U.K. £*
Flambé	350.00	400.00	225.00
Sung	450.00	500.00	250.00

Fish

Model No.: 625
Designer: Charles Noke
Height: 3 1/2" x 5 1/2", 8.9 x 14.0 cm
Glaze: Chinese Jade
Issued: c.1929

Price:	*U.S. $*	*Can. $*	*U.K. £*
Chinese Jade		Very Rare	

Fish (shoal of fish)

Model No.: 632
Designer: Unknown
Height: 6 1/2", 16.5 cm
Glaze: See below
Issued: c.1929
Derivitive: Lamp, Model No. L23

Price:	*U.S. $*	*Can. $*	*U.K. £*
Chinese Jade		Extremely Rare	
Flambé		Very Rare	

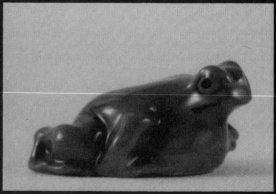

Leaping Salmon

Model No.: 666
Designer: Charles Noke
Height: 12 1/4", 31.1 cm
Glaze: See below
Issued: Flambé: c.1940-1950
Chinese Jade: c.1930

Price:	*U.S. $*	*Can. $*	*U.K. £*
Chinese Jade		Extremely Rare	
Flambé	500.00	600.00	300.00

Frog
Style One - Large

Model No.: 1162
Designer: Unknown
Height: Unknown
Size: Large
Glaze: Flambé
Issued: c.1908-1936

Price:	*U.S. $*	*Can. $*	*U.K. £*
Flambé	475.00	575.00	250.00

Frog
Style One - Medium
Model No.:   1162A
Designer: Unknown
Height: Unknown
Size: Medium
Glaze: Flambé
Issued: c.1908-1936

Price:	*U.S. $*	*Can. $*	*U.K. £*
Flambé	425.00	500.00	225.00

Frog
Style One - Small
Model No.:   1162B
Designer: Unknown
Height: 1 1/4" x 3 1/2", 4.4 x 8.9 cm
Size: Small
Glaze: Flambé
Issued: 1908-1936

Price:	*U.S. $*	*Can. $*	*U.K. £*
Flambé	350.00	400.00	175.00

'Dolphin' (The Leap)
Model No.:   2949
Designer: Adrian Hughes
Height: 8", 20.3 cm
Glaze: Flambé
Issued: 1983-1983
Varieties: HN 3522

Price:	*U.S. $*	*Can. $*	*U.K. £*
Flambé	250.00	300.00	150.00

This figure was test marketed at the RDICC Gallery
in London and other selected outlets

Dog of Fo
Model No.:   2957
Designer: William K. Harper
Height: 5 1/4", 13.3 cm
Glaze: Flambé
Issued: 1982-1982
Series: RDICC

Price:	*U.S. $*	*Can. $*	*U.K. £*
Flambé	250.00	325.00	140.00

Dragon

Model No.:	2085
Designer:	John Bromley
Height:	7 1/2", 19.0 cm
Glaze:	Flambé
Issued:	1973 to the present

Price:	*U.S. $*	*Can. $*	*U.K. £*
Flambé	1,000.00	1,375.00	335.00

Dragon (HN 3552)

Model No.:	4315
Designer:	Robert Tabbenor
Height:	5 1/4", 13.3 cm
Glaze:	Flambé
Issued:	1993 to the present
Series:	RDICC

Price:	*U.S. $*	*Can. $*	*U.K. £*
Flambé	260.00	350.00	160.00

DOG HEADS

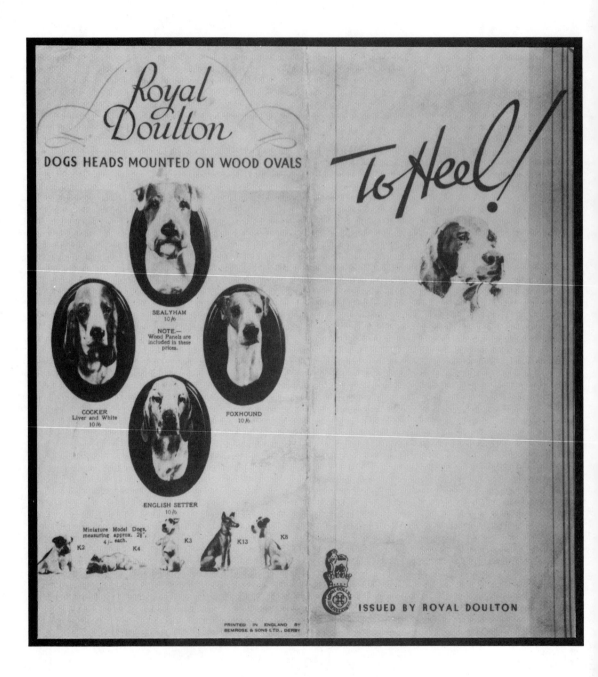

WALL MOUNTS

In the 1930's Doulton produced a series of dogs' heads, plain and mounted on oval wooden panels as wall hangings. Similar heads were also mounted for bookends.

Ten different models have been recorded, one in two colourways. The heads are numbered SK-21, to SK-31 but (possibly due to size) they show only the "K" and not "SK" resulting in possible confusion with the "K" series. Not all pieces have the Royal Doulton backstamp.

The original issue prices of the models were: Without plinths 5/-; With plinths 6/-; On bookends 8/- each

SK 25 Foxhound
Plain

SK 25 Foxhound
Mounted

Number	Style	Type	Colour	Size	U.S.$	Price Can. $	U.K. £
SK 21	English Setter	Plain Mounted Bookend	Black and White	3 1/2" 8.9 cm	1,250.00 1,250.00 1,250.00	1,700.00 1,700.00 1,700.00	825.00 825.00 825.00
SK 22	Irish Setter	Plain Mounted Bookend	Reddish brown and Black	3 1/2" 8.9 cm	1,250.00 1,250.00 1,250.00	1,700.00 1,700.00 1,700.00	825.00 825.00 825.00
SK 23	Cocker Spaniel	Plain Mounted Bookend	Liver and White	4" 10.1 cm	1,250.00 1,250.00 1,250.00	1,700.00 1,700.00 1,700.00	825.00 825.00 825.00
SK 24	Cocker Spaniel	Plain Mounted Bookend	Black	4" 10.1 cm	1,250.00 1,250.00 1,250.00	1,700.00 1,700.00 1,700.00	825.00 825.00 825.00
SK 25	Foxhound	Plain Mounted Bookend	Brown and White	3" 7.6 cm	1,250.00 1,250.00 1,250.00	1,700.00 1,700.00 1,700.00	825.00 825.00 825.00
SK 26	Smooth Haired Fox Terrier	Plain Mounted Bookend	White and Dark Brown	3" 7.6 cm	1,250.00 1,250.00 1,250.00	1,700.00 1,700.00 1,700.00	825.00 825.00 825.00

English Setter

Cocker Spaniel

Sealyham

Pekinese

Number	Style	Type	Colour	Size	U.S.$	Price Can. $	U.K. £
SK 27	Sealyham	Plain	White	3 1/2"	1,250.00	1,700.00	825.00
		Mounted	and	8.9 cm	1,250.00	1,700.00	825.00
		Bookend	Brown		1,250.00	1,700.00	825.00
SK 28	Airedale	Plain	Brown	3 1/2"	1,250.00	1,700.00	825.00
		Mounted	and	8.9 cm	1,250.00	1,700.00	825.00
		Bookend	Black		1,250.00	1,700.00	825.00
SK 29	Scottish Terrier	Plain	Black	3"	1,250.00	1,700.00	825.00
		Mounted		7.6 cm	1,250.00	1,700.00	825.00
		Bookend			1,250.00	1,700.00	825.00
SK 30	Cairn	Plain	Black	3 1/2"	1,250.00	1,700.00	825.00
		Mounted	and	8.9 cm	1,250.00	1,700.00	825.00
		Bookend	Grey		1,250.00	1,700.00	825.00
SK 31	Pekinese	Plain	Brown	4 3/4"	1,250.00	1,700.00	825.00
		Mounted	and	12.1 cm	1,250.00	1,700.00	825.00
		Bookend	Black		1,250.00	1,700.00	825.00

CHAMPIONSHIP DOG BOOKENDS

The following medium size dog models were available by order as bookends. They were mounted on mahogany and sold by order for 21/10d to 22/- a pair. The bookends utilized the medium size (M/S) dogs in all known cases. The listing below is in alphabetical order cross-referenced with HN numbers for the medium size dogs in question.

Style	HN No.	Colour	Size	U.S. $	Price: Can. $	U.K.
Bulldog	HN 1043	Dark Brown and White	Medium	1,250.00	1,650.00	700.00
Cairn	HN 1034	Black and Grey	Medium	700.00	900.00	350.00
Cocker Spaniel	HN 1109	Black and White	Medium	450.00	575.00	200.00
Cocker Spaniel with Pheasant	HN 1028	White and Brown dog Reddish brown Pheasant	Medium	650.00	850.00	300.00
English Setter	HN 2621	Liver and White	Medium	3,600.00	4,900.00	2,500.00
Irish Setter	HN 1055	Reddish Brown and Black	Medium	400.00	500.00	200.00
Pekinese	HN 1012	Brown and Black	Medium	300.00	450.00	180.00
Rough Haired Terrier	HN 1013	White, black and Brown	Medium	800.00	1,000.00	400.00
Scottish Terrier	HN 1015	Black	Medium	800.00	1,000.00	400.00
Sealyham	HN 1031	White and Brown	Medium	900.00	1,200.00	450.00

ROYAL DOULTON BROOCHES

Produced during the 1930's these china items had pin backs for use as jewellery brooches.

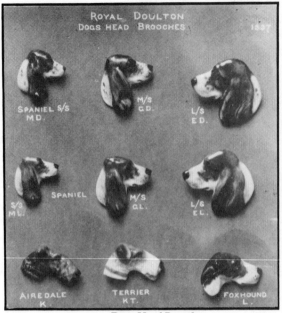

Dogs Head Brooches   Kingfisher Brooch

Style	Type	Colour	Size	U.S. $	Price: Can. $	U.K. £
Dogs	Airedale	Dark brown and black	N/A	300.00	450.00	200.00
	Cairn	Black and Grey	N/A	300.00	450.00	200.00
	Cocker Spaniel	Liver and White	S/S	300.00	450.00	200.00
			M/S	300.00	450.00	200.00
			L/S	300.00	450.00	200.00
	Cocker Spaniel	Black and White	S/S	300.00	450.00	200.00
			M/S	300.00	450.00	200.00
			L/S	300.00	450.00	200.00
	Foxhound	Brown and white	N/A	300.00	450.00	200.00
	Fox Terrier	White and dark brown	N/A	300.00	450.00	200.00
	Greyhound	Dark brown and white	N/A	300.00	450.00	200.00
	Pekinese	Brown and black	N/A	300.00	450.00	200.00
	Pomeranian	Golden brown	N/A	300.00	450.00	200.00
	Seaylham	White and brown	N/A	300.00	450.00	200.00
	Terrier	White and dark brown	N/A	300.00	450.00	200.00
Misc.	Butterfly	Pink	N/A	125.00	175.00	75.00
		Peach	N/A	125.00	175.00	75.00
	Fox	Brown	N/A	125.00	175.00	75.00
	Kingfisher	Unknown	1 1/4"	125.00	175.00	75.00
	Persian Cat	Cream with green eyes	1 1/2"	125.00	175.00	75.00

* N/A - Not Available

ADVERTISING ANIMALS

BERNARD MATHEWS TURKEY
See D 6449 page no. 238 and DA 161 page no. 318

Type: Promotional
Size: 6 1/4", 15.9 cm
Colour: White and red
Issued: 1990

Price: *U.S. $*   *Can. $*   *U.K. £*
                   75.00   125.00   50.00

ERVAN LUCAS BOLS DISTILLERS
Bulldog

Type: Liquor Container
Size: 6", 15.2 cm
Colour: White with Union Jack
Issued: 1932

Price: *U.S. $*   *Can. $*   *U.K. £*
                   600.00   800.00   400.00

ERVAN LUCAS BOLS DISTILLERS
Salmon

Type: Liquor Container
Size: 9 1/2", 24.0 cm
Colour: Silver-grey
Issued: 1940

Price: *U.S. $*   *Can. $*   *U.K. £*
                   450.00   600.00   300.00

ERVAN LUCAS BOLS DISTILLERS
Pekinese

Type: Liquor Container
Size: 6", 15.2 cm
Colour: Brown
Issued: 1940

Price: *U.S. $*   *Can. $*   *U.K. £*
                   2,000.00   2,800.00   1,300.00

FINANCIAL TIMES
Partridge

Type:	Paperweight
Size:	2 1/2", 6.4 cm
Colour:	Cream and brwon
Issued:	1988 in a Limited Edition of 1,200

Price:	*U.S. $*	*Can. $*	*U.K. £*
	300.00	400.00	200.00

GIROLAMA LUXARDO DISTILLERS
Bulldog

Type:	Liquor Container
Size:	11", 27.9 cm
Colour:	White
Issued:	1932

Price:	*U.S. $*	*Can. $*	*U.K. £*
	3,000.00	4,200.00	2,000.00

Photograph
Not Available
at Press Time

GIROLAMA LUXARDO DISTILLERS
Bulldog

Type:	Anniversary
Size:	10 1/2", 26.7 cm
Colour:	White
Issued:	1932

Price:	*U.S. $*	*Can. $*	*U.K. £*
	2,000.00	3,000.00	1,500.00

LOUIS WEARDEN & GUYLEE LTD
Bulldog

Type:	Advertising
Size:	6", 15.2 cm
Colour:	White bulldog with Union Jack
Issued:	1932

Price:	*U.S. $*	*Can. $*	*U.K. £*
	1,000.00	1,500.00	750.00

NATIONAL DISTILLERS CORP.
Old Crow

Type:	Liquor Container		
Size:	12 3/4", 32.0 cm		
Colour:	Black and White		
Issued:	1954		

Price:	*U.S. $*	*Can. $*	*U.K. £*
	175.00	250.00	125.00

PENGUIN BOOKS
Penguin

Type:	Anniversary		
Size:	4 1/2", 11.4 cm		
Colour:	Black and White		
Issued:	1987		

Price:	*U.S. $*	*Can. $*	*U.K. £*
	40.00	50.00	25.00

ROBERT PORTER & CO LTD
Bulldog

Type:	Advertising		
Size:	6", 15.2 cm		
Colour:	White, blue and brown		
Issued:	1915		

Price:	*U.S. $*	*Can. $*	*U.K. £*
	1,000.00	1,250.00	750.00

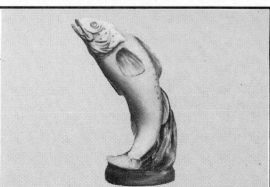

ROYAL DOULTON ANGLING CLUB
Salmon

Type:	Presentation		
Size:	9 1/2", 24.0 cm		
Colour:	Pale green and blue		
Issued:	1985		

Price:	*U.S. $*	*Can. $*	*U.K. £*
	400.00	500.00	250.00

STAUFFER & SON CO.
Begging Dog

Type: Advertising
Size: 8", 20.3 cm
Colour: Black and White
Issued: 1929

Price:	*U.S. $*	*Can. $*	*U.K. £*
	1,000.00	1,250.00	750.00

WHYTE & MACKAY DISTILLERS
Peregrine Falcon

Type: Liquor Container
Modeller: Graham Tongue
Size: 6 1/2", 16.5 cm
Colour: Grey
Issued: 1979

Price:	*U.S. $*	*Can. $*	*U.K. £*
	150.00	200.00	100.00

Photograph
Not Available
at Press Time

WHYTE & MACKAY DISTILLERS
Short Eared Owl

Type: Liquor Container
Modeller: Graham Tongue
Size: 6 1/2", 16.5 cm
Colour: Brown and white
Issued: 1984

Price:	*U.S. $*	*Can. $*	*U.K. £*
	150.00	200.00	100.00

Photograph
Not Available
at Press Time

WHYTE & MACKAY DISTILLERS
Tawny Owl

Type: Liquor Container
Modeller: Graham Tongue
Size: 6 1/2", 16.5 cm
Colour: Brown and white
Issued: 1984

Price:	*U.S. $*	*Can. $*	*U.K. £*
	150.00	200.00	100.00

INDICES

ALPHABETICAL INDEX

A

B

Budgerigar	
Style One	K32
Style Two	
Large	See Royal Adderley Birds Index
Small	See Royal Adderley Birds Index
On Branch (flower holder)	HN 854
On Tree Stump	HN 163A, 163B, 199, Flambé,
Sung	
Budgerigars	See Royal Adderley Birds Index
Budgerigars on Tree Stump	HN 2547
Buffalo	3008S
Bull	
Style One	Flambé
Style Two	Flambé
Bull Terrier	
Lying	K14
Standing	
Style One	HN 1100
Style Two	HN 2511
Bull Terrier Ch. 'Bokos Brock'	
Large	HN 1142
Medium	HN 1143
Small	HN 1144
Also called 'Staffordshire Bull Terrier'	
Bulldog	
Seated	
Style One	Flambé
Style Two	Flambé
Style Three	HN 881A, 881B, Chinese Jade, Flambé
Style Four	HN 129, 948, Flambé
Style Five	K1
Style Six	DA 222
Standing	
Large	HN 1042, 1045, 1072
Medium	HN 1043, 1046, 1073
Small	HN 1044, 1047, 1074
Bulldog Draped in Union Jack	
Without Hat	
Large	D 5913A
Medium	D 5913B
Small	D 5913C
With Derby Hat	
Large	D 6178
Medium	D 6179
Small	D 6180
With Trinity Cap	
Large	D 6181
Medium	D 6182
Small	D 6183
Bulldog Puppy	K2
Bulldog Seated on the Lid of Lustre Bowl	HN 987
Bulldog With Helmet and Haversack (Old Bill)	HN 146
Bulldog With Sailor Suit and Hat	
Large	D 6193A
Medium	D 6193B
Small	D 6193C
Bulldog With Tam O'Shanter and Haversack	HN 153
Bullfinch	
Style One	K31
Style Two	HN 2551
Style Three	HN 2616
Butterfly,	Flambé
Butterfly on Stump	HN 162

C

Cairn Terrier	
Begging	HN 2589
Seated	K11
Standing	
Style One	
Large	HN 1104

Medium	HN 1105
Small	HN 1106
Style Two	DA 118
Cairn Terrier, Ch. 'Charming Eyes'	
Large	HN 1033
Medium	HN 1034
Small	HN 1035
Calf	
Style One	HN 1146, 1161, 1173
Style Two	HN 1147, 1162, 1174
Camberwell Beauty Butterfly	HN 2605
Canada Goose	4400
Canary	See Royal Adderley Birds Index
"Capricorn" Mountain Goat	HN 3523, Flambé
Cardinal	
Style One	K28
Style Two	HN 2554
Style Three	HN 2615
Style Four (female)	
Large	See Royal Adderley Birds Index
Medium	See Royal Adderley Birds Index
Small	See Royal Adderley Birds Index
Style Five (male)	
Large	See Royal Adderley Birds Index
Medium	See Royal Adderley Birds Index
Small	See Royal Adderley Birds Index
Cardinals	See Royal Adderley Birds Index
Cat	
Lying	HN 233, Flambé
Seated	
Style One	HN 109, 120, 967, Flambé, Sung
Style Two	Flambé
Style Three	DA 194
Stalking	DA 149
Walking	DA 148
Cat Asleep, Head on Paw	HN 210, 227
Cat Asleep on a Cushion	HN 993
Cat on a Pillar	HN 203, 244, 245
Cat with Bandaged Paw	DA 195
Cat with Mouse on Tail	HN 201, 202, Flambé, Sung
Cats	HN 234
Cavalier King Charles Spaniel	
Style One	HN 127, Chinese Jade, Flambé
Style Two	DA 121
Cedar Waxwing	4205
Cerval	HN 2500
Chaffinch	
Style One	HN 2550
Style Two	HN 2611
Style Three	See Royal Adderley Birds Index
Style Four	DA 5
'Champion'	DA 35A
Also called 'Moonlight', DA 35B	
Also called 'Sunburst', DA 36	
Character Ape	
In Dunce's Cap with Book	HN 972, Flambé
With Book	
Eyes Closed	HN 961
Eyes Open	HN 960
Character Bird	
Style One	HN 256, 283
Style Two	HN 257, 284
Style Three	HN 258, 285
Style Four	HN 259, 286
Style Five	HN 260, 287
Style Six	HN 261, 288
Style Seven	HN 262, 289
Style Eight	HN 263, 290
Style Nine	HN 264, 291
Style Ten	HN 265, 292
Style Eleven	HN 266, 293

Character Dog	
Lying on Back	HN 1098
Lying, Panting	HN 1101
Running	HN 2510
Running with Ball	HN 1097
With Ball	HN 1103
With Bone	HN 1159
With Plate	HN 1158
With Slipper	HN 2654
Yawning	HN 1099
Character Duck	
Style One	
Large	HN 840, 842, 844
Small	HN 841, 843, 845
Style Two	HN 863, 864, 865
Style Three	HN 973, 974, Flambé
Character Elephant	
Style One	HN 949, 952
Style Two	HN 950, 951
Character Fox	HN 866
Character Fox with Stolen Goose	HN 1096, 1102
Character Kitten	
Curled	
Style One	HN 820, 821, 822
Style Two	HN 823, 824, 825, Chinese Jade
Licking Front Paw	HN 2583
Licking Hind Paw	HN 2580
Looking Up	HN 2584
Lying on Back	HN 2579
On Hind Legs	HN 2582
Sleeping	HN 2581
Character Monkey	HN 182, HN 183, Flambé
Character Parrot on Pillar	
Style One	HN 884
Style Two	HN 885, 886, 888
Character Pig	
Style One	HN 892, 893
Style Two	HN 894
Style Three	HN 895
Style Four	HN 896
Style Five	HN 897
Style Six	HN 902, 903
Character Toucan With Hat	
Style One	HN 913
Style Two	HN 914
Style Three	HN 915
Style Four	HN 916
Style Five	HN 917
Style Six	HN 918
Charolais Bull	DA 27
Charolais Cow and Calf	DA 33
Cheetah	3209S
Chestnut Mare	
Large	HN 2565
Small	HN 2566
Chestnut Mare and Foal	
Large	HN 2522
Small	HN 2533
Chicadee	
Style One	See Royal Adderley Birds Index
Style Two	See Royal Adderley Birds Index
Chicadees	See Royal Adderley Birds Index
Chicks	
One Chick	HN 274, 282, Flambé
Three Chicks	Flambé
Two Chicks	HN 236, Flambé, Sung
Chickens	3303S
Chimpanzees	3406S
Chipping Sparrow	HN 3511

Chow Ch. 'T'Sioh of Kin-Shan'	
Large	HN 2628
Medium	HN 2629
Small	HN 2630
Chow (Shibu Ino)	K15
Christmas Robin	DA 158
Christmas Turkey	D 6449
"Clear Water" (Otter)	HN 3530
Cock Pheasant	HN 2545, 2632
Cockatoo on a Rock	HN 185, 191, 192, 200, 877, Flambé
Cockatoos	Chinese Jade
Cocker Spaniel	
Chewing Handle of Basket	HN 2586
Lying in Basket	HN 2585
Seated	
Style One	K9A, K9B
Style Two	DA 141
Sleeping	HN 2590
Standing	
Large	HN 1002, 1108, 1134, 1186
Medium	HN 1036, 1109, 1135, 1187
Small	HN 1037, 1078, 1136, 1188
With Hare	
Large	HN 1063
Small	HN 1064
With Pheasant	
Large	HN 1001, 1137
Medium	HN 1028, 1138
Small	HN 1029, 1062, 2600
Cocker Spaniel Ch. 'Lucky Star of Ware'	
Large	HN 1000
Medium	HN 1020, Flambé
Small	HN 1021
Also called "Lucky Pride of Ware"	
Cockerel	
Crouching	HN 124, 178, 180, 267, Flambé
Crowing	HN 111, Flambé
Seated	
Style One	HN 157
Style Two	HN 878, 879, 880
Cockerel Bowl	Flambé
Collie	
Seated	HN 105, 106, 112, Flambé
Standing	DA 24
Collies	3307S
Collie Ch. 'Ashstead Applause'	
Large	HN 1057
Medium	HN 1058
Small	HN 1059
Colorado Chipmunks	HN 3506
Comic Brown Bear	HN 170, 270, Flambé
Comic Pig	HN 246
Comical Bird	
On Fluted Ashtray	HN 1092B
On Plain Ashtray	HN 1092A
Common Mallard	See Mallard Duck
Copper Butterfly	HN 2608
Coppersmith Barbet	See Royal Adderley Birds Index
Cormorant Nesting on Tree Stump	HN 857
(flower holder)	
Cottontail Rabbit	3012S
Cougar	
Style One	3004M
Style Two	3014S
Country Mouse	HN 207
"Courtship" (Terns)	HN 3525, 3535
Cows	3304S
Crab	Crystalline, Flambé
Crow Wall Pocket	D 5772B
Cuddlin'	3611S

D

Dachshund
  Seated   K17
  Standing
    Style One   HN 970, Flambé
    Style Two
      Large   HN 1139, Flambé
      Medium   HN 1140, Flambé
      Small   HN 1141, Flambe
    Style Three   DA 116
Dachshund Ch. 'Shrewd Saint'
  Large   HN 1127
  Medium   HN 1128
  Small   HN 1129
Dalmation   DA 85
Dalmation Ch. 'Goworth Victor'
  Large   HN 1111
  Medium   HN 1113
  Small   HN 1114
Dapple Grey   HN 2578
  Also called 'Punch Peon',
  Chestnut Shire, HN 2623
Dapple Grey with Rider   HN 2521
Deer
  Style One   HN 2502, 2503
  Style Two   3400M
  Style Three   3408S
Desert Orchid
  Style One   DA 134
  Style Two   DA 184
Doberman Pinscher   DA 105
Doberman Pinscher
  Ch. 'Rancho Dobe's Storm'   HN 2645, Flambé
Dog of Fo   Flambé
Donkey
  Style One   HN 1149, 1164, 1176
  Style Two   HN 1155, 1170, 1183
Downy Woodpecker
  Style One   HN 3509
  Style Two   4207
Dragon
  Style One   Flambé
  Style Two   HN 3552
Drake
  On Fluted Ashtray   HN 1087B
  On Plain Ashtray   HN 1087A
  On Rock   HN 132, Flambé
  Resting
    Large   HN 977, 1192, Flambé
    Small   HN 148B, Flambé
  Standing
    Large   HN 248, 249, 252, 1198, 2635
    Medium   HN 114, 115, 116, 956, 1191,
                      2555, 2647, Flambé
    Small   HN 806, 807, 2591, Flambé
Duck
  Head stretched forward HN 150, 229, 2556, Flambé
  On Fluted Ashtray   HN 1088B
  On Plain Ashtray   HN 1088A
  Preening
    Style One   HN 235, 298, Flambé
    Style Two   HN 148A, 271, 299
  Resting   HN 148B, Flambé
  Teal   HN 936
Duck and Ladybird (flower holder)   HN 849
Duckling (new born)   HN 188, 189, 190, Flambé
Duckling on a Rock (flower holder)   HN 850
Ducklings
  Standing   HN 205, 206, 275, Flambé
  Resting   HN 239, Flambé
Ducks   3306S

E

Eagle on Rock   HN 139, Titanian
Eagle Crouching on Rock   HN 241, 242
Eastern Bluebird Fledgling   HN 3510
Elephant
  African
    Style One   3201L
    Style Two   3203M
    Style Three   DA 159A, DA 159B
  Asiatic   HN 2506
  Fighter
    Large   HN 1120, 2640, Flambé
    Small   Flambé, Chinese Jade
  Stylized   Chinese Jade
  Trunk down, curled
    Large   HN 1121, Flambé, Sung
    Medium   Flambé
    Small   HN 181, 186, Flambé, Sung
  Trunk in salute
    Large   HN 966, Chinese Jade, Flambé
    Medium   HN 891A, Flambé, Sung
    Small   HN 891B, 941, 2644, Flambé, Sung
  Trunk Stretching   Flambé, Sung
Elephant Calf   3221S
Elephant and Young   HN 3548
Emperor Penguin   See Penguin
English Foxhound Ch. 'Tring Rattler'
  Large   HN 1025
  Medium   HN 1026
  Small   HN 1027
English Robin   See Robin
English St. Bernard   HN 231, Flambé
English Setter
  Large   HN 2620
  Medium   HN 2621
  Small   HN 2622
  With Collar   HN 975
    Also called 'Red Setter with Collar', HN 976
  With Pheasant   HN 2529, 2599
English Setter Ch. 'Maesydd Mustard'
  Large   HN 1049
  Medium   HN 1050
  Small   HN 1051
  See Gordon Setter, Irish Setter

F

Fantail Pigeons   HN 122, Flambé
Farmer's Boy   HN 2520
Fighter Elephant   See Elephant
Finches
  Three   HN 280, Flambé
  Two   HN 278, Flambé
First Born   DA 182
Fish   Chinese Jade
Fish (shoal of fish)   Chinese Jade, Flambé
Fledgling
  Style One   HN 145A, 145B, Flambé
  Style Two   HN 137C, 137D, Flambé
  Style Three   HN 143A, 143B, Flambé
  Style Four   HN 137A, 137B, Flambé
  Style Five   HN 145G, 145H
Fledgling on Rock
  Style One   HN 145C, 145D, 145E, 145F
                             Flambé
  Style Two   HN 279, 281
Foal
  Arab type   DA 80
  Grazing   DA 76
  Large
    Head down   DA 77

Foal (cont.)

Thoroughbred type	DA 81
Lying	DA 75
Small	
Stretched, facing left	DA 78
Stretched, facing right	DA 74
Thoroughbred type, facing left	DA 82
Four Fledglings	HN 171
Also called "Thrush Chicks (four)"	

Fox

Curled	
Style One	HN 147D, Flambé, Matt Red Glaze, Treacle Glaze
Style Two	HN 978, Flambé
Seated	
Style One	
Medium	HN 147C, Flambé, Sung
Small	HN 147C-1, Flambé
Style Two	
Medium	Flambé
Small	HN 147B, Flambé, Sung
Style Three	
Large	HN 130, Flambé
Style Four	HN 963
Style Five	HN 1130, 2527
Style Six	HN 2634
Standing	DA 9
Stalking	
Large	HN 147A, Flambé
Medium	HN 147E, Flambé
Small	HN 147A-1, Chinese Jade, Flambé, Sung
Fox Bowl	Flambé
Fox In Hunting Dress	HN 100
Fox on Pedestal	HN 994, Flambe
Fox with Cub	DA 10

Foxes

Curled	
Style One	HN 117, 179; Flambé, Sung, Treacle Glaze
Style Two	HN 920, 925, Flambé, Matt red glaze
Style Three	HN 926, Flambé

Fox Terrier

Seated	
Style One	HN 900, 901
Style Two	HN 910, 924, Flambé
Style Three	K8
Standing	
Style One	HN 909, 923
Style Two	HN 943, 945, Flambé
Style Three	HN 942, 944

Fox Terrier Puppy

Seated	HN 929, 931

Foxhound

Seated	
Style One	HN 166, Flambé
Style Two	K7
'Freedom' (Otters)	HN 3528
French Poodle	See Poodle
'Friendship' (Borzoi Dog and Cat)	HN 3543
Friesian Bull	DA 23
Friesian Cow	DA 29
Friesian Cow and Calf	DA 30

Frog

Style One	
Large	Flambé
Medium	Flambé
Small	Flambé
Style Two	HN 905
Leopard Frog	3020S

G

Gannet	HN 195, 1197, Flambé
Giant Pandas	3410S
"Gift of Life" Mare and Foal	HN 3524, 3536
Giraffes	
Style One	3402M
Style Two	3412S
"Give Me a Home" (Dog)	DA 196
"Going Home" (Flying Geese)	HN 3527
Golden-Crested Wren	
Style One	HN 2548
Style Two	HN 2613
Style Three	K33
Golden Retriever	DA 142
Golden Retreivers	DA 198
Golden-Crowned Kinglet	HN 3504
Golden Eagle	
Style One	3000L
Style Two	3002M
Style Three	3006S
Style Four	4002
Goldfinch	
Style One	K36
Style Two	See Royal Adderley Birds Index
Gordon Setter	
Large	HN 1079
Medium	HN 1080
Small	HN 1081
See also English Setter, Irish Setter	
"Graceful" (Panthers)	HN 3540
Granny Owl	See Owl
Great-Crested Grebe	HN 175
Great Dane Ch. 'Rebeller of Ouborough'	
Large	HN 2560
Medium	HN 2561
Small	HN 2562
See American Great Dane	
Great Dane's Head - Pencil Holder	HN 962
Great Gray Owl	See Owl
Great Horned Owl	See Owl
Great Tits	See Royal Adderley Birds Index
Greater Scaup	
Female	HN 3517
Male	HN 3514
Green Wing Teal	
Female	HN 3521
Male	HN 3520
Greyhound	
Seated	HN 889, 890, Flambé
Standing	
Large	HN 1065, 1075
Medium	HN 1066, 1076
Small	HN 1067, 1077
Grouse	HN 2619
'Grundy'	DA 20
Gude Grey Mare	
Large	HN 2568
Medium	HN 2569
Small	HN 2570
Gude Grey Mare and Foal	
Large	HN 2519
Small	HN 2532
Guinea Fowl	HN 125, Flambé

H

Harbour Seals	HN 3507
Hare	
Crouching	
Style One	HN 107, 126, 142, 273, 803,
	Flambé, Sung
Style Two	K37
Style Three	HN 2592
Lying, legs stretched behind	
Large	HN 979, 984, 985, 1071, 2593, Flambé
Small	HN 2594, Flambé
Seated	
Ears Up	K39
Ears Down	K38
Standing	
Style One	Flambé
Style Two	DA 6
Hare In White Coat	HN 102
Also called "Rabbit in Morning Dress", HN 103	
Hare and Leverets	HN 1009
Harvest Mice	3414S
Hereford Cow and Calf	DA 34
Herefordshire Bull	DA 19
Heron (flower holder)	HN 250, 251
Heron on Grass Perch (flower holder)	HN 848
Hidin'	3608S
Hippopotamus	3211S
"Homecoming" (Doves)	HN 3532, 3539
'Horse of the Year 1992'	DA 193A
Also called 'My First Horse', DA 193B	
Horse	Chinese Jade
Head tucked, leg up	DA 51
Prancing	HN 1152, 1167, 1180
Stock, jogging mare	DA 44
Swish tail	DA 48
Small thorougbred stallion	DA 56
Hounds	DA 197
Hudsonian Chicadees	See Royal Adderley Birds Index
Huggin'	3612S
Hummingbird	See Royal Adderley Birds Index
Huntsman Fox	D 6448

I

Indian Runner Drake	HN 2636
Irish Setter Champion Pat O'Moy	
Large	HN 1054
Medium	HN 1055
Small	HN 1056
See English Setter, Gordon Setter	

J

Jack Russell	DA 202
Jay	K35
Jumping Goat	HN 1154, 1169, 1182

K

Kangeroos	3416S
'Kateroo', Character Cat	HN 154A, 154B
Kestrel	
Style One	DA 144
Style Two	DA 205
King Charles Spaniel	HN 957, HN 958
King Eider	HN 3502
King Penguin	See Penguin
King Penguin and Chick	See Penguin

Kingfisher	
Style One	HN 268, Flambé
Style Two	HN 2573
Style Three	DA 138
On Fluted Ashtray	HN 1095B
On Plain Ashtray	HN 1095A
On Rock	
Style One	HN 131, 152, Flambé
Style Two	HN 224
On Stand with Kingcups	HN 862B
On Stand with Primroses	HN 862A
On Tree Stump	
Large	HN 2540
Small	HN 2541
On Tree Stump (flower holder)	
Style One	HN 165
Style Two	HN 858, Flambé
Style Three	HN 875
Kissin' Cousins	3603M
Kitten	DA 123
Koala Bears	3418S
Kudu	3213S

L

Labrador	
Seated	DA 86
Standing	
Style One	DA 111
Style Two	DA 145
Labrador Ch. 'Bumblikite of Mansergh'	HN 2667
Labrador and Pup	DA 168
Lamb	
Style One	HN 2504, 2505
Style Two	HN 2595
Style Three	HN 2596
Style Four	HN 2597
Style Five	HN 2598
Langur Monkey	HN 2657
"Leap, Dolphin	HN 3522, Flambé
Leaping Salmon	Chinese Jade, Flambé
Leaping Trout	DA 172
Leopard	
Seated	HN 919
Standing	HN 1094
Leopard on Rock	HN 2638
Leopard Frog	3020S
Lickin' Good	3605M
Life Guard	DA 22
Lion	
Lying	Flambé
Seated	HN 223, Flambé, Treacle glaze
Standing	
Style One	
Large	HN 1085
Small	HN 1086
Style Two	HN 1112
Lion on Alabaster Base	HN 1125
Lion on the Rock	
Style One	HN 1119
Style Two	HN 2641
Lioness	
Style One	3205M
Style Two	3215S
Llama	
Style One	Chinese Jade, Flambé
Style Two	HN 2665
Lop-eared Rabbit	See Rabbit
"Lucky" Black Cat	K12
Also called "Ooloo", HN 818, 819, 827, 828, 829	
Lynx	HN 2501

ALPHABETICAL INDEX TO ROYAL ADDERLEY BIRD STUDIES

ALPHABETICAL INDEX TO THE BRONZE MENAGERIE

INDEX OF MODEL NUMBERS

MODEL NUMBERS PRE 1910

1162 Frog, Flambé
1162A Frog, Flambé
1162B Frog, Flambé
1163 Chicks (Three), Flambé
1163A Chicks (Two), HN 236, Flambé, Sung
1163B Chick, HN 274, 282, Flambé
1164 Mouse on a Cube, HN255, Flambé
1164A Mouse with Nut, Flambé
1164B Mouse (crouching), Flambé;
    On Fluted Ashtray, HN 1090B
    On Plain Ashtray HN 1090A

1165 Lop-Eared Rabbit, Flambé, Matt Red Glaze;
    On Fluted Ashtray, HN 1091B
    On Plain Ashtray HN 1091A
1165A Rabbit (crouching - Style One), Flambé
1165B Rabbit (crouching - Style Two), Sung
1236 Fledgling (Style One), HN 145A, 145B, Flambé
1237 Fledgling (Style Five), HN 145E, 145F
1238 Fledgling (Style Two), HN 137C, 137D, Flambé

MODEL NUMBERS POST 1910

1 Apes, HN 883, Flambé
2 Duck (preening - Style One), HN 235, 298, Flambé
3 Duckling (new born), HN 188, 189, 190, Flambé
4 Duck (preening - Style Two), HN 148A, 271, 299
5 Details Unknown
6 Foxes (curled - Style One), HN 117, 179, Flambé,
    Sung, Treacle Glaze
7 Frog Leaping
8 Frog Sitting
9 Cat (seated - Style One), HN 109, 120, 967, Flambé,
    Sung
10 Fish
11 Butterfly
11A Butterfly
12 Fox (seated - Style One), HN 147C, Flambé, Sung
12A Fox (seated - Style One), HN 147C-1, Flambé
13 Figure
14 Fox (seated - Style Two), HN 147B; Flambé, Sung
14A Fox (seated - Style One), Flambé
15 Fox (curled - Style One), HN 147D, Flambé,
    Treacle glaze
16 Monkey (hand to ear), HN 156; Flambé
17 Cat on Back (Paired with model no. 17)
18 Dog Playing(Paired with model no. 18)
19 Figure
20 Fox Bowl, Flambé
21 Fox on Pedestal, HN 994; Flambé
22 Cormorant on Rock
23 Cat Sleeping, Head on Paw, HN 210, 227
23A Cat on Cushion
24 Cat Asleep on Cushion, HN 993
25 Cockerel (crowing), HN 111
26 Bowl with Double Fox Finial
27 Basket
28 Grotesque
29 Fox (stalking), HN 147E; Flambé

29A Fox (stalking), HN 147A; Flambé
29B Fox (stalking), HN 147A-1, Chinese Jade, Flambé,
    Sung,
30 Cockerel (crouching), HN 124, 178, 180, 267, Flambé
31 Inkstand
32 Details Unknown
33 Butterfly on Square Base
34 Laughing Rabbit
35 Lizard
36 Dachshund (standing - Style One), HN 970
36A Dachshund Flambé
37 Owl in a Crescent Moon-Shaped Dish, HN 222;
    Flambé
38 Bulldog, Flambé
39 Polar Bear (seated), HN 121, Flambé
40 Polar Bear on Dish, Flambé
41 Dog, Flambé
42 Crab, Flambé, Crystalline
43 Raven, HN 135; Flambé
44 Kingfisher on Rock Style One, HN 131, 152, Flambé
44A Kingfisher on Stand with Primroses, HN 862A
44B Kingfisher on Stand with Kingcups, HN 862B
45 Parrot on Pillar, Flambé
46 Fantail Pigeons, HN 122; Flambé
47 Collie (seated), HN 105, 106, 112; Flambé
48 Bloodhound, HN 176, Flambé
49 Labrador on Base, Flambé
50 Cockerel (seated - Style One), HN 157
51 Owl Box
52 Monkies, Mother and Baby, HN 254, Flambé, Sung,
    Yellow and Gold Matt Glaze
53 Monkey (seated, arms folded), HN 118, 253;
    Flambé, Titanian
54 Polar Bears on Ice Floe, Flambé
55 Figure
56 Lion Seated on Rock

57 Comic Pig, HN 246	110B Pig (snoozing), Flambé
58 Comic Brown Bear. HN 170, 270, Flambé	111 Panther, Flambé
59 Lion (seated), HN 223, Flambé, Treacle glaze	111 Tiger (crouching), HN 225, Flambé
61 Pigs (snoozing - Ears Up), HN 213, 238, 802, Flambé	112 Duck (resting), HN 148B, Flambé
62 Pigs (snoozing - Style Two), Flambé	113 Lop-Eared Rabbit, HN 108, 151, 276, Flambé; On Fluted Ashtray, HN 1091B
63 Figure	On Plain Ashtray, HN 1091A
64 Lion (lying), Flambé	114 Pig, Flambé
65 Elephant (trunk down, curled), HN 181, 186, Flambé, Sung	115 Squirrel, HN 138, Flambé On Fluted Ashtray, HN 1093B
66 Dachshund	On Plain Ashtray, HN 1093A
67 Polar Bear on Cube, HN 119, Flambé	116 Puppy (seated), HN 128, Flambé, Sung
68 Cockatoo on a Rock, HN 185, 191, 192, 200, 877, Flambé	117 Hare (Not Issued)
69 Guinea Fowl, HN 125; Flambé	118 Puppy With Bone, HN 232, Flambé
70 Cat (lying), HN 233; Flambé	119 Hare (crouching - Style One), HN 107, 126, 142, 273, 803, Flambé, Sung
71 Owl with Owlet Under Wing, HN 160, Flambé	120 Bulldog (seated), Flambé
72 Pig (snorting) HN 968A, Flambé	121 Terrier Puppy (lying), HN 194, Flambé
72A Pig (snorting) HN 968B, Flambé	122 Bulldog (seated - Style Three), HN 881A, 881B, Chinese Jade, Flambé;
73 Figure	On Lid of Lustre Bowl, HN 987
74 to 75 Novelty Eggs	123 Details Unknown
76 Pedlar Wolf, HN 7, Flambé	124 Grotesque on Rock
77 Figure	125 Pelican (Beak down), HN 295A, 295B, Flambé
78 Scottish Terrier (standing - Style One), HN 964, 965, Flambé	126 Ousel Bird Cover
78A Aberdeen Terrier (s/s)	127 to 134 Grotesque figures on bowls
79 Figure	135 Bulldog (seated - Style Four), HN 129, 948, Flambé
80 Greyhound (seated), HN 889, 890, Flambé	135A Bulldog (seated), Flambé
81 Pigs at Trough, Flambé	136 Bison, HN 172
82 Cavalier King Charles Spaniel (Style One), HN 127, Chinese Jade, Flambé	137 Mallard Drake, (standing) HN 114, 115, 116, 956, 1191, 2555, 2647, Flambé
83 Figure	138 Drake on Rock, HN 132, Flambé
84 Emperor Penguin, HN 113, 296, Flambé	139 Fledgling on Rock (Style One), HN 145C, 145D, 145E, 145F, Flambé
85 Penguin (Style One), HN 104, 134, Flambé	140 Fledgling on Rock (Style Two), HN 279, 281
86 Hare (standing on hind legs), Flambé	141 Butterfly on Stump, HN 162
87 to 90 Figures	142 Butterfly Clip
91 Kingfisher (Style One), HN 268, Flambé	142A Butterfly, Flambé
92 Duck (swimming, looking up)	143 to 144 Figures
93 to 96 Figures	145 Eagle on Rock, HN 139, Titanian
97 Ducklings (Resting), HN 239, Flambé	146 Rabbit Ink Stand
98 Fledgling (Style Three), HN 143A, 143B, Flambé	147 Ape, HN 140
99 Fledgling (Style Four), HN 137A, 137B, Flambé	148 Barn Owl (Style One), HN 169, Flambé
100 Details unknown	149 Monkey (seated, arms folded) ?????
101 Tortoise, HN 193, Flambé, Sung	150 Dog (seated)
101A Tortoise, Flambé, Sung	151 Fox in Hunting Dress HN 100,
102 Fox (seated - Style Three), HN 130, Flambé	152 Rabbit in Morning Dress, HN 101, 102; Also called "Hare in White Coat"
103 Penguins, HN 103, 133, Flambé	153 Owl (Style One) HN 155
104 Robin, HN 144, Flambé; on Fluted Ashtray, HN 1089B	154 Squirrel on Ashtray Fluted, HN 1093B, Plain, HN 1093A
on Plain Ashtray, HN 1089A	155 Robin on Ashtray Fluted HN 1089B, Plain HN 1089A
104 Wren, HN 277	156 to 194 Figures
105 Figure	195 Kingfisher on Box
106 Tiger on Rock (Style One), HN 876, Flambé	196 Swallow on Rock, HN 136, 149; Also called "Blue Bird on Rock", HN 269
107 Rhinoceros (standing) HN 141, Light brown, Orange brown, (Experimental glazes)	197 Figure
108 Figure	198 Pig, HN 968A, 968B
109 Pelican (Beak up), HN 123, Flambé	
110 Pig (snoozing), HN 800, Flambé, Sung	
110A Pig (snoozing), HN 801, Flambé, Sung	

199 Figure
200 Figure
201 Figure
202 Buffalo
203 to 206 Figures
207 Duck (head stretched forward), HN 150, 229, 2556, Flambé
208 Thrush Chicks (four), HN 161, Flambé; Also called "Four Fledglings" HN 171
209 Foxhound (seated - Style One), HN 166, Flambé
210 Bulldog
211 Figure
212 Toucan on Perch, HN 158, 159, 196, 294
213 Character Monkey, HN 182, 183, Flambé
214 "Kateroo" Character Cat, HN 154A, 154B
215 Figure
216 Cat with Mouse on Tail, HN 201, 202, Flambé, Sung
217 Small Ape Figure on Lid of Powder Bowl, HN 177
218 Figure
219 Figure
220 Figure
221 Budgerigar on Tree Stump, HN 163A, 163B, 199, Flambé, Sung
222 to 224 Figures
225 Rooster, HN 164, 184
226 Figure
227 Kingfisher Flying to Tree Stump (flower holder), HN 858, Flambé
228 Granny Owl, HN 173, 187 Also called "Wise Old Owl"
229 to 230 Figures
231 Tern, HN 167, 168, 1193, 1194, Flambé
232 Figure
233 Great-Crested Grebe, HN 175
234 Toucan in Tail Coat and Bow Tie, HN 208
235 Black-Headed Gull (Male), HN 211, 1195, Also called "Seagull" (Female) HN 212, 1196
236 Figure
237 Thrush
238 Figure
239 King Penguin and Chick, HN 198, 297, 998, Flambé
240 Cat on a Pillar, HN 203, 244, 245
241 Figure
242 Persian Kitten (Style One), HN 204, 221, Sung
243 Gannet, HN 195, 1197, Flambé
244 to 245 Figures
246 Bird with Five Chicks, HN 214, 215, 216, 272
247 Ducklings (Standing), HN 205, 206, 275, Flambé
248 Cat on a Pillar
249 Rabbits, HN 209, 217, 218, 219, 969, Flambé
250 Country Mouse, HN 207
251 Weaver Bird on Rock, HN 197, 220
252 Figure
253 Thrush on Rock, HN 240
254 to 255 Figures
256 Town Mouse, HN 226, 228
257 Mrs Gamp Mouse, HN 237
258 Kingfisher on Rock (Style Two), HN 224
259 Cats, HN 234

260 Details Unknown
261 Borzoi
262 English St. Bernard, HN 231, Flambé
263 Finches (two), HN 278, Flambé
264 Finches (three), HN 280, Flambé
265 Eagle Crouching on rock, HN 241, 242
266 to 269 Figures
270 Peahen, HN 247, Flambé
271 to 296 Figures
297 Grotesque Cat
298 to 306 Figures
307 Drake (standing), HN 248, 249, 252, 1198, 2635
308 to 309 Figures
310 Kingfisher
311 Kingfisher
312 to 313 Details Unknown
314 Heron (flower centre), HN 250, 251
315 Bird
316 to 328 Details Unknown
329 to 332 Novelties
333 Character Bird (Style One), HN 256, 283
334 Character Bird (Style Two), HN 257, 284
335 Character Bird (Style Three), HN 258, 285
336 Character Bird (Style Four), HN 259, 286
337 Character Bird (Style Five), HN 260, 287
338 Character Bird (Style Six), HN 261, 288
339 Character Bird (Style Seven), HN 262, 289
340 Character Bird (Style Eight), HN 263, 290
341 Character Bird (Style Nine), HN264, 291
342 Character Bird (Style Ten), HN 265, 292
343 Character Bird (Style Eleven), HN 266, 293
344 to 356 Details Unknown
357 Figure
358 to 364 Details Unknown
365 Character Bird on Plain Ashtray HN 1092A, on Fluted Ashtray HN 1092B
366 Character Bird
367 to 369 Details Unknown
370 to 372 Novelties
373 Details Unknown
374 Figure
375 Pelican
376 to 386 Figures
387 "Bonzo" Character Dog (Style Three), HN 805B, 808, 810, 812
388 Bulldog
389 "Bonzo" Character Dog (Style Two), HN 805A, 809, 811
390 Bulldog
391 Bulldog
392 "Bonzo" Character Dog (Style One), HN 804
393 "Bonzo" Character Dog (Style Four), HN 814, 815, 826
394 Details Unknown
395 Drake, HN 806, 807, 2591, Flambé; On plain Ashtray HN 1087A, on Fluted Ashtray HN 1087B
396 Miniature Bird, HN 813, 867, 868, 869, 870, 871, 872, 873, 874

730	Scottish Terrier
731	Hare with Leverets, HN 1009
732	Details Unknown
733	Scottish Terrier (seated - Style Two), HN 1017
733A	Scottish Terrier (seated - Style Two), HN 1018
733B	Scottish Terrier (seated - Style Two), HN 1019
734	Pekinese Ch. "Biddee of Ifield" (standing) HN 1010
734A	Pekinese Ch. "Biddee of Ifield" (standing) HN 1011
734B	Pekinese Ch. "Biddee of Ifield" (standing) HN 1012
735	Fish
736	Fish
737	Figure
738	Airedale Terrier Ch. "Cotsford Topsail", HN 1022, Flambé
738A	Airedale Terrier Ch. "Cotsford Topsail", HN 1023, Flambé
738B	Airedale Terrier Ch. "Cotsford Topsail", HN 1024
739	Figure
740	English Foxhound Ch. "Tring Rattler", HN 1025
740A	English Foxhound Ch. "Tring Rattler", HN 1026
740B	English Foxhound Ch. "Tring Rattler", HN 1027
741	to 747 Figures
748	Sealyham Ch. "Scotia Stylist", HN 1030, Flambé
748A	Sealyham Ch. "Scotia Stylist", HN 1031
748B	Sealyham Ch. "Scotia Stylist", HN 1032
749	Figure
750	Cairn Ch. "Charming Eyes", HN 1033, also called "Cairn", HN 1104
750A	Cairn Ch. "Charming Eyes", HN 1034, also called "Cairn", HN 1105
750B	Cairn Ch. "Charming Eyes", HN 1035, also called "Cairn", HN 1106
751	Figure
752	Pekinese Ch. "Biddee of Ifield" (seated), HN 1039
752B	Pekinese Ch. "Biddee of Ifield" (seated), HN 1040, Flambé
753	Sealyham Ch. "Scotia Stylist", (lying), HN 1041
753A	Sealyham Ch. "Scotia Stylist", (lying), HN 1052
753B	Sealyham Ch. "Scotia Stylist", (lying), HN 1053
754	Bulldog (standing), HN 1042, 1045, 1072
754A	Bulldog (standing) HN 1043, 1046, 1073
754B	Bulldog (standing) HN 1044, 1047, 1074
755	Cocker Spaniel (Style One), K9A, K9B
756	West Highland Terrier (Style One), HN 1048
757	Airedale Terrier (lying), K5
758	Pekinese (seated), K6
759	Fox Terrier (seated - Style Three), K8
760	Sealyham (begging), K3
761	Scottish Terrier (begging - Style Two), K10
762	Bulldog (seated - Style Two), K1
763	Bulldog Puppy, K2
764	Foxhound (seated - Style Two), K7
765	Sealyham (lying - Style Two), K4
766	Cairn Terrier (seated), K 11
767	Fox (seated - Style Six), HN 2634
768	Figure
769	Peruvian Penguin (Style Three), HN 2633
770	English Setter, Ch. "Maesydd Mustard", HN 1049; Also called English Setter HN 2620

770A	English Setter, Ch. "Maesydd Mustard", HN 1050; Also called English Setter HN 2621
770B	English Setter, Ch. "Maesydd Mustard", HN 1051; Also called English Setter HN 2622
770	Irish Setter, Ch. "Pat O'Moy", HN 1054
770A	Irish Setter, Ch. "Pat O'Moy", HN 1055
770B	Irish Setter, Ch. "Pat O'Moy", HN 1056
770	Gordon Setter, HN 1079
770A	Gordon Setter, HN 1080
770B	Gordon Setter, HN 1081
771	to 778 Figures
779	Collie, Ch. "Ashstead Applause", HN 1057
779A	Collie, Ch. "Ashstead Applause", HN 1058
779B	Collie, Ch. "Ashstead Applause", HN 1059
780	to 783 Figures
784	Cocker Spaniel and Hare, HN 1063
784A	Cocker Spaniel and Hare, HN 1064
785	to 786 Figures
787	Alsatian (seated - Style One), K13
788	to 790 Figures
791	Smooth-haired Terrier, Ch. "Chosen Don of Notts", HN 1068, 2512
791A	Smooth-haired Terrier, Ch. "Chosen Don of Notts", HN 1069, 2513
791B	Smooth-haired Terrier, Ch. "Chosen Don of Notts", HN 1070, 2514
792	Greyhound (standing), HN 1065, 1075
792A	Greyhound (standing), HN 1066, 1076
792B	Greyhound (standing), HN 1067, 1077
793	to 798 Figures
799	Flying Birds (Not Issued)
800	Figure
801	Lion (standing - Style One), HN 1085; Lion on Alabaster Base, HN 1125
801A	Lion (standing - Style One), HN 1086
802	to 803 Figures
804	Fox Head
805	to 808 Figures
809	Tiger (stalking - Style Two), HN 1082, 1125, 2646, Flambé; Tiger on Rock (Style Two), HN 1118 Tiger on Alabaster Base
809A	Tiger (stalking - Style Two), HN 1083
809B	Tiger (stalking - Style Two), HN 1084
809B	Leopard (standing), HN 1094
810	to 822 Figures
823	Horse, Chinese Jade
824	to 826 Figures and Masks
827	Llama (Style One), Chinese Jade, Flambé
828	to 830 Wall Masks
831	to 851 Figures
852	Bull Terrier (standing - Style One), HN 1100
853	Character Dog Running with Ball, HN 1097
854	Character Dog Lying on Back, HN 1098
855	Character Dog with Ball, HN 1103
856	Character Dog Yawning, HN 1099
857	Character Fox with Stolen Goose, HN 1096, 1102
858	Character Dog
859	to 865 Figures
866	Character Dog Lying, Panting, HN 1101

867	to 872 Figures	990	Character Dog
873	Scottish Terrier (standing - Style Four), HN 1110	991	to 992 Figures
874	to 876 Masks	993	Asiatic Elephant, HN 2506
877	to 881 Figures	994	Deer (Style One), HN 2502, 2503
882	Horse, Chinese Jade	995	Lamb (Style One), HN 2504, 2505
883	to 899 Figures	996	Hawk (l/s)
900	Dalmation, Ch. "Goworth Victor", HN 1111	997	Zebu Cow, HN 2507
900A	Dalmation, Ch. "Goworth Victor", HN 1113	998	Details Unknown
900B	Dalmation, Ch. "Goworth Victor", HN 1114	999	to 1008 Figures
901	to 909 Figures	1009	Springer Spaniel, "Ch. Dry Toast", HN 2515
910	Lion (l/s)	1009A	Springer Spaniel, "Ch. Dry Toast", HN 2516
911	to 924 Figures	1009B	Springer Spaniel, "Ch. Dry Toast", HN 2517
925	Alsatian, Ch. "Benign of Picardy", HN 1115	1010	to 1012 Figures
925A	Alsatian, Ch. "Benign of Picardy", HN 1116	1013	Farmer's Boy, HN 2520
925B	Alsatian, Ch. "Benign of Picardy", HN 1117	1014	to 1015 Figures
926	to 937 Figures and Masks	1016	Gude Grey Mare and Foal, HN 2519
938	Dachshund, Ch. "Shrewd Saint", HN 1127, 1139, Flambé	1016A	Gude Grey Mare and Foal, HN 2532
		1017	Dapple Grey and Rider, HN 2521
938A	Dachshund, Ch. "Shrewd Saint", HN 1128, 1140, Flambé	1018	Pride of the Shires and Foal, HN 2518, 2523, 2528
		1018A	Pride of the Shires and Foal, HN 2534, 2536
938B	Dachshund, Ch. "Shrewd Saint", HN 1129, 1141, Flambé	1019	Figure
		1020	Chestnut Mare and Foal, HN 2522
939	to 945 Figures and Masks	1020B	Chestnut Mare and Foal, HN 2533
946	Calf (Style One), HN 1146, 1161, 1173	1021	to 1025 Figures
947	Calf (Style Two), HN 1147, 1162, 1174	1026	American Foxhound, HN 2524
948	Water Buffalo, HN 1148, 1163, 1175	1026A	American Foxhound, HN 2525
949	Donkey (Style One), HN 1149, 1164, 1176	1026B	American Foxhound, HN 2526
950	Young Doe, HN 1150, 1165, 1177	1027	Figure
951	Swiss Goat, HN 1151, 1166, 1178	1028	English Setter with Pheasant, HN 2529, 2599
952	Moufflon (Style One), HN 1145, 1160, 1179	1029	to 1032 Figures
953	Horse (prancing), HN 1152, 1167, 1180	1033	Details Unknown
954	Moufflon (Style Two), HN 1153, 1168, 1181	1033	Lion on Rock (Style Two), HN 2641
955	Jumping Goat, HN 1154, 1169, 1182	1035	Figure
956	Donkey (Style Two), HN 1155, 1170, 1183	1036	Leopard on Rock, HN 2638
957	"Suspicion" (Doe), HN 1156, 1171, 1184	1037	Figure
958	Antelope, HN 1157, 1172, 1185	1038	Tiger on a Rock (Style Three), HN 2535
959	Staffordshire Bull Terrier, HN 1131	1038	Tiger on a Rock (Style Four), HN 2639
959A	Staffordshire Bull Terrier, HN 1132	1039	Merely a Minor, HN 2530, 2531
959B	Staffordshire Bull Terrier, HN 1133	1039A	Merely a Minor, HN 2537, 2538
959	Bull Terrier Ch. "Bokos Brock", HN 1142	1039B	Merely a Minor, HN 2567, 2571
959A	Bull Terrier Ch. "Bokos Brock", HN 1143	1040	Figure
959B	Bull Terrier Ch. "Bokos Brock", HN 1144	1041	Pheasant
960	to 961 Details Unknown	1042	to 1049 Figures
962	Character Dog with Bone, HN 1159	1050	Welsh Corgi, "Ch. Spring Robin", HN 2557
963	Character Dog with Plate, HN 1158	1050A	Welsh Corgi, "Ch. Spring Robin", HN 2558
964	Details Unknown	1050B	Welsh Corgi, "Ch. Spring Robin", HN 2559
965	Figure	1051	Baltimore Oriole (Style One), HN 2542A
966	Lynx, HN 2501	1051	Baltimore Oriole (Style Two), HN 2542B
966	Cerval, HN 2500	1052	Golden-Crested Wren (Style One), HN 2548
967	Details Unknown	1053	Kingfisher on a Tree Stump, HN 2540
968	to 977 Figures	1053A	Kingfisher on a Tree Stump, HN 2541
978	Fox (seated - Style Five) HN 1130, 2527	1054	Budgerigars on a Tree Stump, HN 2547
979	to 983 Figures	1055	to 1056 Details Unknown
984	Dog	1057	Mallard Drake with Spill Vase, HN 2544
985	Sealyham (standing - Style Two), HN 2509	1058	Yellow-Throated Warbler (Style Two), HN 2546
986	Sealyham (seated), HN 2508	1059	Cardinal (Style Two), HN 2554
987	Bull Terrier	1060	English Robin (Style One), HN 2549
988	Bull Terrier (standing - Style Two), HN 2511	1061	Figure
989	Character Dog Running, HN 2510	1062	Bluebird with Lupins (Style One), HN 2543

1063 Cock Pheasant, HN 2545, 2632	1121 Swallowtail on Tree
1064 Details Unknown	1122 Camberwell Beauty on Stump
1065 Figure	1123 Swallowtail on Stump
1066 Chaffinch (Style One), HN 2550	1124 to 1125 Figures
1067 to 1068 Figures	1126 Bullfinch (Style One), K31
1069 Robin Chicks (Style Two), HN 2553	1127 Cardinal (Style One), K28
1070 Bullfinch (Style Two), HN 2551	1128 Yellow-Throated Warbler (Style One), K27
1071 Thrush Chicks (Two), HN 2552, Flambé	1129 Bluebird with Lupins (Style One), K30
1072 Gude Grey Mare, HN 2568	1130 Baltimore Oriole (Style Four), K29
1072A Gude Grey Mare, HN 2569	1131 Cairn Terrier (begging), HN 2589
1072B Gude Grey Mare, HN 2570	1132 Cocker Spaniels Sleeping, HN 2590
1073 Pride of the Shires , HN 2563	1133 Mallard Duck, K26
1073A Pride of the Shires, HN 2564	1134 Dapple Grey, HN 2578; Also called "Punch Peon"
1074 Chestnut Mare, HN 2565	Chestnut Shire, HN 2623
1074A Chestnut Mare, HN 2566	1135 Golden-Crested Wren (Style Three), K33
1075 to 1076 Figures	1136 Red Admiral on Stump
1077 Great Dane, Ch. "Rebeller of Ouborough", HN 2560	1137 Peacock on Stump
1077A Great Dane, Ch. "Rebeller of Ouborough", HN 2561	1138 Small Copper on Stump
1077B Great Dane, Ch. "Rebeller of Ouborough", HN 2562	1139 Tortoiseshell on Stump
1078 Figure	1140 Peacock on Tree
1079 Character Kitten (licking hind paw), HN 2580	1141 Red Admiral on Tree
1080 Character Kitten (lying on back), HN 2579	1142 Tortoiseshell on Tree
1081 Character Kitten (looking up), HN 2584	1143 Copper on Tree
1082 Figure	1144 Budgerigar (Style One), K32
1083 Penguin (Style Eight), K25	1145 Goldfinch (Style One), K36
1084 Penguin with Chick Under Wing, K20	1146 Jay, K35
1085 Character Kitten (sleeping), HN 2581	1147 Figure
1086 Character Kitten (licking front paw), HN 2583	1148 Hare (crouching - Style Three), K37
1087 Character Kitten (on hind legs), HN 2582	1149 Hare (seated - Ears up), K39
1088 to 1091 Figures	1150 Hare (seated - Ears down), K38
1092 Scottish Terrier (seated - Style Three), K18	1151 Magpie. K34
1093 Bull Terrier (lying), K14	1152 Terrier Sitting in Basket, HN 2587
1094 Welsh Corgi, K16	1153 Cocker Spaniel Chewing Handle of Basket, HN 2586
1095 Chow (Shibu Ino), K15	1154 Terrier Puppies in a Basket, HN 2588
1096 Dachshund (seated), K17	1155 Cocker Spaniel Lying in Basket, HN 2585
1097 St. Bernard (lying), K 19	1156 Bird in Dome
1098 Penguin (Style Five), K 22	1157 Hare (crouching - Style Three), HN 2592, Flambé
1099 Penguin (Style Four), K 21	1158 to 1160 Figures
1100 Penguin (Style Seven), K 24	1161 Grouse, HN 2619
1101 Penguin (Style Six), K 23	1162 to 1167 Details Unknown
1102 Mallard Duck (resting), HN 2572	1168 to 1169 Figures
1103 Kingfisher (Style Two), HN 2573	1170 Blue Jay (l/s)
1104 Owl	1171 American Great Dane, HN 2601
1105 Swan, HN 2575	1171A American Great Dane, HN 2602
1106 Peacock, HN 2577	1171B American Great Dane, HN 2603
1107 Pheasant, HN 2576	1172 to 1174 Figures
1108 Seagull on Rock, HN 2574	1175 Swallowtail Butterfly, HN 2606
1109 Figure	1176 Dove
1110 Penguin	1177 Copper Butterfly, HN 2608
1111 Details Unknown	1178 Peacock Butterfly, HN 2604
1112 Lamb (Style Three), HN 2596	1179 Red Admiral Butterfly, HN 2607
1113 Lamb with Tree	1180 Tortoiseshell Butterfly, HN 2609
1114 Lamb (head down, tail up)	1181 Camberwell Beauty Butterfly, HN 2605
1115 Lamb (Style Four), HN 2597	1182 to 1192 Figures
1116 Lamb (Style Five), HN 2598	1193 Details Unknown
1117 Lamb (Style Two), HN 2595	1194 Figure
1118 Ewe with Lamb	1195 Pheasant, HN 2610
1119 Figure	1196 to 1199 Figures
1120 Camberwell Beauty on Tree	1200 Chaffinch (Style Two), HN 2611

1201	Baltimore Oriole (Style Three), HN 2612	1689	Pine Martin, HN 2656, Flambé
1202	Golden-Crested Wren (Style Two), HN 2613	1690	to 1691 Figures
1203	Bluebird, HN 2614	1692	Mountain Sheep, HN 2661
1204	Cardinal (Style Three), HN 2615	1693	Bison
1205	Bullfinch (Style Three), HN 2616	1694	to 1702 Figures
1206	Robin (Style Two), HN 2617	1703	Langur Monkey, HN 2657
1207	Yellow-Throated Warbler (Style Three), HN 2618	1704	River Hog, HN 2663
1208	Figure	1705	Nyala Antelope, HN 2664
1209	Chow Ch. T'Sioh of Kin-Shan, HN 2628	1706	Beaver
1209A	Chow Ch. T'Sioh of Kin-Shan, HN 2629	1707	White-Tailed Deer, HN 2658
1209B	Chow Ch. T'Sioh of Kin-Shan, HN 2630	1708	Badger (Style One), HN 2666, Mandarin
1210	to 1211 Figures	1709	Siamese Cat (standing - Style One), HN 2660
1212	French Poodle, HN 2625	1710	Siamese Cat (lying - Style One), HN 2662
1212A	French Poodle. HN 2631	1711	Figure
1213	to 1228 Figures	1712	Fox
1229	Fish (Not Issued)	1713	to 1769 Figures
1230	to 1273 Figures	1770	Rabbit
1274	Figure	1771	to 1778 Figures
1275	Character Piglet (Style Two), HN 2649	1779	Bull, Flambé
1276	to 1277 Figures	1780	Figure
1278	Piglet (Style Six), HN 2653	1781	Hedgehog, Flambe
1279	Piglet (Style One), HN 2648	1782	to 1785 Figures
1280	Piglet (Style Four), HN 2651	1786	Beaver
1281	Piglet (Style Five), HN 2652	1787	to 1798 Figures
1282	Piglet (Style Three), HN 2650	1799	Bison (Style Two), Flambe
1283	to 1286 Figures	1800	to 1802 Figures
1287	Penguin (Style Three), HN 1199, Flambé	1803	Bear
1288	to 1289 Details Unknown	1804	Bird (Prototype)
1290	Lamb	1805	Ram
1291	Lamb	1806	to 1810 Figures
1292	Red Squirrel in a Pine Tree, (Prototype), HN 2642	1811	to 1846 Figures
1293	to 1311 Figures	1847	Bison (Style Three), Flambé
1312	Pointer (Style One), HN 2624	1848	to 1944 Figures
1313	to 1326 Figures	1945	Beagle
1327	Indian Runner Drake, HN 2636	1946	Labrador, Ch. "Bumblikite of Mansergh", HN 2667
1328	to 1411 Figures	1947	to 2006 Figures
1412	Boxer	2007	Bird
1412A	Boxer Ch. "Warlord of Mazelaine", HN 2643	2008	to 2084 Figures
1413	to 1507 Figures	2085	Dragon, Flambé
1508	Doberman Pinscher Ch. "Rancho Dobe's Storm", HN 2645, Flambe	2086	Figure
		2208	White-Winged Cross Bills, HN 3501
1509	to 1554 Figures	2214	Mouse on Mushroom
1555	Otters	2249	Owl, Flambé
1556	to 1657 Figures	2264	Snowy Owl (male - Style One), HN 2669
1658	Bird on Stand	2268	Black-Throated Loon, HN 3500
1659	Bird on Stand	2269	Cat, Flambé
1660	to 1671 Figures	2289	Puffins, HN 2668
1672	Siamese Cat (seated - Style One), HN 2655	2302	King Eider, HN 3502
1673	Character Dog with Slipper, HN 2654	2319	Roseate Terns, HN 3503
1674	Details Unknown	2389	Snowy Owl (female - Style Two), HN 2670
1675	Squirrel	2404	Colorado Chipmunks, HN 3506
1676	Squirrel	2405	Winter Wren, HN 3505
1677	Squirrel	2406	Golden-Crowned Kinglet, HN 3504
1678	to 1682 Figures	2434	Harbour Seals, HN 3507
1683	Swan	2446	Snowshoe Hares, HN 3508
1684	Bird	2466	Chipping Sparrow, HN 3511
1685	to 1686 Figures	2469	Downy Woodpecker (Style One), HN 3509
1687	Llama (Style Two), HN 2665	2481	Eastern Bluebird Fledgling, HN 3510
1688	Brown Bear (Style Two), HN 2659, Mandarin	2603	Mallard (female), HN 3515

2612 Pintail (female), HN 3516	3140 Peregine Falcon, HN 3541, DA 40
2614 Mallard (male), HN 3512	3187 Pegasus, HN 3547
2620 Greater Scaup (male), HN 3514	3198 "Nestling Down", Swans, HN 3531, 3538
2621 Greater Scaup (female), HN 3517	3304 "Homecoming", Doves, HN 3532, 3539
2643 Merganser (female), HN 3519	3432 "Playful", Lion Cubs, HN 3534
2683 Green Wing Teal (male), HN 3520	3467 "Patience", Heron, HN 3533
2684 Green Wing Teal (female), HN 3521	3548 Elephant and Young, Flambé
2923 "Gift of Life", Mare and Foal, HN 3524, 3536	3573 "Graceful", Panthers, HN 3540
2925 "Going Home", Flying Geese, HN 3527, 3564, Flambé	3658 "Friendship", Borzoi Dog and Cat, HN 3543
	3660 "Serenity", Tropical Shoal of Fish, HN 3542
2930 "Courtship", Terns, HN 3525, 3535	3789 Elephant and Young, HN 3548
2936 "Shadow Play", Cat, HN 3526, Flambé	3864 "Playtime", Cat with Kitten, HN 3544
2949 "The Leap," Dolphin, HN 3522, Flambé	3901 "Motherly Love", Swan and Two Cygnets, HN 3545
2957 Dog of Fo, Flambé	3927 Unicorn, HN 3549
2959 "Capricorn", Mountain Goat, HN 3523, Flambé	4188 "Always and Forever" Doves, HN 3550
3058 "Freedom", Otters, HN 3528	4300 "New Arrival" Chicks, HN 3551
3058A "Bright Water", Otter, HN 3529	4315 Dragon, HN 3552
3058B "Clear Water", Otter, HN 3530	

INDEX OF BESWICK MODEL NUMBERS

The following Beswick Model Numbers were converted to DA (Doulton Animal) numbers and issued by Royal Doulton.

701 Bois Roussel, Race Horse, DA 42	1816 Foal (smaller, thoroughbred type, facing left), DA 82
815 Foal (small, stetched, facing right), DA 74	1867 Persian Cat (seated - Style Two), DA 126
818 Shire Mare, DA 43	1882 Siamese Cat (seated - Style Three), DA 127
855 Horse (stocky, jogging mare), DA 44	1886 Persian Kitten (Style Two), DA 128
915 Foal (lying), DA 75	1887 Siamese Cat (seated - Style Four), DA 129
946 Foal (grazing), DA 76	1897 Siamese Cat (standing - Style Two), DA 130, DA 131
947 Foal (large, head down), DA 77	1898 Persian Cat (standing), DA 132
975 Trotting Horse (cantering shire), DA 45	1991 Mare (small, facing right), DA 55
976 Mare (facing left), DA 46	1992 Horse (small, thoroughbred stallion), DA 56
997 Foal (small, stretched, facing left), DA 78	2058 Old English Sheepdog (standing), DA 100
1014 Prancing Horse (rearing horse), DA 41A, 41B	2065 Arkle, DA 15
1033 Shetland Pony (woolly Shetland mare), DA 47	2139 Siamese Cat (seated - Style Two), DA 83
1034 Shetland Foal, DA 79	2232 Old English Sheepdog (seated), DA 84
1182 Horse (swish tail), DA 48	2271 Dalmation, DA 85
1261 Palomino Horse (prancing Arab type), DA 49	2314 Labrador, DA 86
1265 Arab Horse "Xayal", DA 14, 50	2345 Nijinsky, DA 16
1296 Siamese Kittens, DA 122	2353/2689 "Spirit of Affection", DA 64
1373 Pinto Pony, DA 67	2377 Yorkshire Terrier (Style One), DA 87
1378/3 Traditional Staffordshire Dogs, DA 89-90	2410 Alsatian (seated - Style Two), DA 88
1378/4 Traditional Staffordshire Dogs, DA 91-92	2466 Black Beauty, DA 65
1378/5 Traditional Staffordshire Dogs, DA 93-94	2466/2536 Black Beauty with Foal, DA 17
1378/6 Traditional Staffordshire Dogs, DA 95-96	2510 Red Rum (Style One), DA 18
1378/7 Traditional Staffordshire Dogs, DA 97-98	2536 Black Beauty as a Foal, DA 67
1407 Foal (Arab type), DA 80	2542 Hereford Bull, DA 19
1436 Kitten, DA 123	2558 Grundy, DA 20
1549 Horse (head tucked, leg up), DA 51	2562 Life Guard, DA 22
1558 Siamese Kitten (lying), DA 124, DA 125	2574 Polled Hereford Bull, DA 21
1771 Arab Horse, DA 52	2578 Shire Horse, DA 62
1772 Thoroughbred Horse, DA 53; Also called "Appaloosa", DA 68	2580 Friesian Bull, DA 23
	2581 Alsatian, DA 26
1812 Mare (facing right), DA 54	2587 Collie, DA 24
1813 Foal (larger, thoroughbred type), DA 81	2600 Charolais Bull, DA 27

2605 Morgan Horse, DA 28
2607 Friesian Cow, DA 29
2607 Friesian Cow and Calf, DA 30
2608 The Minstrel, DA 31
2629 Majestic Stag, DA 32
2667/2669 Hereford Cow and Calf, DA 34
2671 Champion, DA 35A; Also called "Moonlight",
     DA 35B and "Sunburst", DA 36
2688 Spirit of the Wind, DA 57
2689 Spirit of Freedom, DA 58
     2689/2536 Spirit of Affection, DA 64
2703 Spirit of Youth, DA 59
2829 Spirit of Fire, DA 60
2837 Springtime, DA 69
2839 Young Spirit, DA 70
2875 Sunlight, DA 71
2876 Adventure, DA 72
2914 Spirit of Earth, DA 61
2916 Spirit of Peace, DA 63
2980 Spaniel, DA 108
2982 Pekinese (begging), DA 113
2984 Norfolk Terrier, DA 114

2985 Poodle on Blue Cushion, DA 115
2986 Setter, DA 109
3011 Pointer (Style Two), DA 110
3013 Dachshund (standing - Style Four), DA 116
3055 Rottweiler, DA 99
3060 Staffordshire Bull Terrier (Style Two), DA 101
3062 Labrador (standing - Style One), DA 111
3066 Retriever (Style One), DA 112
3070 Afghan Hound, DA 102
3073 Alsatian (standing - Style Two), DA 103
3080 Shetland Sheepdog, DA 117
3081 Boxer, DA 104
3082 Cairn Terrier (standing - Style Two), DA 118
3083 Yorkshire Terrier (Style Two), DA 119
3121 Doberman, DA 105
3129 Rough Collie, DA 106
3135 Springer Spaniel, DA 107
3149 West Highland Terrier (Style Two), DA 120
3155 Cavalier King Charles Spaniel (Style Two), DA 121
3358 Alsatian, DA 200
3375 Hounds, DA 197
3376 "Give Me a Home" (dog), DA 196

INDEX OF UNACCOUNTED MODEL NUMBERS

This index lists animal figure subjects by those model numbers assigned by Royal Doulton in their pattern books but subsequently were either not issued or issued but unrecorded.

Some of these model numers may well exist as HN numbers but have not as yet been identified or cross-referenced with the HN system.

5 Fish
7 Frog Leaping
8 Frog Sitting
10 Fish
11 Butterfly
11A Butterfly
17 Cat on Back (Paired with model no. 18)
18 Dog Playing (Paired with model no. 17)
22 Cormorant on Rock
23A Cat on Cushion
26 Bowl with Double Fox Finial
33 Butterfly on Square Base
34 Laughing Rabbit
35 Lizard
51 Owl Box
56 Lion Seated on Rock
66 Dachshund
78A Aberdeen Terrier (s/s)
92 Duck (swimming, looking up)
117 Hare
126 Ousel Bird Cover
142 Butterfly Clip
142A Butterfly, Flambé

146 Rabbit Ink Stand
150 Dog (seated)
195 Kingfisher on Box
202 Buffalo
210 Bulldog
237 Thrush
248 Cat on a Pillar (Style Two)
261 Borzoi
297 Grotesque Cat
310 Kingfisher
311 Kingfisher
315 Bird
365 Character Bird
366 Character Bird
375 Pelican
388 Bulldog
390 Bulldog
391 Bulldog
443 Bear (seated)
456 Ape Sitting in Chair
467 Ape Sitting in Chair
471 Crow in Hat
496 Character Pig (Style Three)

499	Pig	1122	Camberwell Beauty on Stump
500	Pig	1123	Swallowtail on Stump
501	Pig	1136	Red Admiral on Stump
512	Rabbit	1137	Peacock on Stump
534	Comical Elephant	1138	Small Copper on Stump
535	Elephant on back	1139	Tortoiseshell on Stump
536	Elephant with Arms Folded	1140	Peacock on Tree
540	Ram	1141	Red Admiral on Tree
557	Duck (s/s)	1142	Tortoiseshell on Tree
558	Fox (curled)	1143	Copper on Tree
635	Fish Leaping	1156	Bird in Dome
636	Fish	1170	Blue Jay (l/s)
641	Fish	1176	Dove
711	Tiger (snarling)	1229	Fish
730	Scottish Terrier	1290	Lamb
735	Fish	1291	Lamb
736	Fish	1412	Boxer
799	Flying Birds	1555	Otters
804	Fox Head	1658	Bird on Stand
823	Horse, Chinese Jade	1659	Bird on Stand
858	Character Dog	1675	Squirrel
882	Horse, Chinese Jade	1676	Squirrel
910	Lion (l/s)	1677	Squirrel
984	Dog	1683	Swan
987	Bull Terrier	1684	Bird
990	Character Dog	1693	Bison
996	Hawk (l/s)	1706	Beaver
1041	Pheasant	1712	Fox
1104	Owl	1770	Rabbit
1110	Penguin	1786	Beaver
1113	Lamb with Tree	1803	Bear
1114	Lamb (head down, tail up)	1804	Bird (Prototype)
1118	Ewe with Lamb	1805	Ram
1120	Camberwell Beauty on Tree	1945	Beagle
1121	Swallowtail on Tree	2214	Mouse on Mushroom

COLLECTING BY SERIES

"Americana Collection" Bronze Menagerie

Armadillo	3018S
Bighorned Mountain Sheep	3010S
Black Bear	3032S
Buffalo	3008S
Cottontail Rabbit	3012S
Cougar	3004M, 3014S
Golden Eagle	3000L, 3002M, 3006S
Great Grey Owl	3024S
Great Horned Owl	3026S
Leopard Frog	3020S
Northeastern Chipmunk,	016S
Raccoon	3034S
Screech Owl	3028S
Snowshoe Hare	3036S
Snowy Owl	3030S
Wild Burro	3022S

Artist's Signature Series

African Elephant	DA 159B
Kestrel	DA 144
Panda	DA 150B
Peregrine Falcon	HN 3541
Polar Bear	DA 155B
The Tawny Owl, DA 156	

Chatchull Range

Badger	HN 2666
Brown Bear	HN 2659
Langur Monkey	HN 2657
Llama	HN 2665
Mountain Sheep	HN 2661
Nyala Antelope	HN 2664
Pine Martin	HN 2656
River Hog	HN 2663
Siamese Cat (seated)	HN 2655, 2660, 2662
White Tailed Deer	HN 2658

Connoisseur

Majestic Stag	DA 32
"Open Ground" Pheasant	DA 38
Peregrine Falcon	DA 40
"Shire Horse"	DA 62
Vietnamese Pot Bellied Pig	DA 189
"The Watering Hole" Leopard	DA 39

Connoisseur Cattle

Charolais Bull	DA 27
Charolais Cow And Calf	DA33
Friesian Bull	DA 23
Friesian Cow	DA 29
Fresian Cow and Calf	DA 30
Hereford Bull	DA 19
Hereford Cow and Calf	DA 34
Polled Hereford Bull	DA 21

Connoisseur Dogs

Alsatian	DA 26
Collie DA 24	

Connoisseur Horses

Arab Colt "Xayal"	DA14
"Arkle" (Style One)	DA 15
"Black Beauty" and Foal	DA 17A, 17B
"Black Bess"	DA 179
Blues and Royals	DA 25
"Champion"	DA 35A
"Desert Orchid" (Style One)	DA 184
First Born	DA 182
"Grundy"	DA 20
Life Guard	DA 22
"The Minstrel"	DA 31
"Moonlight"	DA 35B
Morgan Horse	DA 28
"Nijinsky"	DA 16
"Red Rum"	DA 18
"Sunburst"	DA 36
"Troy"	DA 37
The Winner	DA 154B

"Country Collection" Bronze Menagerie

Chickens	3303S
Collies	3307S
Cows	3304S
Ducks	3306S
Pigs	3301S
Rooster	3305S
Turkeys	3302S

Dogs and Puppies

Labrador and Pup	DA 168
Retriever and Pup	DA 173
Sheepdog and Pup	DA 176
Spaniel and Pup	DA 174

Endangered Species Edition

African Elephant	DA 159A
Panda	DA 150A
Polar Bear	DA 155A

"Family Collection" Bronze Menagarie

Chimpanzees	3406S
Deer	3400M, 3408S
Giant Pandas	3410S
Giraffes	3402M, 3412S
Harvest Mice	3414S
Kangaroos	3416S
Koala Bears	3418S
Mare and Colt	3404M
Orang-Utans	3422S
Pinto Mare and Colt	3420S
River Otters	3426S
Shaggy Dogs	3424S

"Fine Feathers Collection" Bronze Menagarie "Birds of Prey"

Barred Owl	4000
Golden Eagle	4002

"Fine Feathers Collection"
Bronze Menagarie
"Songbirds"

American Redstart	4215
Belted Kingfisher	4201
Blue Jay	4203
Cedar Waxwing	4205
Downy Woodpecker	4207
Marsh Wren	4209
Mockingbird	4211
Tufted Titmouse	4217
White Breasted Nuthatch	4213

"Fine Feathers Collection"
Bronze Menagarie
"Waterfowl"

Canada Goose	4400
Common Mallard	4402
Whistling Swan	4404
Wood Duck	4406

Fireside Models

Alsatian	DA 88
Dalmatian	DA 85
Labrador	DA 86
Old English Sheepdog	DA 84
Siamese Cat	DA 83
Yorkshire Terrier	DA 87

Garden Birds

Blue Tit with Matches	DA 13
Chaffinch	DA 5
Robin on Apple	DA 12
Robin on Branch	DA 2
Suspended Blue Tit	DA 3
Wren DA 4	

Good Companions

Cairn Terrier	DA 118
Cavalier King Charles Spaniel	DA 121
Dachsund	DA 116
Norfolk Terrier	DA 114
Pekinese	DA 113
Poodle on Blue Cushion	DA 115
Shetland Sheepdog	DA 117
West Highland Terrier	DA 120
Yorkshire Terrier	DA 119

Images Of Fire

"Courtship" Terns	HN 3535
"Elephant and Young"	HN 3548
"Gift of Life" Mare and Foal	HN 3536
"Homecoming" Doves	HN 3539
"Nestling Down" Swans	HN 3538

Images of Nature

"Always and Forever" Doves	HN 3550
"Bright Water" Otter	HN 3529
"Capricorn" Mountain Goat	HN 3523
"Clear Water" Otter	HN 3530
"Courtship" Terns	HN 3525
"Freedom, Otters	HN 3528
"Friendship" Borzoi Dog and Cat	HN 3543
"Gift of Life" Mare and Foal	HN 3524
"Going Home" Flying Geese	HN 3527
"Graceful" Panthers	HN 3540
"Homecoming" Doves	HN 3532
"The Leap" Dolphin	HN 3522
"Motherly Love" Swan and Two Cygnets	HN 3545
"Nestling Down" Swans	HN 3531
"New Arrival" Chicks	HN 3551
"Patience" Heron	HN 3533
"Playful" Lion Cubs	HN 3534
"Playtime" Cat with Kitten	HN 3544
"Serenity" Shoal of Tropical Fish	HN 3542
"Shadow Play" Cat	HN 3526

Jefferson Sculptures

Black-Throated Loon	HN 3500
Chipping Sparrow	HN 3511
Colorado Chipmunks	HN 3506
Downy Woodpecker	HN 3509
Eastern Bluebird Fledgling	HN 3510
Golden-Crowned Kinglet	HN 3504
Harbour Seals	HN 3507
King Eider	HN 3502
Puffins	HN 2668
Roseate Terns	HN 3503
Snowshoe Hares	HN 3508
Snowy Owl (Male)	HN 2669
Snowy Owl (Female)	HN 2670
White-Winged Cross Bills	HN 3501
Winter Wren	HN 3505

Nature Sculptures

Kingfisher, DA 138
Quarter Horse, DA 163A, 163B
Welsh Mountain Pony, DA 164

"Playmate Collection"
Bronze Menagarie

Baby Sittin'	3601M
Cuddlin'	3611S
Hidin'	3608S
Huggin'	3612S
Kissin' Cousins	3603M
Lickin' Good	3605M
Shooin'	3609S
Snoozin'	3606M
Tuggin'	3610S
Wakin'	3607S

Prestige Series

Cock Pheasant	HN 2632
Drake HN 2634	
Fighter Elephant	HN 2640
Fox HN 2634	
Leopard on Rock	HN 2638
Lion on Rock	HN 2641
Puruvian Penguin	HN 2633
Tiger on Rock	HN 2639

R.D.I.C.C.

Dragon	HN 3552
Dog of Fo	Flambe

Roah Schorr

Antelope	HN 1157, 1172, 1185
Calf (Style One)	HN 1146, 1161, 1173
Calf (Style Two)	HN 1147, 1162, 1174
Donkey (Style One)	HN 1149, 1164, 1176
Donkey (Style Two)	HN 1155, 1170, 1183
Horse (prancing)	HN 1152, 1167, 2280
Jumping Goat	HN 1154, 1169, 1182
Moufflon (Style One)	HN 1145, 1160, 1179
Moufflin (Style Two)	HN 1153, 1168, 1181
"Suspicion" Doe	HN 1156, 1171, 1184
Swiss Goat	HN 1151, 1166, 1178
Water Buffalo	HN 1148, 1163, 1175
Youn Doe	HN 1150, 1165, 1177

"Safari Collection" Bronze Menagarie

African Elephant	3201L, 3203M
Baboon	3207S
Cheetah	3209S
Elephant Calf	3221S
Hippopotamus	3211S
Kudu	3213S
Lioness	3205M, 3215S
Markhov Goat	3217S
Tiger	3219S

Spirited Dogs

The Labrador	DA 111
The Pointer	DA 110
The Retriever	DA 112
The Setter	DA 109
The Spaniel	DA 108

Spirited Foals

Adventure	DA 72
Springtime	DA 69
Sunlight	DA 71
Young Spirit	DA 70

Spirited Horses

Spirit of Affection	DA 64
Spirit of Earth	DA 61
Spirit of Fire	DA 60
Spirit of Freedom	DA 58
Spirit of Life	DA 154
Spirit of Love	DA 225
Spirit of Nature	DA 73
Spirit of Peace	DA 63
Spirit of the Wild	DA 183
Spirit of the Wind	DA 57
Spirit of Youth, DA 59	
Spirit of the Land, DA 183	

Wildlife Collection

Badger	DA 8
Barn Owl	DA 1, 137
Fox	DA 9
Fox with Cub	DA 10
Hare	DA 6
Majestic Stag	DA 32
Open Ground	Pheasant, DA 38
Osprey	DA 139
Otter	DA 7
Peregrine Falcon	DA 40
Wood Mice	DA 11
Watering Hole	Leopard, DA 39

Wildlife Decoys

Greater Scaup (Male)	HN 3514
Greater Scaup (Female)	HN 3517
Mallard (Male)	HN 3512
Mallard (Female)	HN 3515
Merganser (Male)	HN 3518
Merganser (Female)	HN 3519
Pintail (Male)	HN 3513
Pintail (Female)	HN 3516

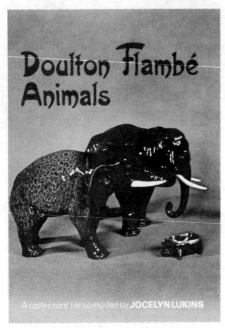
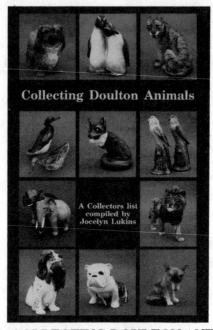

ATTENTION COLLECTORS

OF
DOG FIGURINES & MEMORABILIA

YOU ARE INVITED TO JOIN......

CANINE COLLECTIBLES CLUB OF AMERICA

An organization devoted to the promotion, enjoyment and collection of dog memorabilia.

As a member you will receive:

- A quality publication, fully illustrated with informative and interesting articles about dog collecting, artists profiles, and photographs of fabulous dog collectibles.

- Free classified ads in each issue.

- Annual roster of members specialties

- This and much more....

BUY, SELL, TRADE
MEET FELLOW COLLECTORS

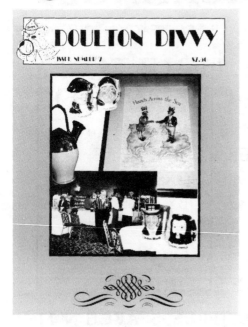

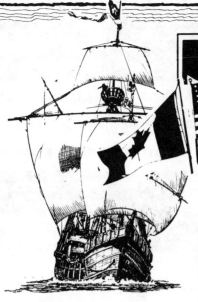

THE CANADIAN DOULTON & BESWICK COLLECTORS FAIR

THE SHERATON TORONTO EAST HOTEL ~ SEPTEMBER 16, 17 & 18, 1994

Canadian, American & U.K. Dealers displaying a wide selection of discontinued Doulton, Beswick, Flambé, Stoneware & Beatrix Potter as well as other fine pottery and porcelain such as Royal Worcester, Moorcroft, Martin Ware and others.

— SHOW TIMES —

Friday 6:00 pm - 10:00 pm ~ $7.50 (3 day pass)
Saturday 10:00 am - 5:00 pm - $4.00; Sunday 11:00 am - 3:30 pm ~ $4.00

FOR RESERVATIONS:

The Sheraton Toronto East Hotel
Tel: 416-299-1500
Fax: 416-299-8959
2035 Kennedy Road,
Scarborough, Ontario, Canada

ORGANIZED BY:

Crown & Lion Productions
W. Laidler - Director
Enquiries:
Fax: 604-535-0682
Tel: 604-535-1884

When calling for reservations mention the show & receive a reduced rate!